PHILIP'S

ROAD ATLAS
Britain
and Ireland

D0259948

www.philips-maps.co.uk

First published in 2009 by Philip's
a division of Octopus Publishing Group Ltd
www.octopusbooks.co.uk
Endeavour House, 189 Shaftesbury Avenue
London WC2H 8JY
An Hachette UK Company
www.hachette.co.uk

Fifth edition 2013
First impression 2013

ISBN 978-1-84907-265-6

Cartography by Philip's
Copyright © 2013 Philip's

Ordnance Survey® This product includes mapping data licensed from Ordnance Survey®, with the permission of the Controller of Her Majesty's Stationery Office. © Crown copyright 2013. All rights reserved. Licence number 100011710

The map of Ireland on pages XVIII–XIX is based on Ordnance Survey Ireland by permission of the Government Permit Number 8847 © Ordnance Survey Ireland and Government of Ireland and Ordnance Survey Northern Ireland on behalf of the Controller of Her Majesty's Stationery Office © Crown copyright 2013 Permit Number 120083.

While every reasonable effort has been made to ensure that the information compiled in this atlas is accurate, complete and up-to-date at the time of publication, some of this information is subject to change and the Publisher cannot guarantee its correctness or completeness.

The information in this atlas is provided without any representation or warranty, express or implied and the Publisher cannot be held liable for any loss or damage due to any use or reliance on the information in this atlas, nor for any errors, omissions or subsequent changes in such information.

The representation in this atlas of any road, drive or track is no evidence of the existence of a right of way.

Data for the speed cameras provided by PocketGPSWorld.com Ltd.

Information for National Parks, Areas of Outstanding Natural Beauty, National Trails and Country Parks in Wales supplied by the Countryside Council for Wales.

Information for National Parks, Areas of Outstanding Natural Beauty, National Trails and Country Parks in England supplied by Natural England. Data for Regional Parks, Long Distance Footpaths and Country Parks in Scotland provided by Scottish Natural Heritage.

Gaelic name forms used in the Western Isles provided by Comhairle nan Eilean.

Data for the National Nature Reserves in England provided by Natural England. Data for the National Nature Reserves in Wales provided by Countryside Council for Wales. Darparwyd data'n ymwneud â Gwarchodfeydd Natur Cenedlaethol Cymru gan Gyngor Cefn Gwlad Cymru.

Information on the location of National Nature Reserves in Scotland was provided by Scottish Natural Heritage.

Data for National Scenic Areas in Scotland provided by the Scottish Executive Office. Crown copyright material is reproduced with the permission of the Controller of HMSO and the Queen's Printer for Scotland. Licence number C02W0003960.

Printed in China.

*Independent research survey, from research carried out by Outlook Research Limited, 2005/06.
**Estimated sales of all Philip's UK road atlases since launch.

Road map symbols

M6 — Motorway, toll motorway

Motorway junction – full, restricted access

Motorway service area – full, restricted access

Motorway under construction

A453 — Primary route – dual, single carriageway

Service area, roundabout, multi-level junction

Numbered junction – full, restricted access

Primary route under construction

Narrow primary route

Derby — Primary destination

A34 — A road – dual, single carriageway

A road under construction, narrow A road

B2135 — B road – dual, single carriageway

B road under construction, narrow B road

Minor road – over 4 metres, under 4 metres wide

Minor road with restricted access

2 — Distance in miles

Scenic route

Speed camera – single, multiple

TOLL — Toll, steep gradient – arrow points downhill

Tunnel

National trail – England and Wales

Long distance footpath – Scotland

Railway with station

Level crossing, tunnel

Preserved railway with station

National boundary

County / unitary authority boundary

Car ferry, catamaran

Passenger ferry, catamaran

Hovercraft

CALAIS 1:30 — Ferry destination, journey time – hrs : mins

Ferry — Car ferry – river crossing

Principal airport, other airport

National park

Area of Outstanding Natural Beauty – England and Wales National Scenic Area – Scotland forest park / regional park / national forest

Woodland

Beach

Linear antiquity

Roman road

Hillfort, battlefield – with date

✕ 1066

795 — Viewpoint, nature reserve, spot height – in metres

Golf course, youth hostel, sporting venue

Camp site, caravan site, camping and caravan site

P&R — Shopping village, park and ride

29 — Adjoining page number – road maps

Approach map symbols

M6 — Motorway

Toll motorway

Motorway junction – full, restricted access

S — Service area

Under construction

A6 — Primary route – dual, single carriageway

S — Service area

Multi-level junction

roundabout

Under construction

A195 — A road – dual, single carriageway

B1288 — B road – dual, single carriageway

Minor road – dual, single carriageway

Ring road

3 — Distance in miles

Congestion charge area

COSELEY — Railway with station

LOXDALE — Tramway with station

M — Underground or metro station

Town plan symbols

Motorway

Primary route – dual, single carriageway

A road – dual, single carriageway

B road – dual, single carriageway

Minor through road

One-way street

Pedestrian roads

Shopping streets

Railway with station

City Hall — Tramway with station

Bus or railway station building

Shopping precinct or retail park

Park

Building of public interest

Theatre, cinema

P — Parking, shopmobility

Bank — Underground station

West St — Metro station

H — Hospital, Police station

PO — Post office

Tourist information

✝ Abbey, cathedral or priory

🛆 Ancient monument

Aquarium

🏛 Art gallery

Bird collection or aviary

Castle

Church

Country park — England and Wales — Scotland

Farm park

❀ Garden

Historic ship

House

House and garden

Motor racing circuit

Museum

Ⓡ Picnic area

Preserved railway

Race course

Roman antiquity

Safari park

Theme park

Tourist information centre
i open all year
i open seasonally

Zoo

✦ Other place of interest

Speed Cameras

Fixed camera locations are shown using the 40 symbol.

In congested areas the 40 symbol is used to show that there are two or more cameras on the road indicated.

Due to the restrictions of scale the camera locations are only approximate and cannot indicate the operating direction of the camera. Mobile camera sites, and cameras located on roads not included on the mapping are not shown. Where two or more cameras are shown on the same road, drivers are warned that this may indicate that a SPEC system is in operation. These cameras use the time taken to drive between the two camera positions to calculate the speed of the vehicle.

Relief

Feet	metres
3000	914
2600	792
2200	671
1800	549
1400	427
1000	305
0	0

Road map scales

1: 200 000 3·15 miles to 1 inch

0 1 2 3 4 5 6 miles

0 1 2 3 4 5 6 7 8 9 10 km

Parts of Scotland

1: 265 000 approximately 4 miles to 1 inch

0 1 2 3 4 5 6 miles

0 2 4 6 8 10 12 km

Scottish Highlands and Islands

1: 332 000 approximately 5 miles to 1 inch

0 1 2 3 4 5 6 7 8 miles

0 2 4 6 8 10 12 km

Orkney and Shetland Islands 1:400 000, approximately 6.25 miles to 1 inch

England

A1(M) Baldock — Extra MSA
🏨 ⛽ ♿ WC 🌉 ✉ ((·))
A1(M) J10 • Northbound and southbound 54 F3 TL23443661
El Mexicana • Greggs • KFC • M&S Simply Food • McDonald's • MooDog • Sorriso café • Starbucks 🏨 Shell 🛏 Days Inn ⓟ 2hrs
✉ A1(M), Junction 10, Baldock, Hertfordshire SG7 5TR
🖥 www.extraservices.co.uk
Ⓒ Forecourt shop, McDonald's and Starbucks open 24 hrs

A1(M) Peterborough — Extra MSA
🏨 ♿ 🌉 ((·))
A1(M) J17 • Northbound and southbound 65 E8 TL13939395
Costa • KFC • Le Petit Four • M&S Simply Food • McDonald's • WH Smith 🏨 Shell, LPG 🛏 Days Inn ⓟ 2hrs ✉ Great North Road, Haddon, Peterborough PE7 8UQ
🖥 www.extraservices.co.uk
Ⓒ Forecourt shop open 24 hrs

A1(M) Blyth — Moto
♿ 🌉 WC ✉ ((·))
A1(M) Junction 34 • Northbound and southbound
89 F7 SK62568827
Burger King • Costa • EDC • Krispy Kreme • M&S Simply Food • WH Smith 🏨 Esso, LPG 🛏 Travelodge ⓟ
✉ Hill Top Roundabout, Blyth S81 8HG 📞 01909 591841
🖥 www.moto-way.co.uk

A1(M) Wetherby — Moto
🏨 ♿ 🌉 WC ✉ ((·))
A1(M): J46 • Northbound and southbound 95 D7 SE41525025
Burger King • Costa • EDC • M&S Simply Food • Upper Crust • West Cornish Pasty • WH Smith 🏨 BP 🛏 Days Inn ⓟ 2hrs
✉ Kirk Deighton, North Yorkshire LS22 5GT 📞 01937 545080
🖥 www.moto-way.co.uk
Ⓒ Forecourt outlets open 24 hrs

A1(M) Durham — RoadChef
🏨 ♿ 🌉 ✉ ((·))
A1(M): J61 • Northbound and southbound 111 F6 NZ30843718
Costa • McDonald's • WH Smith 🏨 Total 🛏 Days Inn ⓟ 2hrs
✉ Tursdale Road, Bowburn, County Durham DH6 5NP
📞 0191 377 9222 🖥 www.roadchef.com Ⓒ Fast food outlet and forecourt shop open 24 hrs

A1(M) Washington — Moto
🏨 ♿ 🌉 WC ✉ ((·))
A1(M) just north of J64 • Northbound and southbound
111 D5 NZ28375506
Burger King • Costa • EDC • WH Smith 🏨 BP 🛏 Travelodge ⓟ 2hrs
✉ Portobello, Birtley, Tyne & Wear DH3 2SJ 📞 0191 410 3435 🖥 www.moto-way.co.uk
Ⓒ WH Smith and forecourt outlets open 24 hrs

M1 London Gateway — Welcome Break
🏨 ♿ 🌉 ✉ ((·))
M1 between J2 and J4 • Northbound and southbound
41 E5 TQ20269369
Burger King • Eat In • Krispy Kreme • Starbucks • Waitrose • WH Smith 🏨 Shell, LPG 🛏 Days Hotel ⓟ 2hrs ✉ M1 J2/4, Mill Hill,

London NW7 3HU 📞 0208 906 0611 @ lgw.enquiry@welcomebreak.co.uk
🖥 www.welcomebreak.co.uk
Ⓒ WH Smith open 24 hrs

M1 Toddington — Moto
🏨 ♿ 🌉 WC ✉ ((·)) 🚚 🏠
M1, 1 mile south of J12 • Northbound and southbound
4 J B3 TL03092878
Burger King • Costa • Cotton Traders (northbound) • EDC • Greggs (northbound) • Krispy Kreme • M&S Simply Food • Starbucks • Upper Crust (northbound) • West Cornish Pasty Company (northbound) • WH Smith 🏨 BP, LPG 🛏 Travelodge ⓟ 2hrs ✉ Toddington, Bedfordshire LU5 6HR 📞 01525 878400 🖥 www.moto-way.co.uk
Ⓒ Forecourt outlets open 24 hrs

M1 Newport Pagnell — Welcome Break
🏨 ♿ 🌉 ✉ ((·)) 🚚 🏠
M1, north of J14 • Northbound and southbound 53 E6
SP85834351
Burger King • Eat In • KFC • Starbucks • Waitrose • WH Smith 🏨 Shell, electric car charge point 🛏 Days Inn ⓟ 2hrs ✉ M1 Motorway, J14/15, Newport Pagnell, Buckinghamshire MK16 8DS
📞 01908 217722 @ newport.enquiry@welcomebreak.co.uk
🖥 www.welcomebreak.co.uk
Ⓒ WH Smith and forecourt shop open 24 hrs

M1 Northampton — RoadChef
♿ 🌉 ✉ ((·)) 🏠
M1 J15A • Northbound and southbound 52 D5 SP72285732
The Burger Company (northbound) • Costa • Hot Food Co (southbound) • McDonald's (southbound) • Restbite! (northbound) • WH Smith 🏨 Shell, LPG ⓟ 2hrs
✉ M1 Junction 15A, Northampton, NN4 9QY 📞 01604 831888 🖥 www.roadchef.com
Ⓒ WH Smith, forecourt shop and (southbound) McDonald's open 24 hrs

M1 Watford Gap — RoadChef
🏨 ♿ 🌉 ✉ ((·)) 🏠
M1 between J16 and J17 • Northbound and southbound
52 C4 SF59956802
Northbound: Costa • Cotton Traders • Fresh Food Co • McDonald's • WH Smith • Southbound: • The Burger Company • Costa • Restbite! • WH Smith 🏨 Shell 🛏 Days Inn (southbound) ⓟ 2hrs ✉ M1 Motorway, Northamptonshire NN6 7UZ 📞 01327 379001 🖥 www.roadchef.com

M1 Leicester Forest East — Welcome Break
🏨 ♿ 🌉 ✉ ((·)) 🏠
M1 between J21 and J21A • Northbound and southbound
64 D2 SK53860267
Burger King • Eat In • KFC • Starbucks • Waitrose • WH Smith 🏨 Shell, LPG 🛏 Days Inn ⓟ 2hrs ✉ Leicester Forest East, M1, Leicester, Leicestershire LE3 3GB 📞 0116 2386801 @ lfe.enquiry@welcomebreak.co.uk 🖥 www.welcomebreak.co.uk Ⓒ Eat In and WH Smith are open 24 hrs

M1 Donington Park — Moto
🏨 ♿ 🌉 ✉ WC ♿ 🌉 ((·)) 🚚
M1 J23A • Northbound and southbound 64 B1 SK46712513
Burger King • Costa • Cotton Traders • EDC • Krispy Kreme • M&S Simply Food • WH Smith 🏨 BP, LPG 🛏 Travelodge ⓟ 2hrs
✉ Castle Donington, Derby, East Midlands DE74 2TN 📞 01509 672220 🖥 www.moto-way.co.uk Ⓒ Forecourt shop and WH Smith open 24 hrs

M1 Woodall — Welcome Break
🏨 ♿ 🌉 ✉ ((·)) 🚚
M1, 2.5 miles north of J30 • Northbound and southbound
89 F5 SK47928006
Burger King • Eat In • KFC • Krispy Kreme • Starbucks • Waitrose • WH Smith 🏨 Shell, LPG 🛏 Days Inn ⓟ 2hrs ✉ M1 Motorway, Sheffield, South Yorkshire S26 7XR 📞 0114 248 7992 @ enquiry@welcomebreak.co.uk
🖥 www.welcomebreak.co.uk Ⓒ Eat In, WH Smith and forecourt outlets open 24 hrs

M1 Woolley Edge — Moto
🏨 ♿ 🌉 WC ♿ 🌉 ((·))
M1, just north of J38 • Northbound and southbound
88 C4 SE29841400
Burger King • Costa • EDC • Krispy Kreme • M&S Simply Food • WH Smith 🏨 BP 🛏 Travelodge ⓟ 2hrs ✉ West Bretton, Wakefield, West Yorkshire WF4 4LG 📞 01924 830371

M1 Trowell — Moto
🏨 ♿ 🌉 WC ♿ 🌉 ((·)) 🏠
M1 between J25 and J26 • Northbound and southbound
76 E4 SK49354073
Burger King • Costa • Krispy Kreme • EDC M&S Simply Food • WH Smith 🏨 BP ⓟ 2hrs ✉ Ilkeston, Trowell, Nottinghamshire NG9 3PL 📞 01159 320291 🖥 www.moto-way.co.uk Ⓒ WH Smith and forecourt outlets are open 24 hrs

M1 Tibshelf — RoadChef
🏨 ♿ 🌉 ✉ ((·))
M1, 2 miles north of J28 • Northbound and southbound
76 C4 SK44856031
The Burger Company (northbound) • McDonald's (southbound) • Restbite! • WH Smith 🏨 Shell,

LPG 🛏 Days Inn (northbound only) ⓟ 2hrs ✉ Newton Wood Lane, Newton, Alfreton DE55 5TZ
📞 01773 876600
🖥 www.roadchef.com
Ⓒ WH Smith and forecourt shop open 24 hrs

M2 Medway — Moto
🏨 ♿ 🌉 WC ♿ 🌉 ((·)) 🏠
M2 between J4 and J5 • Eastbound and westbound 30 C2
TQ81756344
Burger King • Costa • Greggs • Krispy Kreme • WH Smith 🏨 BP, LPG 🛏 Travelodge ⓟ 2hrs
✉ M2, Rainham, Gillingham, Kent ME8 8PQ 📞 01634 236900
🖥 www.moto-way.co.uk
Ⓒ WH Smith and forecourt shop open 24 hrs

M3 Fleet — Welcome Break
🏨 ♿ 🌉 ✉ ((·)) 🚚 🏠
M3 between J4A/J5 • Eastbound and westbound 27 D5
SU79885583
Waitrose • WH Smith • Burger King • Eat In • KFC • Krispy Kreme • Starbucks 🏨 Shell, LPG 🛏 Days Inn ⓟ 2hrs
✉ Fleet, Hampshire GU51 1AA 📞 01252 788 500 @ fleet.enquiry@welcomebreak.co.uk
🖥 www.welcomebreak.co.uk
Ⓒ Eat In and WH Smith open 24 hrs

M3 Winchester — Moto
🏨 ♿ 🌉 WC ♿ ((·))
M3, 4 miles north of J9 • Northbound and southbound
26 F3 SU52303550
Burger King • Costa • EDC • Krispy Kreme • WH Smith 🏨 BP, LPG 🛏 Days Inn ⓟ 2hrs ✉ Shroner Wood, Winchester, Hampshire SO21 1PP 📞 01962 791140
🖥 www.moto-way.co.uk
Ⓒ Forecourt outlets open 24 hrs

M4 Heston — Moto
🏨 ♿ 🌉 WC ♿ 🌉 ((·))
M4 1 mile east of J3 • Eastbound and westbound 28 B2
TQ11777778
Burger King • Costa • EDC (westbound) • Krispy Kreme • WH Smith 🏨 BP, LPG 🛏 Travelodge ⓟ 2hrs ✉ Phoenix Way, Heston, Hounslow, London TW5 9NB
📞 0208 5802152
🖥 www.moto-way.co.uk
Ⓒ WH Smith open 24 hrs

M4 Reading – eastbound — Moto
🏨 ♿ 🌉 ✉ WC ♿ 🌉 ((·))
M4 Junctions 11-12 • Eastbound
26 C4 SU67177012
Burger King • Costa • EDC • Krispy Kreme • M&S Simply Food • West Cornish Pasty • WH Smith 🏨 BP, LPG 🛏 Travelodge ⓟ 2hrs

Symbols
🏨 Accommodation
🍼 Baby change
💇 Barber shop
€$ Bureau de change
£ Cash machine
🌉 Footbridge
⛽ Fuel
✉ Meeting room
ⓟ Free parking
🚿 Showers
🚻 Toilets
WC Disabled toilets
♿ RADAR key scheme
🚚 Truckstop
🚿 Truck wash
((·)) Free WiFi
Work space
✉ Address
📞 Telephone number
@ e-mail address
🖥 website
Ⓒ Details of shops and catering outlets that are normally open 24 hours at the end of each entry. Other listed outlets may not be open 24 hours.

Map labels (Motorway service areas)
Kinross • Stirling • Old Inns • M9 • M90 • M8 • Bothwell • Hamilton • M74 • Happendon • Abington • A74(M) • Annandale Water • Gretna Green • Southwaite • Washington • Durham • A1(M) • M6 • Tebay • Killington Lake • Burton-in-Kendal • Lancaster • Wetherby • A1(M) • M55 • M6 • M65 • Hartshead Moor • Ferrybridge • M62 • Blackburn with Darwen • Charnock Richard • M62 • Doncaster North • Birch • Woolley Edge • M180 • Rivington • Burtonwood • M1 • Blyth • Knutsford • Woodall • Chester • M56 • Sandbach • Tibshelf • Keele • M1 • Trowell • Stafford • Donington Park • Telford • M6 • Norton Canes • Leicester Forest East • Peterborough • M54 • Hilton Park • Tamworth • Corley • M1 • A1(M) • Frankley • M6 • Watford Gap • Hopwood Park • Warwick • Northampton • Strensham • M40 • Newport Pagnell • M50 • Cherwell Valley • Baldock • M11 • Ross Spur • Toddington • A1(M) • Birchanger Green • Pont Abraham • Oxford • South Mimms • M25 • Swansea • M4 • Michaelwood • Beaconsfield • London Gateway • Sarn Park • Cardiff Gate • Magor • M25 • Heston • Thurrock • Cardiff West • Severn View • M4 • Membury • Reading • Medway • M5 • Gordano • Leigh Delamere • Chieveley • Cobham • Maidstone • Sedgemoor • M3 • Fleet • M25 • Clacket Lane • M20 • Stop 24 • Bridgwater • Winchester • M23 • Pease Pottage • Tiverton • M5 • Taunton Deane • Rownhams • Cullompton • M27 • M27 • Exeter

● Motorway service area

Burghfield, Reading RG30 3UQ 01189 566966 www.moto-way.co.uk WH Smith and forecourt outlets open 24 hrs

M4 Reading – westbound *Moto*

M4 Junctions 11-12 • Westbound 26 C4 SU67046985

Burger King • Costa • EDC • Krispy Kreme • M&S Simply Food • Upper Crust • West Cornish Pasty • WH Smith BP, LPG Travelodge 2 hrs Burghfield, Reading RG30 3UQ 01189 566966 www.moto-way.co.uk WH Smith and forecourt outlets open 24 hrs

M4 Chieveley *Moto*

M4 J13 • Eastbound and westbound 26 B2 SU48157268

Burger King • Costa • EDC • Krispy Kreme • M&S Simply Food • West Cornish Pasty • WH Smith BP, LPG Travelodge 2 hrs Oxford Road, Hermitage, Thatcham, Berkshire, RG18 9XX 01635 248024 www.moto-way.co.uk WH Smith open 24 hrs

M4 Membury *Welcome Break*

M4, 4 miles west of J14 • Eastbound and westbound 25 B8 SU30847601

Burger King • Eat In • KFC • Krispy Kreme • Starbucks • Waitrose • WH Smith Shell, LPG, electric car charge point Days Inn 2 hrs Woodlands Road, Membury, near Lambourn, Berkshire RG17 7TZ 01488 674360 membury.enquiry@welcomebreak.co.uk www.welcomebreak.co.uk Eat In, WH Smith and forecourt shop open 24 hrs

M4 Leigh Delamere *Moto*

M4 just west of J17 • Eastbound and westbound 24 B3 ST89077899

Burger King • Costa • Cotton Traders • EDC • Krispy Kreme • M&S Simply Food • West Cornish Pasty • WH Smith BP, LPG Travelodge 2 hrs Chippenham, Wiltshire SN14 6LB 01666 837691 (eastbound); 01666 842015 (westbound) www.moto.co.uk WH Smith and shop and coffee shops in the forecourt open 24 hrs

M5 Frankley *Moto*

M5 J3 • Northbound and southbound 62 F3 SO98938120

Burger King • Costa • EDC • Greggs (northbound) • Krispy Kreme • M&S Simply Food • WH Smith Esso Travelodge 2 hrs Illey Lane, Birmingham, West Midlands B32 4AR 0121 550 3131 www.moto-way.co.uk WH Smith and forecourt outlets open 24 hrs

M5 Strensham – southbound *RoadChef*

M5 southbound, just before J8 • Southbound only 50 F4 SO90413993

Costa • Cotton Traders • Hot Food Co • McDonald's • Soho Coffee Company • WH Smith BP, LPG 2 hrs M5 Motorway, Lower Strensham, Worcestershire WR8 9LJ 01684 290577 www.roadchef.com McDonald's and forecourt outlet open 24 hrs

M5 Strensham – northbound *RoadChef*

M5, 1 mile north of J8 • Northbound only 50 E3 SO89344072

Costa • Cotton Traders • McDonald's • Pizza Hut Express • Subway • WH Smith Texaco, LPG Days Inn 2 hrs M5 Motorway, Lower Strensham, Worcestershire WR8 9LJ 01684 293004 www.roadchef.com McDonald's and forecourt outlets open 24 hrs

M5 Michaelwood *Welcome Break*

M5, just north of J14 • Northbound and southbound 36 E4 ST70409541

Burger King • Eat In • KFC • Krispy Kreme • Starbucks • WH Smith Shell, electric car charge point Days Inn 2 hrs Lower Wick, Dursley, Gloucestershire GL11 6DD 01454 260631 michaelwood.enquiry@welcomebreak.co.uk www.welcomebreak.co.uk WH Smith and forecourt shop open 24 hrs

M5 Gordano *Welcome Break*

M5 J19 • Northbound and southbound 23 B7 ST50977563

Burger King • Eat In • KFC • Krispy Kreme • Starbucks • Waitrose • WH Smith Shell, LPG Days Inn 2 hrs Portbury, Bristol BS20 7XG 01275 373624 gordano.enquiry@welcomebreak.co.uk www.welcomebreak.co.uk WH Smith open 24 hrs

M5 Sedgemoor Southbound *RoadChef*

M5, 7 miles south of J21 23 D5 ST35815259

The Burger Company • Costa • Restbite! • WH Smith Total 2 hrs M5 Southbound Rooksbridge, Axbridge, Somerset BS26 2UF 01934 750888 www.roadchef.com Forecourt shop open 24 hrs

M5 Sedgemoor Northbound *Welcome Break*

M5, 3 miles north of J22 23 D5 ST35815259

Burger King • Eat In • Starbucks • WH Smith Shell, electric car charge point Days Inn 2 hrs M5 Motorway Northbound, Bridgwater, Somerset BS24 0JL 01934 750730 sedgemoor.enquiry@welcomebreak.co.uk www.welcomebreak.co.uk WH Smith and shop on forecourt are open 24 hrs

M5 Bridgwater *Moto*

M5, J24 • Northbound and southbound 22 F5 ST30403441

Burger King • Costa • EDC • Krispy Kreme • West Cornish Pasty • WH Smith BP Travelodge 2 hrs Huntsworth Business Park, Bridgwater, Somerset TA6 6TS 01278 456800 www.moto-way.co.uk WH Smith and forecourt shop open 24 hrs

M5 Taunton Deane *RoadChef*

M5 between J25 and J26 • Northbound and southbound 11 B7 ST19592035

The Burger Company • Costa • Restbite! • WH Smith Shell Days Inn (southbound only) 2 hrs Trull, Taunton, Somerset TA3 7PF 01823 271111 www.roadchef.com Forecourt outlets open 24 hrs

A38 / M5 Tiverton *Moto*

M5 Junction 27 • Northbound and southbound 11 C5 ST04901386

Costa • Burger King Shell Travelodge 2 hrs. No HGVs Tiverton EX16 7HD 01884 829423 www.moto-way.co.uk

M5 Cullompton *Extra MSA*

M5, J28 • Northbound and southbound 10 D5 ST02660798

Costa • McDonald's • WH Smith Shell 2 hrs Old Station Yard, Station Road, Cullompton, Devon EX15 1NS 01522 523737 www.extraservices.co.uk WH Smith and forecourt shop open 24 hrs

M5 Exeter *Moto*

M5 J30 • Northbound and southbound 10 E4 SX96779180

Burger King • Costa • EDS • Harry Ramsden • Krispy Kreme • M&S Simply Food • West Cornish Pasty • WH Smith BP Travelodge 2 hrs Sandygate, Exeter, Devon EX2 7HF 01392 436266 www.moto-way.co.uk WH Smith open 24 hrs

M6 Corley *Welcome Break*

M6, 2.5 miles west of J3 • Eastbound and westbound 63 F7 SP30898604

Burger King • Eat In • KFC • Starbucks • Waitrose • WH Smith Shell, LPG, electric car charge point Days Inn 2 hrs Highfield Lane, Corley, Staffordshire CV7 8NR 01676 540111 corleyenquiry@welcomebreak.co.uk www.welcomebreak.co.uk WH Smith open 24 hrs

M6 Norton Canes *RoadChef*

M6 Toll between JT6 and JT7 • Eastbound and westbound 62 D4 SK02290745

The Burger Company • Costa • Restbite! • WH Smith Shell Days Inn 2 hrs Betty's Lane, Norton Canes, Cannock, Staffordshire WS11 9UX 01543 272540 www.roadchef.co.uk WH Smith and forecourt shop open 24 hrs

M6 Hilton Park *Moto*

M6 J10A and J11 • Northbound and southbound 62 D3 SJ96200500

Burger King • Costa • Cotton Traders (northbound) • EDC • KFC (northbound) • Krispy Kreme • M&S Simply Food • WH Smith BP Travelodge 2 hrs Essington, Wolverhampton, Staffordshire WV11 2AT 01922 412237 www.moto-way.co.uk Coffee shops in forecourt and WH Smith are open 24 hrs

M6 Stafford – northbound *Moto*

M6, 3 miles north of J14 • Northbound only 75 F5 SJ88613186

Burger King • Costa • EDC • Krispy Kreme • M&S Simply Food • WH Smith BP, LPG Travelodge 2 hrs Stone, Staffordshire ST15 0EU 01785 811188 www.moto-way.co.uk Forecourt outlets open 24 hrs

M6 Stafford South *RoadChef*

M6, 7.5 miles south of J15 • Southbound only 75 F5 SJ89243065

The Burger Company • Costa • Restbite! • WH Smith Esso, LPG Days Inn 2 hrs M6 Southbound, Stone, Staffordshire ST15 0EU 01785 826300 www.roadchef.com

M6 Keele *Welcome Break*

M6, 6 miles north of J15 • Northbound and southbound 74 E5 SJ80624406

Burger King • Eat In • KFC • Krispy Kreme • Starbucks • Waitrose • WH Smith Shell, LPG and electric car charge point (both southbound only) 2 hrs Three Mile Lane, Keele, Newcastle under Lyme, Staffordshire ST5 5HG 01782 626221 keele.enquiry@welcomebreak.co.uk www.welcomebreak.co.uk Eat In and WH Smith are open 24 hrs

M6 Sandbach *RoadChef*

M6, just south of J17 • Northbound and southbound 74 C4 SK02290745

Northbound: Costa • Restbite! • WH Smith • Southbound: Costa • Hot Food Co • McDonald's • WH Smith Esso 2 hrs M6 Northbound, Sandbach, Cheshire CW11 2FZ 01270 767134 www.roadchef.co.uk Forecourt outlets and (southbound) McDonald's open 24 hrs

M6 Knutsford *Moto*

M6, between J18 and J19 • Northbound and southbound 74 B4 SJ73267826

Burger King • Costa • EDC • Krispy Kreme • M&S Simply Food • West Cornish Pasty (southbound) • WH Smith BP, LPG Travelodge 2 hrs Northwich Road, Knutsford, Cheshire WA16 0TL 01565 634167 www.moto-way.co.uk Forecourt shop open 24 hrs

M6 Charnock Richard *Welcome Break*

M6, 2.5 miles north of J27 • Northbound and southbound 86 C3 SD54411521

Burger King • Eat In • KFC • Krispy Kreme • Starbucks • WH Smith Shell, LPG (southbound only), electric car charge point Days Inn 2 hrs Mill Lane, Chorley, Lancashire PR7 5LR 01257 791494 charnock.enquiry@welcomebreak.co.uk www.welcomebreak.co.uk Eat In and WH Smith open 24 hrs

M6 Lancaster *Moto*

M6 south of J33 • Northbound and southbound 92 D5 SD50145198

Burger King • Costa • Cotton Traders (northbound) • EDC • Greggs (southbound) • M&S Simply Food • West Cornish Pasty Company (northbound) • WH Smith BP, LPG Travelodge 2 hrs White Carr Lane, Bay Horse, Lancaster, Lancashire LA2 9DU 01524 791775 www.moto-way.co.uk WH Smith and forecourt shop are open 24 hrs

M6 Burton-in-Kendal *Moto*

M6 between J35 and J36 • Northbound only 92 B5 SD52207617

Burger King • Costa • EDC • WH Smith BP 2 hrs Burton West, Carnforth, Lancashire LA6 1JF 01524 781234 www.moto-way.co.uk

M6 Killington Lake *RoadChef*

M6 just south of J37 • Southbound only 99 E7 SD58779111

The Burger Company • Costa • Restbite! • WH Smith BP Days Inn 2 hrs M6 Southbound, near Kendal, Cumbria LA8 0NW 01539 620739 www.roadchef.com WH Smith and forecourt shop open 24 hrs

M6 Tebay – northbound *Westmorland*

M6, just north of J38 • Northbound only 99 D8 NY60510626

Butcher's counter • cafe and coffee shop • farm shop • forecourt shop • takeaway snack bar Total, LPG Westmorland Hotel Yes M6, Old Tebay, Cumbria CA10 3ZA 01539 624511 www.westmorland.com Petrol forecourt shop and takeaway open 24 hours

M6 Tebay – southbound *Westmorland*

M6, 4.5 miles south of J39 • Southbound only 99 D8 NY60790650

Butcher's counter • cafe and coffee shop • farm shop • forecourt shop • takeaway snack bar Total, LPG Yes M6, Old Tebay, Cumbria CA10 3SB 01539 624511 www.westmorland.com Petrol forecourt shop and takeaway open 24 hours

M6 Southwaite *Moto*

M6 Junctions 41-42 • Northbound and southbound 108 E4 NY44164523

Burger King • Costa • Cotton Traders (northbound) • EDC • Greggs • M&S Simply Food (southbound) • West Cornish Pasty Company (southbound) • WH Smith BP Travelodge 2 hrs Broadfield Road, Carlisle CA4 0NT 01697 473476 www.moto-way.co.uk WH Smith and outlets on the forecourts are open 24 hours

M11 Birchanger Green *Welcome Break*

M11 at J8/J8a • Northbound and southbound 41 B8 TL51202149

Burger King • Eat In • KFC • Krispy Kreme • Starbucks • Waitrose • WH Smith Shell, LPG Days Hotel 2 hrs Old Dunmow Road, Bishop's Stortford, Hertfordshire CM23 5QZ 01279 653388 www.welcomebreak.co.uk WH Smith open 24 hrs

M18 Doncaster North *Moto*

M18 J5, at the western end of the M180 • Northbound and southbound 89 C7 SE66791104

Burger King • Costa • EDC • Greggs • Krispy Kreme • WH Smith BP, LPG Travelodge 2 hrs Hatfield, Doncaster, South Yorkshire DN8 5GS 01302 847700 www.moto-way.co.uk WH Smith open 24 hrs

M20 Maidstone *RoadChef*

M20 J8 30 D2 TQ82455523

Costa • Cotton Traders • McDonald's • Restbite! • WH Smith Esso Days Inn 2 hrs M20 J8, Hollingbourne, Maidstone, Kent ME17 1SS 01622 631100 www.roadchef.com McDonald's, WH Smith and forecourt outlets open 24 hrs

M20 Stop24 (Folkestone) *Stop 24*

M20 J11 19 B8 TR13283729

Coffee Stop • Haldane Express • Julian Graves • Just Spuds • KFC • Subway • WH Smith • Wimpy Shell, LPG 2 hrs Junction 11 M20, Stanford Intersection, Stanford, Kent CT21 4BL 01303 760273 info@stop24.co.uk www.stop24.co.uk Forecourt outlets open 24 hrs

M23 Pease Pottage *Moto*

M23 J11 • Northbound and southbound 28 F3 TQ26183310

Burger King • Costa • EDC • Krispy Kreme • M&S Simply Food • West Cornish Pasty • WH Smith BP, LPG 2 hrs Brighton Road, Pease Pottage, Crawley, West Sussex RH11 9AE 01293 562852 www.moto-way.co.uk WH Smith and forecourt outlets open 24 hrs

M25 Clacket Lane — RoadChef

M25 between J5 and J6 • Eastbound and westbound 28 D5 TQ42335457
Costa • Cotton Traders • Hot Food Co • McDonald's • WH Smith — Total, electric car charge point — Days Inn (westbound only) P 2hrs — M25 Westbound, Westerham, Kent TN16 2ER C 01959 565577 — www.roadchef.com — McDonald's open 24 hrs

M25 Cobham — Extra MSA

M25 J9-10 • Clockwise and anti-clockwise 28 D2 TQ11345768
Chozen Noodle • Eat Inn • El Mexicana • Greggs • KFC • M&S Simply Food • McDonald's • MooDog • Sorriso café • Starbucks • WH Smith — Shell, LPG — Days Inn P 2hrs — M25 J9/10, Downside, Cobham, Surrey KT11 3DB — www.extraservices.co.uk — Forecourt outlets open 24 hrs

M25 South Mimms — Welcome Break

M25 J23 and A1(M) J1 • Clockwise and anti-clockwise 41 D5 TL23000C23
Burger King • Eat Inn • KFC • Krispy Kreme • Starbucks • Waitrose • WH Smith — Shell, electric car charge point — Days Inn P 2 hr — Bignells Corner, Potters Bar, Hertfordshire EN6 3QQ C 01707 621001 @ mimms.enquiry@welcomebreak.co.uk — www.welcomebreak.co.uk — Eat In, WH Smith and forecourt outlets open 24 hrs

M25 Thurrock — Moto

M25, signposted from J30/J31 • Clockwise and anti-clockwise 29 B6 TQ57837947
Burger King • Costa • EDC • Krispy Kreme • M&S Simply Food • WH Smith — Esso — Travelodge P 2 hrs — Arterial Road, West Thurrock, Grays, Essex RM16 33G C 01708 865487 — www.moto-way.co.uk — WH Smith and forecourt outlet open 24 hrs

M27 Rownhams — RoadChef

M27, between J3 and J4 • Eastbound and westbound 14 C4 SU38791769
Costa • McDonald's (westbound) • Restbite! • WH Smith — Esso, LPG — Days Inn (westbound) P 2 hrs — M27 Southbound, Southampton, Hampshire SO16 8AP C 02380 734480 — www.roadchef.com — The outlets in the forecourts are open 24 hrs

M40 Beaconsfield — Extra MSA

M40 J2 • Eastbound and westbound 40 F2 SU95098897
Carvery Express • Chozen Noodle • El Mexicana • Greggs • KFC • Le Petit Four • M&S Simply Food • McDonald's • MooDog • Starbucks — Shell, LPG — Ibis P 2 hrs — A355 Windsor Drive, Beaconsfield, Bucks HP9 2SE — www.extraservices.co.uk — McDonald's and forecourt outlet open 24 hrs

M40 Oxford — Welcome Break

M40 J8A • Northbound and southbound 39 D6 SP62440479
Burger King • Eat In • KFC • Krispy Kreme • Starbucks • Waitrose • WH Smith — Shell, electric car charge point — Days Inn P 2 hrs — M40 Junction 8A, Waterstock, Oxfordshire OX33 1LJ C 01865 8770C7 @ oxford.enquiry@welcomebreak.co.uk — www.welcomebreak.co.uk — McDonald's and Starbucks open 24 hours

M40 Cherwell Valley — Moto

M40 J10 • Northbound and southbound 39 B5 SP55162822
Burger King • Costa • Cotton Traders • EDC • Krispy Kreme • M&S Simply Food • Upper Crust • West Cornish Pasty • WH Smith — Esso, electric car charge point — Travelodge P 2 hrs — Northampton Road, Ardley, Bicester, Oxfordshire OX27 7RD C 01869 346060 — www.moto-way.co.uk — WH Smith open 24 hrs

M40 Warwick South — Welcome Break

M40 between J12 and J13 • Southbound 51 D8 SP34075801
Burger King • Eat In • Krispy Kreme • KFC • Starbucks • Waitrose • WH Smith — Shell — Days Inn P 2 hrs — Banbury Road, Ashorne, Warwick CV35 0AA C 01926 650168 @ warwicksouth.enquiry@welcomebreak.co.uk — www.welcomebreak.co.uk — Eat In, WH Smith and forecourt outlets open 24 hrs

M40 Warwick North — Welcome Break

M40 between J12 and J13 • Northbound 51 D8 SP33885770
Burger King • Eat In • KFC • Krispy Kreme • Starbucks • Waitrose • WH Smith — Shell — Days Inn P 2 hrs — Banbury Road, Ashorne, Warwick CV35 0AA C 01926 650168 @ warwicknorth.enquiry@welcomebreak.co.uk — www.welcomebreak.co.uk — Eat In and WH Smith open 24 hrs

M42 Hopwood Park — Welcome Break

M42 Junction 2 • Eastbound and westbound 50 B5 SP03637389
Burger King • Eat In • KFC • Krispy Kreme • Starbucks • Waitrose • WH Smith — Shell, LPG, electric car charge point P 2 hrs — Redditch Road, Alvechurch B48 7AU C 0121 4474000 @ hopwood.enquiry@welcomebreak.co.uk — www.welcomebreak.co.uk

M42 Tamworth — Moto

M42, just north of J10 • Northbound and southbound 63 D6 SK24440112
Burger King • Costa • EDC • Krispy Kreme • M&S Simply Food • WH Smith — Esso — Travelodge P 2 hrs — Green Lane, Tamworth, Staffordshire B77 5PS

C 01827 260120 — www.moto-way.co.uk — WH Smith and forecourt outlets are open 24 hrs

M48 Severn View — Moto

M48 J1 • Eastbound and westbound 36 F2 ST57118959
Burger King • Costa • Krispy Kreme • WH Smith — BP — Travelodge P 2 hrs — Aust, South Gloucestershire BS35 4BH C 01454 623851 — www.moto-way.co.uk — Forecourt outlets open 24 hrs

M50/A40 Ross Spur — Eurogarages

On A40, just west of M50 J4 • Southbound only 36 B3 SO6147125970
Coffee Nation • KFC • Spar • Starbucks • Subway — BF P 2 hrs — Trunk Road, Ross on Wye, Herefordshire HR9 7QL C 01989563493 (BP) — www.eurogarages.com — Forecourt outlets open 24 hours. KFC/Starbucks drive-thru).

M54 Telford — Welcome Break

M54 J4 • Eastbound and westbound 61 D7 SJ73050890
Burger King • Eat In • Starbucks • WH Smith — Shell, LPG available — Days Inn P 2 hrs — Prioslee Road, Shifnal, Telford, Shropshire TF11 8TG C 01952 238444 @ telford.enquiry@welcomebreak.co.uk — www.welcomebreak.co.uk — WH Smith and shop on forecourt open 24 hrs

M56 Chester — RoadChef

M56 J14 • Eastbound and westbound 73 B8 SJ46537491
Costa • Cotton Traders • Hot Food Co • McDonald's • WH Smith — Shell — Days Inn P 2 hrs — Elton, Chester, Cheshire CH2 4QZ C 01928 728500 — www.roadchef.com — Costa and McDonald's open 24 hrs

M61 Rivington – northbound — Euro Garages

M61 between J6 and J8 • Northbound and southbound 36 C4 SD62111168
Burger King • Spar • Starbucks • Subway — BP P 2 hrs — M61, Horwich, Bolton, Lancashire BL6 5UZ C 01254 56070 @ enquiries@eurogarages.com — www.eurogarages.com — Forecourt outlets open 24 hrs

M61 Rivington – southbound — Euro Garages

M61 between J8 and J6 • Northbound and southbound 36 C4 SD62111168
Burger King • Spar • Starbucks • Subway — BP — Rivington Lodge P 2 hrs — M61, Horwich, Bolton, Lancashire BL6 5UZ C 01254 56070 @ enquiries@eurogarages.com — www.eurogarages.com — Forecourt outlets open 24 hrs

M62 Burtonwood — Welcome Break

M62 J8 • Eastbound and westbound 86 E3 SJ57749129
KFC • Starbucks • WH Smith

— Shell P 2 hrs — M62 Great Sankey, Warrington, Cheshire WA5 3AX C 01925 651656 @ burtonwood.enquiry@welcomebreak.co.uk — www.welcomebreak.co.uk — WH Smith open 24 hrs

M62 Birch – eastbound — Moto

M62 1.5 miles east of J18 • Eastbound and westbound 87 D6 SD84700797
Burger King • Costa • EDC • Greggs • Krispy Kreme • M&S Simply Food • WH Smith — BP P 2 hrs — Heywood, Lancashire OL10 2HQ C 0161 643 0911 — www.moto-way.co.uk — WH Smith is open 24 hrs

M62 Birch – westbound — Moto

M62 1.5 miles east of J18 • Eastbound and westbound 87 D6 SD84700797
Burger King • Costa • EDC • Krispy Kreme • M&S Simply Food • WH Smith — BP — Travelodge P 2 hrs — Heywood, Lancashire OL10 2HQ C 0161 643 0911 — www.moto-way.co.uk — WH Smith is open 24 hrs

M62 Hartshead Moor — Welcome Break

M62, between J25 and J26 • Eastbound and westbound 88 B2 SE16892413
Burger King • Eat In • KFC • Krispy Kreme • Starbucks • WH Smith — Shell — Days Inn P 2 hrs — Clifton, Brighouse, W Yorks HD6 4JX C 01274 876584 @ hartshead.enquiry@welcomebreak.co.uk — www.welcomebreak.co.uk — Eat In and WH Smith open 24 hrs

M62 Ferrybridge — Moto

M62 Junction 33. Also A1(M) J40 (northbound) or J41 (southbound) • Northbound and southbound 89 B5 SE48512262
Burger King • Costa • EDC • Greggs • Krispy Kreme • M&S Simply Food • WH Smith — Travelodge P 2 hrs — Ferrybridge, Knottingly West Yorkshire WF11 0AF C 01977 672767 — www.moto-way.co.uk — Coffee Nation and WH Smith open 24 hrs

M65 Blackburn with Darwen — Extra MSA

M65 J4 • Eastbound and westbound 86 B4 SD68592414
Co-op • Costa • Greggs • McDonald's — Shell, LPG — Travelodge P 2 hrs — Darwen Motorway Services Area, Darwen, Lancashire BB3 0AT — www.extraservices.co.uk — Forecourt shop open 24 hrs

Scotland

M9 Stirling — Moto

M9 J9 • Northbound and southbound 127 F7 NS80438870
Burger King • Costa • EDC • WH Smith — BP — Travelodge P 2 hrs — Pirnhall, Stirling FK7 8EU C 01786 813614

M74 Bothwell — RoadChef

M74, south of J4 • southbound only 119 D7 NS70855980
Costa • Restbite! • WH Smith — BP P 2hrs — M74 Southbound, Bothwell, Lanarkshire G71 8BG C 01698 854123 — www.roadchef.com — Forecourt shop is open 24 hrs

M74 Hamilton — RoadChef

M74, 1 mile north of J6 • northbound only 119 D7 NS72525672
Costa • Restbite! • WH Smith — BP — Days Inn P 2hrs — M74 Northbound, Hamilton, S Lanarks, ML3 6JW C 01698 282176 — www.roadchef.com — Forecourt shop is open 24hrs

M74 Happendon — Cairn Lodge

M74 between J11 and J12 on B7078 • Northbound and southbound 119 F8 NS85243364
Coffee shop • restaurant • retail shop — Shell P 2hrs — Cairn Lodge, Douglas, Lanark, S Lanarkshire ML11 0RJ C 01555 851880

A74(M) Abington — Welcome Break

A74(M) J13 • Northbound and southbound 114 B2 NS93022505
Burger King • Eat In • Starbucks • WH Smith — Shell, LPG — Days Inn P 2 hrs — Abington, Biggar, South Lanarkshire ML12 6RG C 01864 502637 @ abington.enquiry@welcomebreak.co.uk — www.welcomebreak.co.uk — Eat In open 24 hrs. Tourist information office

A74(M) Annandale Water — RoadChef

A74(M) J16 • Northbound and southbound 114 E4 NY10389261
The Burger Company • Costa • Restbite! • WH Smith — BP — Days Inn P 2 hrs — Johnstone Bridge, near Lockerbie, DG11 1HD C 01576 470870 — www.roadchef.com — Restbite and forecourt shop are open 24 hrs

A74(M) Gretna Green — Welcome Break

A74(M), just north of J22 • Northbound and southbound 108 C3 NY30746872
Burger King • Eat In • KFC • Krispy Kreme • Starbucks • Waitrose • WH Smith — Shell — Days Inn P 2 hrs — M74A Trunk Road, Gretna Green, Dumfries and Galloway DG16 5HQ C 01461 337567 @ gretna.enquiry@welcomebreak.co.uk — www.welcomebreak.co.uk — Eat In open 24 hrs

M80 Old Inns —

M80 • Eastbound and Westbound 119 B7 NS77187671
Shell Select • Old Inns Cafe • Silk Cottage Cantonese buffet and takeaway — Shell P — Castlecary Road, Cumbernauld G68 0BJ C 0843 2590190 (filling station) — www.shell.co.uk • www.oldinnscafe.com

M90 Kinross — Moto

M90 J6 • Northbound and southbound 128 D3 NO10800282
Burger King • Costa • EDC • WH Smith — BP — Travelodge P 2 hrs — M90, Kinross, KY13 7NQ C 01577 863123 — www.moto-way.co.uk — WH Smith and forecourt shop open 24 hrs

Wales

M4 Magor — RoadChef

M4 J23A • Eastbound and westbound 35 F8 ST42068796
Costa • Cotton Traders • McDonald's • Restbite! • WH Smith — Esso — Days Inn P 2 hours — M4 Magor, Caldicot, Monmouthshire NP26 3YL C 01633 881515 @ info@firstmotorway.co.uk — www.roadchef.com — McDonald's open 24 hrs

M4 Cardiff Gate — Welcome Break

M4 J30 • Eastbound and westbound 35 F6 ST21658283
Burger King • Krispy Kreme • Starbucks • Waitrose • WH Smith — Shell P 2 hrs — Cardiff Gate Business Park, Cardiff, South Glamorgan CF23 8RA C 02920 541122 @ cardiff.enquiry@welcomebreak.co.uk — www.welcomebreak.co.uk — Forecourt shop open 24 hrs

M4 Cardiff West — Moto

M4, off J33 • Eastbound and westbound 22 B2 ST09417967
Burger King • Costa • Krispy Kreme • WH Smith — Esso — Travelodge P 2 hrs — Pontyclun, Mid Glamorgan CF72 8SA C 02920 891141 — www.moto-way.co.uk — WH Smith is open 24 hrs

M4 Sarn Park — Welcome Break

M4 J36 • Eastbound and westbound 34 F3 SS90688290
Burger King • Starbucks • WH Smith — Shell — Days Inn P 2 hrs — M4 Motorway, Junction 36, Sarn Park, Bridgend CF32 9RW C 01656 655332 @ sarn.enquiry@welcomebreak.co.uk — www.welcomebreak.co.uk — WH Smith and forecourt shop open 24 hrs

M4 Swansea — Moto

M4 at J47 • Eastbound and westbound 33 E7 SS62159969
Burger King • Costa • WH Smith — BP — Travelodge P 2 hrs — Penllergaer, Swansea, West Glamorgan SA4 1GT C 01792 896222 — www.moto-way.co.uk — Forecourt outlets open 24 hrs

M4 Pont Abraham — RoadChef

M4 J49 • Eastbound and westbound 33 D6 SN57470743
Costa • Restbite! • WH Smith — Texaco P 2 hours — Llanedi, Pontarddulais, Swansea SA4 0FU C 01792 884 663 — www.roadchef.com — Forecourt outlets open 24 hrs

Restricted motorway junctions

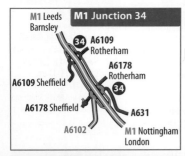

M1 Junction 34
M1 Leeds Barnsley · 34 · A6109 Rotherham · A6178 Rotherham · A6109 Sheffield · A6178 Sheffield · 34 · A631 · A6102 · M1 Nottingham London

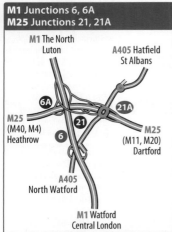

M1 Junctions 6, 6A
M25 Junctions 21, 21A
M1 The North Luton · A405 Hatfield St Albans · 6A · 21A · M25 (M40, M4) Heathrow · 21 · 6 · M25 (M11, M20) Dartford · A405 North Watford · M1 Watford Central London

M4 Junctions 25, 25A, 26
A4042 Abergavenny Cwmbran · A4051 Cwmbran · 25A · 25 · B4596 Caerleon · 26 · A4042 A4051 Newport B4596 · M4 Chepstow London · M4 Cardiff

M5 Junction 11A
A417 Gloucester · M5 Cheltenham (A40) · 11A · B4641 · A417 Cirencester · M5 Bristol

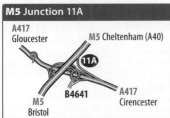

M8 Junctions 8, 9 · M73 Junctions 1, 2
M74 Junctions 2A, 3, 3A, 4
M8 Glasgow · 9 · M73 Stirling · 8 · A89 Coatbridge · 2 · A8 Edinburgh · B7058 · A74 · B765 · A74 · M73 · M74 Glasgow · 2A · 3 · M74 · B7001 · 3A · A721 · A763 · B758 · M74 Carlisle · B7071

M1	Northbound	Southbound
2	No exit	No access
4	No exit	No access
6A	No exit. Access from M25 only	No access. Exit to M25 only
7	No exit. Access from A414 only	No access. Exit to A414 only
17	No access. Exit to M45 only	No exit. Access from M45 only
19	No exit to A14	No access from A14
21A	No access	No exit
23A		Exit to A42 only
24A	No exit	No access
35A	No access	No exit
43	No access. Exit to M621 only	No exit. Access from M621 only
48	No exit to A1(M) southbound	

M3	Eastbound	Westbound
8	No exit	No access
10	No access	No exit
13	No access to M27 eastbound	
14	No exit	No access

M4	Eastbound	Westbound
1	Exit to A4 eastbound only	Access from A4 westbound only
2	Access from A4 eastbound only	Access to A4 westbound only
21	No exit	No access
23	No access	No exit
25	No exit	No access
25A	No exit	No access
29	No exit	No access
38		No access
39	No exit or access	No exit
41	No access	No exit
41A	No exit	No access
42	Access from A483 only	Exit to A483 only

M5	Northbound	Southbound
10	No exit	No access
11A	No access from A417 eastbound	No exit to A417 westbound

M6	Northbound	Southbound
3A	No access. Exit to M42 northbound only	No exit. Access from M6 eastbound only
4A	No exit. Access from M42 southbound only	No access. Exit to M42 only
5	No access	No exit
10A	No access. Exit to M54 only	No exit. Access from M54 only
11A	No exit. Access from M6 Toll only	No access. Exit to M6 Toll only
20	No exit to M56 eastbound	No access from M56 westbound
24	No exit	No access
25	No access	No exit
30	No exit. Access from M61 northbound only	No access. Exit to M61 southbound only
31A	No access	No exit
45	No access	No exit

M6 Toll	Northbound	Southbound
T1		No exit
T2	No exit, no access	No access
T5	No exit	No access
T7	No access	No exit
T8	No access	No exit

M8	Eastbound	Westbound
8	No exit to M73 northbound	No access from M73 southbound
9	No access	No exit
13	No exit southbound	Access from M73 southbound only
14	No access	No exit
16	No exit	No access
17	No exit	No access
18		No exit
19	No exit to A814 eastbound	No access from A814 westbound
20	No exit	No access
21	No access from M74	No exit
22	No exit. Access from M77 only	No access. Exit to M77 only
23	No exit	No access
25	Exit to A739 northbound only. Access from A739 southbound only	Access from A739 southbound only
25A	No exit	No access
28	No exit	No access
28A	No exit	No access

M9	Eastbound	Westbound
1A	No exit	No access
2	No access	No exit
3	No exit	No access
6	No access	No exit
8	No exit	No access

M11	Northbound	Southbound
4	No exit	No access
5	No access	No exit
9	No access	No exit
13	No access	No exit
14	No exit to A428 westbound	No exit. Access from A14 westbound only

M20	Eastbound	Westbound
2	No access	No exit
3	No exit. Access from M26 eastbound only	No access. Exit to M26 westbound only
11A	No access	No exit

M23	Northbound	Southbound
7	No exit to A23 southbound	No access from A23 northbound
10A	No exit	No access

M25	Clockwise	Anticlockwise
5	No exit to M26 eastbound	No access from M26 westbound
19	No access	No exit
21	No exit to M1 southbound. Access from M1 southbound only	No exit to M1 southbound. Access from M1. southbound only
31	No exit	No access

M27	Eastbound	Westbound
10	No exit	No access
12	No access	No exit

M40	Eastbound	Westbound
3	No exit	No access
7	No exit	No access
8	No exit	No access
13	No exit	No access
14	No access	No exit
16	No access	No exit

M42	Northbound	Southbound
1	No exit	No access
7	No access. Exit to M6 northbound only	No exit. Access from M6 northbound only
7A	No access. Exit to M6 southbound only	No exit
8	No exit. Access from M6 southbound only	Exit to M6 northbound only. Access from M6 southbound only

M45		Eastbound	Westbound
M1 J17		Access to M1 southbound only	No access from M1 southbound
With A45		No access	No exit

M48		Eastbound	Westbound
M4 J21		No exit to M4 westbound	No access from M4 eastbound
M4 J23		No access from M4 westbound	No exit to M4 eastbound

M49	Southbound	Northbound
18A	No exit to M5 northbound	No access from M5 southbound

M53	Northbound	Southbound
11	Exit to M56 eastbound only. Access from M56 westbound only	Exit to M56 eastbnd only. Access from M56 westbound only

M56	Eastbound	Westbound
2	No exit	No access
3	No access	No exit
4	No exit	No access
7		No access
8	No exit or access	No access
9	No access from M6 northbound	No access to M6 southbound
15	No exit to M53	No access from M53 northbound

M57	Northbound	Southbound
3	No exit	No access
5	No exit	No access

M58	Eastbound	Westbound
1	No exit	No access

M60	Clockwise	Anticlockwise
2	No exit	No access
3	No exit to A34 northbound	No exit to A34 northbound
4	No access from M56	No exit to M56
5	No exit to A5103 southbound	No exit to A5103 northbound
14	No exit	No access
16	No exit	No access
20	No access	No exit
22		No access
25	No access	
26		No exit or access
27	No exit	No access

M61	Northbound	Southbound
2	No access from A580 eastbound	No exit to A580 westbound
3	No access from A580 eastbound. No access from A666 southbound	No exit to A580 westbound
M6 J30	No exit to M6 southbound	No access from M6 northbound

M62	Eastbound	Westbound
23	No access	No exit

M65	Eastbound	Westbound
9	No access	No exit
11	No exit	No access

M66	Northbound	Southbound
1	No access	No exit

M67	Eastbound	Westbound
1A	No access	No exit
2	No exit	No access

M69	Northbound	Southbound
2	No exit	No access

M73	Northbound	Southbound
2	No access from M8 or A89 eastbound. No exit to A89	No exit to M8 or A89 westbound. No access from A89

M74	Northbound	Southbound
3	No access	No exit
3A	No exit	No access
7	No exit	No access
9	No exit or access	No access
10		No exit
11	No access	No exit
12	No access	No exit

M77	Northbound	Southbound
4	No exit	No access
6	No exit	No access
7	No exit or access	
8	No access	No access

M80	Northbound	Southbound
4A	No access	No exit
6A	No exit	
8	Exit to M876 northbound only. No access	Access from M876 southbound only. No exit

M90	Northbound	Southbound
2A	No access	No exit
7	No exit	No access
8	No access	No exit
10	No access from A912	No exit to A912

M180	Eastbound	Westbound
1	No access	No exit

M621	Eastbound	Westbound
2A	No exit	No access
4	No exit	
5	No exit	No access
6	No access	No exit

M876	Northbound	Southbound
2	No access	No exit

A1(M)	Northbound	Southbound
2	No access	No exit
3		No access
5	No exit	No access
14	No exit	No access
40	No access	No access
43	No exit. Access from M1 only	No access. Exit to M1 only
57	No access	No exit
65	No access	No exit

A3(M)	Northbound	Southbound
1	No exit	No access
4	No access	No exit

A38(M)	Northbound	Southbound
With Victoria Rd, (Park Circus) Birmingham	No exit	No access

A48(M)	Northbound	Southbound
M4 Junc 29	Exit to M4 eastbound only	Access from M4 westbound only
29A	Access from A48 eastbound only	Exit to A48 westbound only

A57(M)	Eastbound	Westbound
With A5103	No access	No exit
With A34	No access	No exit

A58(M)		Southbound
With Park Lane and Westgate, Leeds		No access

A64(M)	Eastbound	Westbound
With A58 Clay Pit Lane, Leeds	No access	No exit
With Regent Street, Leeds	No access	No access

A74(M)	Northbound	Southbound
18	No access	No exit
22		No exit

A194(M)	Northbound	Southbound
A1(M) J65 Gateshead Western Bypass	Access from A1(M) northbound only	Exit to A1(M) southbound only

M3 Junctions 13, 14 · **M27** Junction 4

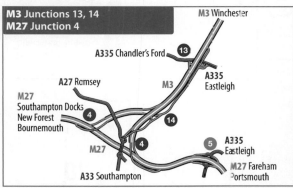

M6 Junctions 3A, 4A · **M42** Junctions 7, 7A, 8, 9
M6 Toll Junctions T1, T2

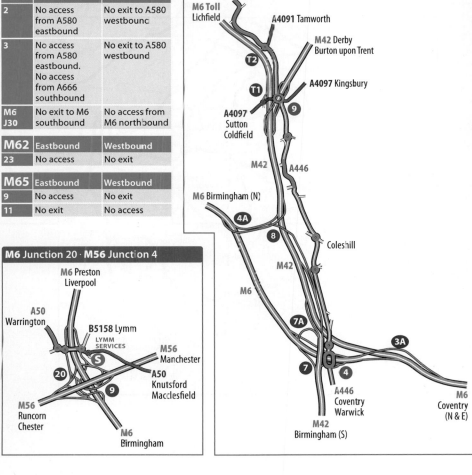

M6 Junction 20 · **M56** Junction 4

M62 Junctions 32A, 33 · **A1(M)** Junctions 40, 41

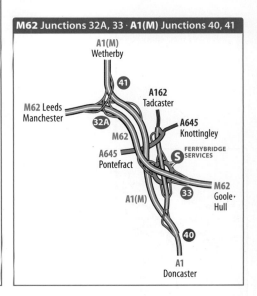

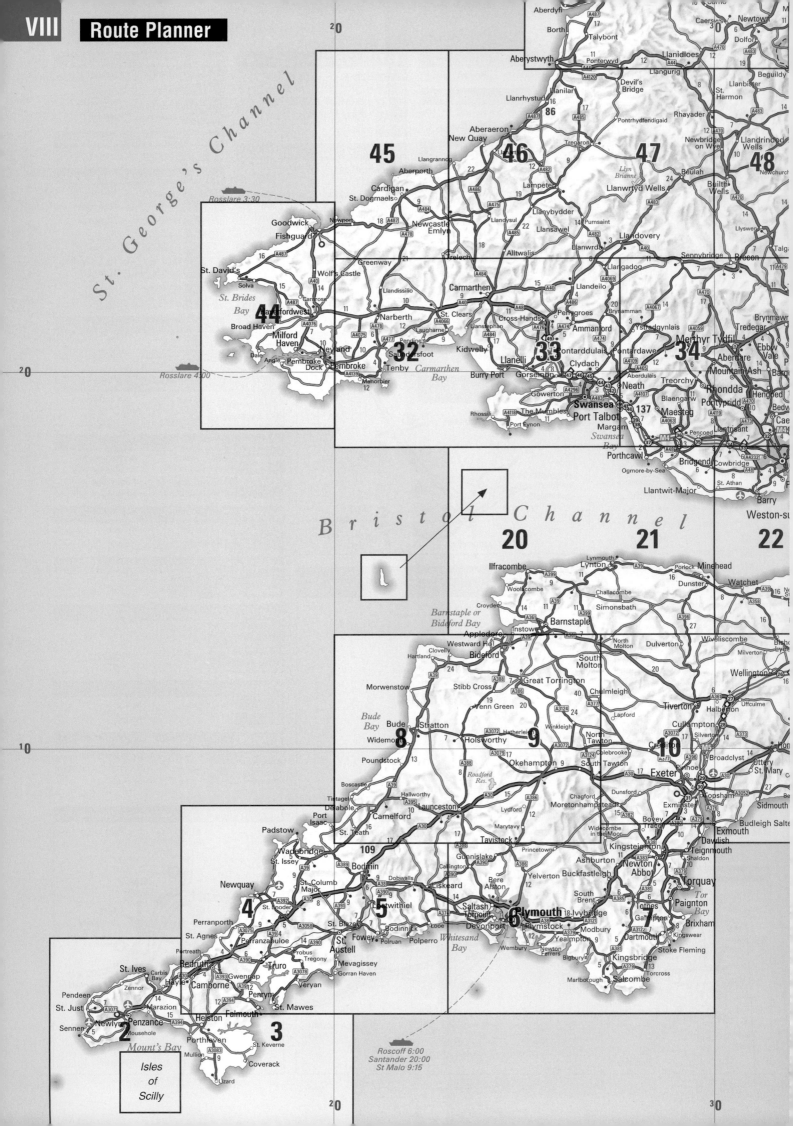

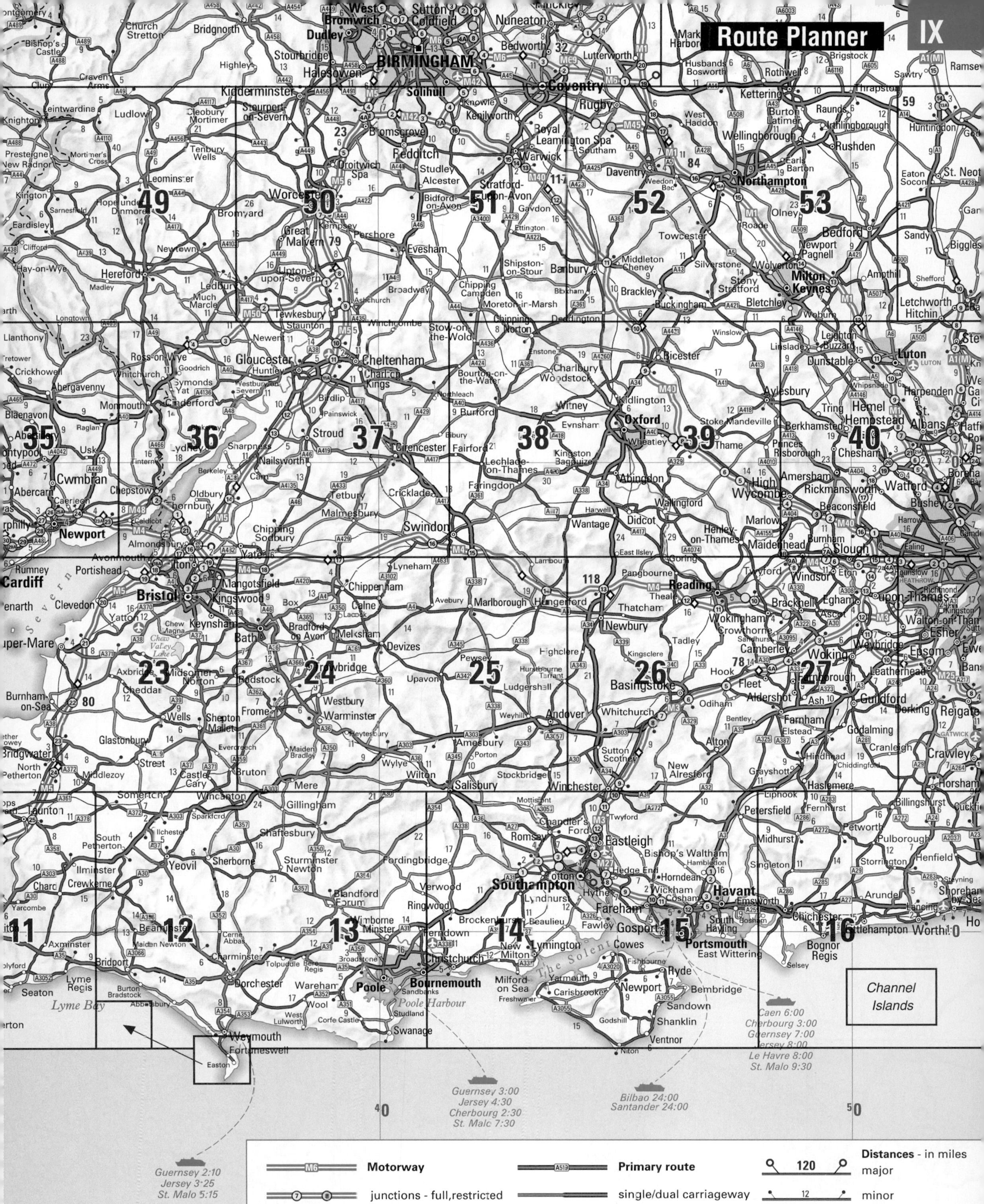

M6	**Motorway**	A519	**Primary route**	120	**Distances** - in miles major
7 8	junctions - full, restricted		single/dual carriageway	12	minor
	Toll motorway	A519	**A Road**		**Railway**
	Services		**B Road**		**National boundary**
Dieppe 4:00	**Ferry route**		**Airport**		

Scale **1:1000000 1cm = 10km 1 inch = 15.78 miles**

0 5 10 15 20 25 30 35 40 45 50 miles

0 10 20 30 40 50 60 70 80 km

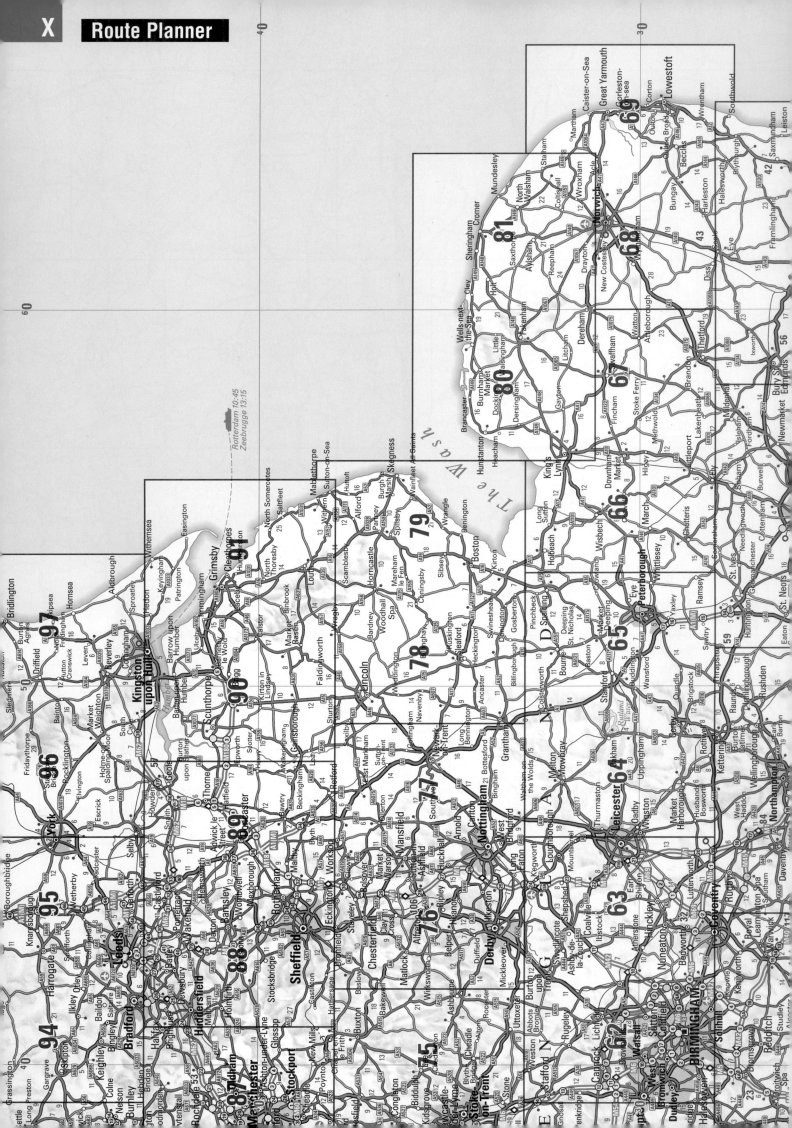

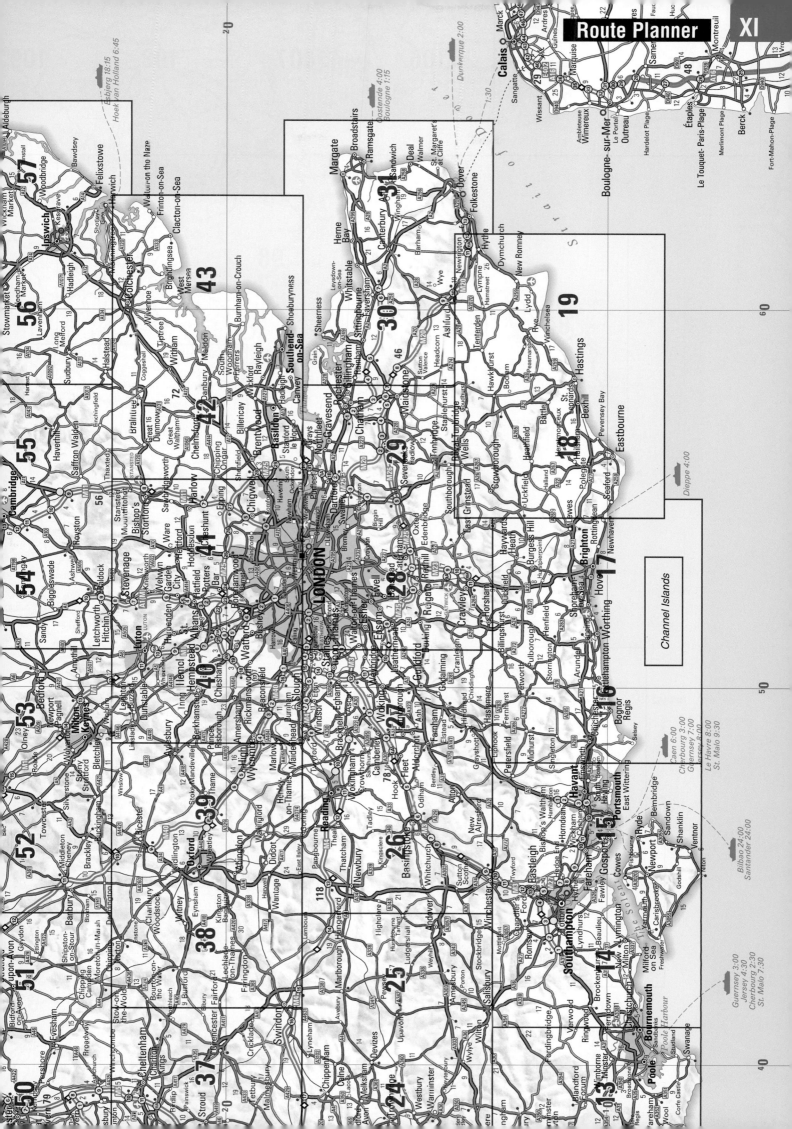

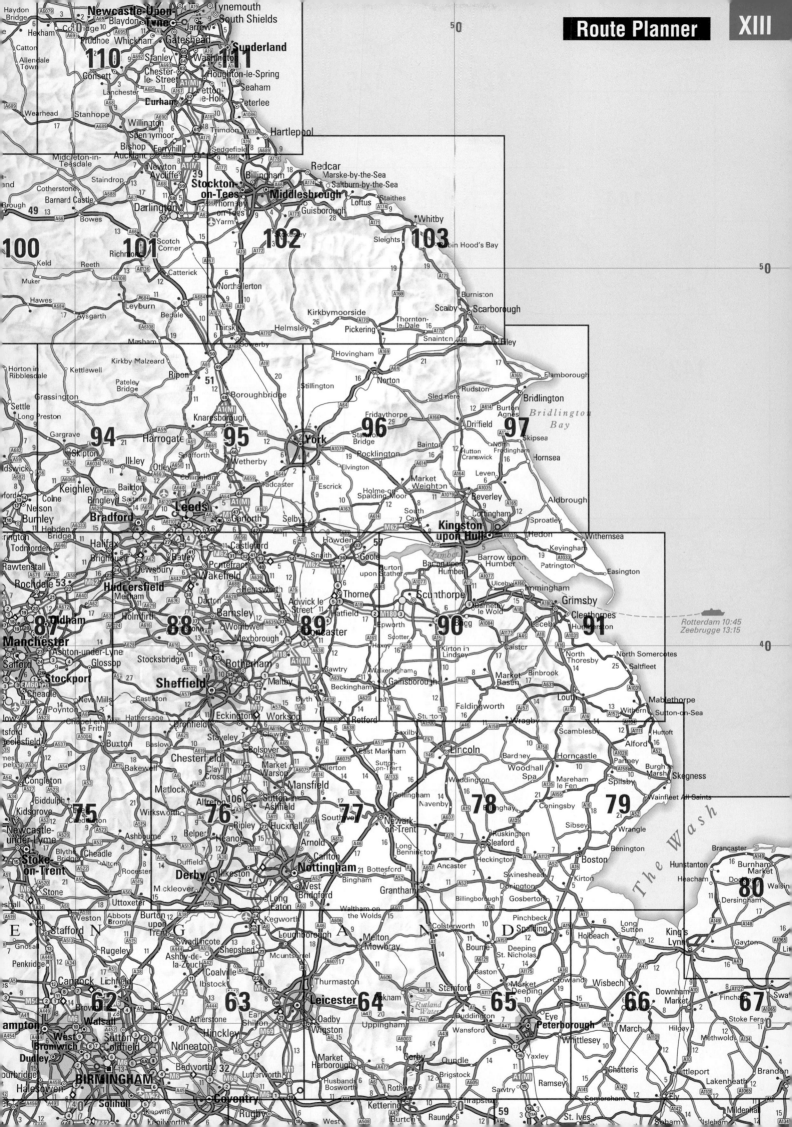

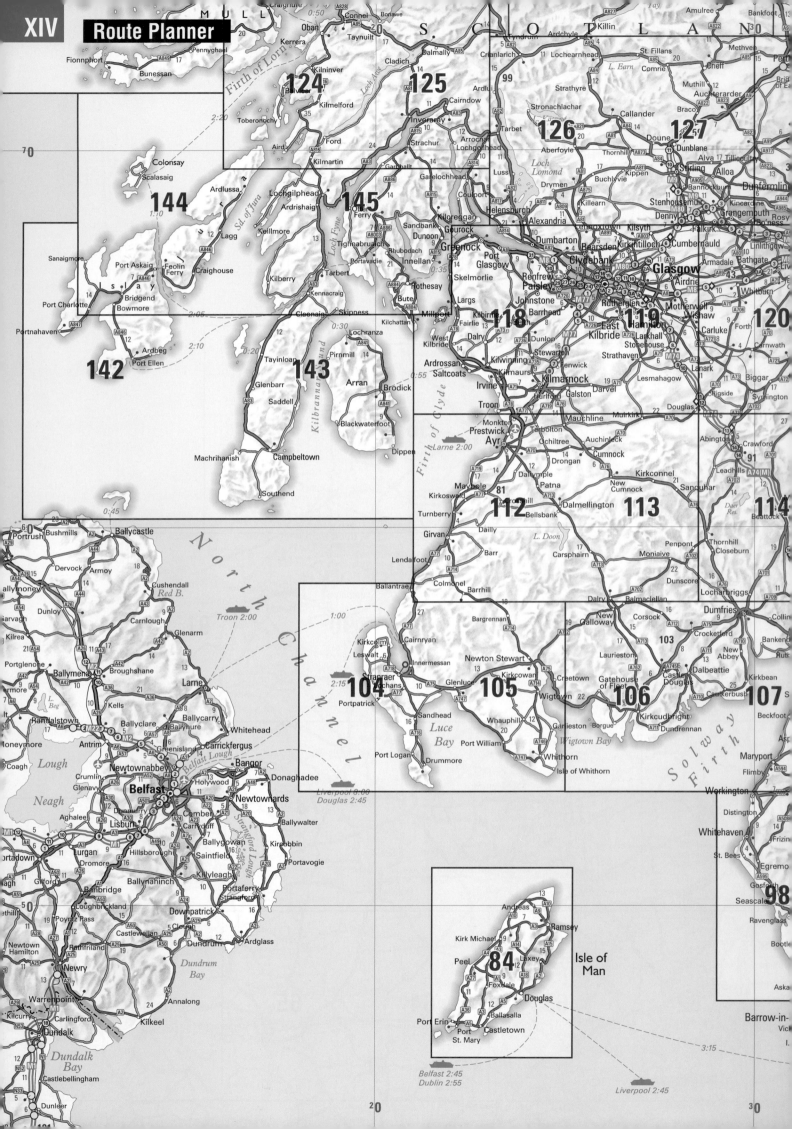

NORTH

SEA

Amsterdam 15:30

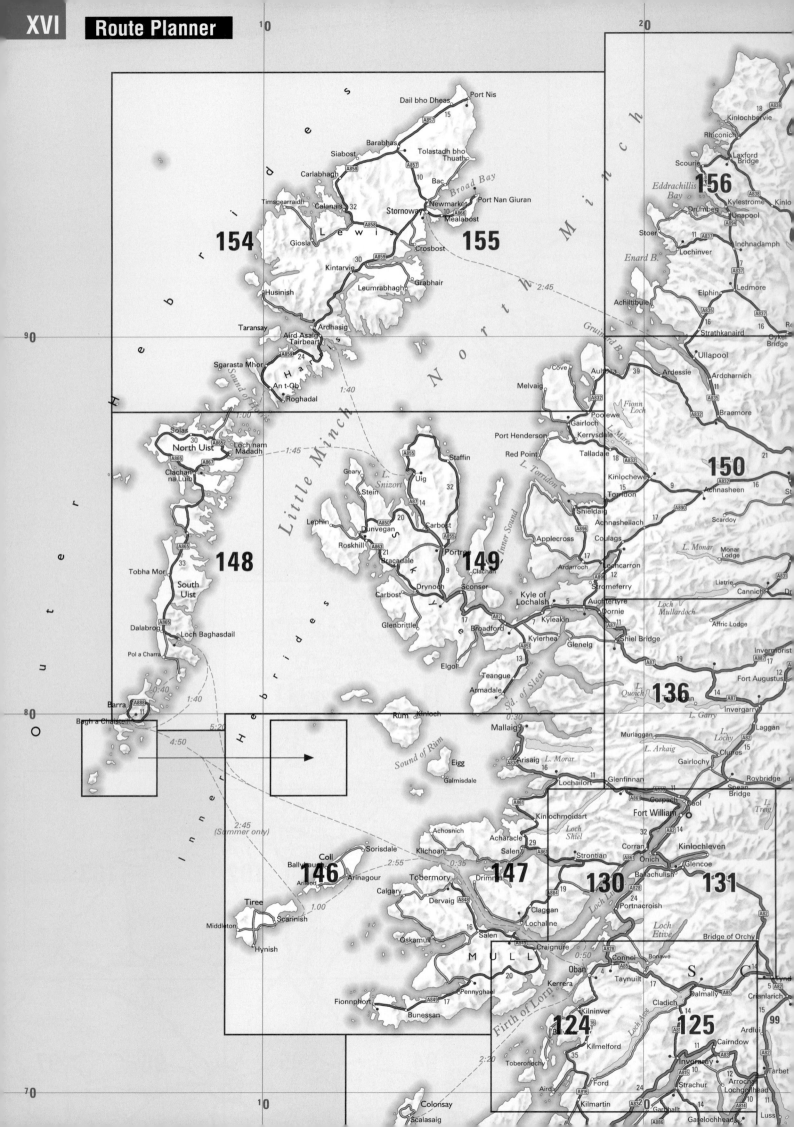

Port Nis
Dail bho Dheas
15
A857
Barabhas
Siabost
Tolastadh bho
Thuath
Carlabhagh
A858
A857
10
Bac
Broad Bay
Timsgearraidh
Calanais
32
Newmarket
Port Nan Giuran
A866
Stornoway
Mealabost
154
Lewis
A858
10
155
Giosla
Crosbost
30
A859
Kintarvie
Grabhair
Husinish
Leumrabhagh
2:45
Taransay
Ardhasig
Aird Asaig
Tairbeart
Harris
A859
24
Sgarasta Mhor
1:40
An t-Ob
Roghadal
1:00
1:45

North Minch

Enard B.

18
A838
Kinlochbervie
Rhiconich
Scourie
Laxford
Bridge
156
Eddrachillis
Bay
Drumbeg
A894
Kylestrome
Kinlo
Stoer
11
A837
Inchnadamph
Lochinver
Elphin
A837
Ledmore
7
Achiltibuie
16
Strathkanaird
Oykel
Bridge

90

Solas
30
A865
Loch nam
Madadh
North Uist
A865
A867
Clachan
na Luib
A865
148
Tobha Mor
33
*South
Uist*
A865
Dalabrog
Loch Baghasdail
Pol a Charra
0:40
1:40
0:40
Barra
A888
11
Bagh a Chaisteil

Little Minch

Geary
Stein
L.
Snizort
A855
Staffin
Uig
32
A87
14
Lephin
A850
20
Dunvegan
Carbost
A855
Roskhill
A863
21
Portree
S k y e
9
Bracadale
Clachan
Drynoch
Sconser
Carbost
17
Glenbrittle
Elgol

Cove
Aultbea
39
Melvaig
A832
*Fionn
Loch*
Poolewe
Gairloch
A832
Port Henderson
Kerrysdale
Red Point
Talladale
18
L. Maree
L. Torridon
Kinlochewe
15
Torridon
Shieldaig
A896
Achnashellach
Applecross
Coulags
17
Ardarroch
Lochcarron
Stromeferry
12
Kyle of
Lochalsh
5
Auchtertyre
A87
Dornie
Kyleakin
A87
11
Shiel Bridge
Broadford
Kylerhea
Glenelg
A851
Teangue
13
Armadale
Sd. of Sleat

150
A832
Ardessie
Ardcharnich
11
A835
Braemore
Ullapool
A835
21
A890
Achnasheen
Scardoy
A831
Monar
Liatrie
Lodge
Cannich
L. Monar
A890
L.
Mullardoch
Affric Lodge
19
A87
17
Invermorist
A87
136
A87
14
Fort Augustus
12
L. Garry
Invergarry
L.
Quoich
L.
Lochy
A82
Laggan

80

2:45
(Summer only)
4:50
5:20

Rum
Kinloch
0:30
Mallaig
Sound of Rum
Eigg
A830
Arisaig
L. Morar
16
Galmisdale
Lochailort
A861

Murlaggan
L. Arkaig
Gairlochy
Glenfinnan
A830
11
A861
Corpach
Kaol
Fort William
32
Clunes
15
Roybridge
Spean
7
Bridge
L.
Treig

Inner Hebrides

Coll
Sorisdale
Ballygown
Arinagour
Arinot
1.00
146
Tiree
Scarinish
Middleton
Hynish
2:55
Kilchoan
0:35
147
Achosnich
Acharacle
29
Salen
A861
Drimnin
Tobermory
Dervaig
Calgary
A848
Claggan
Lochaline
16
Oskamull
Salen
A849

M U L L

Kilbride
Craignure
0:50
20
Pennyghael
A849
17
Fionnphort
Bunessan

Loch
Shiel
Strontian
Corran
130
A884
19
Onich
Ballachulish
A828
Portnacroish
Loch Linnhe
24

Kinlochmoidart

Kinlochleven
Glencoe
131
Loch
Etive
Bridge of Orchy
A82

Connel
Bonawe
0:50
Oban
4
Taynuilt
Kerrera
124
Kilninver
Kilmelford
11
35
Toberonochy
Aird
A816
Ford
24
Kilmartin
A832
0
Colonsay
Scalasaig

Dalmally
A85
Cladich
125
A819
11
Inveraray
A83
A815
10
Strachur
Lochgoilhead
Aird
A816

Cairndow
S
C
Crianlarich
15
Ardlui
99
A82
Garelochhead
12
Arrochar
Lussa

70

1
10
2
20

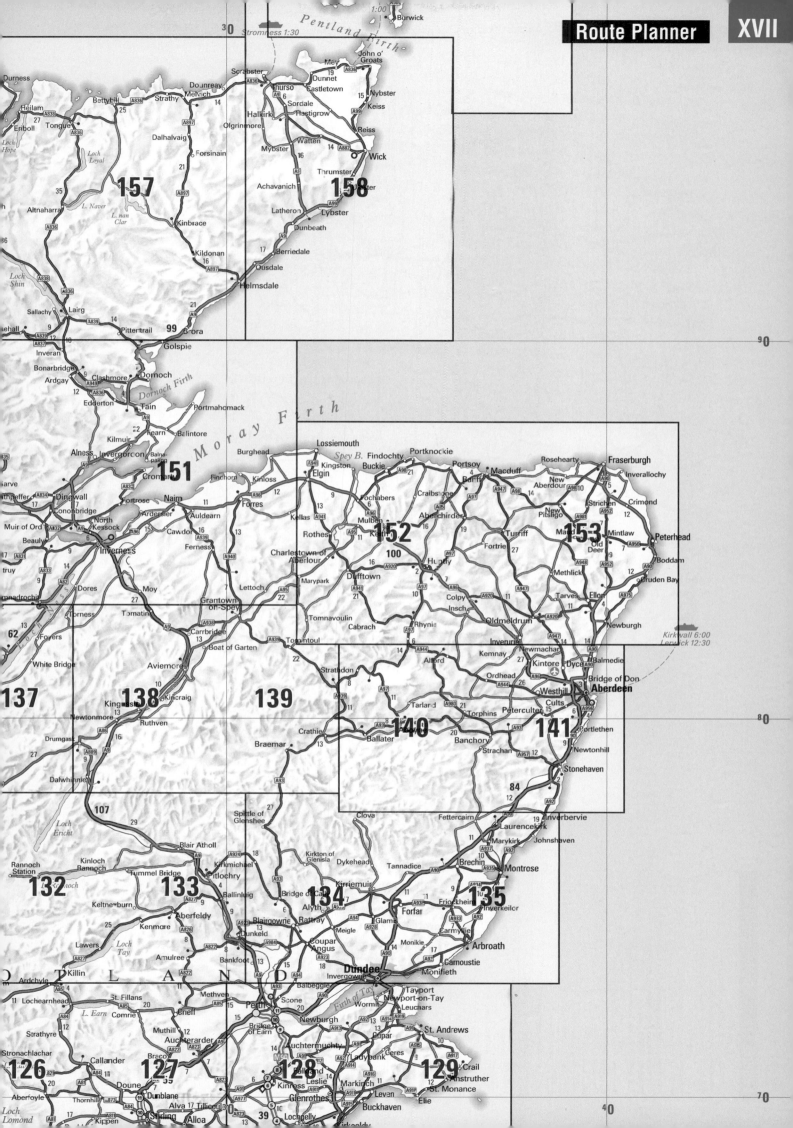

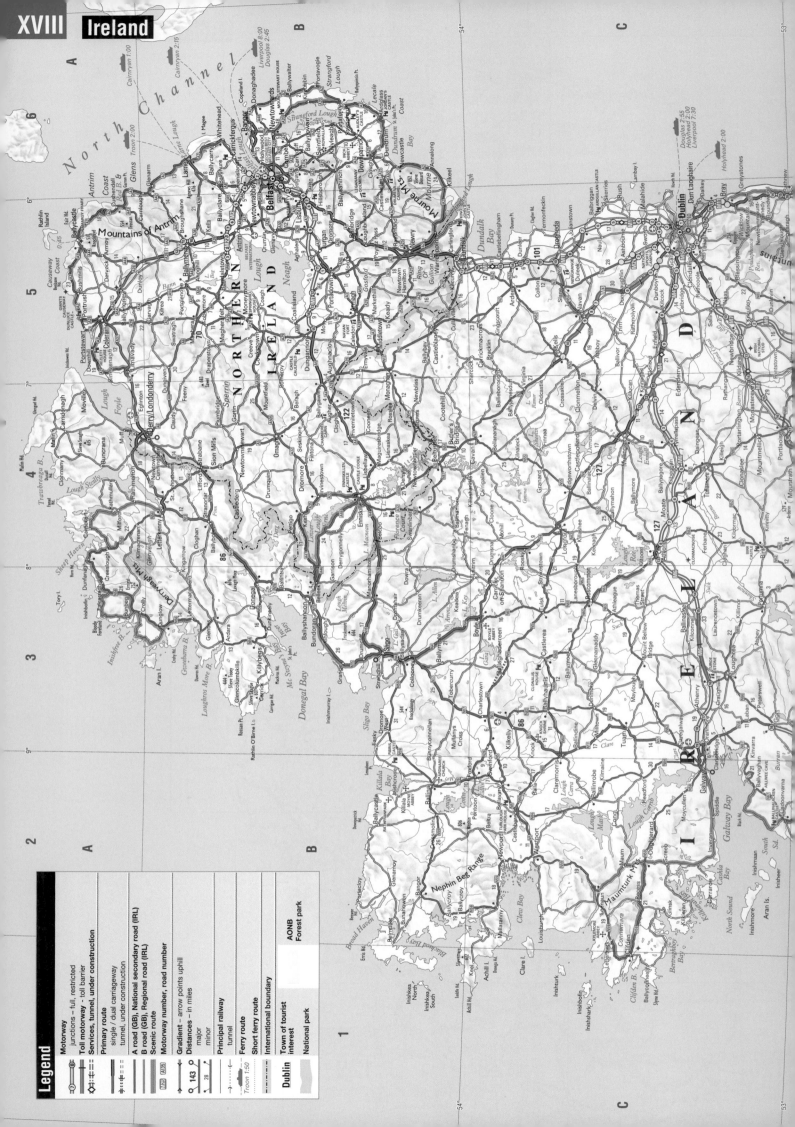

Legend

Motorway
junctions – full, restricted
Toll motorway – toll barrier
Services, tunnel, under construction

Primary route
single / dual carriageway
tunnel, under construction
A road (GB), National secondary road (IRL)
B road (GB), Regional road (IRL)
Scenic route
Motorway number, road number

Gradient – arrow points uphill
Distances – in miles
major
minor

Principal railway
tunnel

Ferry route
Short ferry route

International boundary

Town of tourist interest
Dublin

National park

AONB
Forest park

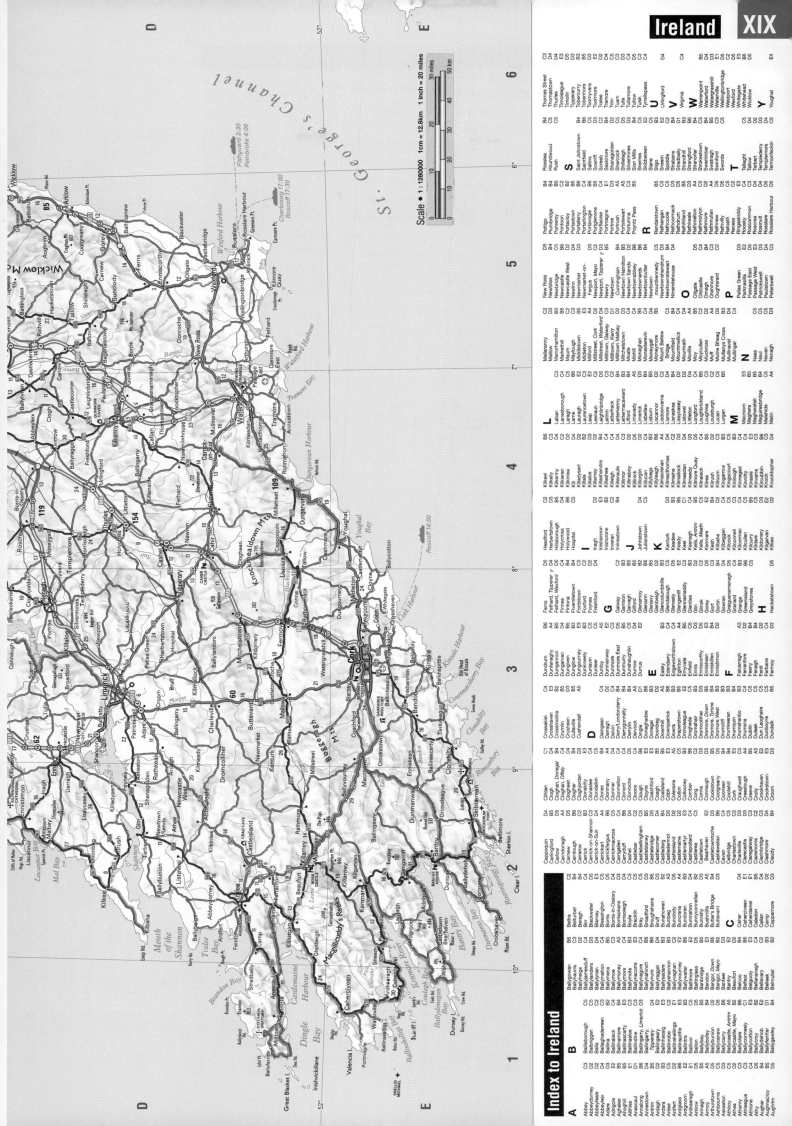

Distance table

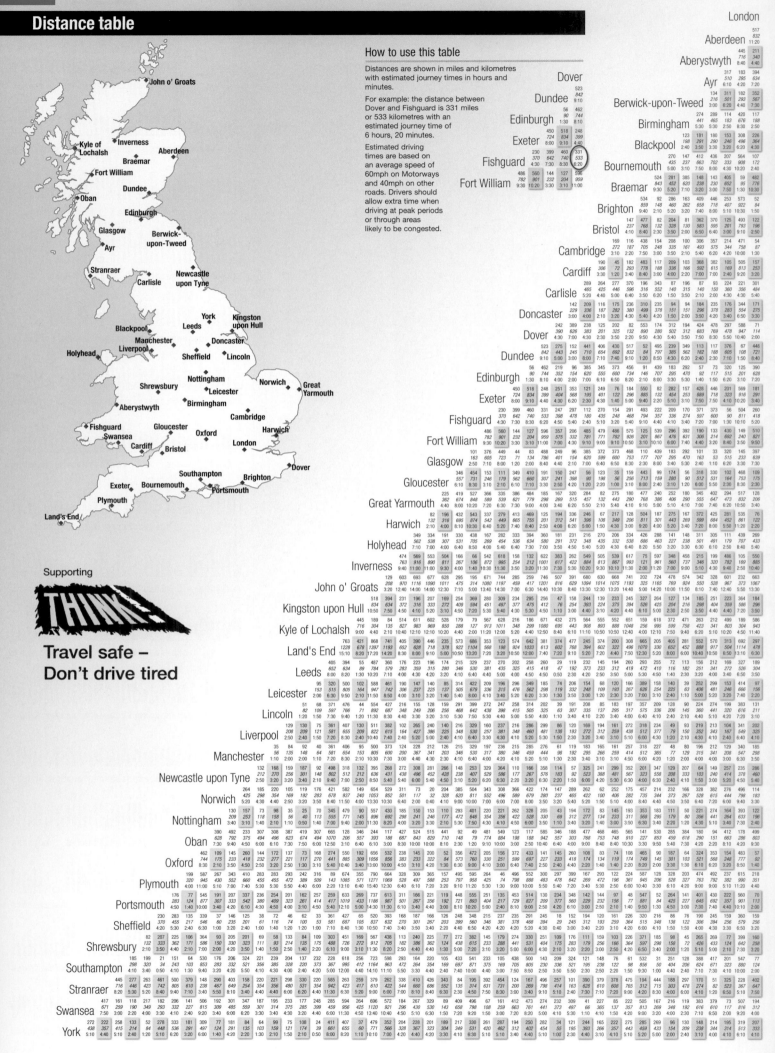

How to use this table

Distances are shown in miles and kilometres with estimated journey times in hours and minutes.

For example: the distance between Dover and Fishguard is 331 miles or 533 kilometres with an estimated journey time of 6 hours, 20 minutes.

Estimated driving times are based on an average speed of 60mph on Motorways and 40mph on other roads. Drivers should allow extra time when driving at peak periods or through areas likely to be congested.

Supporting

THINK!

Travel safe –
Don't drive tired

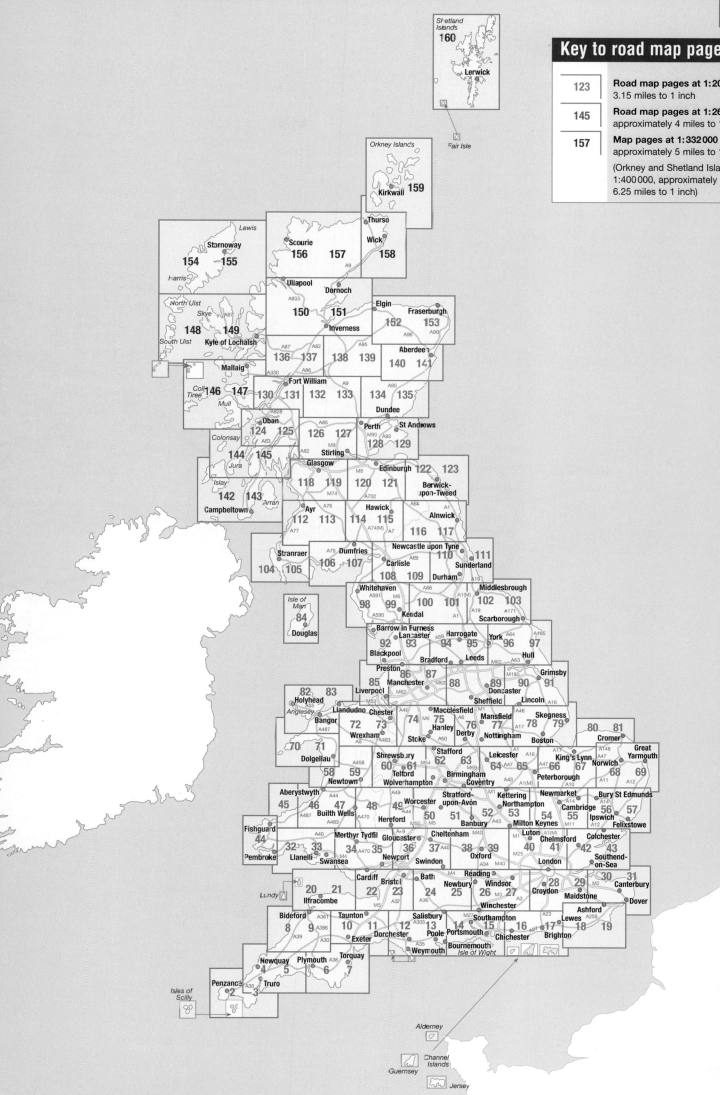

Key to road map pages

123	**Road map pages at 1:200 000** 3.15 miles to 1 inch
145	**Road map pages at 1:265 000** approximately 4 miles to 1 inch
157	**Map pages at 1:332 000** approximately 5 miles to 1 inch (Orkney and Shetland Islands at 1:400 000, approximately 6.25 miles to 1 inch)

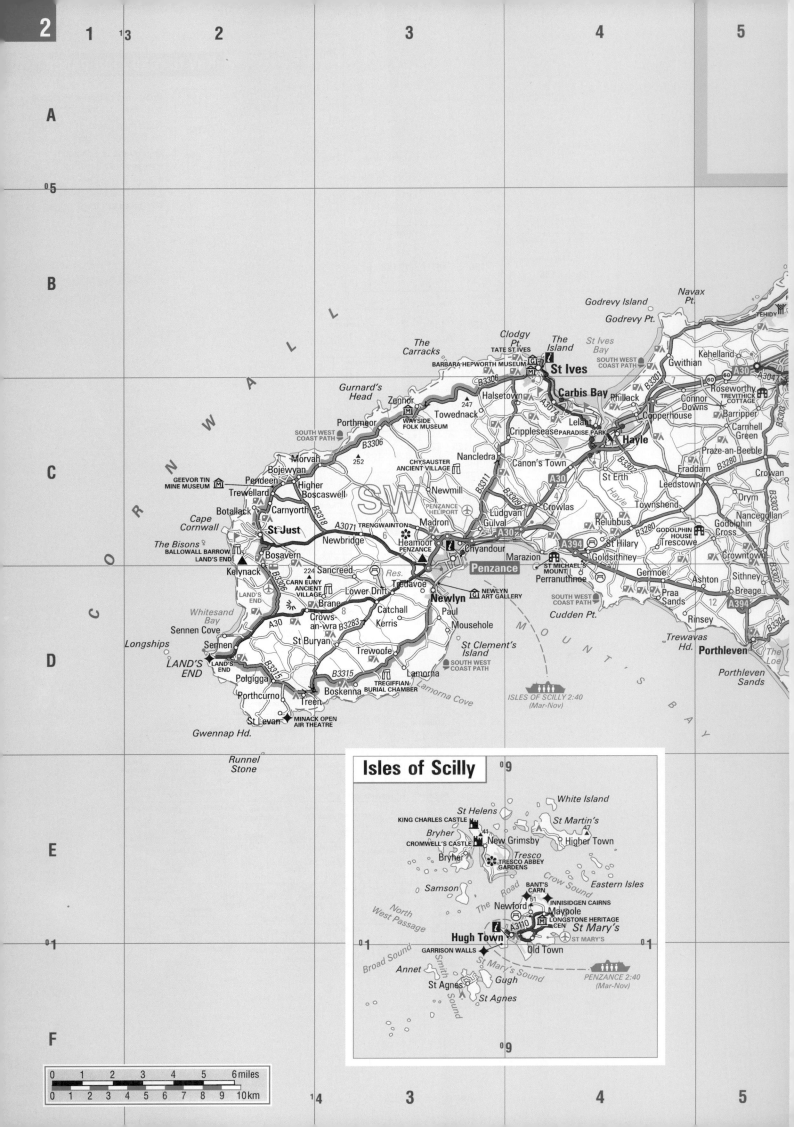

A
⁰5

B

C

D

E
⁰1   ⁰1

F

CORNWALL

Navax Pt.

Godrevy Island
Godrevy Pt.
TEHIDY

The Carracks
Clodgy Pt.
TATE ST IVES
The Island
St Ives Bay
SOUTH WEST COAST PATH
Gwithian
Kehelland
A30   A3047

BARBARA HEPWORTH MUSEUM
St Ives
B3301
ℹ
Roseworthy
TREVITHICK COTTAGE
60   A30

Gurnard's Head
Zennor
Halsetown
Carbis Bay
Phillack
Connor Downs
Barripper
B3303

Porthmeor
WAYSIDE FOLK MUSEUM
Towednack
247
A3074
Lelant
Copperhouse
Praze-an-Beeble
Carnhell Green

SOUTH WEST COAST PATH
B3306
Cripplesease
PARADISE PARK
Hayle
Crowan
Drym

Morvah
252
CHYSAUSTER ANCIENT VILLAGE
Nancledra
Canon's Town
St Erth
Leedstown
Fraddam
B3280
Nancegollan

Bojewyan
Newmill
A30
Townshend
Godolphin Cross

GEEVOR TIN MINE MUSEUM
Pendeen
Higher Boscaswell
PENZANCE HELIPORT
B3311
B3309
Crowlas
Relubbus
B3280
GODOLPHIN HOUSE
Growntown

Trewellard
SW
Ludgvan
Gulval
Hayle
St Hilary
Trescowe

Botallack
Carnyorth
TRENGWAINTON
Madron
A30
A394
Goldsithney
Sithney

Cape Cornwall
St Just
A3071
Heamoor
PENZANCE
Chyandour
Marazion
ST MICHAEL'S MOUNT
Germoe
Ashton
Breage

The Bisons
BALLOWALL BARROW
LAND'S END
Bosavern
Newbridge
6
ℹ
Penzance
Perranuthnoe
Praa Sands
A394

Kelynack
224
Sancreed
CARN EUNY ANCIENT VILLAGE
Lower Drift
Tredavoe
NEWLYN ART GALLERY
Cudden Pt.
SOUTH WEST COAST PATH
Rinsey
B3304

B3306
Brane
8
Catchall
Kerris
Newlyn
Paul
Trewavas Hd.
Porthleven
The Loe

Whitesand Bay
A30
Crows-an-wra
B3283
Mousehole
St Clement's Island
M
O
U
N
T
'
S
Porthleven Sands

Sennen Cove
Sennen
St Buryan
Trewoofe
St Clement's Island

Longships
LAND'S END
LAND'S END
B3315
Lamorna
SOUTH WEST COAST PATH
ISLES OF SCILLY 2:40 (Mar-Nov)
B
A
Y

LAND'S END
Polgigga
Boskenna
B3315
TREGIFFIAN BURIAL CHAMBER
Lamorna Cove

Porthcurno
Treen

St Levan
MINACK OPEN AIR THEATRE

Gwennap Hd.

Runnel Stone

Isles of Scilly

⁰9

White Island

St Helens
St Martin's
47

KING CHARLES CASTLE
41
Higher Town

Bryher
New Grimsby
CROMWELL'S CASTLE

Bryher
Tresco
TRESCO ABBEY GARDENS

Samson
Crow Sound
Eastern Isles

The Road
BANT'S CARN
51
INNISIDGEN CAIRNS

North West Passage
Newford
Maypole
LONGSTONE HERITAGE CEN

ℹ
A3110
St Mary's

Hugh Town
A3110
Old Town
ST MARY'S

GARRISON WALLS

Annet
Smith Sound
St Mary's Sound
PENZANCE 2:40 (Mar-Nov)

St Agnes
Gugh
St Agnes

Broad Sound

⁰9

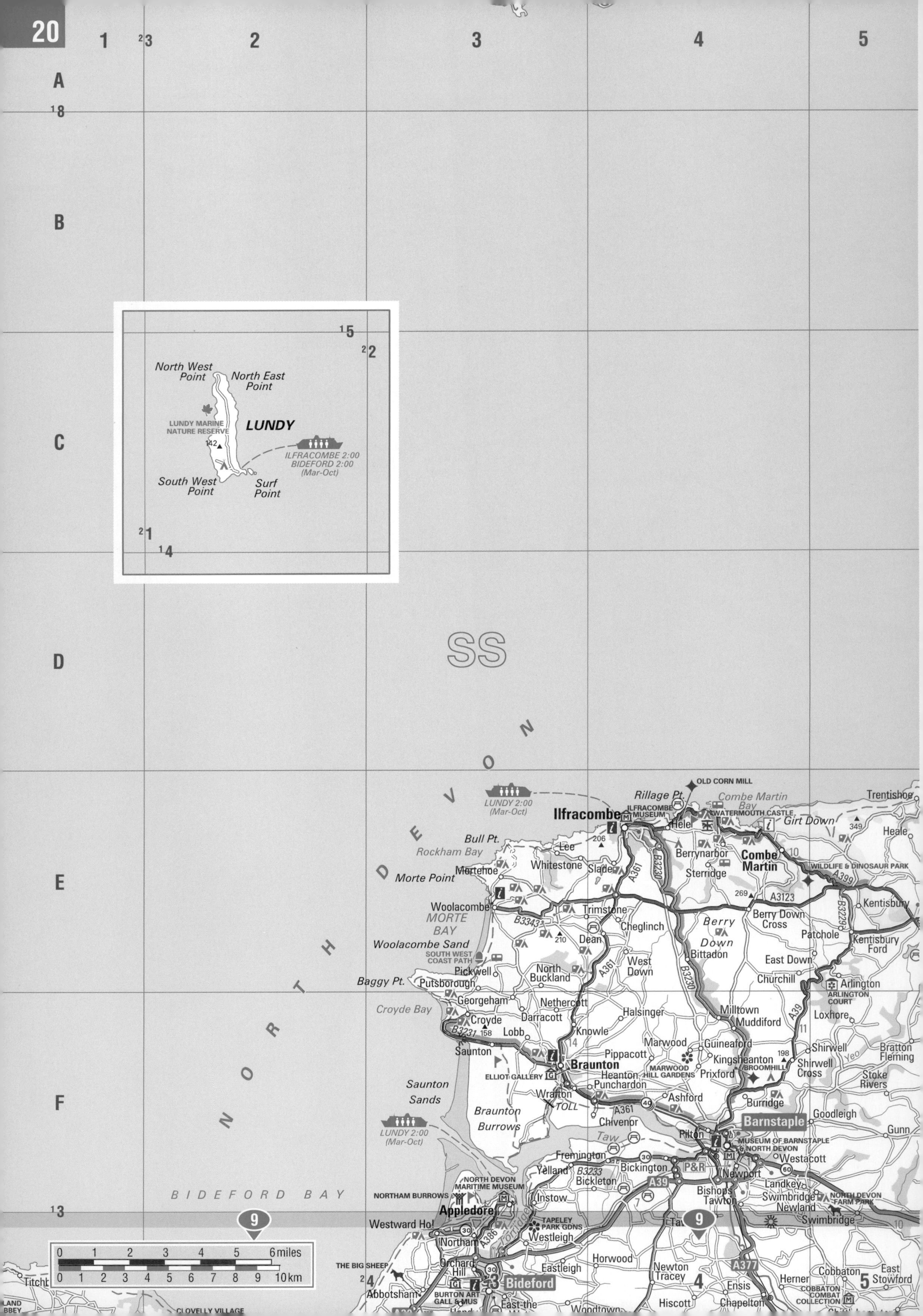

1   2 3   2   3   4   5

A
1 8

B

C

15
2 2

North West
Point   *North East*
                Point

LUNDY MARINE
NATURE RESERVE   **LUNDY**

142▲   *ILFRACOMBE 2:00*
                        BIDEFORD 2:00
South West   *(Mar-Oct)*
Point   *Surf*
               Point

2 1
1 4

D   SS

                                                    N
                                                    O
                                                    V
                                                    E
                                                    D

                        LUNDY 2:00   *Rillage Pt.*   *Combe Martin*   Trentishoe
                        (Mar-Oct)   *Bay*
                                            Ilfracombe   ILFRACOMBE   WATERMOUTH CASTLE   *Girt Down*
                                                             MUSEUM   349
E   *Bull Pt.*   Hele   Berrynarbor   **Combe**   Heale
                        Rockham Bay   206   Sterridge **Martin** 10 WILDLIFE & DINOSAUR PARK
                        Mortehoe   Lee   A399
          Morte Point   Whitestone   Slade   Kentisbury
                        Mortehoe   A361 B3230   269   A3123   B3229
                        N   Trimstone   *Berry*   Berry Down   Kentisbury
          O   O   B3343   Cheglinch   *Down*   Cross   Patchole   Ford
          H   *Woolacombe*   210 Dean West   Bittadon   East Down
                        MORTE   Down B3230   Churchill
                        BAY   North   Arlington
          T   *Woolacombe Sand*   Buckland Nethercott   Milltown   ARLINGTON
                        SOUTH WEST   Halsinger Muddiford Loxhore   COURT
          R   COAST PATH   Georgeham Darracott   11 Shirwell Bratton
                Baggy Pt. Putsborough   Knowle Marwood Guineaford   Shirwell Fleming
F   Croyde   *Croyde Bay*   Lobb 158 Pippacott MARWOOD Kingsheanton 198 Cross   Stoke
          D   B3231   14   HILL GARDENS Prixford BROOMHILL   Rivers
                        Saunton   ELLIOT GALLERY **Braunton** Heanton   Goodleigh
          O   *Saunton*   Wrafton Punchardon Ashford   Burridge
          N   *Sands*   TOLL A361 49   Gunn
                        Braunton   Chivenor   Pilton **Barnstaple**
          T   *Burrows*   *LUNDY 2:00*   Taw   MUSEUM OF BARNSTAPLE Westacott
                        (Mar-Oct)   Fremington 30   & NORTH DEVON
                                      Yelland B3233 Bickington P&R Newport Landkey
          BIDEFORD BAY   NORTH DEVON Instow A39   Bishops   NORTH DEVON
1 3   MARITIME MUSEUM   Tawton Swimbridge FARM PARK
                                      NORTHAM BURROWS   9 TAPELEY   Swimbridge 10
                        Appledore   PARK GDNS
                        Westward Ho! Northam A386 Westleigh   A377
                                      Orchard   Newton   Herner Cobbaton East
0 1 2 3 4 5 6miles THE BIG SHEEP Hill 30   Tracey   Cobbaton COMBAT Stowford
0 1 2 3 4 5 6 7 8 9 10km   2 4   Ensis Chapelton COLLECTION
Titch   Abbotsham BURTON ART **Bideford** 4   5
LAND   GALL & MUS East-the
BBEY CLOVELLY VILLAGE   Wood Hiscott

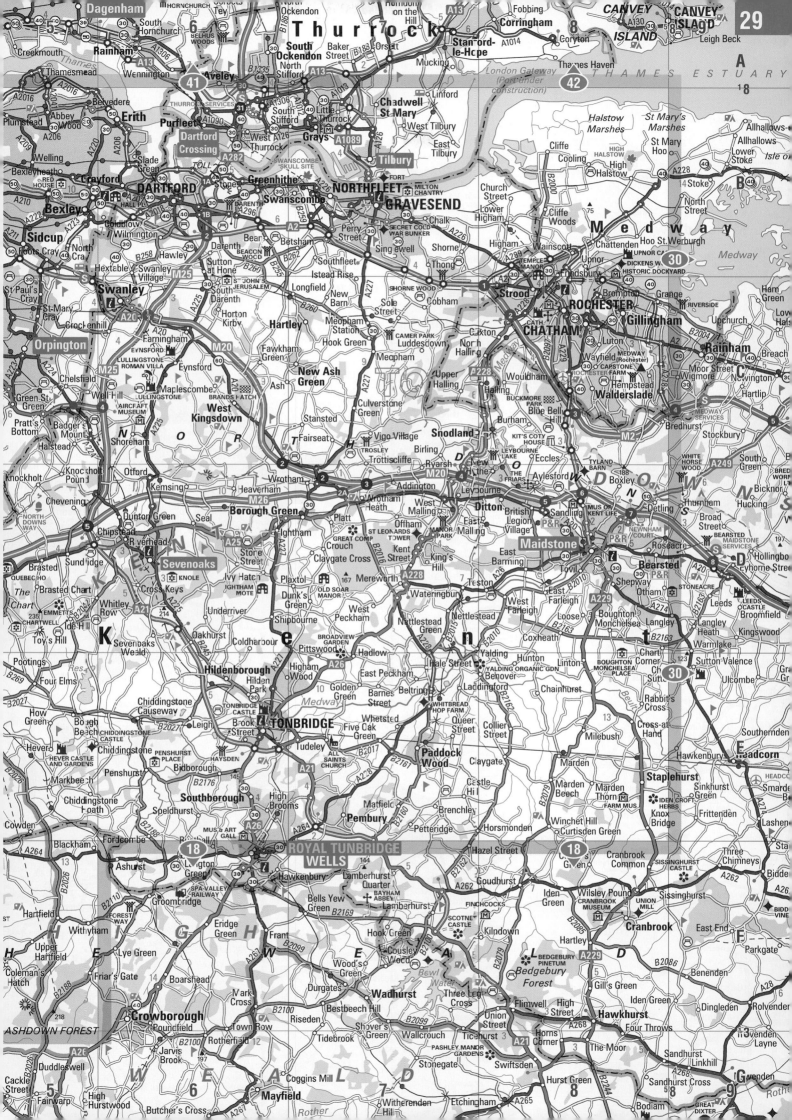

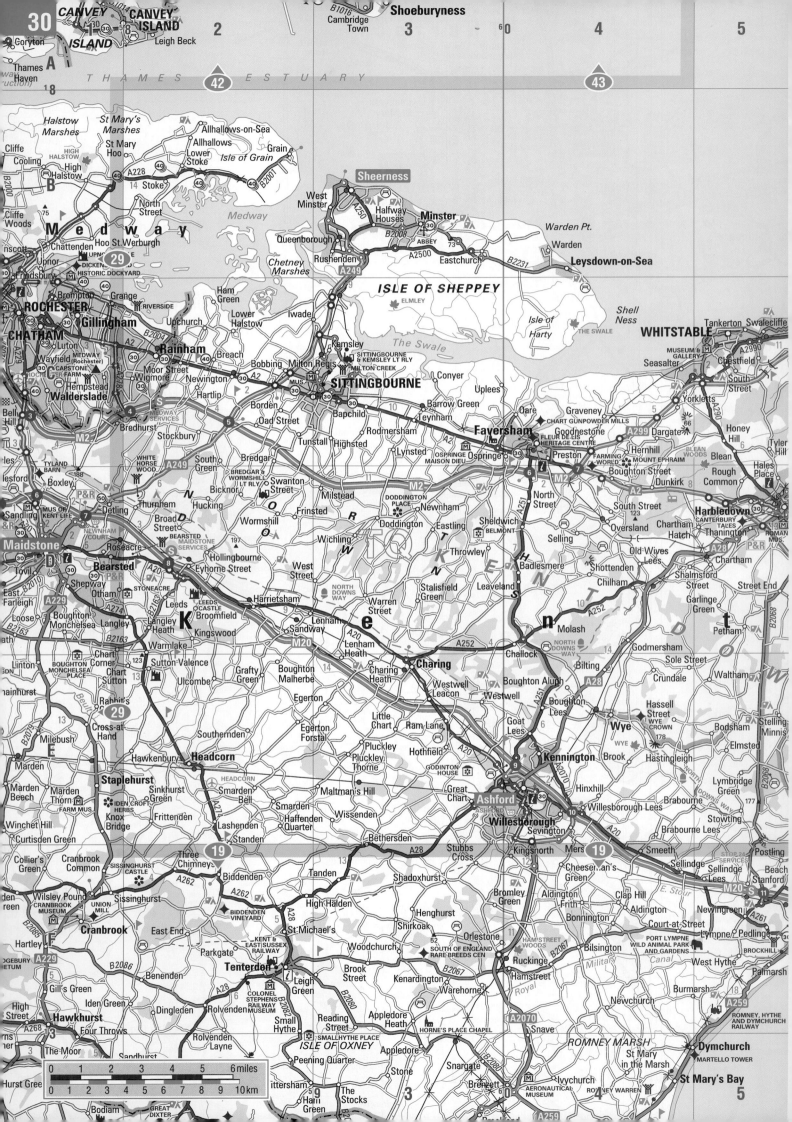

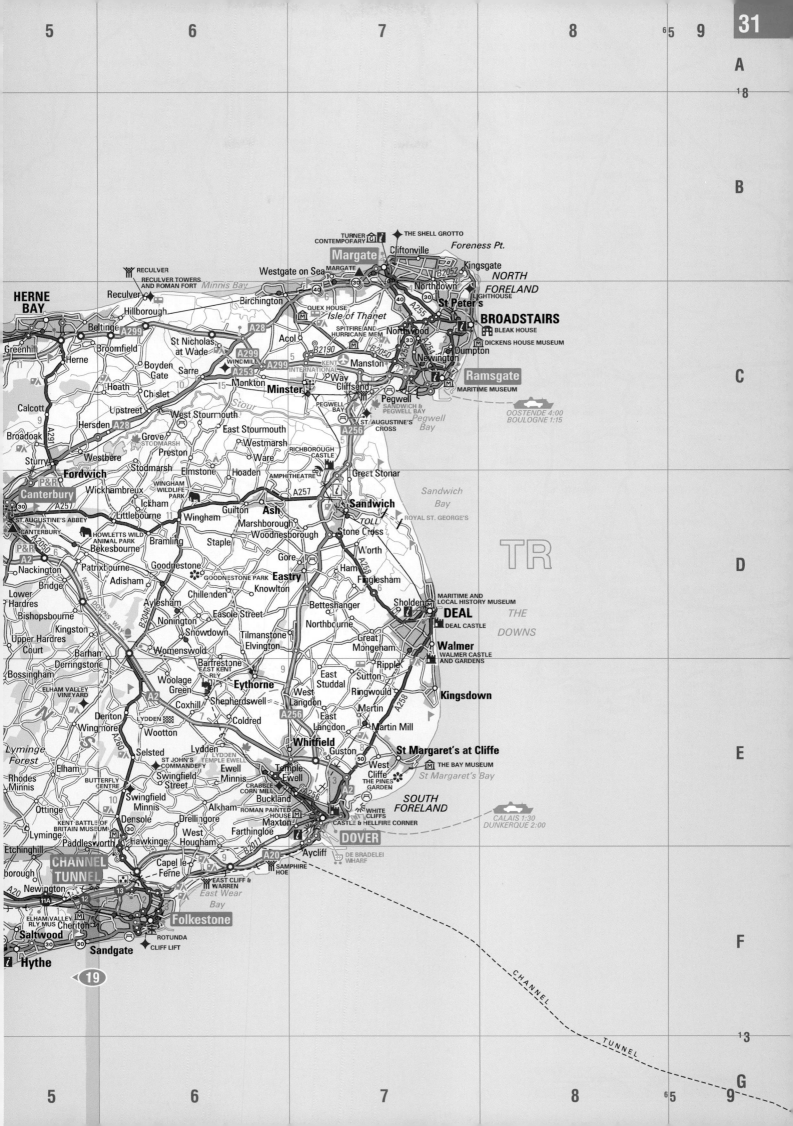

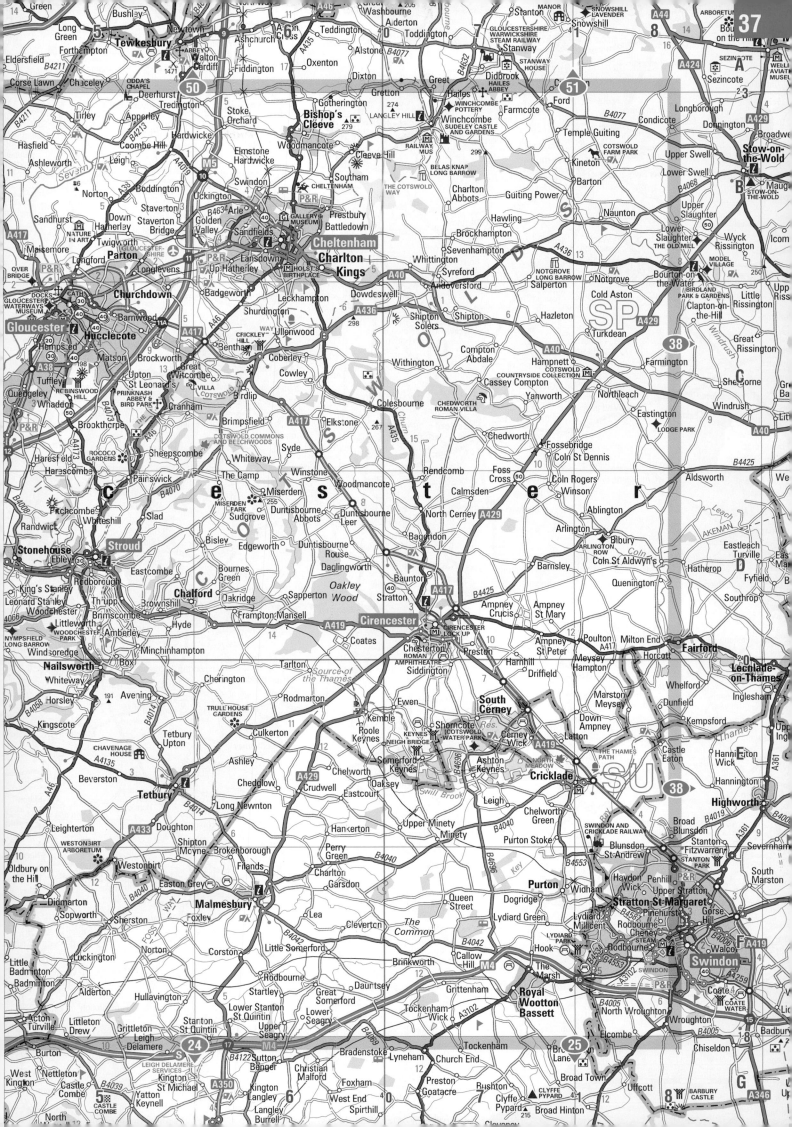

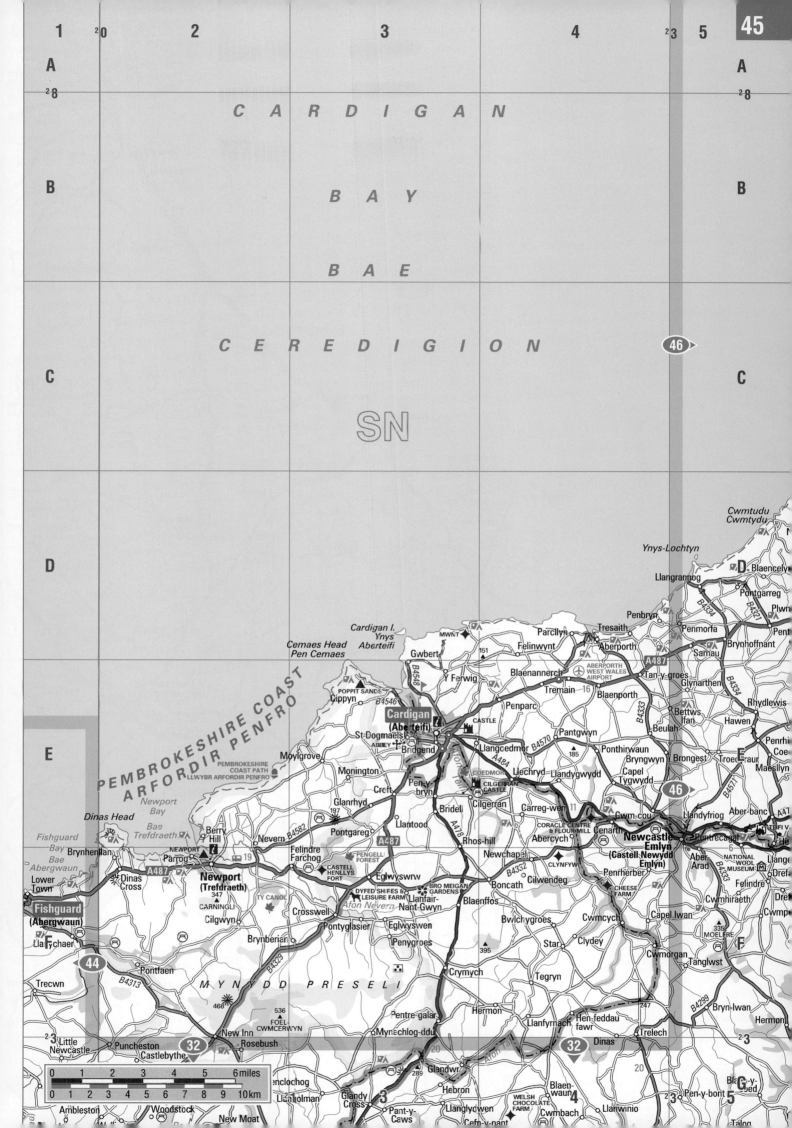

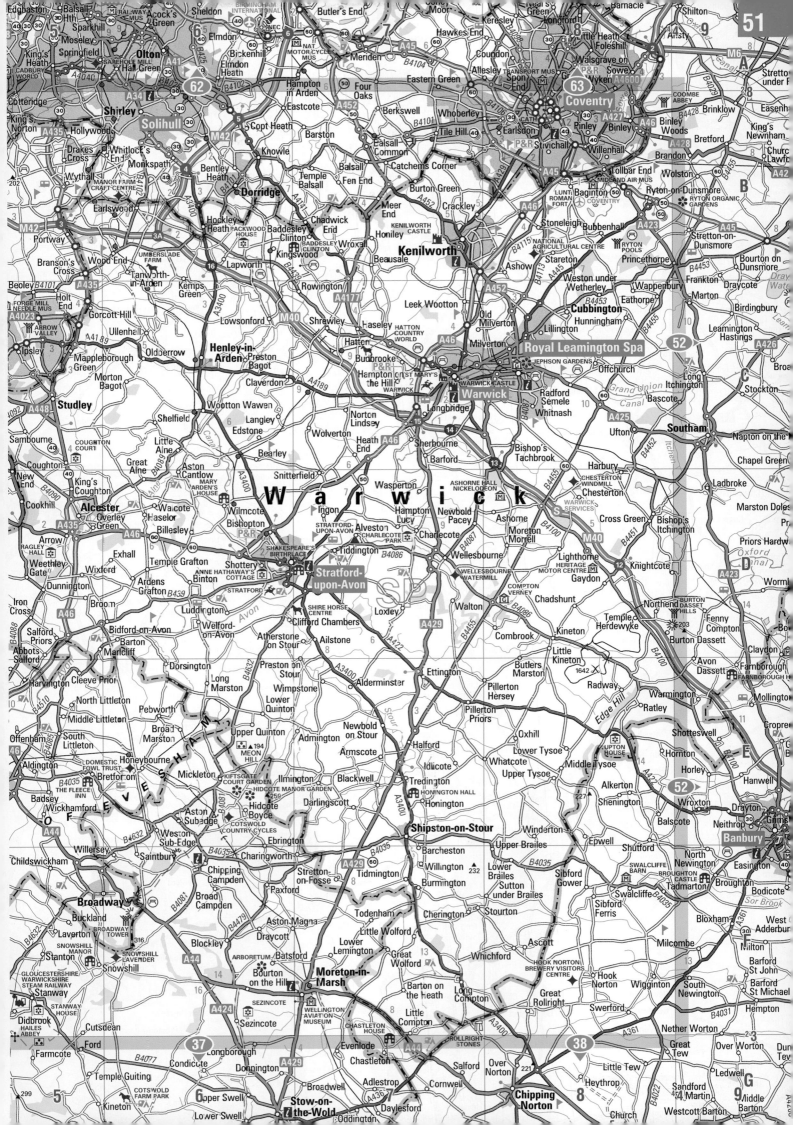

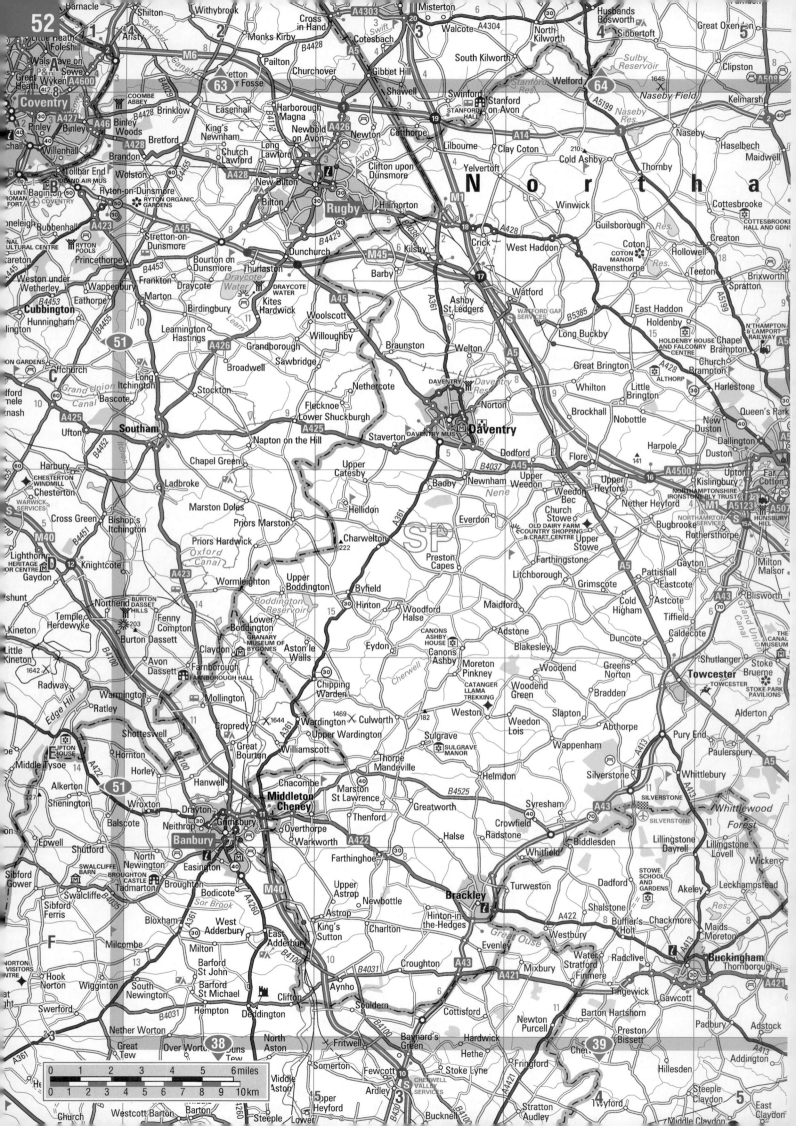

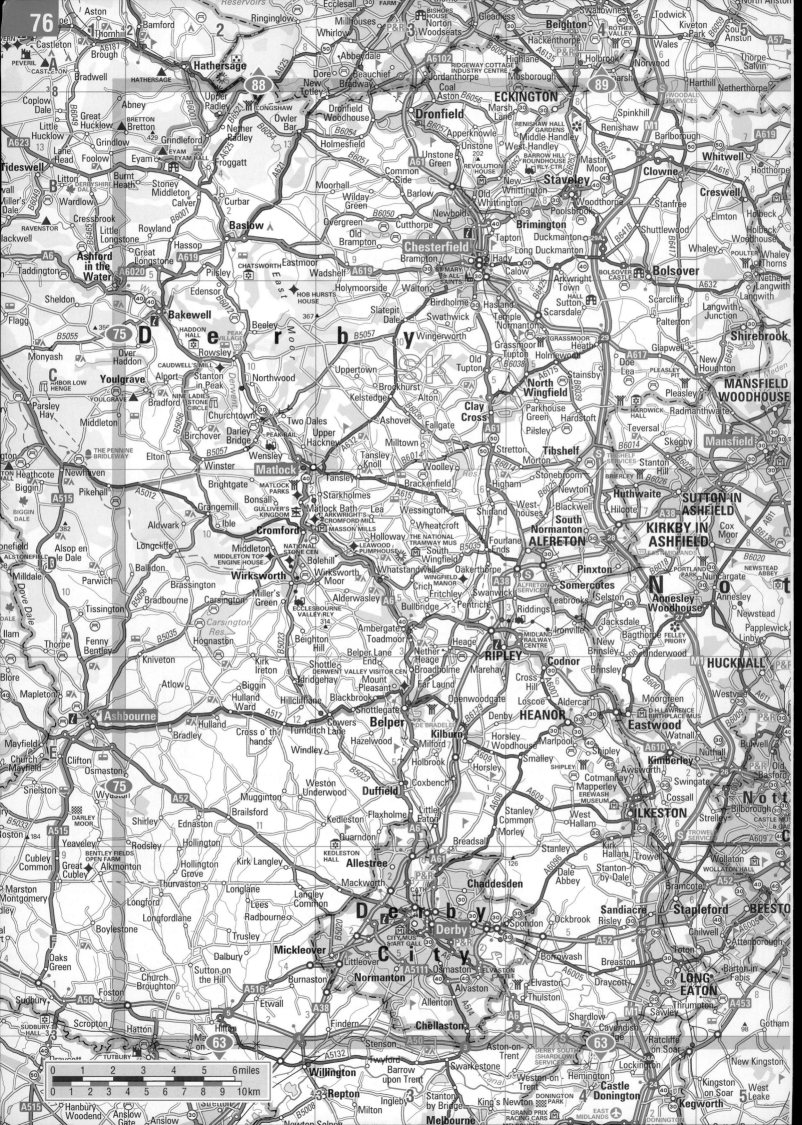

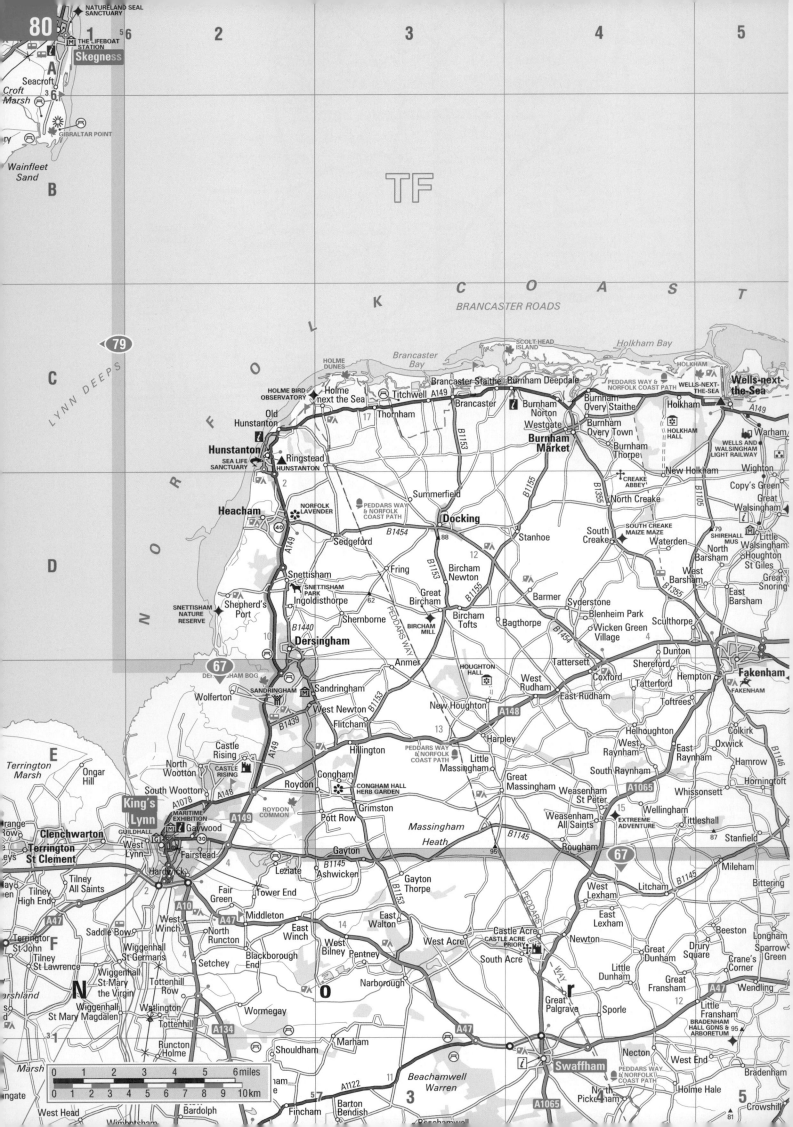

Map grid and labels

Isle of Anglesey

Anglesey

(Sir Ynys Môn)

SH

Locations

The Skerries
Ynysoedd y
Moelrhoniaid

Wilfa Head
Pen Wilfa

Cemaes Bay
Bae Cemaes

Bull Bay
Porth llechog

Point Lynas
Trwyn Eilian

Carmel Head
Pen Carmel

WYLFA POWER STATION
AND OBSERVATION TOWER

Tregele
Cemaes
Llanbadrig
Porthllechog
Burwen
Amlwch
Amlwch Port
Llaneilian

Llanfairynghornwy
Llanfechell
Rhosbeirio
Bodewryd
Rhosgoch
Carreglefn
Llanbabo
Rhosybol
Tyn-y-pwll

Church Bay
Porth Swtan

Rhydwyn
Llanrhyddlad

Pengorffwysfa
Penysarn
Nebo
Dulas
Dulas Bay
Bae Dulas

HOLYHEAD BAY
BAE CAERGYBI

Llanfaethlu
LLYNON WINDMILL
Llanddeusant
Gwredog
City Dulas
Brynrefail
Moelfre

DUBLIN 2:00
DUN LAOGHAIRE 2:00
(Apr-Sept)

DUBLIN 3:15

Elim
Llantrisant
Carmel
Llanerchymedd
Bachau
Hebron
Llandyfrydog
Mynydd Bodafon
Ty-mawr
Llanallgo
Marianglas

North Stack
BREAKWATER
Llantwrog
Pen-llyn Res.
B5112
Capel Coch
Maenaddwyn
Brynteg
Tynygongl
Benllech

HOLYHEAD MOUNTAIN
Llaingoch
Holyhead
(Caergybi)
Llanfachraeth
Llanynghenedl
Llechcynfarwy
CORS ERDDREINIOG
Llanbedrgoch
CORS GOCH
Red Wharf Bay

South Stack
ELLINS TOWER RSPB RESERVE
Goferydd
Kingsland
Valley
Bodedern
Trefor
Tregaian
Llangwyllog
Glan Gors
Rhosmeirch
Llanddyfnan
Tan-y-graig
Pentraeth

PENRHOS FEILW STANDING STONES
Penrhosfeilw
ANGLESEY
Caergeiliog
Llanfihangel yn Nhowyn
Bryngwran
Gwalchmai
Bodffordd
ORIEL YNYS MÔN
THE STONE SCIENCE
CORS BODEILIO
Pen-y-garnedd

Penrhyn Mawr
Trearddur
Glan-traeth
Four Mile Bridge
B4545
Llynfaes
Heneglwys
Talwrn
Rhoscefnir

Holy Island
Ynys Gybi
Rhoscolyn
Cymyran Bay
Bae Cymyran
Llanfaelog
Capel-gwyn
Ddrydwy
Pencarnisiog
Cerrigceinwen
Llangristiolus
HENBLAS COUNTRY PARK
Pentre Berw
Ceint
Penmynydd
JAMES PRINGLE WEAVERS
PILI PALAS

Rhosneigr
Bryn Du
Soar
Capel Mawr
Gaerwen
Llanfairpwll -gwyngyll
Llanddaniel Fab
PLAS NEWYDD
Capel-y-graig

WALES COAST PATH
Bethel
Trefdraeth
B4419
Afon Cefni
B4421
PLAS COCH GARDEN ZOO
GREENW... CENTRE
Seion

Llangwyfan-isaf
Aberffraw
Hermon
Llangadwaladr
Malltraeth
Llangaffo
Brynsiencyn
SEA ZOO
Y Felinheli
Llanddeiniolen
Bethel
Saron

Bodorgan
B4421
Dwyran
B4419
MENAI STRAIT AFON MENAI
Llanrug
Pont-rug
BRYN BRA CASTL

NEWBOROUGH WARREN AND YNYS LLANDDWYN
Newborough
Pen-lôn
MODEL VILLAGE
BIRD WORLD
FOEL FARM PARK
Waterloo Port
SEGONTIUM FORT
Cwm-y-glo

Malltraeth Bay
Bae Malltraeth
Newborough Forest
SEIONT II MARITIME MUSEUM
CASTLE & REGIMENTAL MUS
Caeathro
Ceunant

Llanddwyn I.
Ynys Llanddwyn
The Bar
Abermenai Pt.
Trwyn Abermenai
Caernarfon
INIGO JONES TUDOR SLATEWORKS
Groeslon
Waunfawr

CAERNARFON AIR MUSEUM
Llanfaglan
WELSH HIGHLAND RAILWAY
Croesywaun

Morfa Dinlle
Glan-rhyd
Saron
Bontnewydd
Rhostryfan
Rhosgadfan

Dinas Dinlle
Ffrwd
Penyffridd
Groeslon
Betws-Garmon

Llandwrog
Penrhos
Fron
Carmel
Nantlle
B4418

GLYNLLIFON
A487
Penygroes
Cilgwyn
Talysarn

Pontllyfni
Tân-yr-allt
Llanllyfni
Nebo

Aberdesach
Clynnog-fawr

Gyrn-goch
Bryn-yr-eryr
Capel Uc...
Tainlon
Nasareth
Pant-glas

BWLCH MAWR
U...er Clynnog
Dafarn Faig
Trefor
GYRN DDU
Afon Dwyfor

CAERNARFON BAY
BAE
CAERNARFON

Scale bar

0 1 2 3 4 5 6 miles
0 1 2 3 4 5 6 7 8 9 10 km

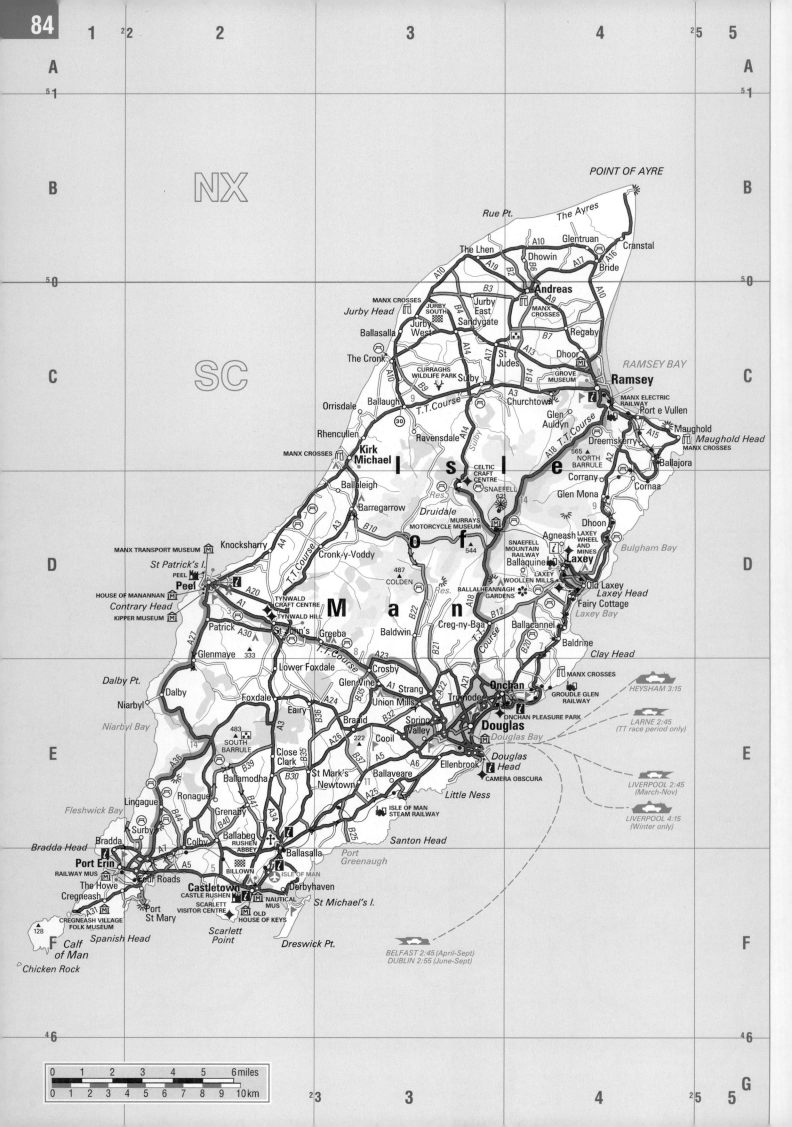

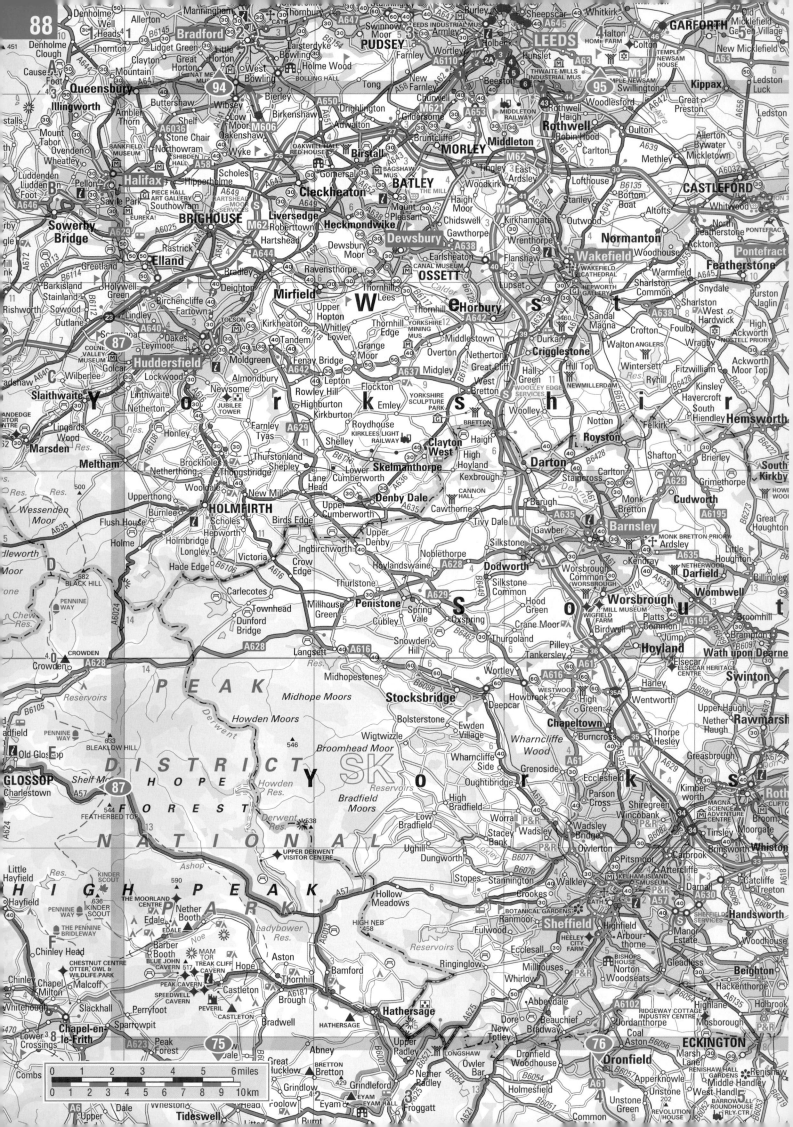

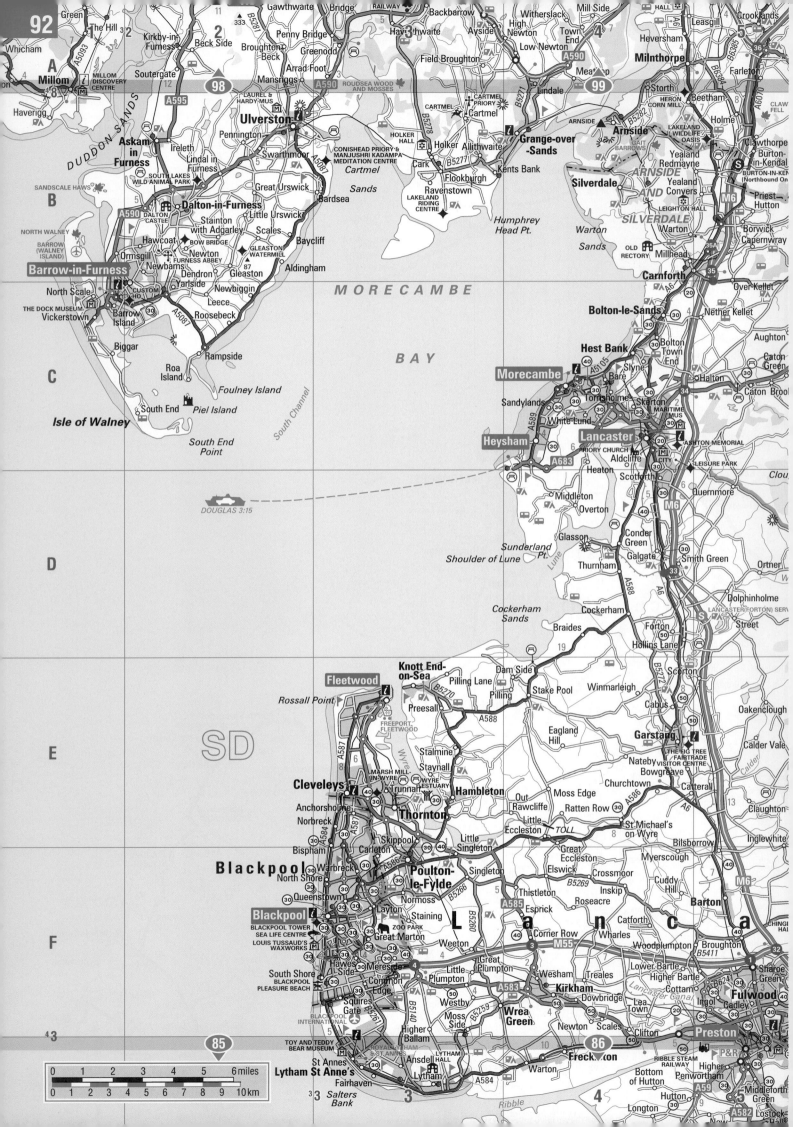

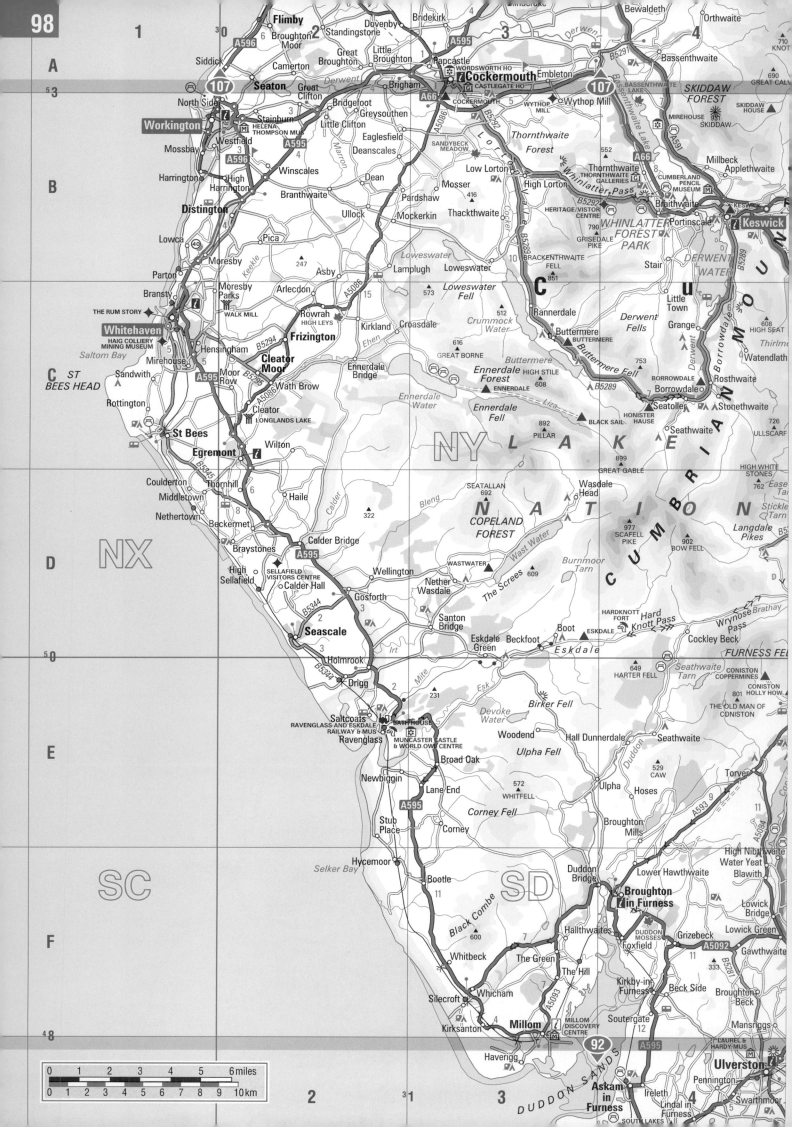

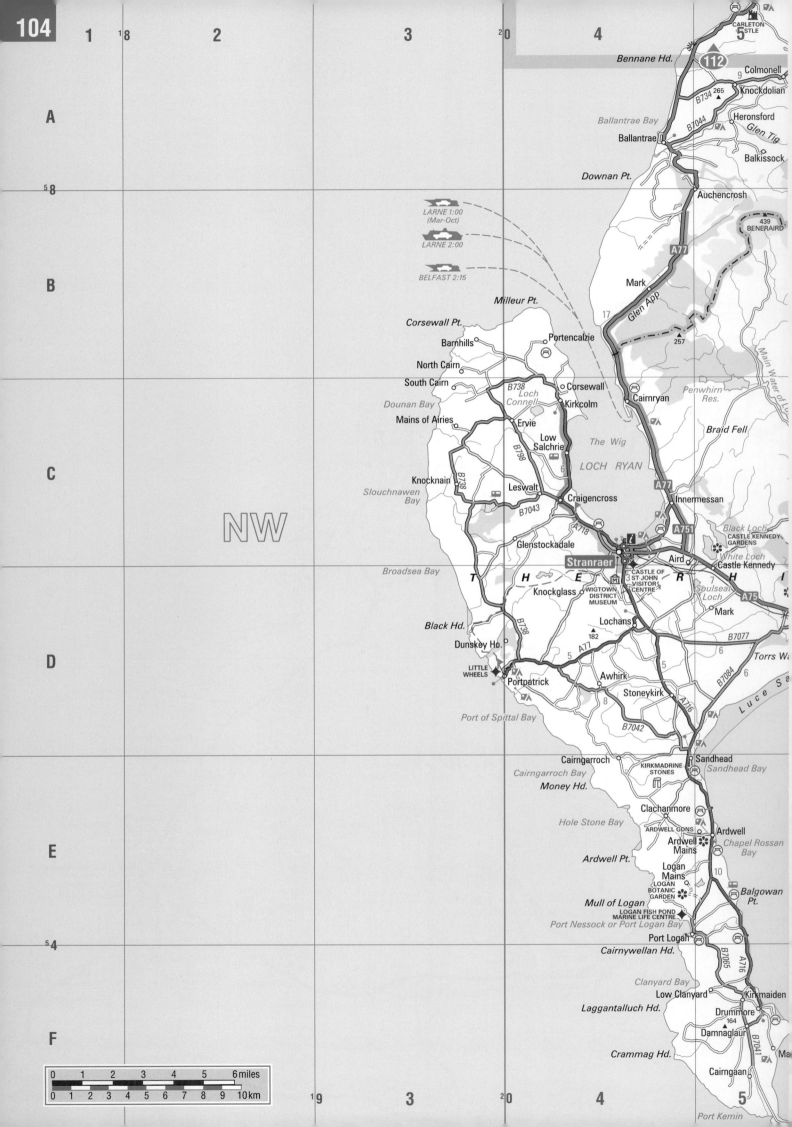

NW

LARNE 1:00
(Mar-Oct)
LARNE 2:00
BELFAST 2:15

Bennane Hd.
CARLETON
CASTLE
Colmonell
Knockdolian
B734 265
B7044
Heronsford
Glen Tig
Ballantrae Bay
Ballantrae
Balkissock
Downan Pt.
Auchencrosh
A77
439
BENERAIRD
257
Glen App
Mark
Main Water of Lu
Milleur Pt.
Corsewall Pt.
Portencalzie
Penwhirn
Res.
Barnhills
North Cairn
Corsewall
B738
Loch
Connell
Cairnryan
Braid Fell
South Cairn
Kirkcolm
Dounan Bay
Mains of Airies
Ervie
B798
The Wig
Low
Salchrie
LOCH RYAN
Knocknain
B738
Leswalt
Innermessan
A77
Slouchnawen
Bay
Craigencross
B7043
A718
A751
CASTLE KENNEDY
GARDENS
Black Loch
White Loch
Glenstockadale
Stranraer
CASTLE OF
ST JOHN
VISITOR
CENTRE
Aird
Castle Kennedy
Broadsea Bay
T H E   E   R   H   I
Knockglass
WIGTOWN
DISTRICT
MUSEUM
Mark
Soulseat
Loch
A75
Black Hd.
B738
Lochans
182
B7077
Dunskey Ho.
5 A77
5
Torrs Wa
LITTLE
WHEELS
Awhirk
B7084
6
Luce Sa
Portpatrick
Stoneykirk
8
A716
Port of Spittal Bay
B7042
Cairngarroch
Sandhead
Cairngarroch Bay
KIRKMADRINE
STONES
Sandhead Bay
Money Hd.
Clachanmore
Hole Stone Bay
ARDWELL GDNS
Ardwell
Ardwell
Mains
Chapel Rossan
Bay
Ardwell Pt.
Logan
Mains
10
LOGAN
BOTANIC
GARDEN
Balgowan
Pt.
Mull of Logan
LOGAN FISH POND
MARINE LIFE CENTRE
Port Nessock or Port Logan Bay
Port Logan
Cairnywellan Hd.
A716
B7065
Clanyard Bay
Low Clanyard
Kirkmaiden
Laggantalluch Hd.
Drummore
164
B7041
Damnaglaur
Crammag Hd.
Cairngaan
Port Kemin

0 1 2 3 4 5 6 miles
0 1 2 3 4 5 6 7 8 9 10km

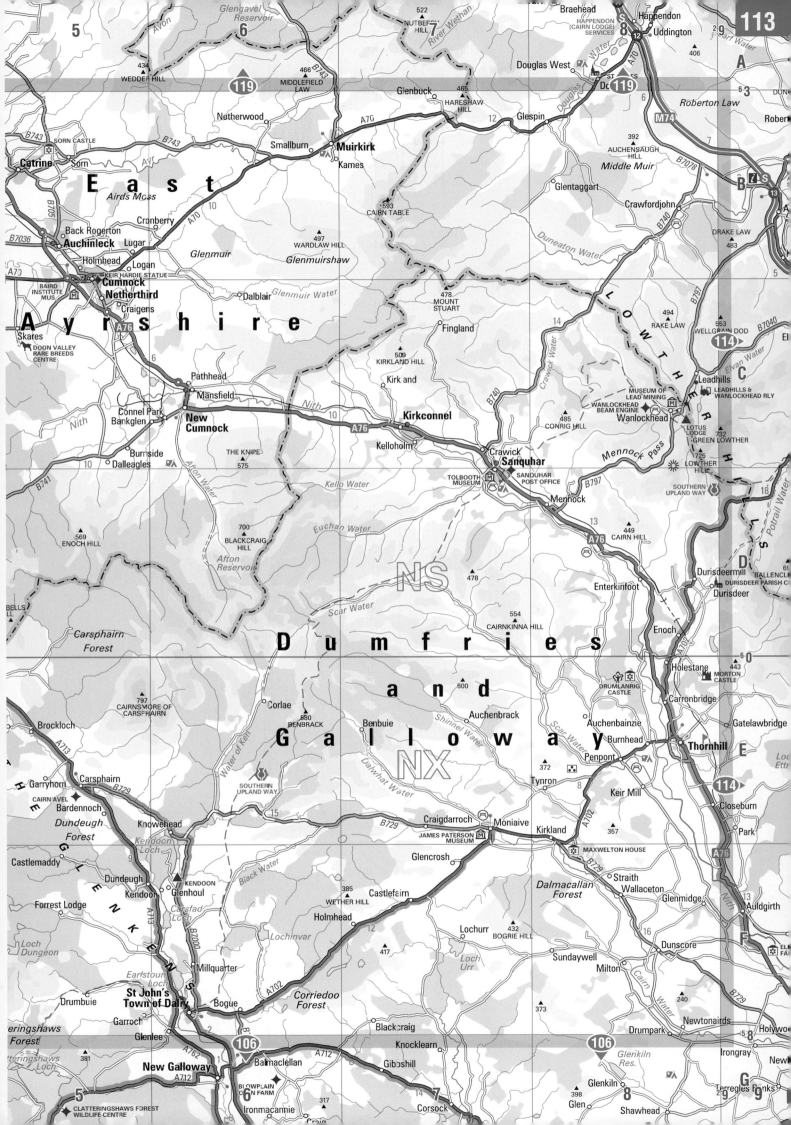

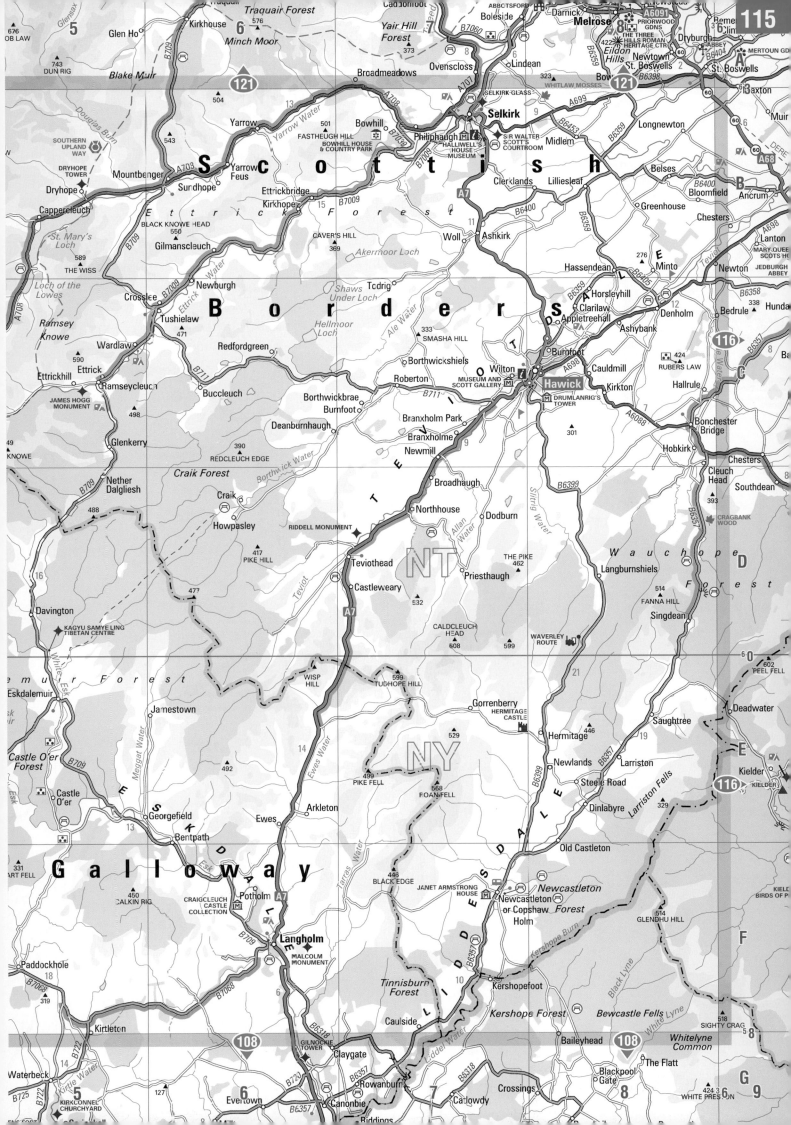

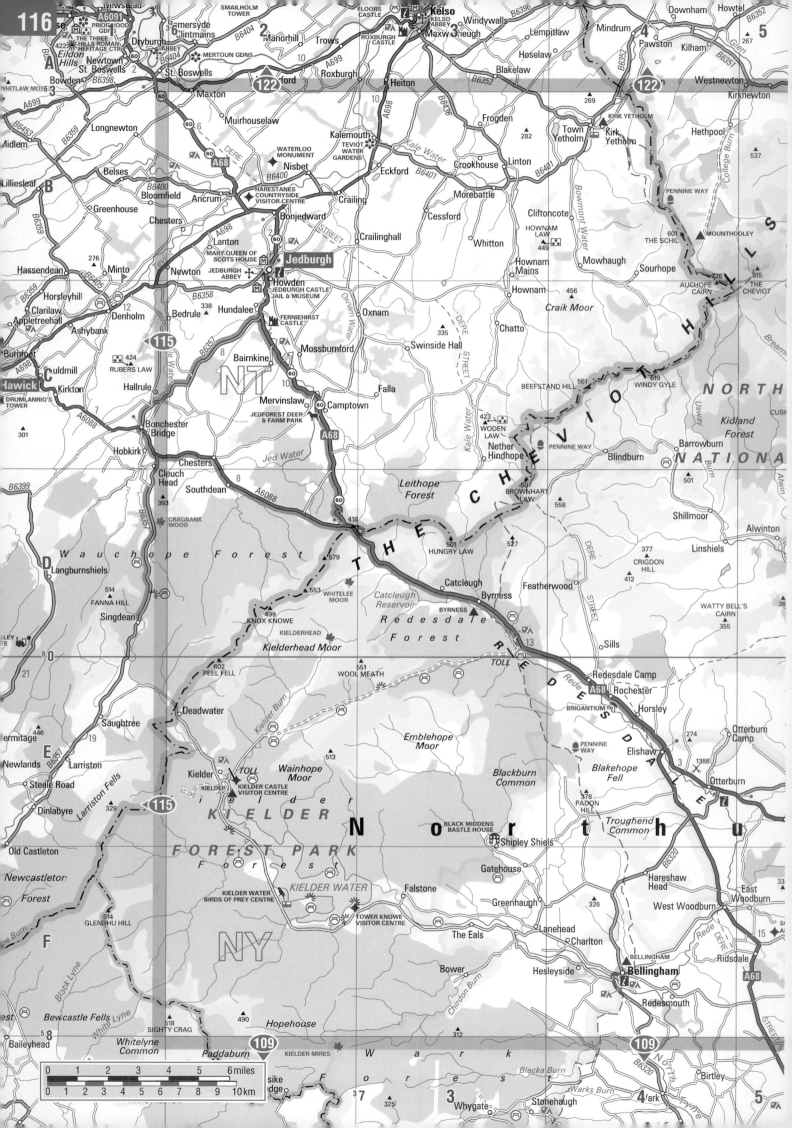

A

B

C

EYEMOUTH MUSEUM

Burnmouth

Lamberton Beach

Lamberton

1333

Highfields

Berwick-upon-Tweed

B6461

BARRACKS MUSEUM & RAMPARTS
BERWICK

East Ord

Tweedmouth

Spittal

Prior Park

Redshin Cove

A698

108

Murton

Thornton

Scremerston

West Allerdean

Shoresdean

Cheswick

Ancroft

Goswick

B6354

Berrington

Haggerston

Bowsden

Beal

Barmoor Castle

Barmoor Lane End

West Kyloe

Fenwick

Fenham

HUT SMITHY WOOD WORKSHOP

Lowick

Kyloe Hills

East Kyloe

Buckton

ERSLAW MILL

LADY WATERFORD HALL

B6353

157

ST CUTHBERTS WAY

Holburn

Detchant

Elwick

Ross

Kimmerston

Nesbit

Hetton Steads

North Hazelrigg

Middleton

211

Belford

Easington

Budle

Budle Bay

Fenton Town

Doddington

200

South Hazelrigg

Spindlestone

Waren Mill

BAMBURGH CASTLE

Bamburgh

Newtown

West Horton

East Horton

Mousen

Bradford

Glororum

Burton

Akeld

1402

B6525

Weetwood Hall

Warenton

Bellshill

Adderstone

Elford

North Sunderland

Seahouses

Humbleton

B6348

10

117

B6348

Chatton

Greendikes

A1

Warenford

Newham Hall

Beal

117

Benthall

Wooler

WOOLER

166

Newham

Newstead

Swinhoe

Beadnell Bay

Earle

Haugh Head

CHILLINGHAM CASTLE

Chillingham

WILD CATTLE OF CHILLINGHAM

Rosebrough

Chathill

Ellingham

Preston

High Newton-by-the-Sea

Middleton Hall

Newton

NORTH NU

NORTHUMBERLAND COAST

LINDISFARNE

Emmanuel Hd.

Holy Island (Lindisfarne)

LINDISFARNE CASTLE

Castle Pt.

Causeway Holy Island Sands

Holy Island

LINDISFARNE PRIORY

HERITAGE CENTRE

Guile Pt.

Farne Islands

Staple Sound

FARNE ISLANDS

Inner Sound

DEVIL'S CAUSEWAY

North Low

South Low

82

12

B6353

B1342

B6349

B1340

B1341

B1340

D

E

F

G

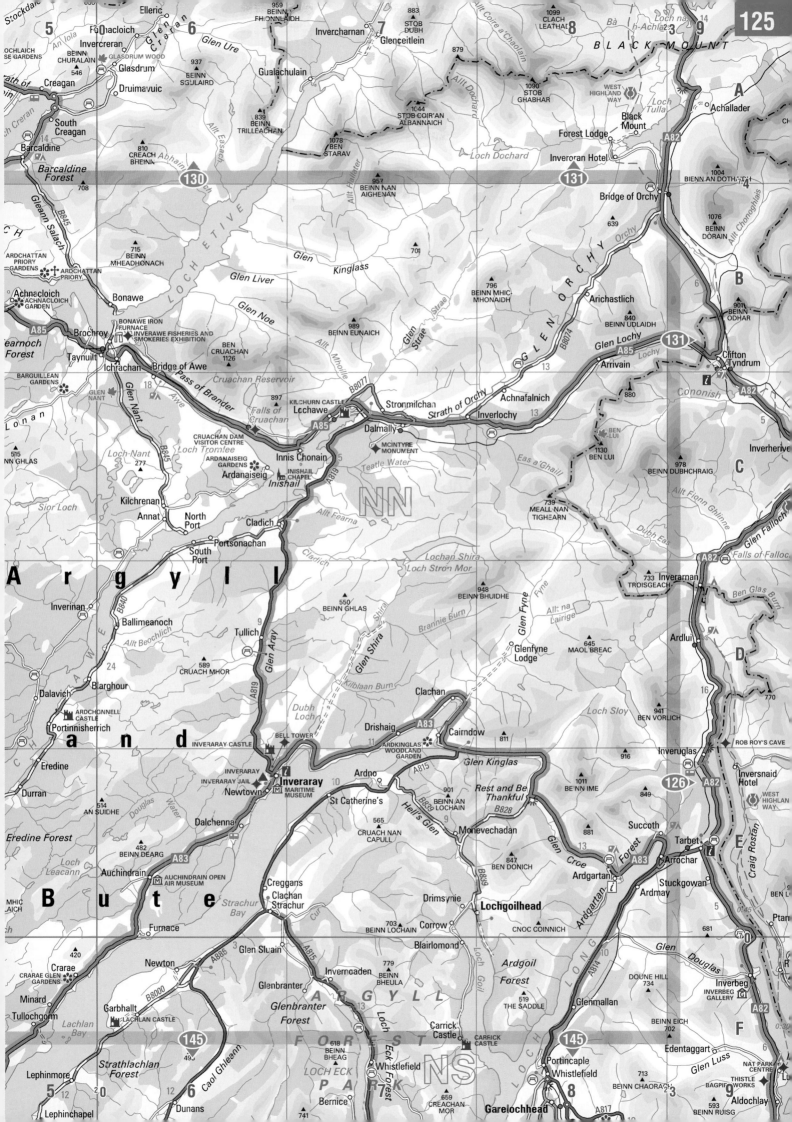

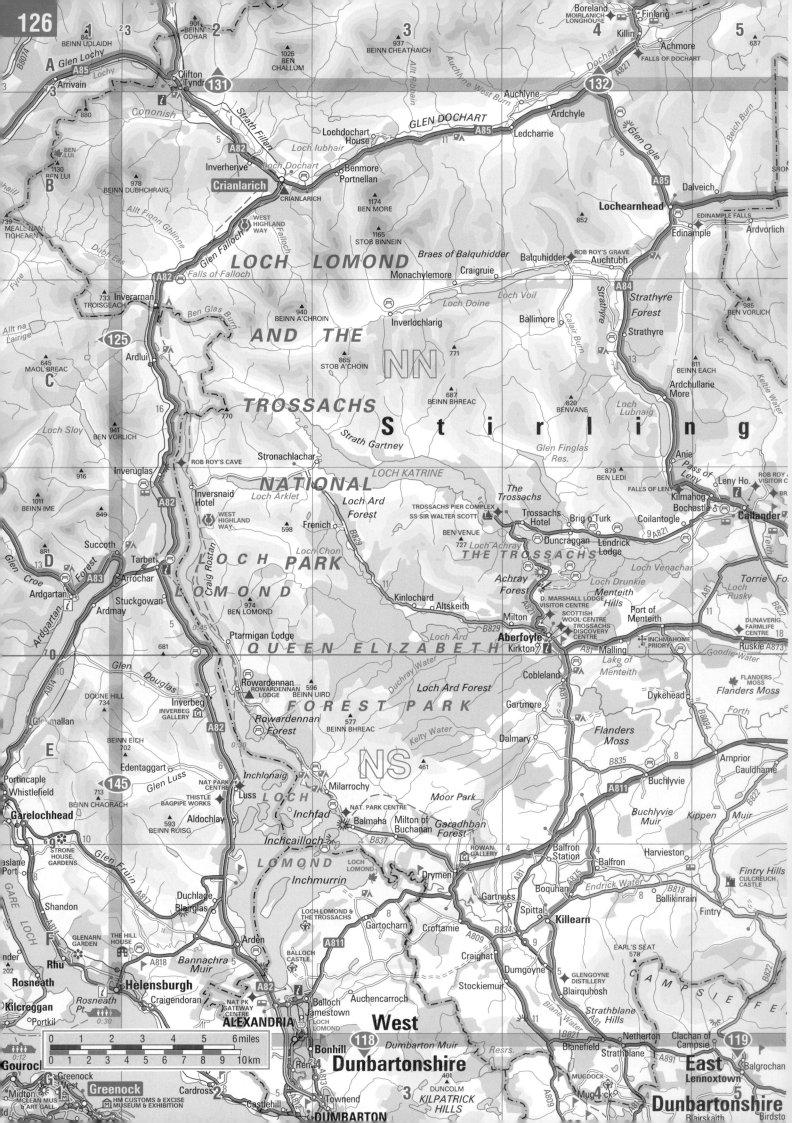

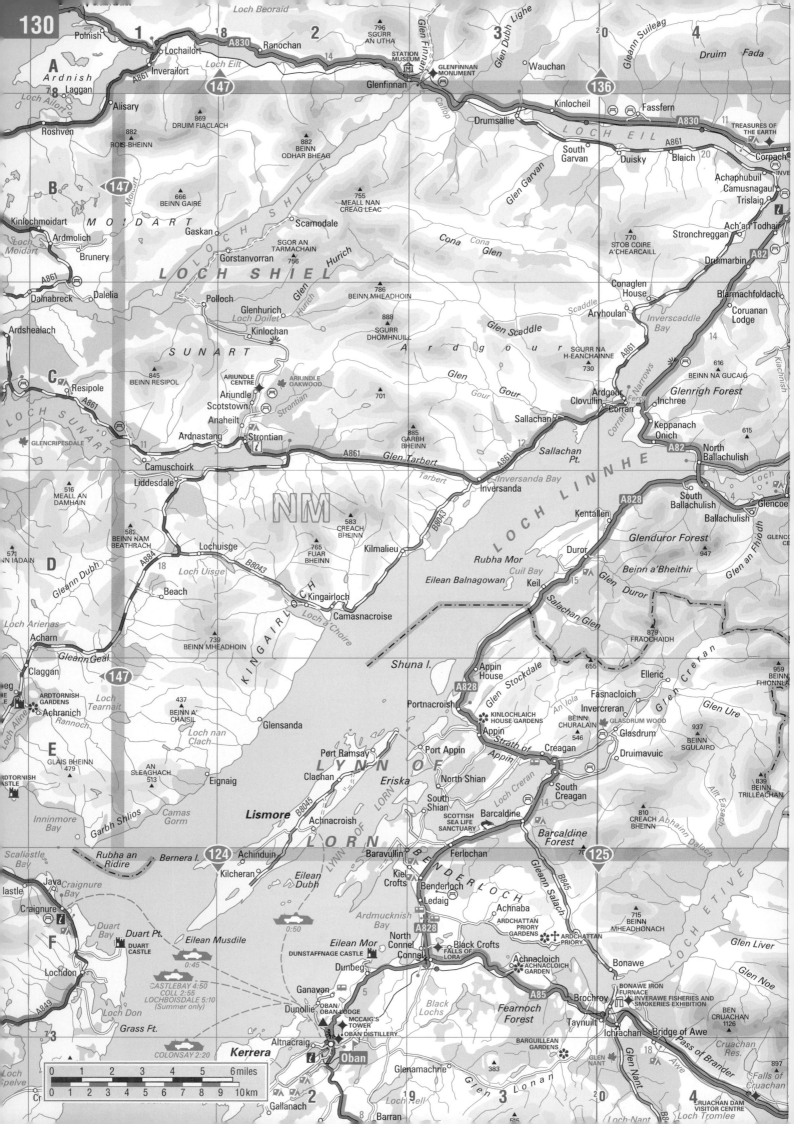

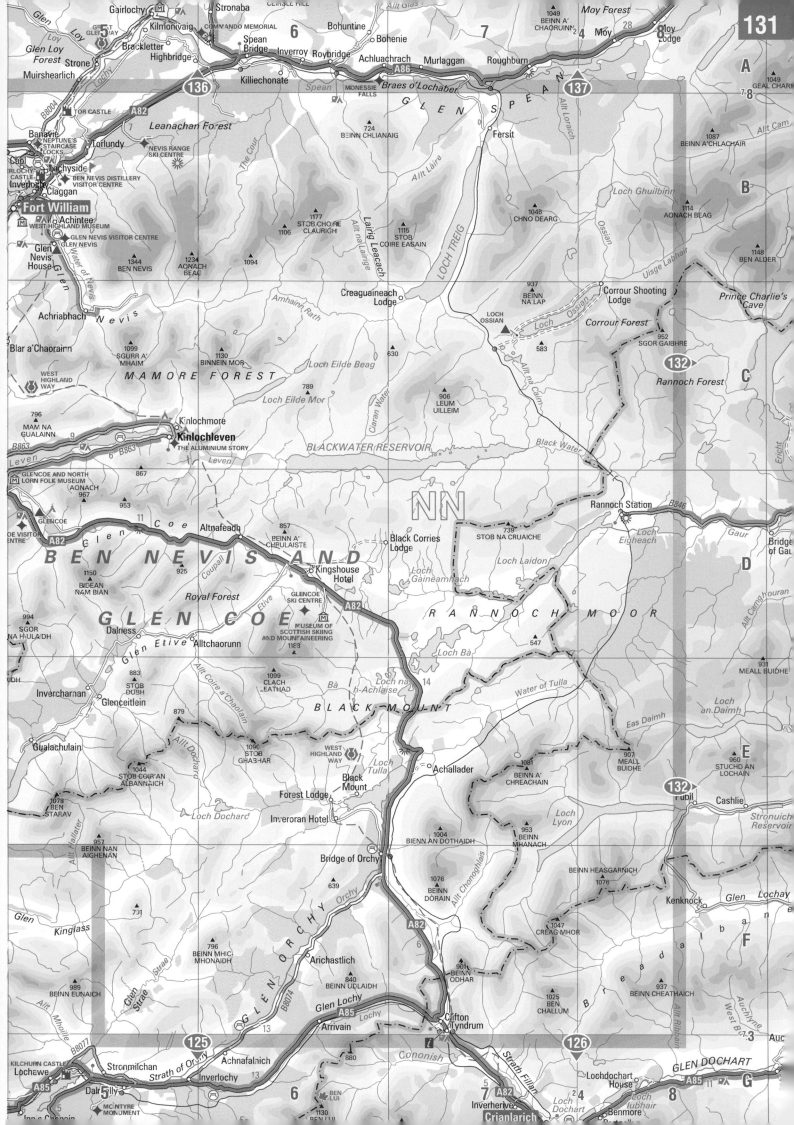

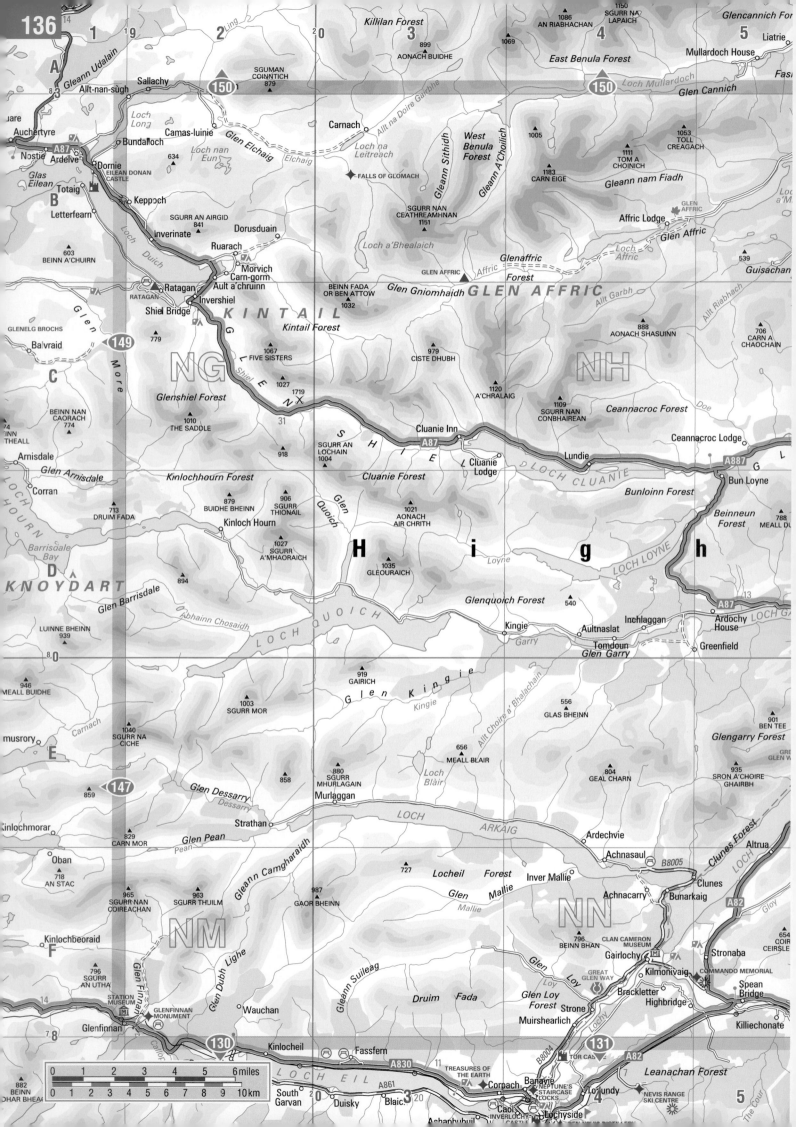

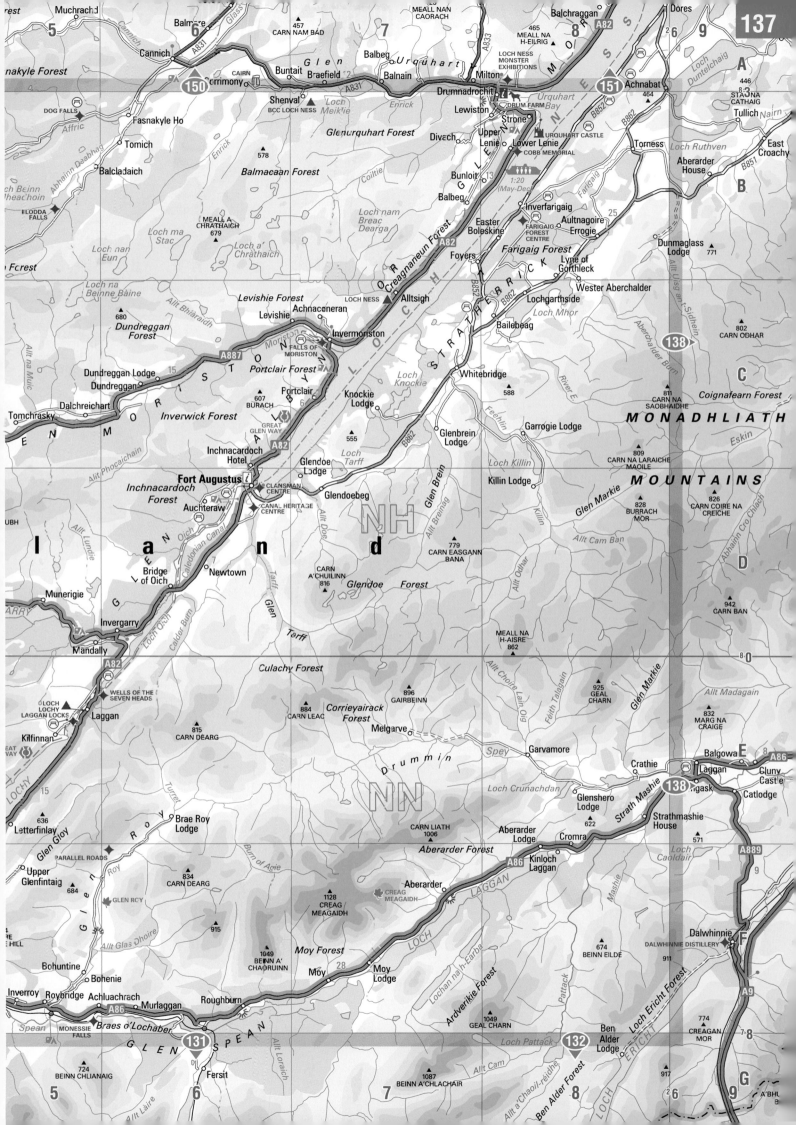

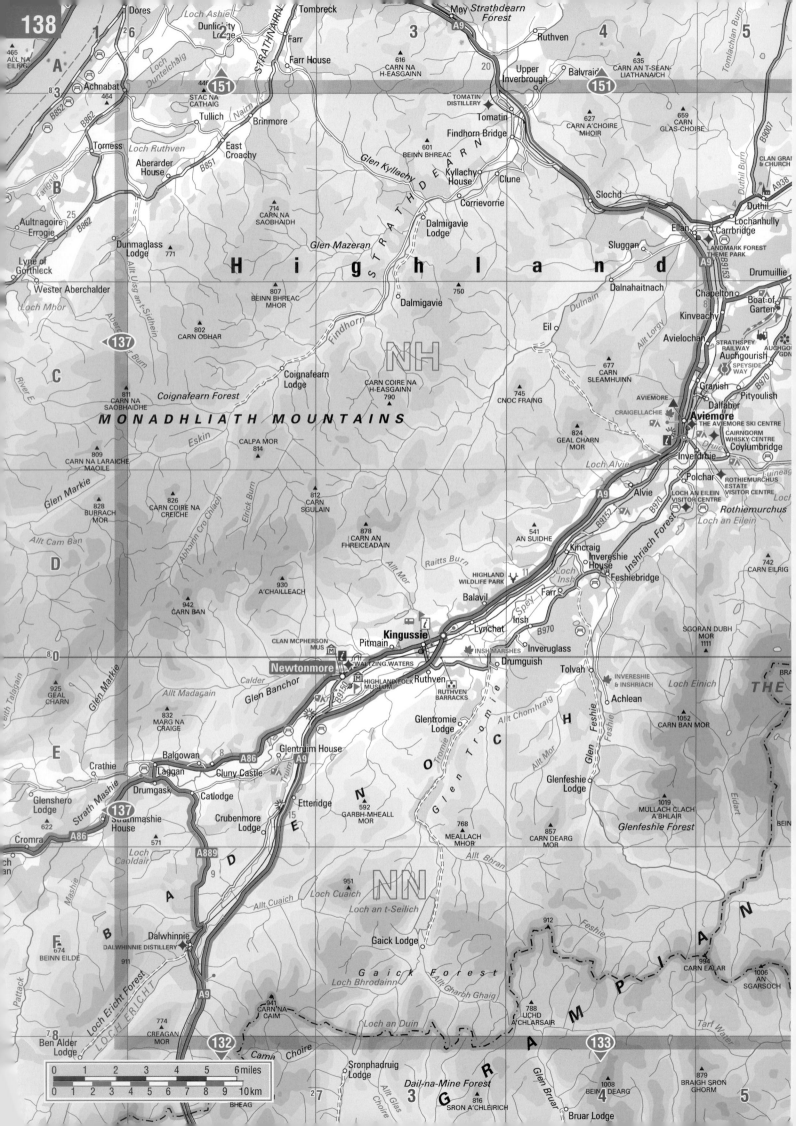

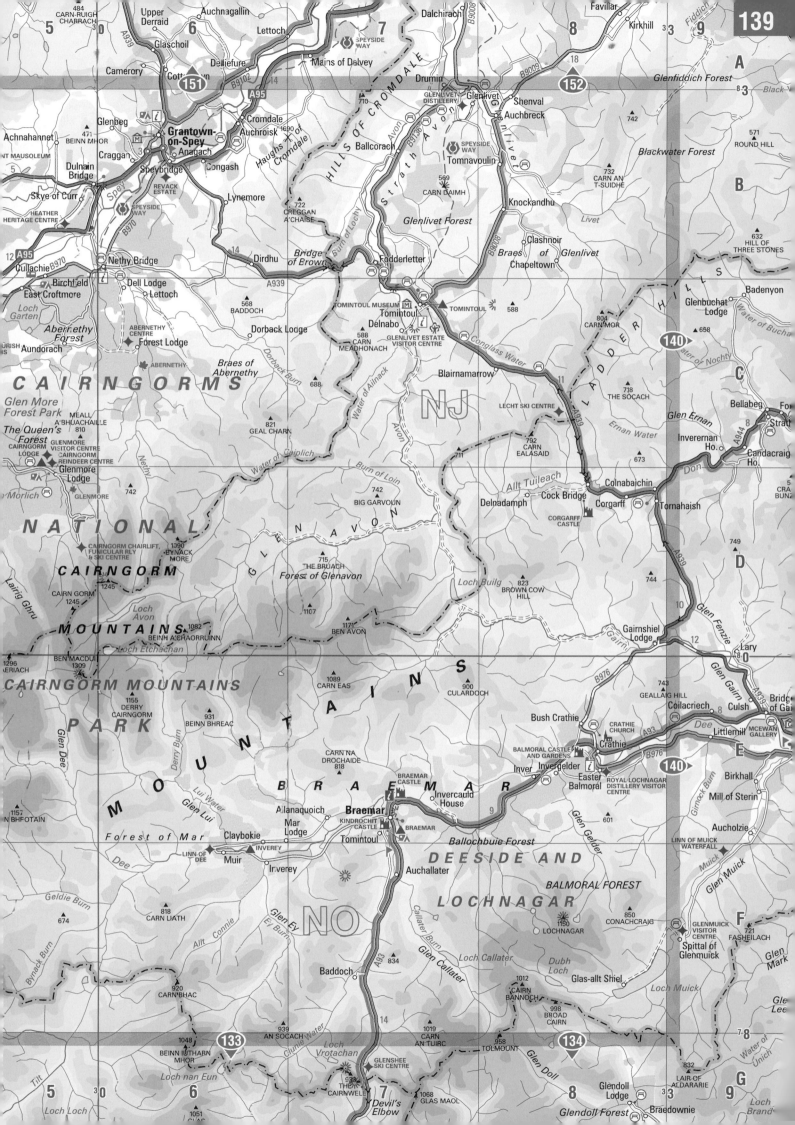

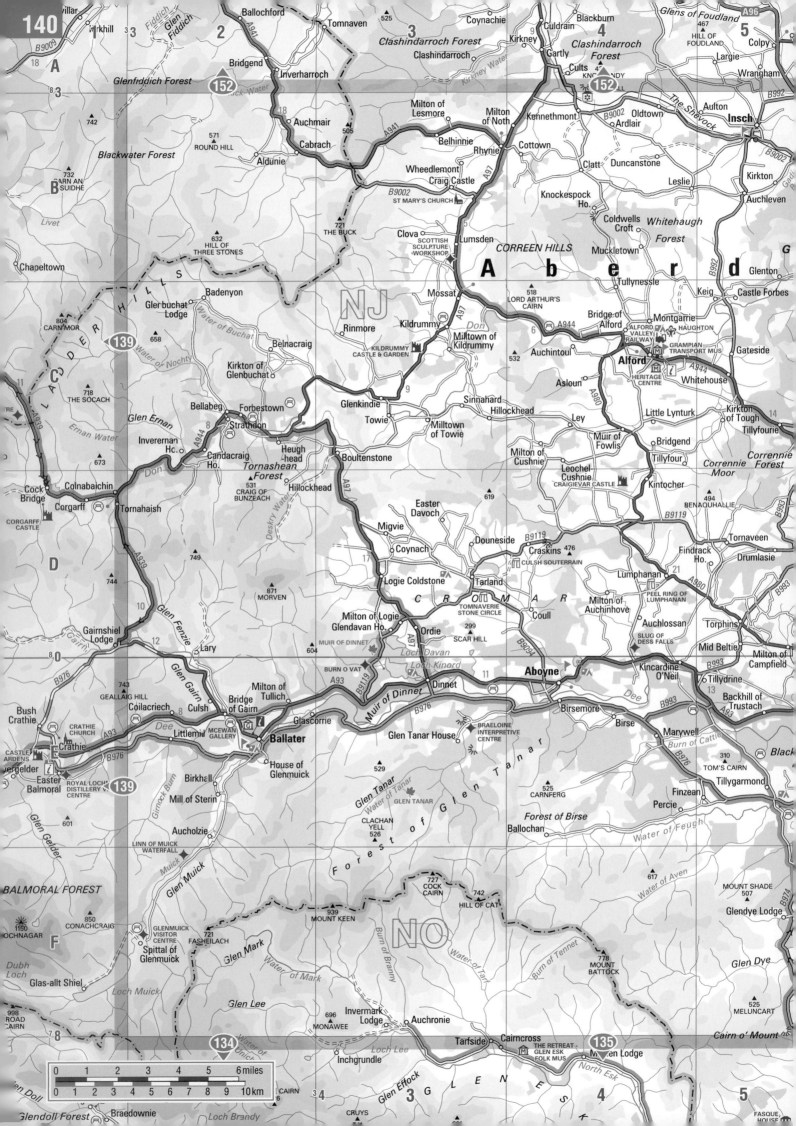

A B C D E F G H

1 2 3 4 5 6

Rubha a'Mhail

COLONSAY 1:10
(Summer only)

Rubha Bholsa

Loch an Aircill

439

Nave Island

Ardnave Pt.

Gortantaoid

SCARBH
BREAC

364

J U R A

785

755

*Loch a Chnuic
Bhric*

PAPS OF JURA

JURA FOREST

Carraig Bhan

Ardnave

Killinallan

Bunnahabhain

BUNNAHABHAIN
DISTILLERY

316

Gleann Astaile

Leargybreck

561

Loch

An Clachan

Sanaigmore

Leckgruinart

Caol Ila

Loch Gruinart

CAOL ILA DISTILLERY

Port Askaig

Feolin Ferry

144

Corran

Braigo

FINLAGGAN
CENTRE

*Loch
Finlaggan*

Keills

Keils

Gleann Uilibh

Craighouse

Ballinaby

Carnduncan

LOCH GRUINART NATURE
RESERVE VISITORS CENTRE

Craigens

Ballygrant

Loch Cam

Kilmeny

8

ISLE OF JURA
DISTILLERY

Aoradh

Coull

Saligo Bay

*Loch
Gorm*

I S L A Y

8

342

BRAT BHEINN

Coul Pt.

Sunderland

Blackrock

Redhouses

Daill

Sorn

Cabrach

Machir Bay

Kilchoman

Conisby

Bridgend

267
BEINN DUBH

Am Fraoch
Eilean

Rubha na Tràill

Brosdale I.

Kilchiaran Bay

Bruichladdich

Kilchiaran

ISLAY LIFE
MUSEUM

Bowmore

BOWMORE
ROUND
CHURCH

7

A846

A r g y l l

McArthur's Hd.

RHINNS

Islay

Mulindry

Tormisdale

Port
Charlotte

15

Kilennan

471
BEINN BHAN

491
BEINN
BHEIGEIR

Carraig Mhòr

Lossit

232

O F

Nerabus

L O C H   I N D A A L

Laggan

Duich

*Loch Beinn
Uraraidh*

Ardtalla

*Claggain
Bay*

Lossit Pt.

ISLAY

Laggan
Pt.

Laggan

13

B8016

Rubha na Faing

Portnahaven

A847

*Laggan
Pt.*

Glenegedale

347

Kintour

Ardmore Pt.

Port Wemyss

Orsay

Rinns Pt.

LAGGAN
BAY

Islay

BEINN SHOLUM

KILDALTON CHURCH
AND CROSSES

Eilean Craobhach

Port Alsaig

Rubha Mòr

Kintra

Leorin

A846

Ardbeg

Eilean a'Chuirn

ARDBEG
DISTILLERY

Eilean Bhride

Cornabus

Imeraval

4

Lagavulin

Eilean Imersay

Dùn Mór Ghil

Lower Cragabus

152

Port Ellen

LAGAVULIN DISTILLERY

T H E   O A

Risabus

LAPHROAIG
DISTILLERY

Laphroaig

Lower
Killeyan

Texa

Inerval

NR

AMERICAN MONUMENT

Mull of Oa

202

Rubha nan Leacan

N O R T H   C H A N N E L

Rathlin Island

NF

A

B

C

D

E

NL

F

G

H

J

K

Canna
Garrisdale Pt.
A'Chill
Sanday
Canna Harbour
Rubha Shamhnan Insir
Sound of Canna
Kilmory
Guirdil Bay
Rubha na Roinne
A'Bhrideanach
Kinloch Glen
Loch Scresort
Kinloch
388
RÙM
571 ORVAL
RÙM
KINLOCH CASTLE
Rubha Port na Caranean
Schooner Pt.
Harris
Glen Harris
812 ASKIVAL
Rubha Sgorr an t-Snidhe
781 AINSHVAL
Rubha nam Meirleach

THE SMALL ISLES
SOUND OF RÙM

Bay of Laig
Cleadale
Rubha an Fhasaidh
Eigg
393 AN SGURR
Kildonnan
Galmisdale
Eileas

SOUND OF EIGG
Oigh-sgeir
Eilean nan Each
Muck
137
Port Mor
0:35

Oigh-sgeir

Bhatarsaigh (Vatersay)
Uidh
Bagh Bhatarsaigh
Bhatarsaigh
148
Caolas Shanndraigh
Flodaigh (Flodday)
Sanndraigh (Sandray)
207
Lingeigh (Lingay)
Greanamul
Caolas Phabaigh
Theisgeir (Heiskers)
171
Pabaidh (Pabbay)
Caolas Mhiul Laigh
Miùgh Laigh (Mingulay)
273
Bearnaraigh (Berneray)
Caolas Bhearnaraigh
Barra Hd.

Sanna Point
Sanna Bay
Sanna
Portuairk
Achnaha
Point of Ardnamurchan
ARDNAMURCHAN LIGHTHOUSE
Achosnich
An Acairseid
Ormsaigmore
Ormsaigbeg
Kilchoan
Kilchoan Bay

Cairns of Coll
Rubha Mor
Eilean Mor
Sorisdale
Bousd
Cliad Bay
Arnabost
Gallanach
Grishipol
B8072
Ballyhaugh
Loch Cliad
73
COLL
OBAN 2:55
Hogh Bay
104
B8071
Arinagour
B8070
Feall Bay
Anleod
Totronald
Acha
Loch Eatharna
Eilean Ornsay
Breachacha Castle
Friesland
Loch Breachacha
Calgary Pt.
Gunna
Crossapol Bay
Soa

Ardmore Bay
Ardmore Pt.
Bloody B
Glengorm Castle
MULL MUSEUM
Quinish Pt.
Caliach Pt.
Rubha an Aird
Sunipol
Mishnish
S AIRDE-BEINN
292
Mornish
Penmore Mill
Dervaig
Achnadrish
Calgary Bay
Calgary
THE OLD BYRE HERITAGE CENTRE
SPENH

CASTLEBAY 2:45 (Summer only)

Hough Skerries
TIREE
Vaul Bay
Balephetrish Bay
Vaul
Salum
Caolas
Rubha Dubh
Balevullin
R. Chraiginis
Kenovay
Gott Bay
Ruaig
Soa
1:00
Kilkenneth
Moss
B8069
TIREE
Scarinish
Heanish
Rubha Traigh an Duin
Middleton
Heylipol
B8065
Crossapol
Hynish Bay
Port Mor
Barrapol
B8067
Balemartine
Rinn Thorbhais
Balephuil
141
Mannal
Balephuil Bay
Hynish
Port Snoig

Treshnish Pt.
Ensay
340 CARN MOR
Rubh a'Chaoil
Haunn
Burg
Kilninian
Achleck
23
Fanmore
390
Treshnish Isles
Fladda
LOCH TUATH
Ballygown
Eilean Dioghlum
Lunga
Gometra
Beamus 313
Laggan Bay
424 BEINN NA DRISE
Lagganulva
Oskamull
ULVA
Killiemor
Ulva House
Killiemor

Bac Mor

LOCH NA KEAL
Little Colonsay
Eorsa
ISLE OF
Staffa
STAFFA
FINGAL'S CAVE
INCH KENNETH CHAPEL
Inch Kenneth
Derryguaig
Balnahard
Erisgeir
MACKINNON'S CAVE
519
ARDMEANACH
BEINN NA SREINE
Killiemore House
Kilfinich
THE BURG
561
Glen Seilisdeir

MACLEAN'S CROSS
Eilean Annraidh
Rubha nan Cearc
100
IONA ABBEY AND CATHEDRAL
Kintra
IONA HERITAGE CENTRE
Baile Mor
ST COLUMBA EXHIBITION & WELCOME CENTRE
Iona
Aridhglas
Eorabus
LOCH SCRIDAIN
Torrans
BRC
Stac an Aoineach
Fionnphort
A849
Lee
18
Fidden
Tiraghoil
Bunessan
376 CRUACHAN MIN
Erraid
Loch Assapol
ROSS OF MULL
Lisken
Scoor
Ardalanish
125
Ardchiavaig
Soa I.
Eilean a'Chalmain
Rubha nam Braithrean
Rubh Ardalanish
144
Torran Rocks
Malcolm's Pt.

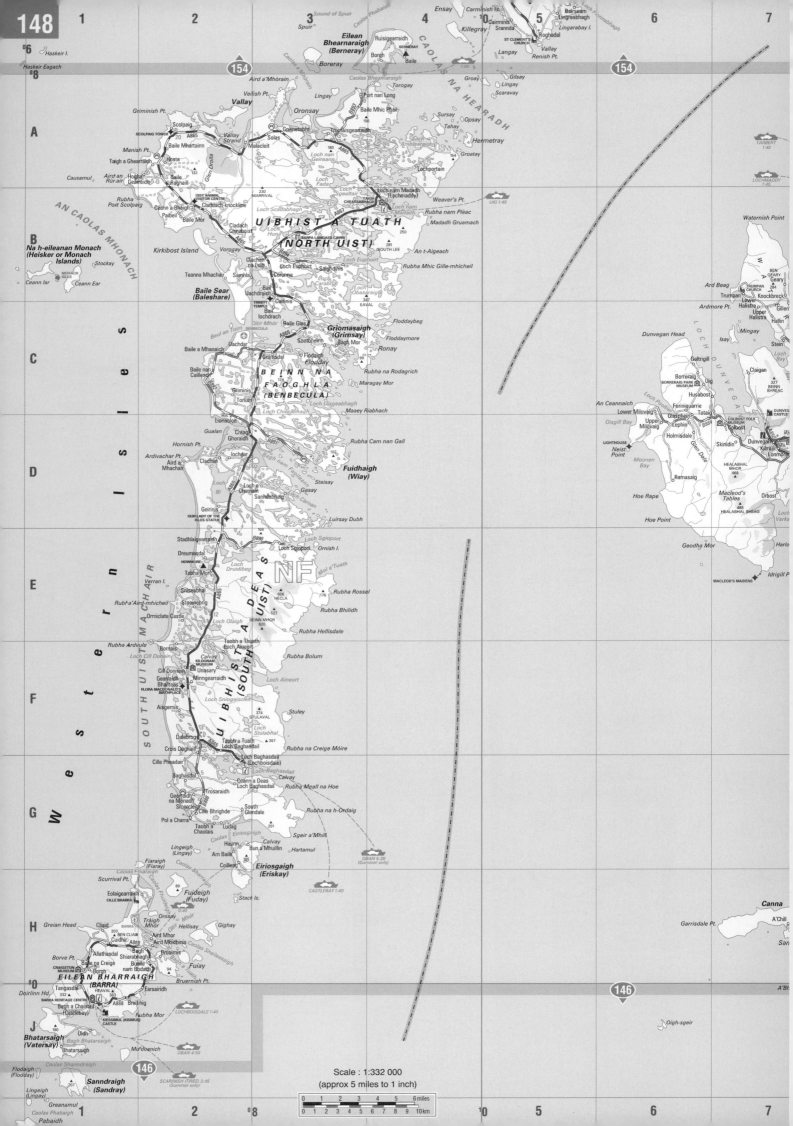

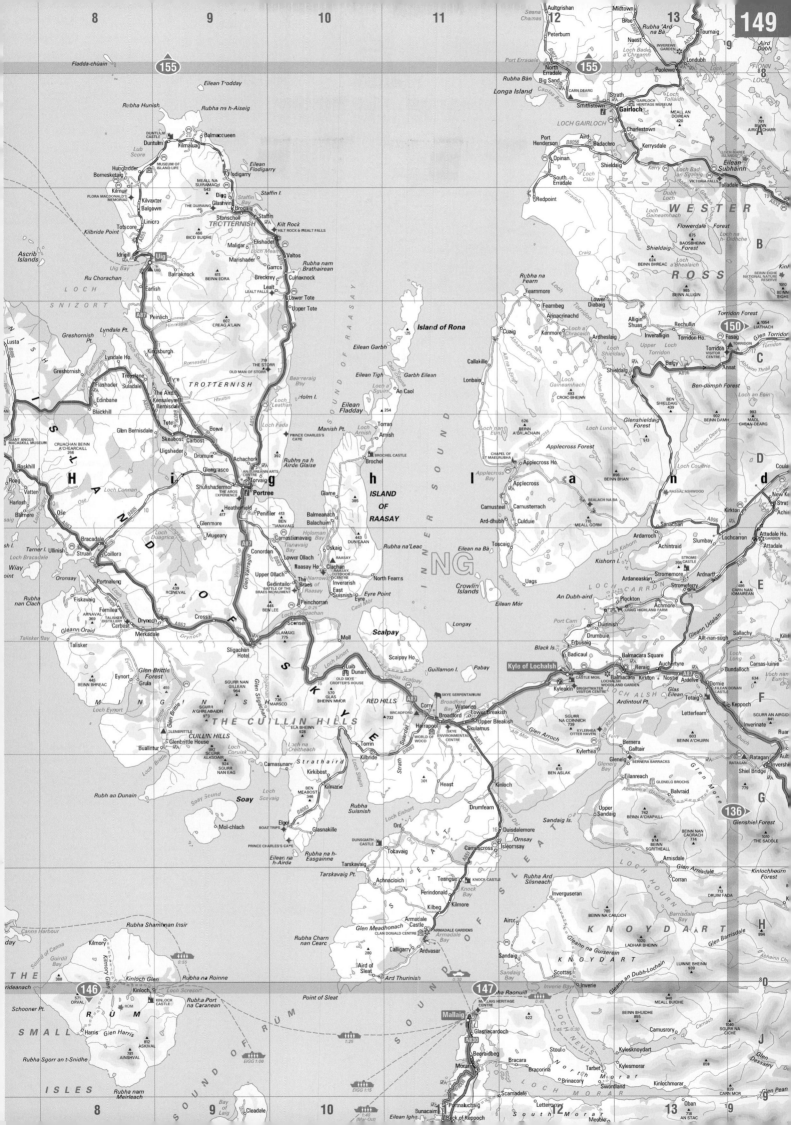

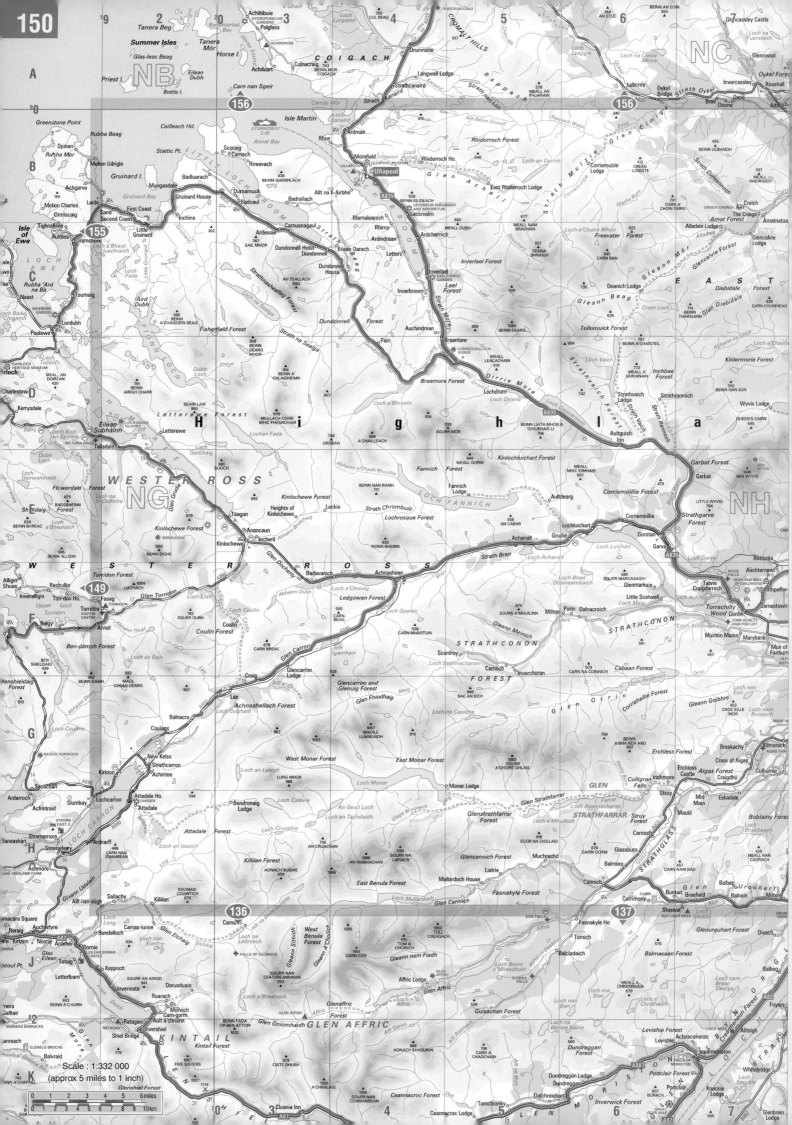

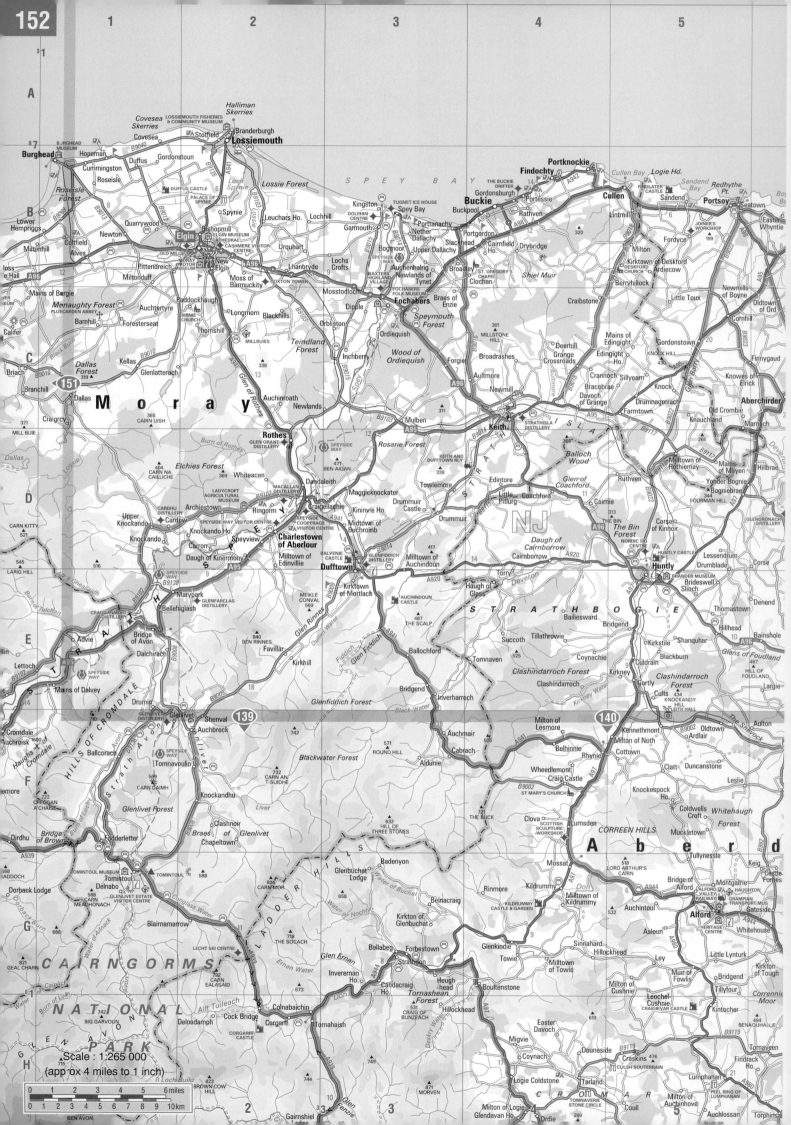

NA

St. Kilda

NA

NF

Boreray
384 ▲

CNOC GLAS 376 ▲ *Soay*
Loch a' Ghlinne
CONACHAIR 376 ▲
MULLACH BI 358 ▲
ST KILDA
Bàgh a Bhaille
Dun
ST KILDA

St Kilda or Hirta (Hiort)

Na h-Eileanan Flannach

W e s t e r n

I s l e s

Haskeir I.
Haskeir Eagach

NF

Gaisgeir

Kearstay
308 ▲
Bràighe Mòr
Scarp
Huisinis
679 ▲
Hushinish Pt.
489 ▲
Bàgh Huisinis
Caolas
Gobhaig
Horsanish
Arda Móra
Loch a' Ghlinne
679 ▲ TIRGA MOR
659 ▲ ULLAVAL

Taransay Glorigs
Soay Beag
Cliasmol
Soay Mòr
Carnus an t-suithean
Tarasaigh (Taransay)
436 ▲ BEN LUSKENTYRE

Rubha Sgeirigin
Paible
99 ▲
Caolas Tharasaigh
Luskentyre Beach
LUSKENTYRE BEACH
Losgaintir
467 ▲
South Harris Forest

Toe Head
Coppay
Seilebost
Borve Lodge
Buirgh
23
CHAIPAVAL 365 ▲
Sgarasta Mhor
398 ▲ BLEAVAL
Shillay
Little Shillay
Rubha 'an Teampuill
Sound of Shillay
Taobh Tuath
SEALLAM!

Pabaidh (Pabbay)
Quinish
Brenish Pt.
196 ▲
Sound of Spuir
Spuir

Eilean Bhearnaraigh (Berneray)
Ruisi gearraidh
Borgh
BERNERAY
Baile
Boreray
Langay
Renish Pt.
Vallay
ST CLEMENT'S CHURCH

Ensay
Carminish Is.
Cairinis Srannda
Killegray

Caolas Phabaich
Caolas a' Mhorain

Vallay
Aird a'Mhòrain
Veilish Pt.
Lingay
Griminish Pt.
Scolpaig
A865
Oronsay
Valley Strand
Baile Mhartainn
Grèinetobht
Solas
Malacleit
Trumaisgearraidh
180 ▲
Port nan Long
Baile Mhic Phail
B893

Sursay
Tahay
Opsay
Groay
Gilsay
Lingay
Scaravay
Hermetray

CAOLAS NA HEARADH

Siabost bho Thuath
SHAWBOST NORSE MILL
Siabost bho Dheas
Bàgh Dhail Beag
Pairc Shiaboist
261 ▲ BEIN BRAC
20
GEARRANNAN BLACKHOUSE VILLAGE
GARENIN
Na Gearrannan
Dail Beag
Dail Mòr
Borghastan
Carlabhagh
Campay
Loch Chàrlabhaigh
DUN CARLOWAY BROCH
Little Bernera
Floday
Cirbhig
Harsgeir
Carlabhagh
IRON AGE HOUSE
A858
Loch Lacasbhad Ard
An Galan Uigeach
Aird Uig
AN CAOLAS
Pabay Mòr
Tobson
Great Bernera
Crothair
Breacleit
Vacsay
Circebost
Keava
Breasclete
Cliobh
Miabhig
Bhaltos
Riof
Vuia Mòr
Barraglom
Eilean Kearstay
CALANAIS VISITOR CENTRE
Timsgearraidh
205 ▲
Uigen
Tobharol
Floday
Vuia Beag
CALANAIS STANDING STONES
Linsiadar
Gearraidh na h-Aibhne
Cradhlastadh
Cairisiadar
Crulabhig
Loch Ròg
B8011
Ard More Mangersta
Carnais
Eadar Dha Fhadhail
SUAINAVAL 429 ▲
Geisiadar
256 ▲
Mangurstadh
Loch Smuasbhaigh
Aird Fenish
Loch Ròg
Einacleite
Loch Tungabhat
B8011
Aird Brenish
574 ▲ MEALISVAL
Islibhig
Loch Grunabhat
Giosla
Breanais
Giosla
Loch Fuaroil
19
Loch Chaolartan
Loch Airigh na h-Airde
Loch Morsgail
397 ▲ BEINN MHEADHONACH
Loch Cro Criosdaig
Loch Coirigerod
Loch Beinnseabhal
Morsgail Forest
Loch Langabhat
Loch Strandabhat
Mealasta Island
Loch Bodabhat
Loch Tamnabhaigh
Loch Reasort

LOCH LANGABHAT
Ceann Tarabhaigh
A859
Aird an Troim
Airidh a' Bhruaich
Aline Lodge
Seaforth I.
Loch Seaforth
572 ▲ BEINN MHOR
STULAVAL 579 ▲
UISGNAVAL MORE 729 ▲
Scaladal
449 ▲
17
Aird a' Mhulaidh
Forest of Harris
Abhainn Suidhe
HARRIS AND CEANN A TUATH NA HEARADH
CLISHAM 799 ▲
B887
Miabhag
Bun Abhainn Eadarra
A859
S O U T H   L E W I S
13
559 ▲
Maraig
OLD WHALING STATION
Rhenigidale
Reinigeadal
Loch Trollamarig
N O R T H   U I S T
Isay
Aird Asaig
Lochan Lacasdail
Teirbeart (Tarbert)
Urgha
Carragraich
Caolas Scalpaigh
Carnach
Sgeotasaigh
Rudha Crago
Drinisiadar
Loch Ceann Dibig
Miabhag
Scalpay
Eilean Scalpa (Scalp
NA HEARADH (HARRIS)
Kennacley
Plocropol Pt.
Loch an Tairbeart
A859
Greosabhagh
Aird Mhighe
386 ▲
Leac a Li
Plocropol
Liceasto
Geocrab
Scadabhagh
Caolas Stocinis
Cluthar
Rubha Bhocaig
Beacrabhaic
Loch Langabhat
Fleodabhagh
Manais
Stockinish I.
Aird Mhighe
Boirseam Lingreabhagh
Lingarabay I.
Cuidhtinis
Loch Fhinnsbhaigh

Aird
An t-Ob (Leverburgh)
Fionnsbhagh
ROINEABHAL
Roghadal
Loch an Amhlsarraidh

UIG 1:40

A859

G R A C E *(no visible)*

Scale : 1:332 000
(approx 5 miles to 1 inch)

0 1 2 3 4 5 6 miles
0 1 2 3 4 5 6 7 8 9 10km

148
148

B

C
Papa Westray
North Ronaldsay
NORTH RONALDSAY
Hollandstoun
BROCH OF BURRIAN
Aikerness KNAP OF HOWAR Holland
Holm of Papa
Backaskaill
Gayfield
NOUP HEAD
PIEROWALL CHURCH Rackwick
Pierowall
Broughton
NOLTLAND CASTLE Braehead
NORTH RONALDSAY FIRTH
Scar
Burness
Sellibister
Lettan

D
WESTRAY
THE NORTH SOUND
Lady
FITTY HILL 169
Midbea
Skelwick
KIRKWALL 1:25
Langskaill
WESTSIDE CHURCH
Sulland
Rapness
Broughtown
Overbister
Newark
SANDAY
START PT.
B9068
B9069

E
WESTRAY FIRTH
HY
Calf of Eday
Carrick Ho.
Carrick House
Calfsound
Laminess
Kettletoft
QUOYNESS CHAMBERED CAIRN
Faray
Braeswick
Guith
Millbounds
Stove
Loth
SANDAY SOUND
EDA
Backaland
EDAY
Veness
Odie
STRONSAY Papa Stronsay
Wasbister
ROUSAY
Sourin
Skaill
ST MAGNUS CHURCH
Whitehall Village
MIDHOWE BROCH Eynhallow
Westness 227
Brinian
Muckle Green Holm
Wardhill
Everbay
STRONSAY
EYNHALLOW CHURCH Costa
KNOWE OF YARSO CAIRN
Egilsay
Linga Holm
Grobister
Kirbister

F
BROUGH HEAD
BROUGH OF BIRSAY
Abune-the-Hill
Burgar
Frotoft
CUBBIE ROO'S CASTLE AND ST MARY'S CHAPEL
STRONSAY
Rothiesholm
Dishes
Holland
EARL'S PALACE The Barony
Stenso
BROCH OF GURNESS
Wyre
MARWICK HEAD NATURE RESERVE
Stara
K'byuster
Redland
Marwick
Twatt
159
Tingwall
Scarwell
Quoyloo
B9057
Click Mill
CLICK MILL
Beaquoy
102
Gairsay
Northdyke
Dounby
A966
Hackland
Skaill
Kierfield Ho.
Mirbister
221
Gorseness
Edmonstone
SKAILL HOUSE
Brough
CORRIGALL FARM MUSEUM
Settiscarth
Isbister
Shapinsay
FIRTH
Aith
Heslwall
Netherbrough
Bimbister
Breck of Cruan
BALFOUR CASTLE
Auskerry

G
Yesnaby
Voy
Arion
STANDING STONES
Bridge of Waith
A965
MAES HOWE
Quholm
RING OF BROGAR
158
Outertown
PIER ARTS CENTRE
Stromness
STROMNESS MUSEUM
Finstown
TORMISTON MILL
Heddle
Clouston
Nisthouse
A965
225
Grimbister
WIRELESS MUSEUM
Work
Balfour
Newlot
ORKNEY MUSEUM
Kirkwall
ST MAGNUS CATHEDRAL
BISHOP'S & EARL'S PALACE
Berstane
HIGHLAND PARK DISTILLERY
Hall of Tankerness
Orkney
ABERDEEN 6:00 LERWICK 7:45

H
HOY AND WEST MAINLAND
Ireland
Kirbister
Scapa
Tradespack
Whitecleat
North Halley
43
Skaill
Breckan
Clestrain
Hobbister
A964
Greengoe
Deerness
B9050
Grindigar
Murra
Graemsay
Petertown
Crya
Smoogro
Waulkmill Lodge
Toab
Foubister
Gritley
NORTH HOY NATURE RESERVE
Linksness
Oucyness
Houton
Swanbister
Gyre
ST NICHOLAS CHURCH
North Bown
NORWOOD MUSEUM
Upper Sanday
SCRABSTER 1:30
Hoy
433
479 WARD HILL
DWARFIE STANE
Cava
ITALIAN CHAPEL
Braehead

J
OLD MAN OF HOY
304
Rackwick
399 KNAP OF TROWIEGLEN
Ryse Little
Fara
St Mary's
Cornquoy
RORA HEAD
FOSSIL AND VINTAGE CENTRE
Northtown
HOY
236
SCAPA FLOW VISITOR CENTRE
Lyness
Rinnicill
Bow
Pan
Uppertown
Hunda
Hillside
Burray
Lynes
Little Ayre
Crockness
Wyng
Hackness
Switha
St. Margaret's Hope
Burray Village
Southtown
Grimness
FLOTTA
Melsetter
Longhope
MARTELLO TOWERS
Herston
Quindry
Papley
B9047
Hurliness
Brims
SOUTH WALLS
Widewall
Aikers
Sandwick
Suckquoy
Lythes
SOUTH RONALDSAY

K
Swona
Dundas Ho.
Cleat
TOMB OF THE EAGLES AND BRONZE AGE HOUSE
Burwick
Liddel
B9041

PENTLAND FIRTH

158

Nethertown
Island of Stroma
Uppertown
DUNCANSBY HEAD

L
DUNNET HEAD
Scarfskerry
East Mey
Brough
CASTLE OF MEY
Kirkstyle
Huna
Hunspow
Ham
Rattar
Mey
Gills
John o'Groats
STROMNESS 1:30
MARY ANN'S COTTAGE
Corsback
Canisby
A836
DUNNET BAY
Dunnet
Scrabster
THURSO CASTLE
FOLK MUSEUM
Barrock
Clardon
Murkle
Castlehill
Inkstack
Thurso
INTERPRETATIVE TRAIL
Castletown
Brabster
Skirza

M
East
Haimer
CASTLETOWN Tain
Lochend
Freswick
Milbank
AE36
Castleton
Geise
Oling Ho.
Reaster
141
BUCHOLLY CASTLE
Waydale
Hilliclay
Durran
Alterwall
Slickly
Scale : 1:400 000 (approx 6¼ miles to 1 inch)
Buckies
LYTH ARTS CENTRE
Nybster
16
Lieuray
Achingills
Bowermadden
Lyth
Sortat
CAITHNESS BROCH CENTRE
Auckengill
Sordale
Knockdee
Stemster Ho.
Barrock Ho.
Howe
KEISS CASTLE

N
Calder Mains
Braal Castle
Roadside
Gillock
Mireland
Keiss
ND
Scotscalder Station
Halkirk
Banniskirk Ho.
Kirk
North Watten
Myrelandhorn
SINCLAIR'S BAY
Mains of Watten
176
Killimster
CASTLE GIRNIGOE

Town plan symbols

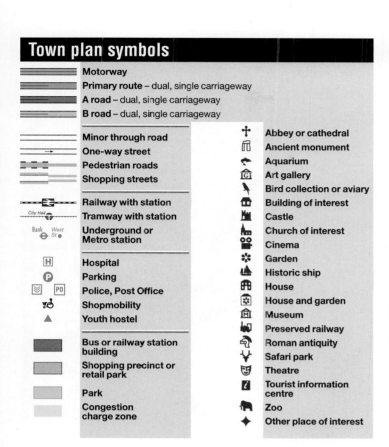

Motorway	
Primary route – dual, single carriageway	
A road – dual, single carriageway	
B road – dual, single carriageway	
Minor through road	
One-way street	
Pedestrian roads	
Shopping streets	
Railway with station	
Tramway with station	
Underground or Metro station	
H Hospital	
P Parking	
Police, Post Office	
Shopmobility	
▲ Youth hostel	
Bus or railway station building	
Shopping precinct or retail park	
Park	
Congestion charge zone	

✝	Abbey or cathedral
	Ancient monument
	Aquarium
G	Art gallery
	Bird collection or aviary
	Building of interest
	Castle
	Church of interest
	Cinema
✳	Garden
	Historic ship
	House
	House and garden
	Museum
	Preserved railway
	Roman antiquity
⋎	Safari park
	Theatre
i	Tourist information centre
	Zoo
✦	Other place of interest

Aberdeen

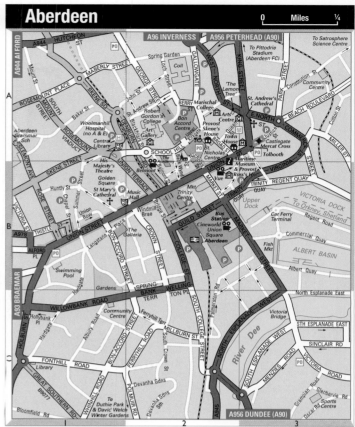

Birmingham

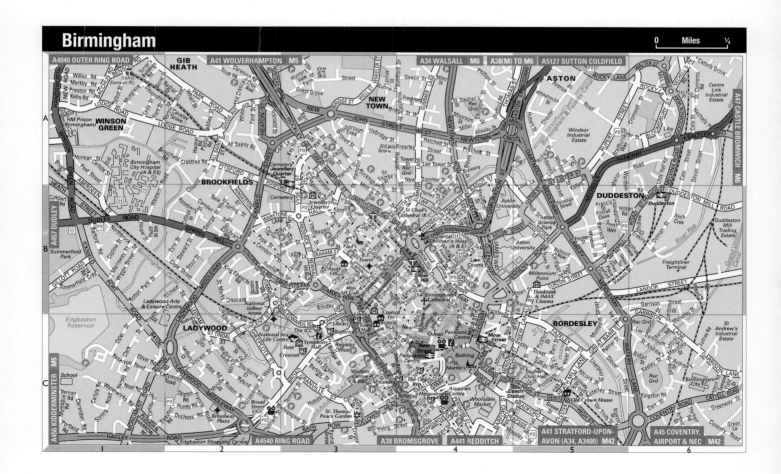

Bath

0 Miles ¼

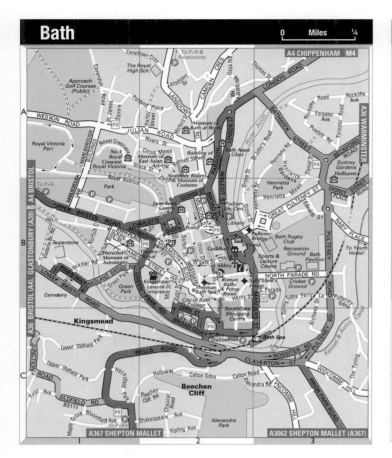

Bradford

0 Miles ¼

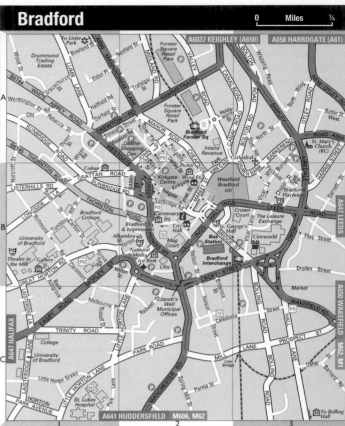

Bristol

0 Miles ¼

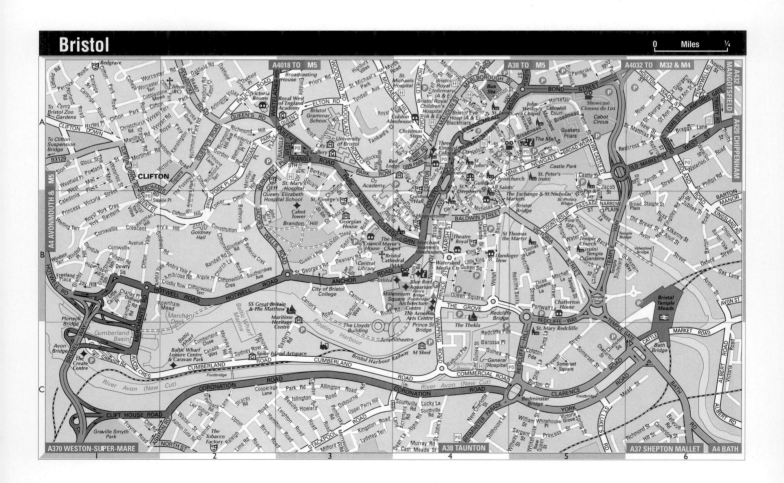

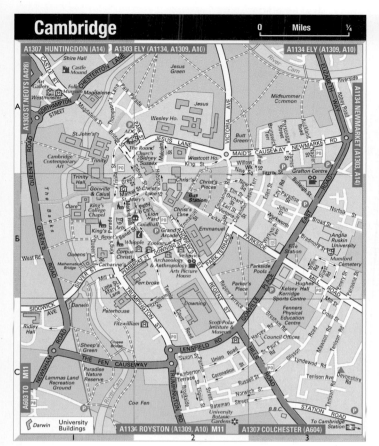

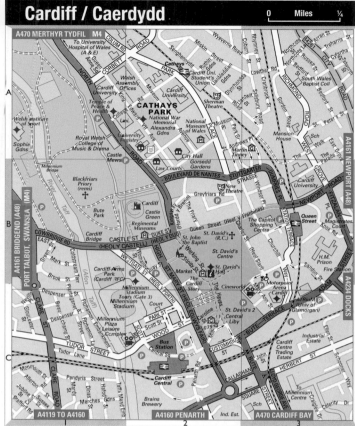

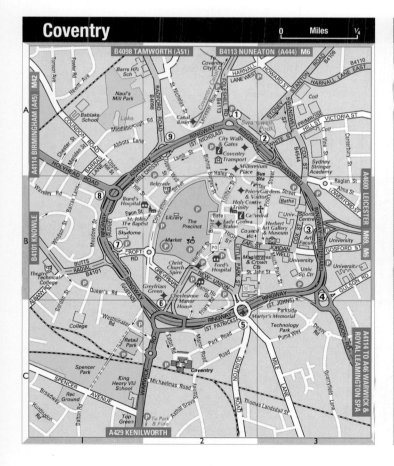

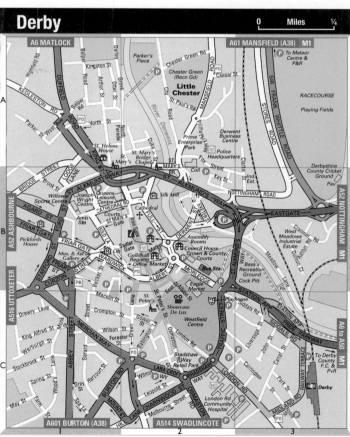

Edinburgh

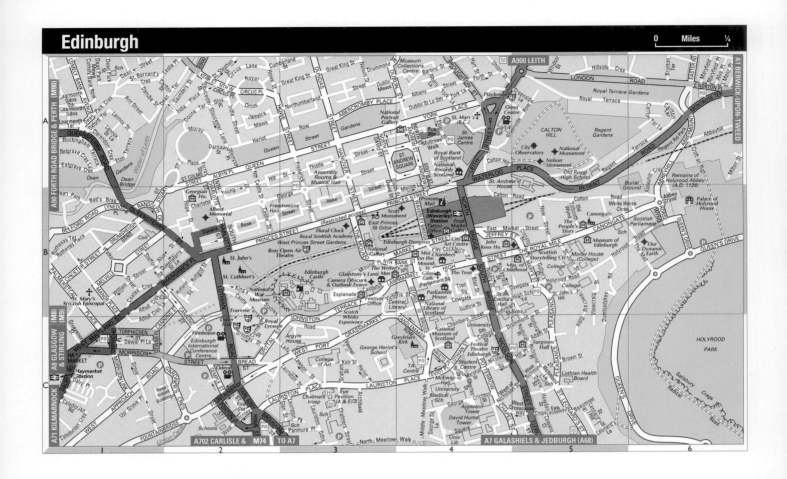

Glasgow

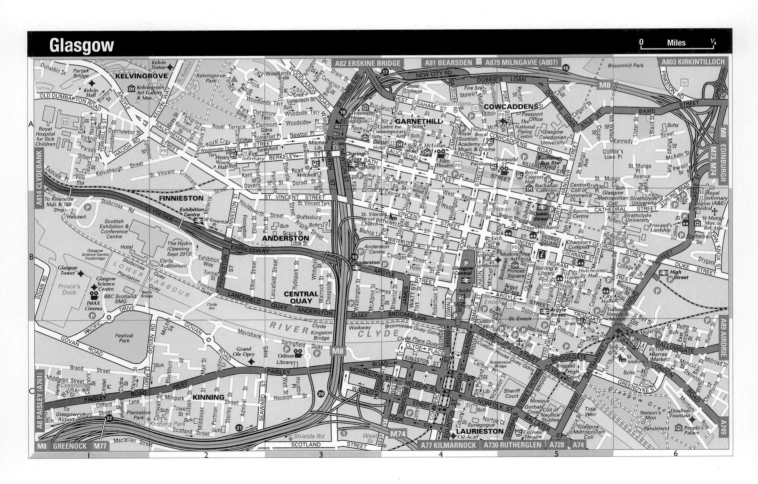

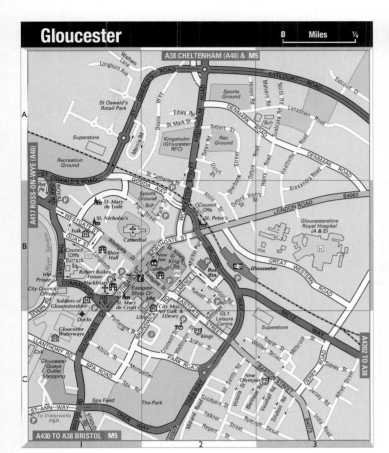

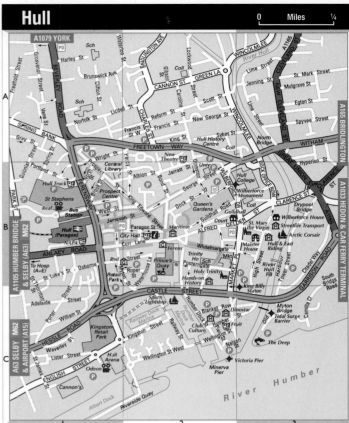

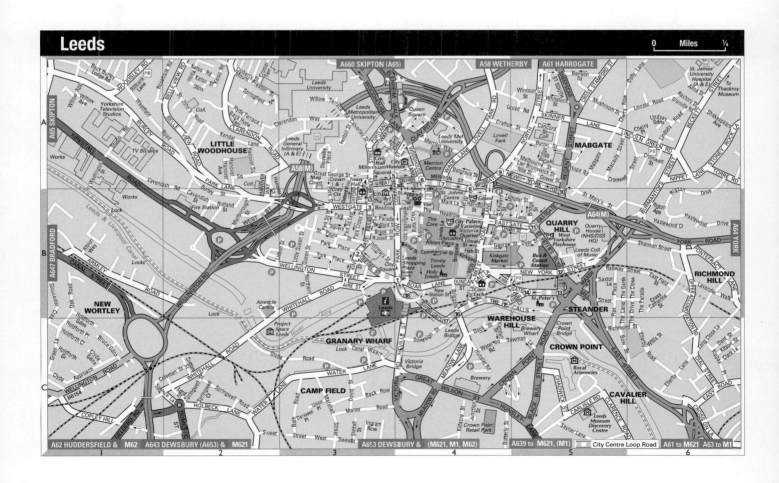

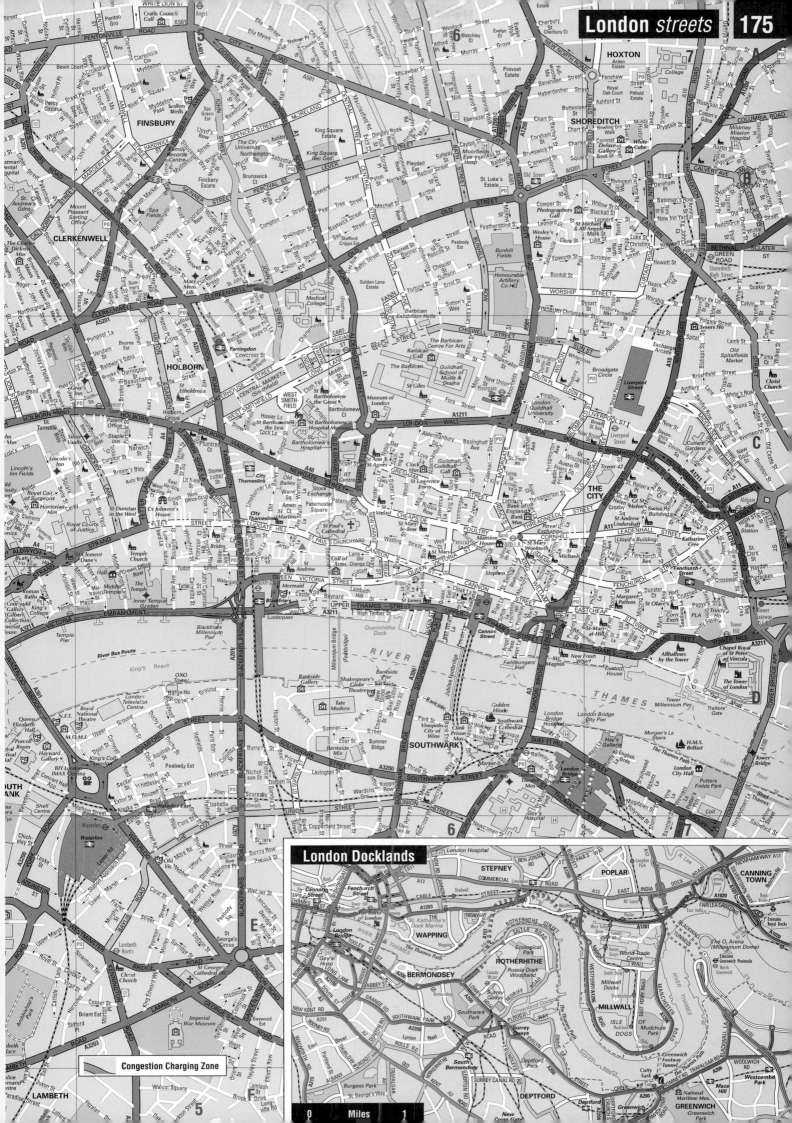

Congestion Charging Zone

London Docklands

0   Miles   1

Liverpool

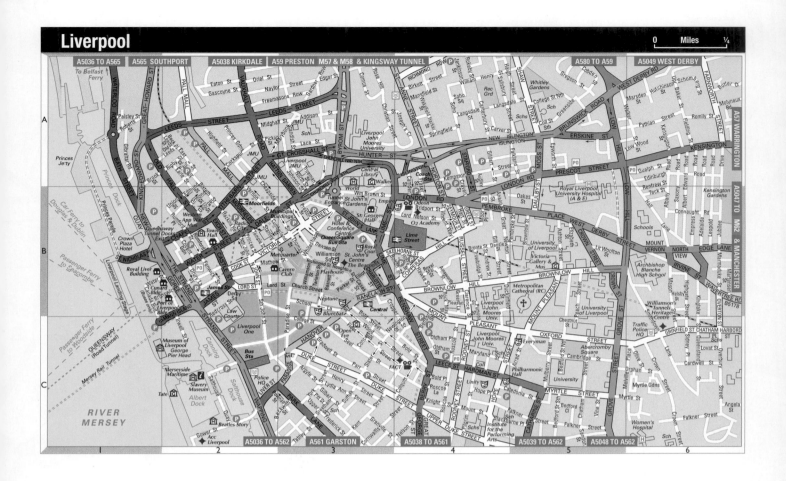

Manchester

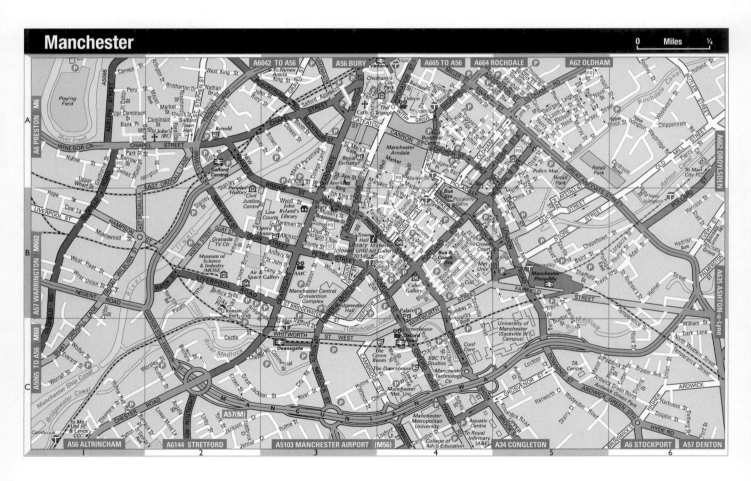

Leicester

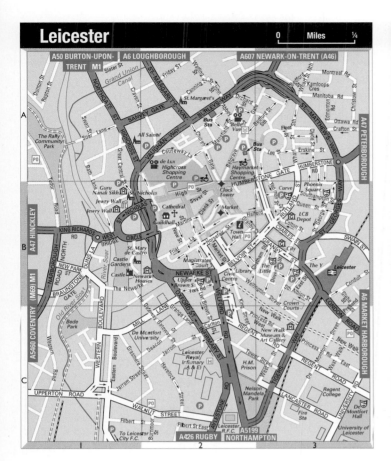

Middlesbrough

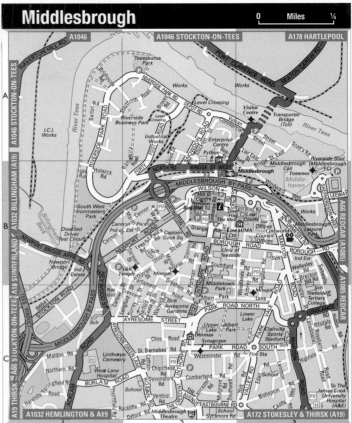

Newcastle upon Tyne

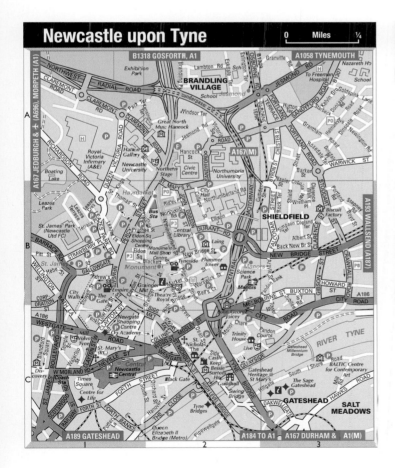

Norwich

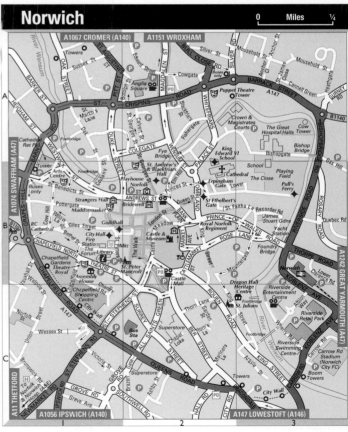

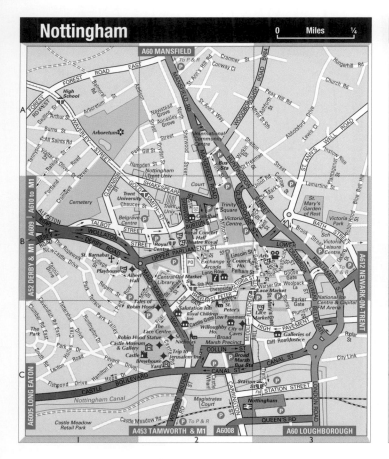

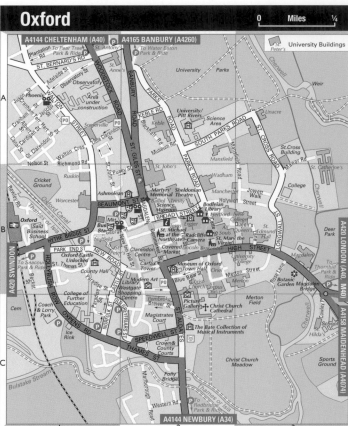

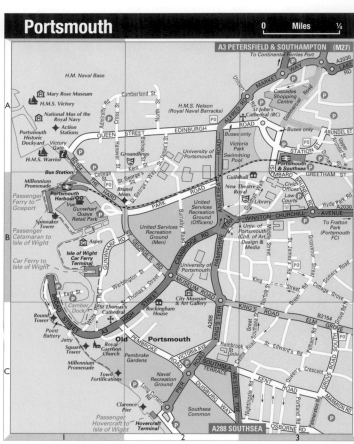

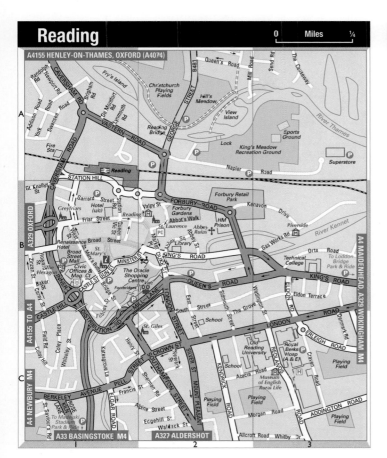

Reading

0 Miles ¼

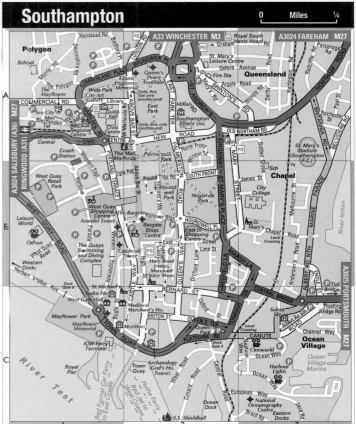

Southampton

0 Miles ¼

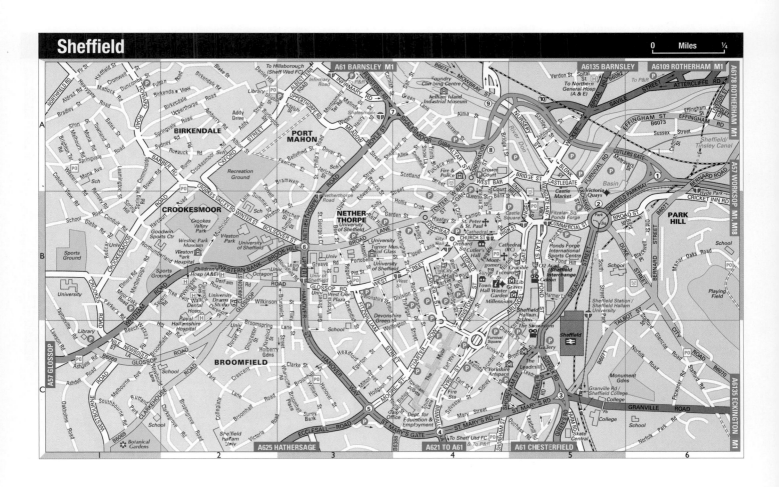

Sheffield

0 Miles ¼

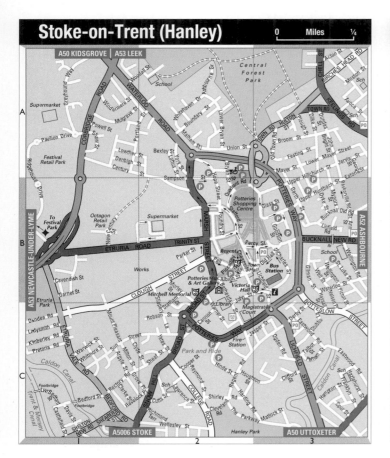

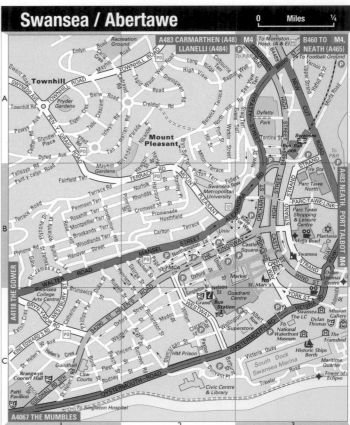

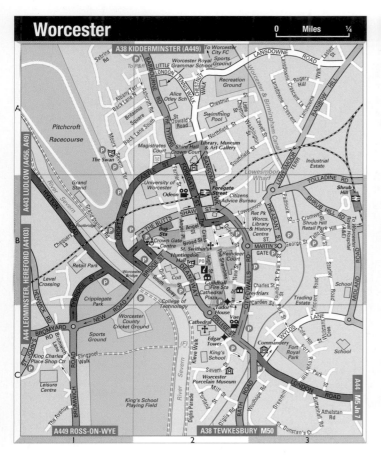

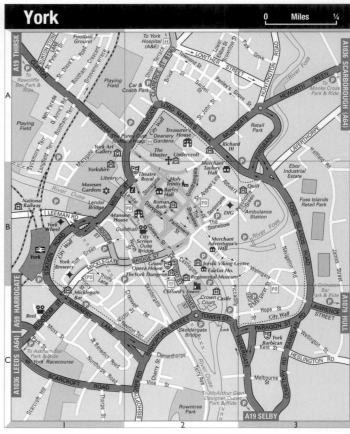

Abbreviations used in the index

Aberdeen	Aberdeen City
Aberds	Aberdeenshire
Ald	Alderney
Anglesey	Isle of Anglesey
Angus	Angus
Argyll	Argyll and Bute
Bath	Bath and North East Somerset
Bedford	Bedford
Bl Gwent	Blaenau Gwent
Blackburn	Blackburn with Darwen
Blackpool	Blackpool
Bmouth	Bournemouth
Borders	Scottish Borders
Brack	Bracknell
Bridgend	Bridgend
Brighton	City of Brighton and Hove
Bristol	City and County of Bristol
Bucks	Buckinghamshire
C Beds	Central Bedfordshire
Caerph	Caerphilly
Cambs	Cambridgeshire
Cardiff	Cardiff
Carms	Carmarthenshire
Ceredig	Ceredigion
Ches E	Cheshire East
Ches W	Cheshire West and Chester
Clack	Clackmannanshire
Conwy	Conwy
Corn	Cornwall
Cumb	Cumbria
Darl	Darlington
Denb	Denbighshire
Derby	City of Derby
Derbys	Derbyshire
Devon	Devon
Dorset	Dorset
Dumfries	Dumfries and Galloway
Dundee	Dundee City
Durham	Durham
E Ayrs	East Ayrshire
E Dunb	East Dunbartonshire
E Loth	East Lothian
E Renf	East Renfrewshire
E Sus	East Sussex
E Yorks	East Riding of Yorkshire
Edin	City of Edinburgh
Essex	Essex
Falk	Falkirk
Fife	Fife
Flint	Flintshire
Glasgow	City of Glasgow
Glos	Gloucestershire
Gtr Man	Greater Manchester
Guern	Guernsey
Gwyn	Gwynedd
Halton	Halton
Hants	Hampshire
Hereford	Herefordshire
Herts	Hertfordshire
Highld	Highland
Hrtlpl	Hartlepool
Hull	Hull
IoM	Isle of Man
IoW	Isle of Wight
Invclyd	Inverclyde
Jersey	Jersey
Kent	Kent
Lancs	Lancashire
Leicester	City of Leicester
Leics	Leicestershire
Lincs	Lincolnshire
London	Greater London
Luton	Luton
M Keynes	Milton Keynes
M Tydf	Merthyr Tydfil
Mbro	Middlesbrough
Medway	Medway
Mers	Merseyside
Midloth	Midlothian
Mon	Monmouthshire
Moray	Moray
N Ayrs	North Ayrshire
N Lincs	North Lincolnshire
N Lanark	North Lanarkshire
N Som	North Somerset
N Yorks	North Yorkshire
NE Lincs	North East Lincolnshire
Neath	Neath Port Talbot
Newport	City and County of Newport
Norf	Norfolk
Northants	Northamptonshire
Northumb	Northumberland
Nottingham	City of Nottingham
Notts	Nottinghamshire
Orkney	Orkney
Oxon	Oxfordshire
Pboro	Peterborough
Pembs	Pembrokeshire
Perth	Perth and Kinross
Plym	Plymouth
Poole	Poole
Powys	Powys
Ptsmth	Portsmouth
Reading	Reading
Redcar	Redcar and Cleveland
Renfs	Renfrewshire
Rhondda	Rhondda Cynon Taff
Rutland	Rutland
S Ayrs	South Ayrshire
S Glos	South Gloucestershire
S Lanark	South Lanarkshire
S Yorks	South Yorkshire
Scilly	Scilly
Shetland	Shetland
Shrops	Shropshire
Slough	Slough
Som	Somerset
Soton	Southampton
Staffs	Staffordshire
Southend	Southend-on-Sea
Stirling	Stirling
Stockton	Stockton-on-Tees
Stoke	Stoke-on-Trent
Suff	Suffolk
Sur	Surrey
Swansea	Swansea
Swindon	Swindon
T&W	Tyne and Wear
Telford	Telford and Wrekin
Thurrock	Thurrock
Torbay	Torbay
Torf	Torfaen
V Glam	The Vale of Glamorgan
W Berks	West Berkshire
W Dunb	West Dunbartonshire
W Isles	Western Isles
W Loth	West Lothian
W Mid	West Midlands
W Sus	West Sussex
W Yorks	West Yorkshire
Warks	Warwickshire
Warr	Warrington
Wilts	Wiltshire
Windsor	Windsor and Maidenhead
Wokingham	Wokingham
Worcs	Worcestershire
Wrex	Wrexham
York	City of York

How to use the index

Example

Trudoxhill Som **24** E2

- grid square
- page number
- county or unitary authority

Index to road maps of Britain

Ansty Wilts 13 B7
Anthill Common Hants 15 C7
Anthorn Cumb 107 D8
Antingham Norf 81 D8
Anton's Gowt Lincs 79 E5
Antonshill Falk 127 F7
Antony Corn 5 D8
Anwick Lincs 78 D4
Anwoth Dumfries 106 D2
Aoradh Argyll 142 B3
Apes Hall Cambs 67 E5
Apethorpe Northants 65 E7
Apeton Staffs 62 C2
Apley Lincs 78 B4
Apperknowle Derbys 76 B3
Apperley Glos 37 B5
Apperley Bridge W Yorks 94 F4
Appersett N Yorks 100 E3
Appin Argyll 130 E3
Appin House Argyll 130 E3
Appleby N Lincs 90 C3
Appleby-in-Westmorland Cumb 100 B1
Appleby Magna Leics 63 D7
Appleby Parva Leics 63 D7
Applecross Highld 149 D12
Applecross Ho. Highld 149 D12
Appledore Devon 11 C5
Appledore Devon 20 F3
Appledore Kent 19 C6
Appledore Heath Kent 19 B6
Appleford Oxon 39 E5
Applegarthtown Dumfries 114 F4
Appleshaw Hants 25 E8
Applethwaite Cumb 98 B4
Appleton Halton 86 F3
Appleton Oxon 38 D4
Appleton-le-Moors N Yorks 103 F5
Appleton-le-Street N Yorks 96 B3
Appleton Roebuck N Yorks 95 E8
Appleton Thorn Warr 86 F4
Appleton Wiske N Yorks 102 D1
Appletreehall Borders 115 C8
Appletreewick N Yorks 94 C3
Appley Som 11 B5
Appley Bridge Lancs 86 D3
Apse Heath IoW 15 F6
Apsley End C Beds 54 F2
Apuldram W Sus 16 D2
Aquhythie Aberds 141 C6
Arabella Highld 151 D11
Arbeadie Aberds 141 E5
Arberth = Narberth Pembs 32 C2
Arbirlot Angus 135 E6
Arboll Highld 151 C11
Arborfield Wokingham 27 C5
Arborfield Cross Wokingham 27 C5
Arborfield Garrison Wokingham 27 C5
Arbour-thorne S Yorks 88 F4
Arbroath Angus 135 E6
Arbuthnott Aberds 135 B7
Archiestown Moray 152 D2
Arclid Ches E 74 C4
Ard-dhubh Highld 149 D12
Ardachu Highld 157 J9
Ardalanish Argyll 146 K6
Ardanaiseig Argyll 125 C6
Ardaneaskan Highld 149 E13
Ardanstur Argyll 124 D4
Ardargie House Hotel Perth 128 C2
Ardarroch Highld 149 E13
Ardbeg Argyll 142 D5
Ardbeg Argyll 145 E10
Ardcharnich Highld 150 C4
Ardchiavaig Argyll 146 K6
Ardchullarie More Stirling 126 C4
Ardchyle Stirling 126 B4
Arddleen Powys 60 C2
Ardechvie Highld 136 E4
Ardeley Herts 41 B6
Ardelve Highld 149 F13
Arden Argyll 126 F2
Ardens Grafton Warks 51 D6
Ardentinny Argyll 145 E10
Ardentraive Argyll 145 F9
Ardeonaig Stirling 132 F3
Ardersier Highld 151 F10
Ardessie Highld 150 C3
Ardfern Argyll 124 E4
Ardgartan Argyll 125 E8
Ardgay Highld 151 B8
Ardgour Highld 130 C4
Ardheslaig Highld 149 C12
Ardiecow Moray 152 B5
Ardindrean Highld 150 C4
Ardingly W Sus 17 B7
Ardington Oxon 38 F4
Ardlair Aberds 140 B4
Ardlamont Ho. Argyll 145 G8
Ardleigh Essex 43 B6
Ardler Perth 134 E2
Ardley Oxon 39 B5
Ardlui Argyll 126 C2
Ardlussa Argyll 144 E5
Ardmair Highld 150 B4
Ardmay Argyll 125 E8
Ardminish Argyll 143 D7
Ardmolich Highld 147 D10
Ardmore Argyll 124 C3
Ardmore Highld 151 C10
Ardmore Highld 156 D5
Ardnacross Argyll 147 G8
Ardnadam Argyll 145 F10
Ardnagrask Highld 151 G8
Ardnarff Highld 149 E13
Ardnastang Highld 130 C2
Ardnave Argyll 142 A3
Ardno Argyll 125 E7
Ardo Aberds 153 E8
Ardo Ho. Aberds 141 B8
Ardoch Perth 133 F7
Ardochy House Highld 136 D5
Ardoyne Aberds 141 B5
Ardpatrick Argyll 144 G6
Ardpatrick Ho. Argyll 144 H6
Ardpeaton Argyll 145 E11
Ardrishaig Argyll 145 E7
Ardross Fife 129 D7
Ardross Highld 151 D9
Ardross Castle Highld 151 D9
Ardrossan N Ayrs 118 E2
Ardshealach Highld 147 E9
Ardsley S Yorks 88 D4
Ardslignish Highld 147 E8
Ardtalla Argyll 142 C5
Ardtalnaig Perth 132 F4
Ardtoe Highld 147 D9
Ardtrostan Perth 127 B5
Arduaine Argyll 124 D3
Ardullie Highld 151 E8
Ardvasar Highld 149 H11
Ardvorlich Perth 126 B5
Ardwell Dumfries 104 E5
Ardwell Mains Dumfries 104 E5
Ardwick Gtr Man 87 E6
Areley Kings Worcs 50 B3
Arford Hants 27 F6
Argoed Caerph 35 E5
Argoed Mill Powys 47 C8
Arichamish Argyll 124 E5
Arichastlich Argyll 125 B8
Aridhglas Argyll 146 J6
Arileod Argyll 146 F4
Arinacrinachd Highld 149 C12
Arinagour Argyll 146 F5
Arion Orkney 159 G3
Arisaig Highld 147 C9
Ariundle Highld 130 C2
Arkendale N Yorks 95 C6
Arkesden Essex 55 F5
Arkholme Lancs 93 B5
Arkle Town N Yorks 101 D5
Arkleton Dumfries 115 E6
Arkley London 41 E5
Arksey S Yorks 89 D6
Arkwright Town Derbys 76 B4
Arle Glos 37 B6
Arlecdon Cumb 98 C2
Arlesey C Beds 54 F2
Arleston Telford 61 C6
Arley Ches E 86 F4
Arlingham Glos 36 C4
Arlington Devon 20 E5
Arlington E Sus 18 E2
Arlington Glos 37 D8
Armadale Highld 157 C10
Armadale W Loth 120 C2
Armadale Castle Highld 149 H11
Armathwaite Cumb 108 E5
Arminghall Norf 69 D5
Armitage Staffs 62 C4
Armley W Yorks 95 F5
Armscote Warks 51 E7
Armthorpe S Yorks 89 D7
Arnabost Argyll 146 F5
Arncliffe N Yorks 94 B2
Arncroach Fife 129 D7
Arne Dorset 13 F7
Arnesby Leics 64 E3
Arngask Perth 128 C3
Arnisdale Highld 149 G13
Arnish Highld 149 D10
Arniston Engine Midloth 121 C6
Arnol W Isles 155 C8
Arnold E Yorks 97 E7
Arnold Notts 77 E5
Arnprior Stirling 126 E5
Arnside Cumb 92 B4
Aros Mains Argyll 147 G8
Arowry Wrex 73 F8
Arpafeelie Highld 151 F9
Arrad Foot Cumb 99 F5
Arram E Yorks 97 E6
Arrathorne N Yorks 101 E7
Arreton IoW 15 F6
Arrington Cambs 54 D4
Arrivain Argyll 125 B8
Arrochar Argyll 125 E8
Arrow Warks 51 D5
Arthington W Yorks 95 E5
Arthingworth Northants 64 F4
Arthog Gwyn 58 C3
Arthrath Aberds 153 E9
Arthurstone Perth 134 E2
Artrochie Aberds 153 E10
Arundel W Sus 16 D4
Aryhoulan Highld 130 C4
Asby Cumb 98 B2
Ascog Argyll 145 G10
Ascot Windsor 27 C7
Ascott Warks 51 F8
Ascott-under-Wychwood Oxon 38 C3
Asenby N Yorks 95 B6
Asfordby Leics 64 C4
Asfordby Hill Leics 64 C4
Asgarby Lincs 78 E4
Asgarby Lincs 79 C6
Ash Kent 29 C6
Ash Kent 31 D6
Ash Som 12 B2
Ash Sur 27 D6
Ash Bullayne Devon 10 D2
Ash Green Warks 63 F7
Ash Magna Shrops 74 F2
Ash Mill Devon 10 B2
Ash Priors Som 11 B6
Ash Street Suff 56 E4
Ash Thomas Devon 10 C5
Ash Vale Sur 27 D6
Ashampstead W Berks 26 B3
Ashbocking Suff 57 D5
Ashbourne Derbys 75 E8
Ashbrittle Som 11 B5
Ashburton Devon 7 C5
Ashbury Devon 9 E7
Ashbury Oxon 38 F2
Ashby N Lincs 90 D3
Ashby by Partney Lincs 79 C7
Ashby cum Fenby NE Lincs 91 D6
Ashby de la Launde Lincs 78 D3
Ashby-de-la-Zouch Leics 63 C7
Ashby Folville Leics 64 C4
Ashby Magna Leics 64 E2
Ashby Parva Leics 64 F2
Ashby Puerorum Lincs 79 B6
Ashby St Ledgers Northants 52 C3
Ashby St Mary Norf 69 D6
Ashchurch Glos 50 F4
Ashcombe Devon 7 B7
Ashcott Som 23 F6
Ashdon Essex 55 E6
Ashe Hants 26 E3
Asheldham Essex 43 D5
Ashen Essex 55 E8
Ashendon Bucks 39 C7
Ashfield Carms 33 B7
Ashfield Stirling 127 D6
Ashfield Suff 57 C6
Ashfield Green Suff 57 B6
Ashfold Crossways W Sus 17 B6
Ashford Devon 20 F4
Ashford Hants 14 C2
Ashford Kent 30 E4
Ashford Sur 27 B8
Ashford Bowdler Shrops 49 B7
Ashford Carbonell Shrops 49 B7
Ashford Hill Hants 26 C3
Ashford in the Water Derbys 75 C8
Ashgill S Lanark 119 E7
Ashill Devon 11 C5
Ashill Norf 67 D8
Ashill Som 11 C8
Ashingdon Essex 42 E4
Ashington Northumb 117 F8
Ashington Som 12 B3
Ashington W Sus 16 C5
Ashintully Castle Perth 133 C8
Ashkirk Borders 115 B7
Ashlett Hants 15 D5
Ashleworth Glos 37 B5
Ashley Cambs 55 C7
Ashley Ches E 87 F5
Ashley Devon 9 C8
Ashley Dorset 14 D2
Ashley Glos 37 E6
Ashley Hants 14 E3
Ashley Hants 25 F8
Ashley Northants 64 E4
Ashley Staffs 74 F4
Ashley Green Bucks 40 D2
Ashley Heath Dorset 14 D2
Ashley Heath Staffs 74 F4
Ashmanhaugh Norf 69 B6
Ashmansworth Hants 26 D2
Ashmansworthy Devon 8 C5
Ashmore Dorset 13 C7
Ashorne Warks 51 D8
Ashover Derbys 76 C3
Ashow Warks 51 B8
Ashprington Devon 7 D6
Ashreigney Devon 9 C8
Ashtead Sur 28 D2
Ashton Ches W 74 C2
Ashton Corn 2 D5
Ashton Hants 15 C6
Ashton Hereford 49 C7
Ashton Invclyd 118 B2
Ashton Northants 53 E5
Ashton Northants 65 F7
Ashton Common Wilts 24 D3
Ashton-In-Makerfield Gtr Man 86 E3
Ashton Keynes Wilts 37 E7
Ashton under Hill Worcs 50 F4
Ashton-under-Lyne Gtr Man 87 E7
Ashton upon Mersey Gtr Man 87 E5
Ashurst Hants 14 C4
Ashurst Kent 18 B2
Ashurst W Sus 17 C5
Ashurstwood W Sus 28 F5
Ashwater Devon 9 E5
Ashwell Herts 54 F3
Ashwell Rutland 65 C5
Ashwell Som 11 C8
Ashwellthorpe Norf 68 E4
Ashwick Som 23 E8
Ashwicken Norf 67 C7
Ashybank Borders 115 C8
Askam in Furness Cumb 92 B2
Askern S Yorks 89 C6
Askerswell Dorset 12 E3
Askett Bucks 39 D8
Askham Cumb 99 B7
Askham Notts 77 B7
Askham Bryan York 95 E8
Askham Richard York 95 E8
Asknish Argyll 145 D8
Askrigg N Yorks 100 E4
Askwith N Yorks 94 E4
Aslackby Lincs 78 F3
Aslacton Norf 68 E4
Aslockton Notts 77 F7
Asloun Aberds 140 C4
Aspatria Cumb 107 E8
Aspenden Herts 41 B6
Asperton Lincs 79 F5
Aspley Guise C Beds 53 F7
Aspley Heath C Beds 53 F7
Aspull Gtr Man 86 D4
Asselby E Yorks 89 B8
Asserby Lincs 79 B7
Assington Suff 56 F3
Assynt Ho. Highld 151 E8
Astbury Ches E 74 C5
Astcote Northants 52 D4
Asterley Shrops 60 D3
Asterton Shrops 60 E3
Asthall Oxon 38 C2
Asthall Leigh Oxon 38 C3
Astley Shrops 60 C5
Astley Warks 63 F7
Astley Worcs 50 C2
Astley Abbotts Shrops 61 E7
Astley Bridge Gtr Man 86 C5
Astley Cross Worcs 50 C3
Astley Green Gtr Man 86 E5
Aston Ches E 74 E3
Aston Ches W 74 B2
Aston Derbys 88 F2
Aston Hereford 49 B6
Aston Herts 41 B5
Aston Oxon 38 D3
Aston S Yorks 89 F5
Aston Shrops 60 B5
Aston Staffs 74 E4
Aston Telford 61 D6
Aston W Mid 62 F4
Aston Wokingham 39 F7
Aston Abbotts Bucks 39 B8
Aston Botterell Shrops 61 F6
Aston-By-Stone Staffs 75 F6
Aston Cantlow Warks 51 D6
Aston Clinton Bucks 40 C1
Aston Crews Hereford 36 B3
Aston Cross Glos 50 F4
Aston End Herts 41 B5
Aston Eyre Shrops 61 E6
Aston Fields Worcs 50 C4
Aston Flamville Leics 63 E8
Aston Ingham Hereford 36 B3
Aston juxta Mondrum Ches E 74 D3
Aston le Walls Northants 52 D2
Aston Magna Glos 51 F6
Aston Munslow Shrops 60 F5
Aston on Clun Shrops 60 F3
Aston-on-Trent Derbys 63 B8
Aston Rogers Shrops 60 D3
Aston Rowant Oxon 39 E7
Aston Sandford Bucks 39 D7
Aston Somerville Worcs 50 F5
Aston Subedge Glos 51 E6
Aston Tirrold Oxon 39 F5
Aston Upthorpe Oxon 39 F5
Astrop Northants 52 F3
Astwick C Beds 54 F3
Astwood M Keynes 53 E7
Astwood Worcs 50 D3
Astwood Bank Worcs 50 C5
Aswarby Lincs 78 F3
Aswardby Lincs 79 B6
Atch Lench Worcs 50 D5
Atcham Shrops 60 D5
Athelhampton Dorset 13 E5
Athelington Suff 57 B6
Athelney Som 11 B8
Athelstaneford E Loth 121 B8
Atherington Devon 9 B7
Atherstone Warks 63 E7
Atherstone on Stour Warks 51 D7
Atherton Gtr Man 86 D4
Atley Hill N Yorks 101 D7
Atlow Derbys 76 E2
Attadale Highld 150 H2
Attadale Ho. Highld 150 H2
Attenborough Notts 76 F5
Atterby Lincs 90 E3
Attercliffe S Yorks 88 F4
Attleborough Norf 68 E3
Attleborough Warks 63 E7
Attlebridge Norf 68 C4
Atwick E Yorks 97 D7
Atworth Wilts 24 C3
Aubourn Lincs 78 C2
Auchagallon N Ayrs 143 E9
Auchallater Aberds 139 F7
Aucharnie Aberds 153 D6
Auchattie Aberds 141 E5
Auchavan Angus 134 C1
Auchbreck Moray 139 B8
Auchenback E Renf 118 D5
Auchenbainzie Dumfries 113 E8
Auchenblae Aberds 135 B7
Auchenbrack Dumfries 113 E7
Auchenbreck Argyll 145 E9
Auchencairn Dumfries 106 D4
Auchencairn Dumfries 114 F2
Auchencairn N Ayrs 143 F11
Auchencrosh S Ayrs 105 B5
Auchencrow Borders 122 C4
Auchendinny Midloth 121 C5
Auchengray S Lanark 120 D2
Auchenhalrig Moray 152 B3
Auchenheath S Lanark 119 E8
Auchenlochan Argyll 145 F8
Auchenmalg Dumfries 105 D6
Auchensoul S Ayrs 112 E2
Auchentiber N Ayrs 118 E3
Auchertyre Highld 149 F13
Auchgourish Highld 138 C5
Auchincarroch W Dunb 126 F3
Auchindrain Argyll 125 E6
Auchindrean Highld 150 C4
Auchininna Aberds 153 D6
Auchinleck E Ayrs 113 B5
Auchinloch N Lanark 119 B6
Auchinroath Moray 152 C2
Auchintoul Aberds 140 C4
Auchiries Aberds 153 E10
Auchlee Aberds 141 E7
Auchleven Aberds 140 B5
Auchlochan S Lanark 119 F8
Auchlossan Aberds 140 D4
Auchlunies Aberds 141 E7
Auchlyne Stirling 126 B4
Auchmacoy Aberds 153 E9
Auchmair Moray 140 B2
Auchmantle Dumfries 105 C5
Auchmillan E Ayrs 112 B5
Auchmithie Angus 135 E6
Auchmuirbridge Fife 128 D4
Auchmull Angus 135 B5
Auchnacree Angus 134 C4
Auchnagallin Highld 151 H13
Auchnagatt Aberds 153 D9
Auchnaha Argyll 145 E8
Auchnashelloch Perth 127 C6
Aucholzie Aberds 140 E2
Auchrannie Angus 134 D2
Auchroisk Highld 139 B6
Auchronie Angus 140 F3
Auchterarder Perth 127 C8
Auchteraw Highld 137 D6
Auchterderran Fife 128 E4
Auchterhouse Angus 134 F3
Auchtermuchty Fife 128 C4
Auchterneed Highld 150 F7
Auchtertool Fife 128 E4
Auchtertyre Moray 152 C1
Auchtubh Stirling 126 B4
Auckengill Highld 158 D5
Auckley S Yorks 89 D7
Audenshaw Gtr Man 87 E7
Audlem Ches E 74 E3
Audley Staffs 74 D4
Audley End Essex 56 F2
Auds Aberds 153 B6
Aughton E Yorks 96 F3
Aughton Lancs 85 D4
Aughton Lancs 93 C5
Aughton S Yorks 89 F5
Aughton Wilts 25 D7
Aughton Park Lancs 86 D2
Auldearn Highld 151 F12
Aulden Hereford 49 D6
Auldgirth Dumfries 114 F2
Auldhame E Loth 129 F7
Auldhouse S Lanark 119 D6
Ault a'chruinn Highld 136 B2
Aultanrynie Highld 156 F6
Aultbea Highld 155 J13
Aultdearg Highld 150 E5
Aultgrishan Highld 155 J12
Aultguish Inn Highld 150 D6
Aultibea Highld 157 G13
Aultiphurst Highld 157 C11
Aultmore Moray 152 C4
Aultnagoire Highld 137 B8
Aultnamain Inn Highld 151 C9
Aultnaslat Highld 136 D4
Aulton Aberds 140 B5
Aundorach Highld 139 C5
Aunsby Lincs 78 F3
Auquhorthies Aberds 141 B7
Aust S Glos 36 F2
Austendike Lincs 66 B2
Austerfield S Yorks 89 E7
Austrey Warks 63 D6
Austwick N Yorks 93 C7
Authorpe Lincs 91 F8
Authorpe Row Lincs 79 B8
Avebury Wilts 25 C6
Aveley Thurrock 42 F1
Avening Glos 37 E5
Averham Notts 77 D7
Aveton Gifford Devon 6 E4
Avielochan Highld 138 C5
Aviemore Highld 138 C4
Avington Hants 26 F3
Avington W Berks 25 C8
Avoch Highld 151 F10
Avon Hants 14 E2
Avon Dassett Warks 52 E2
Avonbridge Falk 120 B2
Avonmouth Bristol 23 B7
Avonwick Devon 6 D5
Awbridge Hants 14 B4
Awhirk Dumfries 104 D4
Awkley S Glos 36 F2
Awliscombe Devon 11 D6
Awre Glos 36 D4
Awsworth Notts 76 E4
Axbridge Som 23 D6
Axford Hants 26 E4
Axford Wilts 25 B7
Axminster Devon 11 E7
Axmouth Devon 11 E7
Axton Flint 85 F2
Aycliff Kent 31 E7
Aycliffe Durham 101 B7
Aydon Northumb 110 C3
Aylburton Glos 36 D3
Ayle Northumb 109 E7
Aylesbeare Devon 10 E5
Aylesbury Bucks 39 C8
Aylesby NE Lincs 91 D6
Aylesford Kent 29 D8
Aylesham Kent 31 D6
Aylestone Leicester 64 D2
Aylmerton Norf 81 D7
Aylsham Norf 81 E7
Aylton Hereford 49 F8
Aymestrey Hereford 49 C6
Aynho Northants 52 F3
Ayot St Lawrence Herts 40 C4
Ayot St Peter Herts 41 C5
Ayr S Ayrs 112 B3
Aysgarth N Yorks 101 F5
Ayside Cumb 99 F5
Ayston Rutland 65 D5
Aythorpe Roding Essex 42 C1
Ayton Borders 122 C5
Aywick Shetland 160 E7
Azerley N Yorks 95 B5

B

Babbacombe Torbay 7 C7
Babbinswood Shrops 73 F7
Babcary Som 12 B3
Babel Carms 47 F7
Babell Flint 73 B5
Babraham Cambs 55 D6
Babworth Notts 89 F7
Bac W Isles 155 C9
Bachau Anglesey 82 C4
Back of Keppoch Highld 147 C9
Back Rogerton E Ayrs 113 B5
Backaland Orkney 159 E6
Backaskaill Orkney 159 C5
Backbarrow Cumb 99 F5
Backe Carms 32 C3
Backfolds Aberds 153 C10
Backford Ches W 73 B8
Backford Cross Ches W 73 B7
Backhill Aberds 153 E7
Backhill Aberds 153 E10
Backhill of Clackriach Aberds 153 D9
Backhill of Fortree Aberds 153 D9
Backhill of Trustach Aberds 140 E5
Backies Highld 157 J11
Backlass Highld 158 E4
Backwell N Som 23 C6
Backworth T&W 111 B6
Bacon End Essex 42 C2
Baconsthorpe Norf 81 D7
Bacton Hereford 49 F5
Bacton Norf 81 D9
Bacton Suff 56 C4
Bacton Green Suff 56 C4
Bacup Lancs 87 B6
Badachro Highld 149 A12
Badanloch Lodge Highld 157 F10
Badavanich Highld 150 F4
Badbury Swindon 38 F1
Badby Northants 52 D3
Badcall Highld 156 D5
Badcaul Highld 150 B3
Baddeley Green Stoke 75 D6
Baddesley Clinton Warks 51 B7
Baddesley Ensor Warks 63 E6
Baddidarach Highld 156 G3
Baddoch Aberds 139 F7
Baddock Highld 151 F10
Badenscoth Aberds 153 E7
Badenyon Aberds 140 C2
Badger Shrops 61 E7
Badger's Mount Kent 29 C5
Badgeworth Glos 37 C6
Badgworth Som 23 D5
Badicaul Highld 149 F12
Badingham Suff 57 C7
Badlesmere Kent 30 D4
Badlipster Highld 158 F4
Badluarach Highld 150 B2
Badminton S Glos 37 F5
Badnaban Highld 156 G3
Badninish Highld 151 B10
Badrallach Highld 150 B3
Badsey Worcs 51 E5
Badshot Lea Sur 27 E6
Badsworth W Yorks 89 C5
Badwell Ash Suff 56 C3
Bae Colwyn = Colwyn Bay Conwy 83 D8
Bag Enderby Lincs 79 B6
Bagby N Yorks 102 F2
Bagendon Glos 37 D7
Bagh a Chaisteil = Castlebay W Isles 148 J1
Bagh Mor W Isles 148 C3
Bagh Shiarabhagh W Isles 148 H2
Baghasdal W Isles 148 G2
Bagillt Flint 73 B6
Baginton Warks 51 B8
Baglan Neath 33 E8
Bagley Shrops 60 B4
Bagnall Staffs 75 D6
Bagnor W Berks 26 C2
Bagshot Sur 27 C7
Bagshot Wilts 25 C8
Bagthorpe Norf 80 D3
Bagthorpe Notts 76 D4
Bagworth Leics 63 D8
Bagwy Llydiart Hereford 35 B8
Bail Àrd Bhuirgh W Isles 155 B9
Bail Uachdraich W Isles 148 B3
Baildon W Yorks 94 F4
Baile W Isles 154 J4
Baile a Mhanaich W Isles 148 C2
Baile Ailein W Isles 155 E7
Baile an Truiseil W Isles 155 B8
Baile Boidheach Argyll 144 F6
Baile Glas W Isles 148 C3
Baile Mhartainn W Isles 148 A2
Baile Mhic Phail W Isles 148 A3
Baile Mor Argyll 146 J5
Baile Mor W Isles 148 B2
Baile na Creige W Isles 148 H1
Baile nan Cailleach W Isles 148 C2
Baile Raghaill W Isles 148 A2
Bailebeag Highld 137 C8
Baileyhead Cumb 108 B5
Bailiesward Aberds 152 E4
Baillieston Glasgow 119 C6
Bail'lochdrach W Isles 148 C3
Bail'Ur Tholastaidh W Isles 155 C10
Bainbridge N Yorks 100 E4
Bainsford Falk 127 F7
Bainshole Aberds 152 E6
Bainton E Yorks 97 D5
Bainton Pboro 65 D7
Bairnkine Borders 116 C2
Baker Street Thurrock 42 F2
Baker's End Herts 41 C6
Bakewell Derbys 76 C2
Bala = Y Bala Gwyn 72 F3
Balachuirn Highld 149 D10
Balavil Highld 138 D3
Balbeg Highld 137 B7
Balbeg Highld 150 H7
Balbeggie Perth 128 B3
Balbithan Aberds 141 C6
Balbithan Ho. Aberds 141 C7
Balblair Highld 151 B8
Balblair Highld 151 E10
Balby S Yorks 89 D6
Balchladich Highld 156 F3
Balchraggan Highld 151 G8
Balchraggan Highld 151 H8
Balchrick Highld 156 D4
Balchrystie Fife 129 D6
Balcladaich Highld 137 B5
Balcombe W Sus 28 F4
Balcombe Lane W Sus 28 F4
Balcomie Fife 129 C8
Balcurvie Fife 128 D5
Baldersby N Yorks 95 B6
Baldersby St James N Yorks 95 B6
Balderstone Lancs 93 F6
Balderton Ches W 73 C7
Balderton Notts 77 D8
Baldhu Corn 3 B6
Baldinnie Fife 129 C6
Baldock Herts 54 F3
Baldovie Dundee 134 F4
Baldrine IoM 84 D4
Baldslow E Sus 18 D4
Baldwin IoM 84 D3
Baldwinholme Cumb 108 D3
Baldwin's Gate Staffs 74 E4
Bale Norf 81 D6
Balearn Aberds 153 C10
Balemartine Argyll 146 G2
Balephuil Argyll 146 G2
Balerno Edin 120 C4
Balevullin Argyll 146 G2
Balfield Angus 135 C5
Balfour Orkney 159 G5
Balfron Stirling 126 F4
Balfron Station Stirling 126 F4
Balgaveny Aberds 153 D6
Balgavies Angus 135 D5
Balgonar Fife 128 E2
Balgove Aberds 153 E8
Balgowan Highld 138 E2
Balgown Highld 149 B8
Balgrochan E Dunb 119 B6
Balgy Highld 149 C13
Balhaldie Stirling 127 D7
Balhalgardy Aberds 141 B6
Balham London 28 B3
Balhary Perth 134 E2
Baliasta Shetland 160 C8
Baligill Highld 157 C11
Balintore Angus 134 D2
Balintore Highld 151 D11
Balintraid Highld 151 D10
Balk N Yorks 102 F2
Balkeerie Angus 134 E3
Balkemback Angus 134 F3
Balkholme E Yorks 89 B8
Balkissock S Ayrs 104 A5
Ball Shrops 60 B3
Ball Haye Green Staffs 75 D6
Ball Hill Hants 26 C2
Ballabeg IoM 84 E2
Ballacannel IoM 84 D4
Ballachulish Highld 130 D4
Ballajora IoM 84 C4
Ballaleigh IoM 84 D3
Ballamodha IoM 84 E2
Ballantrae S Ayrs 104 A4
Ballaquine IoM 84 D4
Ballards Gore Essex 43 E5
Ballasalla IoM 84 C3
Ballasalla IoM 84 E2
Ballater Aberds 140 E2
Ballaugh IoM 84 C3
Ballaveare IoM 84 E3
Ballcorach Moray 139 B7
Ballechin Perth 133 D6
Balleigh Highld 151 C10
Ballencrieff E Loth 121 B7
Ballentoul Perth 133 C5
Ballidon Derbys 76 D2
Balliemore Argyll 124 C4
Balliemore Argyll 145 E9
Ballikinrain Stirling 126 F4
Ballimeanoch Argyll 125 D6
Ballimore Argyll 145 E8
Ballimore Stirling 126 C4
Ballinaby Argyll 142 B3
Ballindean Perth 128 B4
Ballingdon Suff 56 E2
Ballinger Common Bucks 40 D2
Ballingham Hereford 49 F7
Ballingry Fife 128 E3
Ballinlick Perth 133 E6
Ballinluig Perth 133 D6
Ballintuim Perth 133 D8
Balloch Angus 134 D3
Balloch Highld 151 G10
Balloch N Lanark 119 B7
Balloch W Dunb 126 F2
Ballochan Aberds 140 E4
Ballochford Moray 152 E3
Ballochmorrie S Ayrs 112 F2
Balls Cross W Sus 16 B3
Balls Green Essex 43 B6
Ballygown Argyll 146 G7
Ballygrant Argyll 142 B4
Ballyhaugh Argyll 146 F4
Balmacara Highld 149 F13
Balmacara Square Highld 149 F13
Balmaclellan Dumfries 106 B3
Balmacneil Perth 133 D6
Balmacqueen Highld 149 A9
Balmae Dumfries 106 E3
Balmaha Stirling 126 E3
Balmalcolm Fife 128 D5
Balmeanach Highld 149 D10
Balmedie Aberds 141 C8
Balmer Heath Shrops 73 F8
Balmerino Fife 129 B5
Balmerlawn Hants 14 D4
Balmichael N Ayrs 143 E10
Balmirmer Angus 135 F5
Balmore Highld 149 D7
Balmore Highld 150 H6
Balmore Highld 151 G11
Balmore Perth 133 D6
Balmule Fife 128 F4
Balmullo Fife 129 B6
Balmungie Highld 151 F10
Balnaboth Angus 134 C3
Balnabruaich Highld 151 E10
Balnabruich Highld 158 H3
Balnacoil Highld 157 H11
Balnacra Highld 150 G2
Balnafoich Highld 151 H9
Balnagall Highld 151 C11
Balnaguard Perth 133 D6
Balnahard Argyll 144 D3
Balnahard Argyll 146 H7
Balnain Highld 150 H7
Balnakeil Highld 156 C6
Balnaknock Highld 149 B9
Balnapaling Highld 151 E10
Balne N Yorks 89 C6
Balochroy Argyll 143 C8
Balone Fife 129 C6
Balornock Glasgow 119 C6
Balquharn Perth 133 F7
Balquhidder Stirling 126 B4
Balsall W Mid 51 B7
Balsall Common W Mid 51 B7
Balsall Heath W Mid 62 F4
Balscott Oxon 51 E8
Balsham Cambs 55 D6
Baltasound Shetland 160 C8
Balterley Staffs 74 D4
Baltersan Dumfries 105 C8
Balthangie Aberds 153 C8
Baltonsborough Som 23 F7
Balvaird Highld 151 F8
Balvicar Argyll 124 D3
Balvraid Highld 149 G13
Balvraid Highld 151 H11
Bamber Bridge Lancs 86 B3
Bambers Green Essex 42 B1
Bamburgh Northumb 123 F7
Bamff Perth 134 D2
Bamford Derbys 88 F3
Bamford Gtr Man 87 C6
Bampton Cumb 99 C7
Bampton Devon 10 B4
Bampton Oxon 38 D3
Bampton Grange Cumb 99 C7
Banavie Highld 131 B5
Banbury Oxon 52 E2
Bancffosfelen Carms 33 C5
Banchory Aberds 141 E5
Banchory-Devenick Aberds 141 D8
Bancycapel Carms 33 C5
Bancyfelin Carms 32 C4
Bancyffordd Carms 46 F3
Bandirran Perth 134 F2
Banff Aberds 153 B6
Bangor Gwyn 83 D5
Bangor-is-y-coed Wrex 73 E7
Banham Norf 68 F3
Bank Hants 14 D3
Bank Newton N Yorks 94 D2
Bank Street Worcs 49 C8
Bankend Dumfries 107 C7
Bankfoot Perth 133 F7
Bankglen E Ayrs 113 C6
Bankhead Aberdeen 141 C7
Bankhead Aberds 141 D5
Banknock Falk 119 B7
Banks Cumb 109 C5
Banks Lancs 85 B4
Bankshill Dumfries 114 F4
Banningham Norf 81 E8
Banniskirk Ho. Highld 158 E3
Bannister Green Essex 42 B2
Bannockburn Stirling 127 E7
Banstead Sur 28 D3
Bantham Devon 6 E4
Banton N Lanark 119 B7
Banwell N Som 23 D5
Banyard's Green Suff 57 B6
Bapchild Kent 30 C3
Bar Hill Cambs 54 C4
Barabhas W Isles 155 C8
Barabhas Iarach W Isles 155 C8
Barabhas Uarach W Isles 155 B8
Barachandroman Argyll 124 C2
Barassie S Ayrs 118 F3
Baravullin Argyll 124 E4
Barbaraville Highld 151 D10
Barber Booth Derbys 88 F2
Barbieston S Ayrs 112 C4
Barbon Cumb 99 F8
Barbridge Ches E 74 D3
Barbrook Devon 21 E6
Barby Northants 52 B3
Barcaldine Argyll 130 E3
Barcheston Warks 51 F7
Barcombe E Sus 17 C8
Barcombe Cross E Sus 17 C8
Barden N Yorks 101 E6
Barden Scale N Yorks 94 D3
Bardennoch Dumfries 113 E5
Bardfield Saling Essex 42 B2
Bardister Shetland 160 F5
Bardney Lincs 78 C4
Bardon Leics 63 C8
Bardon Mill Northumb 109 C7
Bardowie E Dunb 119 B5
Bardrainney Invclyd 118 B3
Bardsea Cumb 92 B3
Bardsey W Yorks 95 E6
Bardwell Suff 56 B3
Bare Lancs 92 C4
Barfad Argyll 145 G7
Barford Norf 68 D4
Barford Warks 51 C7
Barford St John Oxon 52 F2
Barford St Martin Wilts 25 F5
Barford St Michael Oxon 52 F2
Barfrestone Kent 31 D6
Bargod = Bargoed Caerph 35 E5
Bargoed = Bargod Caerph 35 E5
Bargrennan Dumfries 105 B7
Barham Cambs 54 B2
Barham Kent 31 D6
Barham Suff 56 D5
Barharrow Dumfries 106 D3
Barhill Dumfries 106 C5
Barholm Lincs 65 C7
Barkby Leics 64 D3
Barkestone-le-Vale Leics 77 F7
Barkham Wokingham 27 C5
Barking London 41 F7
Barking Suff 56 D4
Barking Tye Suff 56 D4
Barkingside London 41 F7
Barkisland W Yorks 87 C8
Barkston Lincs 78 E2
Barkston N Yorks 95 F7
Barkway Herts 54 F4
Barlaston Staffs 75 F5
Barlavington W Sus 16 C3
Barlborough Derbys 76 B4
Barlby N Yorks 96 F2
Barlestone Leics 63 D8
Barley Herts 54 F4
Barley Lancs 93 E8
Barley Mow T&W 111 D5
Barleythorpe Rutland 64 D5
Barling Essex 43 F5
Barlow Derbys 76 B3
Barlow N Yorks 89 B7
Barlow T&W 110 C4
Barmby Moor E Yorks 96 E3
Barmby on the Marsh E Yorks 89 B7
Barmer Norf 80 D4
Barmoor Castle Northumb 123 F5
Barmoor Lane End Northumb 123 F6
Barmouth = Abermaw Gwyn 58 C3
Barmpton Darl 101 C8
Barmston E Yorks 97 D7
Barnack Pboro 65 D7
Barnacle Warks 63 F7
Barnard Castle Durham 101 C5
Barnard Gate Oxon 38 C4
Barnardiston Suff 55 E8
Barnbarroch Dumfries 106 D5
Barnburgh S Yorks 89 D5
Barnby Suff 69 F7
Barnby Dun S Yorks 89 D7
Barnby in the Willows Notts 77 D8
Barnby Moor Notts 89 F7
Barnes Street Kent 29 E7
Barnet London 41 E5
Barnetby le Wold N Lincs 90 D4
Barney Norf 81 D5
Barnham Suff 56 B2
Barnham W Sus 16 D3
Barnham Broom Norf 68 D3
Barnhead Angus 135 D6
Barnhill Ches W 73 D8
Barnhill Dundee 134 F4
Barnhill Moray 152 C1
Barnhills Dumfries 104 B3
Barningham Durham 101 C5
Barningham Suff 56 B3
Barnoldby le Beck NE Lincs 91 D6
Barnoldswick Lancs 93 E8
Barns Green W Sus 16 B5
Barnsley Glos 37 D7
Barnsley S Yorks 88 D4
Barnstaple Devon 20 F4
Barnston Essex 42 C2
Barnston Mers 85 F3
Barnstone Notts 77 F7
Barnt Green Worcs 50 B5
Barnton Ches W 74 B3
Barnton Edin 120 B4
Barnwell All Saints Northants 65 F7
Barnwell St Andrew Northants 65 F7
Barnwood Glos 37 C5
Barochreal Argyll 124 C4
Barons Cross Hereford 49 D6
Barr S Ayrs 112 E2
Barra Castle Aberds 141 B6
Barrachan Dumfries 105 E7
Barrack Aberds 153 D8
Barraglom W Isles 154 D6
Barrahormid Argyll 144 E6
Barran Argyll 124 C4
Barrapol Argyll 146 G2
Barras Aberds 141 F7
Barras Cumb 100 C3
Barrasford Northumb 110 B2
Barravullin Argyll 124 E4
Barregarrow IoM 84 D3
Barrhead E Renf 118 D4
Barrhill S Ayrs 112 F2
Barrington Cambs 54 E4
Barrington Som 11 C8
Barripper Corn 2 C5
Barrmill N Ayrs 118 D3
Barrock Highld 158 C4
Barrock Ho. Highld 158 D4
Barrow Lancs 93 F7
Barrow Rutland 65 C5
Barrow Suff 55 C8
Barrow Green Kent 30 C3
Barrow Gurney N Som 23 C7
Barrow Haven N Lincs 90 B4
Barrow-in-Furness Cumb 92 C2
Barrow Island Cumb 92 C1
Barrow Nook Lancs 86 D2
Barrow Street Wilts 24 F3
Barrow upon Humber N Lincs 90 B4
Barrow upon Soar Leics 64 C2
Barrow upon Trent Derbys 63 B7
Barroway Drove Norf 67 D5
Barrowburn Northumb 116 C4
Barrowby Lincs 77 F8
Barrowcliff N Yorks 103 F8
Barrowden Rutland 65 D6
Barrowford Lancs 93 F8
Barrows Green Ches E 74 D3
Barrows Green Cumb 99 F7
Barrow's Green Mers 86 F3
Barry Angus 135 F5
Barry = Y Barri V Glam 22 C3
Barry Island V Glam 22 C3
Barsby Leics 64 C3
Barsham Suff 69 F6
Barston W Mid 51 B7
Bartestree Hereford 49 E7
Barthol Chapel Aberds 153 E8
Barthomley Ches E 74 D4
Bartley Hants 14 C4
Bartley Green W Mid 62 F4
Bartlow Cambs 55 E6
Barton Cambs 54 D5
Barton Ches W 73 D8
Barton Glos 37 B8
Barton Lancs 85 D4
Barton Lancs 92 F5
Barton N Yorks 101 D7
Barton Oxon 39 D5
Barton Torbay 7 C7
Barton Warks 51 D6
Barton Bendish Norf 67 D7
Barton Hartshorn Bucks 52 F4
Barton in Fabis Notts 76 F5
Barton in the Beans Leics 63 D7
Barton-le-Clay C Beds 53 F8
Barton-le-Street N Yorks 96 B3
Barton-le-Willows N Yorks 96 C3
Barton Mills Suff 55 B8
Barton on Sea Hants 14 E3
Barton on the Heath Warks 51 F7
Barton St David Som 23 F7
Barton Seagrave Northants 53 B6
Barton Stacey Hants 26 E2
Barton Turf Norf 69 B6
Barton-under-Needwood Staffs 63 C5
Barton-upon-Humber N Lincs 90 B4
Barton Waterside N Lincs 90 B4
Barugh S Yorks 88 D4
Barway Cambs 55 B6
Barwell Leics 63 E8
Barwick Herts 41 C6
Barwick Som 12 C3
Barwick in Elmet W Yorks 95 F6
Baschurch Shrops 60 B4
Bascote Warks 52 C2
Basford Green Staffs 75 D6
Bashall Eaves Lancs 93 E6
Bashley Hants 14 E3
Basildon Essex 42 F3
Basingstoke Hants 26 D4
Baslow Derbys 76 B2
Bason Bridge Som 22 E5
Bassaleg Newport 35 F6
Bassenthwaite Cumb 108 F2
Bassett Soton 14 C5
Bassingbourn Cambs 54 E4
Bassingfield Notts 77 F6
Bassingham Lincs 78 C2
Bassingthorpe Lincs 65 B6
Basta Shetland 160 D7
Baston Lincs 65 C8
Bastwick Norf 69 C7
Baswick Steer E Yorks 97 E6
Batchworth Heath Herts 40 E3
Batcombe Dorset 12 D4
Batcombe Som 23 F8
Bate Heath Ches E 74 B3
Batford Herts 40 C4
Bath Bath 24 C2
Bathampton Bath 24 C2
Bathealton Som 11 B5
Batheaston Bath 24 C2
Bathford Bath 24 C2
Bathgate W Loth 120 C2
Bathley Notts 77 D7
Bathpool Corn 5 B7
Bathpool Som 11 B7
Bathville W Loth 120 C2
Batley W Yorks 88 B3
Batsford Glos 51 F6
Battersby N Yorks 102 D3
Battersea London 28 B3
Battisborough Cross Devon 6 E3
Battisford Suff 56 D4
Battisford Tye Suff 56 D4
Battle E Sus 18 D4
Battle Powys 48 F2
Battledown Glos 37 B6
Battlefield Shrops 60 C5
Battlesbridge Essex 42 E3
Battlesden C Beds 40 B2
Battlesea Green Suff 57 B6
Battleton Som 10 B4
Battram Leics 63 D8
Battramsley Hants 14 E4
Baughton Worcs 50 E3
Baughurst Hants 26 D3

184 Bra–Bux

Braaid IoM 84 E3
Braal Castle Highld 158 D3
Brabling Green Suff 57 C6
Brabourne Kent 30 E4
Brabourne Lees Kent 30 E4
Brabster Highld 158 D5
Bracadale Highld 149 E8
Bracara Highld 147 B10
Braceborough Lincs 65 C7
Bracebridge Lincs 78 C2
Bracebridge Heath Lincs 78 C2
Bracebridge Low Fields Lincs 78 C2
Braceby Lincs 78 F3
Bracewell Lancs 93 E8
Brackenfield Derbys 76 D3
Brackenthwaite Cumb 108 E2
Brackenthwaite N Yorks 95 D5
Bracklesham W Sus 16 E2
Brackletter Highld 136 F4
Brackley Argyll 143 D8
Brackley Northants 52 F3
Brackloch Highld 156 G4
Bracknell Brack 27 C6
Braco Perth 127 D7
Bracobrae Moray 152 C5
Bracon Ash Norf 68 E4
Bracorina Highld 147 B10
Bradbourne Derbys 76 D2
Bradbury Durham 101 B8
Bradda IoM 84 F1
Bradden Northants 52 E4
Braddock Corn 5 C6
Bradeley Stoke 75 D5
Bradenham Bucks 39 E8
Bradenham Norf 68 D2
Bradenstoke Wilts 24 B5
Bradfield Essex 56 F5
Bradfield Norf 81 D8
Bradfield W Berks 26 B4
Bradfield Combust Suff 56 D2
Bradfield Green Ches E 74 D3
Bradfield Heath Essex 43 B7
Bradfield St Clare Suff 56 D3
Bradfield St George Suff 56 C3
Bradford Corn 5 B6
Bradford Derbys 76 C2
Bradford Devon 9 D6
Bradford Northumb 123 F7
Bradford W Yorks 94 F4
Bradford Abbas Dorset 12 C3
Bradford Leigh Wilts 24 C3
Bradford-on-Avon Wilts 24 C3
Bradford-on-Tone Som 11 B6
Bradford Peverell Dorset 12 E4
Brading IoW 15 F7
Bradley Derbys 76 E2
Bradley Hants 26 E4
Bradley NE Lincs 91 D6
Bradley Staffs 62 C2
Bradley W Mid 62 E3
Bradley W Yorks 88 B2
Bradley Green Worcs 50 C4
Bradley in the Moors Staffs 75 E7
Bradley Stoke S Glos 36 F3
Bradlow Hereford 50 F2
Bradmore Notts 77 F5
Bradmore W Mid 62 E2
Bradninch Devon 10 D5
Bradnop Staffs 75 D7
Bradpole Dorset 12 E2
Bradshaw Gtr Man 86 C5
Bradshaw W Yorks 87 C8
Bradstone Devon 9 F5
Bradwall Green Ches E 74 C4
Bradway S Yorks 88 F4
Bradwell Derbys 88 F2
Bradwell Essex 42 B4
Bradwell M Keynes 53 F6
Bradwell Norf 69 D8
Bradwell Staffs 74 E5
Bradwell Grove Oxon 38 D2
Bradwell on Sea Essex 43 D6
Bradwell Waterside Essex 43 D5
Bradworthy Devon 8 C5
Bradworthy Cross Devon 8 C5
Brae Dumfries 107 B5
Brae Highld 155 J13
Brae Highld 156 J7
Brae Shetland 160 G5
Brae of Achnahaird Highld 156 H3
Brae Roy Lodge Highld 137 E6
Braeantra Highld 151 D8
Braedownie Angus 134 B2
Braefield Highld 150 H7
Braegrum Perth 128 B2
Braehead Dumfries 105 D8
Braehead Orkney 159 D5
Braehead Orkney 159 H6
Braehead S Lanark 119 F8
Braehead S Lanark 120 D2
Braehead of Lunan Angus 135 D6
Braehoulland Shetland 160 F4
Braehungie Highld 158 G3
Braelangwell Lodge Highld 151 B8
Braemar Aberds 139 E7
Braemore Highld 150 D4
Braemore Highld 158 G2
Braes of Enzie Moray 152 C3
Braeside Involyd 118 B2
Braeswick Orkney 159 E7
Braewick Shetland 160 H5
Brafferton Darl 101 B7
Brafferton N Yorks 95 B7
Brafield-on-the-Green Northants 53 D6
Bragar W Isles 155 C7
Bragbury End Herts 41 B5
Bragleenmore Argyll 124 C5
Braichmelyn Gwyn 83 E6
Braid Edin 120 C5
Braides Lancs 92 D4
Braidley N Yorks 101 F5
Braidwood S Lanark 119 E8
Braigo Argyll 142 B3
Brailsford Derbys 76 E2
Brainshaugh Northumb 117 D8
Braintree Essex 42 B3
Braiseworth Suff 56 B5
Braishfield Hants 14 B4
Braithwaite Cumb 98 B4
Braithwaite S Yorks 89 C7
Braithwaite W Yorks 94 E3
Braithwell S Yorks 89 E6
Bramber W Sus 17 C5
Bramcote Notts 76 F5
Bramcote Warks 63 F8
Bramdean Hants 15 B7
Bramerton Norf 69 D5
Bramfield Herts 41 C5
Bramfield Suff 57 B7
Bramford Suff 56 E5
Bramhall Gtr Man 87 F6
Bramham W Yorks 95 E7
Bramhope W Yorks 95 E5
Bramley Hants 26 D4
Bramley S Yorks 89 E5
Bramley Sur 27 E8
Bramley W Yorks 94 F5
Bramling Kent 31 D6
Brampford Speke Devon 10 E4
Brampton Cambs 54 B3
Brampton Cumb 100 B1
Brampton Cumb 108 C5
Brampton Derbys 76 B3
Brampton Hereford 49 F6
Brampton Lincs 77 B8
Brampton Norf 81 E8
Brampton S Yorks 88 D5
Brampton Suff 69 F7
Brampton Abbotts Hereford 36 B3
Brampton Ash Northants 64 F4
Brampton Bryan Hereford 49 B5
Brampton en le Morthen S Yorks 89 F5
Bramshall Staffs 75 F7
Bramshaw Hants 14 C3
Bramshill Hants 26 C5
Bramshott Hants 27 F6
Bran End Essex 42 B2
Branault Highld 147 E8
Brancaster Norf 80 C3
Brancaster Staithe Norf 80 C3
Brancepeth Durham 110 F5
Branch End Northumb 110 C3
Branchill Moray 151 F13
Brand Green Glos 36 B4
Branderburgh Moray 152 A2
Brandesburton E Yorks 97 E7
Brandeston Suff 57 C6
Brandhill Shrops 49 B6
Brandis Corner Devon 9 D6
Brandiston Norf 81 E7
Brandon Durham 110 F5
Brandon Lincs 78 E2
Brandon Northumb 117 C6
Brandon Suff 67 F7
Brandon Warks 52 B2
Brandon Bank Cambs 67 F6
Brandon Creek Norf 67 E6
Brandon Parva Norf 68 D3
Brandsby N Yorks 95 B8
Brandy Wharf Lincs 90 E4
Brane Corn 2 D3
Branksome Poole 13 E8
Branksome Park Poole 13 E8
Bransby Lincs 77 B8
Branscombe Devon 11 F6
Bransford Worcs 50 D2
Bransgore Hants 14 E2
Branshill Clack 127 E7
Bransholme Hull 97 F7
Branson's Cross Worcs 51 B5
Branston Leics 64 B5
Branston Lincs 78 C3
Branston Staffs 63 B6
Branston Booths Lincs 78 C3
Branstone IoW 15 F6
Bransty Cumb 98 C1
Brant Broughton Lincs 78 D2
Brantham Suff 56 F5
Branthwaite Cumb 98 B2
Branthwaite Cumb 108 F2
Brantingham E Yorks 90 B3
Branton Northumb 117 C6
Branton S Yorks 89 D7
Branxholm Park Borders 115 C7
Branxholme Borders 115 C7
Branxton Northumb 122 F4
Brassey Green Ches W 74 C2
Brassington Derbys 76 D2
Brasted Kent 29 D5
Brasted Chart Kent 29 D5
Brathens Aberds 141 E5
Bratoft Lincs 79 C7
Brattleby Lincs 90 F3
Bratton Telford 61 C6
Bratton Wilts 24 D4
Bratton Clovelly Devon 9 E6
Bratton Fleming Devon 20 F5
Bratton Seymour Som 12 B4
Braughing Herts 41 B6
Braunston Northants 52 C3
Braunston-in-Rutland Rutland 64 D5
Braunstone Town Leicester 64 D2
Braunton Devon 20 F3
Brawby N Yorks 96 B3
Brawl Highld 157 C11
Brawlbin Highld 158 E2
Bray Windsor 27 B7
Bray Shop Corn 5 B8
Bray Wick Windsor 27 B6
Braybrooke Northants 64 F4
Braye Ald 16
Brayford Devon 21 F5
Braystones Cumb 98 D2
Braythorn N Yorks 94 E5
Brayton N Yorks 95 F9
Brazacott Corn 8 E4
Breach Kent 30 C2
Breachacha Castle Argyll 146 F4
Breachwood Green Herts 40 B4
Breacleit W Isles 154 D6
Breaden Heath Shrops 73 F8
Breadsall Derbys 76 F3
Breadstone Glos 36 D4
Breage Corn 2 D5
Breakachy Highld 150 G7
Bream Glos 36 D3
Breamore Hants 14 C2
Brean Som 22 D4
Breanais W Isles 154 E4
Brearton N Yorks 95 C6
Breascleit W Isles 154 D7
Breaston Derbys 76 F4
Brechfa Carms 46 F4
Brechin Angus 135 C5
Breck of Cruan Orkney 159 G4
Breckan Orkney 159 H3
Breckrey Highld 149 B10
Brecon = Aberhonddu Powys 34 B4
Bredbury Gtr Man 87 E7
Brede E Sus 18 D5
Bredenbury Hereford 49 D8
Bredfield Suff 57 D6
Bredgar Kent 30 C2
Bredhurst Kent 29 C8
Bredicot Worcs 50 D4
Bredon Worcs 50 F4
Bredon's Norton Worcs 50 F4
Bredwardine Hereford 48 E5
Breedon on the Hill Leics 63 B8
Breibhig W Isles 148 J1
Breibhig W Isles 155 D9
Breich W Loth 120 C2
Breightmet Gtr Man 86 D5
Breighton E Yorks 96 F3
Breinton Hereford 49 F6
Breinton Common Hereford 49 E6
Breiwick Shetland 160 J6
Bremhill Wilts 24 B4
Bremirehoull Shetland 160 L6
Brenchley Kent 29 E7
Brendon Devon 21 E6
Brenkley T&W 110 B5
Brent Eleigh Suff 56 E3
Brent Knoll Som 22 D5
Brent Pelham Herts 54 F5
Brentford London 28 B2
Brentingby Leics 64 C4
Brentwood Essex 42 E1
Brenzett Kent 19 C7
Brereton Staffs 62 C4
Brereton Green Ches E 74 C4
Brereton Heath Ches E 74 C5
Bressingham Norf 68 F3
Bretby Derbys 63 B6
Bretford Warks 52 B2
Bretforton Worcs 51 E5
Bretherdale Head Cumb 99 D7
Bretherton Lancs 86 B2
Brettabister Shetland 160 H6
Brettenham Norf 68 F2
Brettenham Suff 56 D3
Bretton Derbys 76 B2
Bretton Flint 73 C7
Brewer Street Sur 28 D4
Brewlands Bridge Angus 134 C1
Brewood Staffs 62 D2
Briach Moray 151 F13
Briants Puddle Dorset 13 E6
Brick End Essex 42 B1
Brickendon Herts 41 D6
Bricket Wood Herts 40 D4
Bricklehampton Worcs 50 E4
Bride IoM 84 B4
Bridekirk Cumb 107 F8
Bridell Pembs 45 E3
Bridestowe Devon 9 F7
Brideswell Aberds 152 E5
Bridford Devon 10 F3
Bridfordmills Devon 10 F3
Bridge Kent 31 D5
Bridge End Lincs 78 F4
Bridge Green Essex 55 F5
Bridge Hewick N Yorks 95 B6
Bridge of Alford Aberds 140 C4
Bridge of Allan Stirling 127 E6
Bridge of Avon Moray 152 E1
Bridge of Awe Argyll 125 C6
Bridge of Balgie Perth 132 E2
Bridge of Cally Perth 133 D8
Bridge of Canny Aberds 141 E5
Bridge of Craigisla Angus 134 D2
Bridge of Dee Dumfries 106 D4
Bridge of Don Aberdeen 141 C8
Bridge of Dun Angus 135 D6
Bridge of Dye Aberds 141 F5
Bridge of Earn Perth 128 C3
Bridge of Ericht Perth 132 D2
Bridge of Feugh Aberds 141 E6
Bridge of Forss Highld 157 C13
Bridge of Gairn Aberds 140 E2
Bridge of Gaur Perth 132 D2
Bridge of Muchalls Aberds 141 E7
Bridge of Oich Highld 137 D6
Bridge of Orchy Argyll 125 B8
Bridge of Waith Orkney 159 G3
Bridge of Walls Shetland 160 H4
Bridge of Weir Renfs 118 C3
Bridge Sollers Hereford 49 E6
Bridge Street Suff 56 E2
Bridge Trafford Ches W 73 B8
Bridge Yate S Glos 23 B8
Bridgefoot Angus 134 F3
Bridgefoot Cumb 98 B2
Bridgehampton Som 12 B3
Bridgehill Durham 110 D3
Bridgemary Hants 15 D6
Bridgemont Derbys 87 F8
Bridgend Aberds 140 C4
Bridgend Aberds 152 E5
Bridgend Angus 135 C5
Bridgend Argyll 142 B4
Bridgend Argyll 143 E8
Bridgend Argyll 145 D7
Bridgend = Pen-Y-Bont Ar Ogwr Bridgend 21 B8
Bridgend Cumb 99 C5
Bridgend Fife 129 C5
Bridgend Moray 152 E3
Bridgend N Lanark 119 B6
Bridgend Pembs 45 E3
Bridgend W Loth 120 B3
Bridgend of Lintrathen Angus 134 D2
Bridgerule Devon 8 D4
Bridges Shrops 60 E3
Bridgeton Glasgow 119 C6
Bridgetown Corn 8 F5
Bridgetown Som 21 F8
Bridgham Norf 68 F2
Bridgnorth Shrops 61 E7
Bridgtown Staffs 62 D3
Bridgwater Som 22 F5
Bridlington E Yorks 97 C7
Bridport Dorset 12 E2
Bridstow Hereford 36 B2
Brierfield Lancs 93 F8
Brierley Glos 36 C3
Brierley Hereford 49 D6
Brierley S Yorks 88 C5
Brierley Hill W Mid 62 F3
Briery Hill Bl Gwent 35 D5
Brig o'Turk Stirling 126 D4
Brigg N Lincs 90 D4
Briggswath N Yorks 103 D6
Brigham Cumb 107 F7
Brigham E Yorks 97 D6
Brighouse W Yorks 88 B2
Brighstone IoW 14 F5
Brightgate Derbys 76 D2
Brighthampton Oxon 38 D3
Brightling E Sus 18 C3
Brightlingsea Essex 43 C6
Brighton Brighton 17 D7
Brighton Corn 4 D4
Brighton Hill Hants 26 E4
Brightons Falk 120 B2
Brightwalton W Berks 26 B2
Brightwell Suff 57 E6
Brightwell Baldwin Oxon 39 E6
Brightwell cum Sotwell Oxon 39 E5
Brignall Durham 101 C5
Brigsley NE Lincs 91 D6
Brigsteer Cumb 99 F6
Brigstock Northants 65 F6
Brill Bucks 39 C6
Brilley Hereford 48 E4
Brimaston Pembs 44 C4
Brimfield Hereford 49 C7
Brimington Derbys 76 B4
Brimley Devon 7 B5
Brimpsfield Glos 37 C6
Brimpton W Berks 26 C3
Brims Orkney 159 K3
Brimscombe Glos 37 D5
Brimstage Mers 85 F4
Brinacory Highld 147 B10
Brind E Yorks 96 F3
Brindister Shetland 160 H4
Brindister Shetland 160 K6
Brindle Lancs 86 B4
Brindley Ford Stoke 75 D5
Brineton Staffs 62 C2
Bringhurst Leics 64 E5
Brington Cambs 53 B8
Brinian Orkney 159 F5
Briningham Norf 81 D6
Brinkhill Lincs 79 B6
Brinkley Cambs 55 D7
Brinklow Warks 52 B2
Brinkworth Wilts 37 F7
Brinmore Highld 138 B2
Brinscall Lancs 86 B4
Brinsea N Som 23 C6
Brinsley Notts 76 E4
Brinsop Hereford 49 E6
Brinsworth S Yorks 88 F5
Brinton Norf 81 D6
Brisco Cumb 108 D4
Brisley Norf 81 E5
Brislington Bristol 23 B8
Bristol Bristol 23 B7
Briston Norf 81 D6
Britannia Lancs 87 B6
Britford Wilts 14 B2
Brithdir Gwyn 58 C4
British Legion Village Kent 29 D8
Briton Ferry Neath 33 E8
Britwell Salome Oxon 39 E6
Brixham Torbay 7 D7
Brixton Devon 6 D3
Brixton London 28 B4
Brixton Deverill Wilts 24 F3
Brixworth Northants 52 B5
Brize Norton Oxon 38 D3
Broad Blunsdon Swindon 38 E1
Broad Campden Glos 51 F6
Broad Chalke Wilts 13 B8
Broad Green C Beds 53 E7
Broad Green Essex 42 B4
Broad Green Worcs 50 D2
Broad Haven Pembs 44 D3
Broad Heath Worcs 49 C8
Broad Hill Cambs 55 B6
Broad Hinton Wilts 25 B6
Broad Laying Hants 26 C2
Broad Marston Worcs 51 E6
Broad Oak Carms 33 B6
Broad Oak Cumb 98 E3
Broad Oak Dorset 12 E2
Broad Oak Dorset 13 C5
Broad Oak E Sus 18 C3
Broad Oak E Sus 18 D5
Broad Oak Hereford 36 B1
Broad Oak Mers 86 E3
Broad Street Kent 30 D2
Broad Street Green Essex 42 D4
Broad Town Wilts 25 B5
Broadbottom Gtr Man 87 E7
Broadbridge W Sus 16 D2
Broadbridge Heath W Sus 28 F2
Broadclyst Devon 10 E4
Broadfield Gtr Man 87 C6
Broadfield Lancs 86 B3
Broadfield Pembs 32 D2
Broadfield W Sus 28 F3
Broadford Highld 149 F11
Broadford Bridge W Sus 16 B4
Broadhaugh Borders 115 D7
Broadhaven Highld 158 E5
Broadheath Gtr Man 87 F5
Broadhembury Devon 11 D6
Broadhempston Devon 7 C6
Broadholme Derbys 76 E3
Broadholme Lincs 77 B8
Broadland Row E Sus 18 D5
Broadlay Carms 32 D4
Broadley Lancs 87 C6
Broadley Moray 152 B3
Broadley Common Essex 41 D7
Broadmayne Dorset 12 F5
Broadmeadows Borders 121 F7
Broadmere Hants 26 E4
Broadmoor Pembs 32 D1
Broadoak Kent 31 C5
Broadrashes Moray 152 C4
Broadsea Aberds 153 B9
Broadstairs Kent 31 C7
Broadstone Poole 13 E8
Broadstone Shrops 60 F5
Broadtown Lane Wilts 25 B5
Broadwas Worcs 50 D2
Broadwater Herts 41 B5
Broadwater W Sus 17 D5
Broadway Carms 32 D3
Broadway Pembs 44 D3
Broadway Som 11 C8
Broadway Suff 57 B7
Broadway Worcs 51 F5
Broadwell Glos 36 C2
Broadwell Glos 38 B2
Broadwell Oxon 38 D2
Broadwell Warks 52 C2
Broadwell House Northumb 110 D2
Broadwey Dorset 12 F4
Broadwindsor Dorset 12 D2
Broadwood Kelly Devon 9 D8
Broadwoodwidger Devon 9 F6
Brobury Hereford 48 E5
Brochel Highld 149 D10
Brochloch Dumfries 113 E5
Brochroy Argyll 125 B6
Brockamin Worcs 50 D2
Brockbridge Hants 15 C7
Brockdam Northumb 117 B7
Brockdish Norf 57 B6
Brockenhurst Hants 14 D4
Brocketsbrae S Lanark 119 F8
Brockford Street Suff 56 C5
Brockhall Northants 52 C4
Brockham Sur 28 E2
Brockhampton Glos 37 B7
Brockhampton Hereford 49 F7
Brockholes W Yorks 88 C2
Brockhurst Derbys 76 C3
Brockhurst Hants 15 D7
Brocklebank Cumb 108 E3
Brocklesby Lincs 90 C5
Brockley N Som 23 C6
Brockley Green Suff 56 D2
Brockleymoor Cumb 108 F4
Brockton Shrops 60 D3
Brockton Shrops 60 F3
Brockton Shrops 61 D7
Brockton Shrops 61 E5
Brockton Telford 61 C7
Brockweir Glos 36 D2
Brockwood Hants 15 B7
Brockworth Glos 37 C5
Brocton Staffs 62 C3
Brodick N Ayrs 143 E11
Brodsworth S Yorks 89 D6
Brogaig Highld 149 B9
Brogborough C Beds 53 F7
Broken Cross Ches E 75 B5
Broken Cross Ches W 74 B3
Brokenborough Wilts 37 F6
Bromborough Mers 85 F4
Brome Suff 56 B5
Brome Street Suff 57 B5
Bromeswell Suff 57 D7
Bromfield Cumb 107 E8
Bromfield Shrops 49 B6
Bromham Bedford 53 D8
Bromham Wilts 24 C4
Bromley London 28 C5
Bromley W Mid 62 F3
Bromley Common London 28 C5
Bromley Green Kent 19 B6
Brompton Medway 29 C8
Brompton N Yorks 102 E1
Brompton N Yorks 103 F7
Brompton-on-Swale N Yorks 101 E7
Brompton Ralph Som 22 F2
Brompton Regis Som 21 F8
Bromsash Hereford 36 B3
Bromsberrow Heath Glos 50 F2
Bromsgrove Worcs 50 B4
Bromyard Hereford 49 D8
Bromyard Downs Hereford 49 D8
Bronaber Gwyn 71 D8
Brongest Ceredig 46 E2
Bronington Wrex 73 F8
Bronllys Powys 48 F3
Bronnant Ceredig 46 C5
Bronwydd Arms Carms 33 B5
Bronydd Powys 48 E4
Bronygarth Shrops 73 F6
Brook Carms 32 D3
Brook Hants 14 B4
Brook Hants 14 C3
Brook IoW 14 F4
Brook Kent 30 E4
Brook Sur 27 E8
Brook Sur 27 F7
Brook End Bedford 53 C8
Brook Hill Hants 14 C3
Brook Street Kent 19 B6
Brook Street Kent 29 E6
Brook Street W Sus 17 B7
Brooke Norf 69 E5
Brooke Rutland 64 D5
Brookenby Lincs 91 E6
Brookend Glos 36 E2
Brookfield Renfs 118 C4
Brookhouse Lancs 92 C5
Brookhouse Green Ches E 74 C5
Brookland Kent 19 C6
Brooklands Dumfries 106 B5
Brooklands Gtr Man 87 E5
Brooklands Shrops 74 E2
Brookmans Park Herts 41 D5
Brooks Powys 59 E8
Brooks Green W Sus 16 B5
Brookthorpe Glos 37 C5
Brookville Norf 67 E7
Brookwood Sur 27 D7
Broom C Beds 54 E2
Broom S Yorks 88 E5
Broom Warks 51 D5
Broom Worcs 50 B4
Broom Green Norf 81 E5
Broom Hill Dorset 13 D8
Broome Norf 69 E6
Broome Shrops 60 F4
Broome Park Northumb 117 C7
Broomedge Warr 86 F5
Broomer's Corner W Sus 16 B5
Broomfield Aberds 153 E9
Broomfield Essex 42 C3
Broomfield Kent 30 D2
Broomfield Kent 31 C5
Broomfield Som 22 F4
Broomfleet E Yorks 90 B2
Broomhall Ches E 74 E3
Broomhall Windsor 27 C7
Broomhaugh Northumb 110 C3
Broomhill Norf 67 D6
Broomhill Northumb 117 D8
Broomhill S Yorks 88 D5
Broomholm Norf 81 D9
Broomley Northumb 110 C3
Broompark Durham 110 E5
Broom's Green Glos 50 F2
Broomy Lodge Hants 14 C3
Brora Highld 157 J12
Broseley Shrops 61 D6
Brotherhouse Bar Lincs 66 C2
Brotherstone Borders 122 F2
Brothertoft Lincs 79 E5
Brotherton N Yorks 89 B5
Brotton Redcar 102 C4
Broubster Highld 157 C13
Brough Cumb 100 C2
Brough Derbys 88 F2
Brough E Yorks 90 B3
Brough Highld 158 C4
Brough Notts 77 D8
Brough Orkney 159 G4
Brough Shetland 160 F6
Brough Shetland 160 F7
Brough Shetland 160 G7
Brough Shetland 160 H6
Brough Shetland 160 J7
Brough Lodge Shetland 160 D7
Brough Sowerby Cumb 100 C2
Broughall Shrops 74 E2
Broughton Borders 120 F4
Broughton Cambs 54 B3
Broughton Flint 73 C7
Broughton Hants 25 F8
Broughton Lancs 92 F5
Broughton M Keynes 53 E6
Broughton N Lincs 90 D3
Broughton N Yorks 94 D2
Broughton N Yorks 96 B3
Broughton Northants 53 B6
Broughton Orkney 159 D5
Broughton Oxon 52 F2
Broughton V Glam 21 B8
Broughton Astley Leics 64 E2
Broughton Beck Cumb 98 F4
Broughton Common Wilts 24 C3
Broughton Gifford Wilts 24 C3
Broughton Hackett Worcs 50 D4
Broughton in Furness Cumb 98 F4
Broughton Mills Cumb 98 E4
Broughton Moor Cumb 107 F7
Broughton Park Gtr Man 87 D6
Broughton Poggs Oxon 38 D2
Broughtown Orkney 159 D7
Broughty Ferry Dundee 134 F4
Browhouses Dumfries 108 C2
Browland Shetland 160 H4
Brown Candover Hants 26 F3
Brown Edge Lancs 85 C4
Brown Edge Staffs 75 D6
Brown Heath Ches W 73 C8
Brownhill Aberds 153 D6
Brownhill Aberds 153 D8
Brownhill Blackburn 93 F6
Brownhill Shrops 60 B4
Brownhills Fife 129 C7
Brownhills W Mid 62 D4
Brownlow Ches E 74 C5
Brownlow Heath Ches E 74 C5
Brownmuir Aberds 135 B7
Brown's End Glos 50 F2
Brownshill Glos 37 D5
Brownston Devon 6 D4
Brownyside Northumb 117 B7
Broxa N Yorks 103 E7
Broxbourne Herts 41 D6
Broxburn E Loth 122 B2
Broxburn W Loth 120 B3
Broxholme Lincs 78 B2
Broxted Essex 42 B1
Broxton Ches W 73 D8
Broxwood Hereford 49 D5
Broyle Side E Sus 17 C8
Brù W Isles 155 C8
Bruairnis W Isles 148 H2
Bruan Highld 158 G5
Bruar Lodge Perth 133 B5
Brucehill W Dunb 118 B3
Bruera Ches W 73 C8
Bruern Abbey Oxon 38 B2
Bruichladdich Argyll 142 B3
Bruisyard Suff 57 C7
Brumby N Lincs 90 D2
Brund Staffs 75 C8
Brundall Norf 69 D6
Brundish Suff 57 C6
Brundish Street Suff 57 B6
Brunery Highld 147 D10
Brunshaw Lancs 93 F8
Brunswick Village T&W 110 B5
Bruntcliffe W Yorks 88 B3
Bruntingthorpe Leics 64 E3
Brunton Fife 128 B5
Brunton Northumb 117 B8
Brunton Wilts 25 D7
Brushford Devon 9 D8
Brushford Som 10 B4
Bruton Som 23 F8
Bryanston Dorset 13 D6
Brydekirk Dumfries 107 B8
Bryher Scilly 2 E3
Brymbo Wrex 73 D6
Brympton Som 12 C3
Bryn Carms 33 D6
Bryn Gtr Man 86 D3
Bryn Neath 34 E2
Bryn Shrops 60 F2
Bryn-coch Neath 33 E8
Bryn Du Anglesey 82 D3
Bryn Gates Gtr Man 86 D3
Bryn-glas Conwy 83 E8
Bryn Golau Rhondda 34 F3
Bryn-Iwan Carms 46 F2
Bryn-mawr Gwyn 70 D3
Bryn-nantllech Conwy 72 C3
Bryn-penarth Powys 59 D8
Bryn Rhyd-yr-Arian Conwy 72 C3
Bryn Saith Marchog Denb 72 D4
Bryn Sion Gwyn 59 C5
Bryn-y-gwenin Mon 35 C7
Bryn-y-maen Conwy 83 D8
Bryn-yr-eryr Gwyn 70 C4
Brynamman Carms 33 C8
Brynberian Pembs 45 F3
Brynbryddan Neath 34 E1
Brynbuga = Usk Mon 35 D7
Bryncae Rhondda 34 F3
Bryncethin Bridgend 34 F3
Bryncir Gwyn 71 C5
Bryncroes Gwyn 70 D3
Bryncrug Gwyn 58 D3
Bryneglwys Denb 72 E5
Brynford Flint 73 B5
Bryngwran Anglesey 82 D3
Bryngwyn Ceredig 45 E4
Bryngwyn Mon 35 D7
Bryngwyn Powys 48 E3
Brynhenllan Pembs 45 F2
Brynhoffnant Ceredig 46 D2
Brynithel Bl Gwent 35 D6
Brynmawr Bl Gwent 35 C5
Brynmenyn Bridgend 34 F3
Brynmill Swansea 33 E7
Brynna Rhondda 34 F3
Brynrefail Anglesey 82 C4
Brynrefail Gwyn 83 E5
Brynsadler Rhondda 34 F4
Brynsiencyn Anglesey 82 E4
Brynteg Anglesey 82 C4
Brynteg Ceredig 46 E3
Buaile nam Bodach W Isles 148 H2
Bualintur Highld 149 F9
Buarthmeini Gwyn 72 F2
Bubbenhall Warks 51 B8
Bubwith E Yorks 96 F3
Buccleuch Borders 115 C6
Buchanhaven Aberds 153 D11
Buchanty Perth 127 B8
Buchlyvie Stirling 126 E4
Buckabank Cumb 108 E3
Buckden Cambs 54 C2
Buckden N Yorks 94 B2
Buckenham Norf 69 D6
Buckerell Devon 11 D6
Buckfast Devon 6 C5
Buckfastleigh Devon 6 C5
Buckhaven Fife 129 E5
Buckholm Borders 121 F7
Buckholt Mon 36 C2
Buckhorn Weston Dorset 13 B5
Buckhurst Hill Essex 41 E7
Buckie Moray 152 B4
Buckies Highld 158 D3
Buckingham Bucks 52 F4
Buckland Bucks 40 C1
Buckland Devon 6 E4
Buckland Glos 51 F5
Buckland Hants 14 E4
Buckland Herts 54 F4
Buckland Kent 31 E7
Buckland Oxon 38 E3
Buckland Sur 28 D3
Buckland Brewer Devon 9 B6
Buckland Common Bucks 40 D2
Buckland Dinham Som 24 D2
Buckland Filleigh Devon 9 D6
Buckland in the Moor Devon 6 B5
Buckland Monachorum Devon 6 C2
Buckland Newton Dorset 12 D4
Buckland St Mary Som 11 C7
Bucklebury W Berks 26 B3
Bucklegate Lincs 79 F6
Bucklerheads Angus 134 F4
Bucklers Hard Hants 14 E5
Bucklesham Suff 57 E6
Buckley = Bwcle Flint 73 C6
Bucklow Hill Ches E 86 F5
Buckminster Leics 65 B5
Bucknall Lincs 78 C4
Bucknall Stoke 75 E6
Bucknell Oxon 39 B5
Bucknell Shrops 49 B5
Buckpool Moray 152 B4
Buck's Cross Devon 8 B5
Bucks Green W Sus 27 F8
Bucks Horn Oak Hants 27 E6
Buck's Mills Devon 9 B5
Bucksburn Aberdeen 141 D7
Buckshaw Village Lancs 86 B3
Buckskin Hants 26 D4
Buckton E Yorks 97 B7
Buckton Hereford 49 B5
Buckton Northumb 123 F6
Buckworth Cambs 54 B2
Budbrooke Warks 51 C7
Budby Notts 77 C6
Budd's Titson Corn 8 D4
Bude Corn 8 D4
Budlake Devon 10 E4
Budle Northumb 123 F7
Budleigh Salterton Devon 11 F5
Budock Water Corn 3 C6
Buerton Ches E 74 E3
Buffler's Holt Bucks 52 F4
Bugbrooke Northants 52 D4
Buglawton Ches E 75 C5
Bugle Corn 4 D5
Bugley Wilts 24 E3
Bugthorpe E Yorks 96 D3
Buildwas Shrops 61 D6
Builth Road Powys 48 D2
Builth Wells = Llanfair-Ym-Muallt Powys 48 D2
Buirgh W Isles 154 H5
Bulby Lincs 65 B7
Bulcote Notts 77 E6
Buldoo Highld 157 C12
Bulford Wilts 25 E6
Bulford Camp Wilts 25 E6
Bulkeley Ches E 74 D2
Bulkington Warks 63 F7
Bulkington Wilts 24 D4
Bulkworthy Devon 9 C5
Bull Hill Hants 14 E4
Bullamoor N Yorks 102 E1
Bullbridge Derbys 76 D3
Bullbrook Brack 27 C6
Bulley Glos 36 C4
Bullgill Cumb 107 F7
Bullington Hants 26 E2
Bullington Lincs 78 B3
Bull's Green Herts 41 C5
Bullwood Argyll 145 F10
Bulmer Essex 56 E2
Bulmer N Yorks 96 C2
Bulmer Tye Essex 56 F2
Bulphan Thurrock 42 F2
Bulverhythe E Sus 18 E4
Bulwark Aberds 153 D9
Bulwell Nottingham 76 E5
Bulwick Northants 65 E6
Bumble's Green Essex 41 D7
Bun a'Mhuillin W Isles 148 G2
Bun Abhainn Eadarra W Isles 154 G6
Bun Loyne Highld 136 D5
Bunacaimb Highld 147 C9
Bunarkaig Highld 136 F4
Bunbury Ches E 74 D2
Bunbury Heath Ches E 74 D2
Bunchrew Highld 151 G9
Bundalloch Highld 149 F13
Buness Shetland 160 C8
Bunessan Argyll 146 J6
Bungay Suff 69 F6
Bunker's Hill Lincs 78 B2
Bunker's Hill Lincs 79 D5
Bunkers Hill Oxon 38 C4
Bunloit Highld 137 B8
Bunnahabhain Argyll 142 A5
Bunny Notts 64 B2
Buntait Highld 150 H6
Buntingford Herts 41 B6
Bunwell Norf 68 E4
Burbage Derbys 75 B7
Burbage Leics 63 E8
Burbage Wilts 25 C7
Burchett's Green Windsor 39 F8
Burcombe Wilts 25 F5
Burcot Oxon 39 E5
Burcott Bucks 40 B1
Burdon T&W 111 D6
Bures Suff 56 F3
Bures Green Suff 56 F3
Burford Ches E 74 D3
Burford Oxon 38 C2
Burford Shrops 49 C7
Burg Argyll 146 G6
Burgar Orkney 159 F4
Burgate Hants 14 C2
Burgate Suff 56 B4
Burgess Hill W Sus 17 C7
Burgh Suff 57 D6
Burgh by Sands Cumb 108 D3
Burgh Castle Norf 69 D7
Burgh Heath Sur 28 D3
Burgh le Marsh Lincs 79 C8
Burgh Muir Aberds 141 B6
Burgh next Aylsham Norf 81 E8
Burgh on Bain Lincs 91 F6
Burgh St Margaret Norf 69 C7
Burgh St Peter Norf 69 E7
Burghclere Hants 26 C2
Burghead Moray 151 E14
Burghfield W Berks 26 C4
Burghfield Common W Berks 26 C4
Burghfield Hill W Berks 26 C4
Burghill Hereford 49 E6
Burghwallis S Yorks 89 C6
Burham Kent 29 C8
Buriton Hants 15 B8
Burland Ches E 74 D3
Burlawn Corn 4 B4
Burleigh Brack 27 C6
Burlescombe Devon 11 C5
Burleston Dorset 13 E5
Burley Hants 14 D3
Burley Rutland 65 C5
Burley W Yorks 95 F5
Burley Gate Hereford 49 E7
Burley in Wharfedale W Yorks 94 E4
Burley Lodge Hants 14 D3
Burley Street Hants 14 D3
Burleydam Ches E 74 E3
Burlingjobb Powys 48 D4
Burlow E Sus 18 D2
Burlton Shrops 60 B4
Burmarsh Kent 19 B7
Burmington Warks 51 F7
Burn N Yorks 89 B6
Burn of Cambus Stirling 127 D6
Burnaston Derbys 76 F2
Burnbank S Lanark 119 D7
Burnby E Yorks 96 E4
Burncross S Yorks 88 E4
Burneside Cumb 99 E7
Burness Orkney 159 D7
Burneston N Yorks 101 F8
Burnett Bath 23 C8
Burnfoot Borders 115 C7
Burnfoot Borders 115 C8
Burnfoot E Ayrs 112 D4
Burnfoot Perth 127 D8
Burnham Bucks 40 F2
Burnham N Lincs 90 C4
Burnham Deepdale Norf 80 C4
Burnham Green Herts 41 C5
Burnham Market Norf 80 C4
Burnham Norton Norf 80 C4
Burnham-on-Crouch Essex 43 E5
Burnham-on-Sea Som 22 E5
Burnham Overy Staithe Norf 80 C4
Burnham Overy Town Norf 80 C4
Burnham Thorpe Norf 80 C4
Burnhead Dumfries 113 E8
Burnhead S Ayrs 112 D2
Burnhervie Aberds 141 C6
Burnhill Green Staffs 61 D7
Burnhope Durham 110 E4
Burnhouse N Ayrs 118 D3
Burniston N Yorks 103 E8
Burnlee W Yorks 88 D2
Burnley Lancs 93 F8
Burnley Lane Lancs 93 F8
Burnmouth Borders 123 C5
Burnopfield Durham 110 D4
Burnsall N Yorks 94 C3
Burnside Angus 135 D5
Burnside E Ayrs 113 C5
Burnside Fife 128 D3
Burnside S Lanark 119 C6
Burnside Shetland 160 F4
Burnside W Loth 120 B3
Burnside of Duntrune Angus 134 F4
Burnswark Dumfries 107 B8
Burnt Heath Derbys 76 B2
Burnt Houses Durham 101 B6
Burnt Yates N Yorks 95 C5
Burntcommon Sur 27 D8
Burnthouse Corn 3 C6
Burntisland Fife 128 F4
Burnton E Ayrs 112 D4
Burntwood Staffs 62 D4
Burnwynd Edin 120 C4
Burpham Sur 27 D8
Burpham W Sus 16 D4
Burradon Northumb 117 D5
Burradon T&W 111 B5
Burrafirth Shetland 160 B8
Burraland Shetland 160 F5
Burraland Shetland 160 J4
Burras Corn 3 C5
Burravoe Shetland 160 F7
Burravoe Shetland 160 G5
Burray Village Orkney 159 J5
Burrells Cumb 100 C1
Burrelton Perth 134 F2
Burridge Devon 20 F4
Burridge Hants 15 C6
Burrill N Yorks 101 F7
Burringham N Lincs 90 D2
Burrington Devon 9 C8
Burrington Hereford 49 B6
Burrington N Som 23 D6
Burrough Green Cambs 55 D7
Burrough on the Hill Leics 64 C4
Burrow-bridge Som 11 B8
Burrowhill Sur 27 C7
Burry Swansea 33 E5
Burry Green Swansea 33 E5
Burry Port = Porth Tywyn Carms 33 D5
Burscough Lancs 86 C2
Burscough Bridge Lancs 86 C2
Bursea E Yorks 96 F4
Burshill E Yorks 97 E6
Bursledon Hants 15 D5
Burslem Stoke 75 E5
Burstall Suff 56 E4
Burstock Dorset 12 D2
Burston Norf 68 F4
Burston Staffs 75 F6
Burstow Sur 28 E4
Burstwick E Yorks 91 B6
Burtersett N Yorks 100 F3
Burtle Som 23 E5
Burton Ches W 73 B7
Burton Ches W 74 C2
Burton Dorset 14 E2
Burton Lincs 78 B2
Burton Northumb 123 F7
Burton Pembs 44 E4
Burton Som 22 E3
Burton Wilts 24 B3
Burton Agnes E Yorks 97 C7
Burton Bradstock Dorset 12 F2
Burton Dassett Warks 51 D8
Burton Fleming E Yorks 97 B6
Burton Green W Mid 51 B7
Burton Green Wrex 73 D7
Burton Hastings Warks 63 E8
Burton-in-Kendal Cumb 92 B5
Burton in Lonsdale N Yorks 93 B6
Burton Joyce Notts 77 E6
Burton Latimer Northants 53 B7
Burton Lazars Leics 64 C4
Burton-le-Coggles Lincs 65 B6
Burton Leonard N Yorks 95 C6
Burton on the Wolds Leics 64 B2
Burton Overy Leics 64 E3
Burton Pedwardine Lincs 78 E4
Burton Pidsea E Yorks 97 F8
Burton Salmon N Yorks 89 B5
Burton Stather N Lincs 90 C2
Burton upon Stather N Lincs 90 C2
Burton upon Trent Staffs 63 B6
Burtonwood Warr 86 E3
Burwardsley Ches W 74 D2
Burwarton Shrops 61 F6
Burwash E Sus 18 C3
Burwash Common E Sus 18 C3
Burwash Weald E Sus 18 C3
Burwell Cambs 55 C6
Burwell Lincs 79 B6
Burwen Anglesey 82 B4
Burwick Orkney 159 K5
Bury Cambs 66 F2
Bury Gtr Man 87 C6
Bury Som 10 B4
Bury W Sus 16 C4
Bury Green Herts 41 B7
Bury St Edmunds Suff 56 C2
Burythorpe N Yorks 96 C3
Busby E Renf 119 D5
Buscot Oxon 38 E2
Bush Bank Hereford 49 D6
Bush Crathie Aberds 139 E8
Bush Green Norf 68 F5
Bushbury W Mid 62 D3
Bushby Leics 64 D3
Bushey Herts 40 E4
Bushey Heath Herts 40 E4
Bushley Worcs 50 F3
Bushton Wilts 25 B5
Buslingthorpe Lincs 90 F4
Busta Shetland 160 G5
Butcher's Cross E Sus 18 C2
Butcombe N Som 23 C7
Butetown Cardiff 22 B3
Butleigh Som 23 F7
Butleigh Wootton Som 23 F7
Butler's Cross Bucks 39 D8
Butler's End Warks 63 F6
Butlers Marston Warks 51 E8
Butley Suff 57 D7
Butley High Corner Suff 57 E7
Butt Green Ches E 74 D3
Butterburn Cumb 109 B6
Buttercrambe N Yorks 96 D3
Butterknowle Durham 101 B6
Butterleigh Devon 10 D4
Buttermere Cumb 98 C3
Buttermere Wilts 25 C8
Buttershaw W Yorks 88 B2
Butterstone Perth 133 E7
Butterton Staffs 75 D7
Butterwick Durham 102 B1
Butterwick Lincs 79 E6
Butterwick N Yorks 96 B3
Butterwick N Yorks 97 B5
Buttington Powys 60 D2
Buttonoak Worcs 50 B2
Butt's Green Hants 14 B4
Buttsash Hants 14 D5
Buxhall Suff 56 D4
Buxhall Fen Street Suff 56 D4
Buxley Borders 122 D4
Buxted E Sus 17 B8
Buxton Derbys 75 B7

Crofton Wilts 25 C7
Crofts of Benachielt Highld 158 G3
Crofts of Haddo Aberds 153 E8
Crofts of Inverthernie Aberds 153 D7
Crofts of Meikle Ardo Aberds 153 D8
Crofty Swansea 33 E6
Croggan Argyll 124 C3
Croglin Cumb 109 E5
Croich Highld 150 B7
Crois Dughaill W Isles 148 F2
Cromarty Highld 151 E10
Cromblet Aberds 153 E7
Cromdale Highld 139 B6
Cromer Herts 41 B5
Cromer Norf 81 C8
Cromford Derbys 76 D2
Cromhall S Glos 36 E3
Cromhall Common S Glos 36 F3
Cromor W Isles 155 E9
Cromra Highld 137 E8
Cromwell Notts 77 C7
Cronberry E Ayrs 113 B6
Crondall Hants 27 E5
Cronk-y-Voddy IoM 84 D3
Cronton Mers 86 F2
Crook Cumb 99 E6
Crook Durham 110 F4
Crook of Devon Perth 128 D2
Crookedholm E Ayrs 118 F4
Crookes S Yorks 88 F4
Crookham Northumb 122 F5
Crookham W Berks 26 C3
Crookham Village Hants 27 D5
Crookhaugh Borders 114 B4
Crookhouse Borders 116 B3
Crooklands Cumb 99 F7
Cropredy Oxon 52 E2
Cropston Leics 64 C2
Cropthorne Worcs 50 E4
Cropton N Yorks 103 F5
Cropwell Bishop Notts 77 F6
Cropwell Butler Notts 77 F6
Cros W Isles 155 A10
Crosbost W Isles 155 E8
Crosby Cumb 107 F7
Crosby IoM 84 E3
Crosby N Lincs 90 C2
Crosby Garrett Cumb 100 D2
Crosby Ravensworth Cumb 99 C8
Crosby Villa Cumb 107 F7
Croscombe Som 23 E7
Cross Som 23 D6
Cross Ash Mon 35 C8
Cross-at-Hand Kent 29 E8
Cross Green Devon 9 F5
Cross Green Suff 56 D2
Cross Green Suff 56 D3
Cross Green Warks 51 D8
Cross-hands Carms 32 B2
Cross Hands Carms 33 C6
Cross Hands Pembs 32 C1
Cross Hill Derbys 76 E4
Cross Houses Shrops 60 D5
Cross in Hand E Sus 18 C2
Cross in Hand Leics 64 F2
Cross Inn Ceredig 46 C4
Cross Inn Ceredig 46 D2
Cross Inn Rhondda 34 F4
Cross Keys Kent 29 D6
Cross Lane Head Shrops 61 E7
Cross Lanes Corn 3 D5
Cross Lanes N Yorks 95 C8
Cross Lanes Wrex 73 E7
Cross Oak Powys 35 B5
Cross of Jackston Aberds 153 E7
Cross o'th'hands Derbys 76 E2
Cross Street Suff 57 B5
Crossaig Argyll 143 C9
Crossal Highld 149 E9
Crossapol Argyll 146 G2
Crossburn Falk 119 B8
Crossbush W Sus 16 D4
Crosscanonby Cumb 107 F7
Crossdale Street Norf 81 D8
Crossens Mers 85 C4
Crossflatts W Yorks 94 E4
Crossford Fife 128 F2
Crossford S Lanark 119 E8
Crossgate Lincs 66 B2
Crossgatehall E Loth 121 C6
Crossgates Fife 128 F3
Crossgates Powys 48 C2
Crossgill Lancs 93 C5
Crosshill E Ayrs 112 B4
Crosshill Fife 128 E3
Crosshill S Ayrs 112 D3
Crosshouse E Ayrs 118 F3
Crossings Cumb 108 B5
Crosskeys Caerph 35 E6
Crosskirk Highld 157 B13
Crosslanes Shrops 60 C3
Crosslee Borders 115 C6
Crosslee Renfs 118 C4
Crossmichael Dumfries 106 C4
Crossmoor Lancs 92 F4
Crossroads Aberds 141 E6
Crossroads E Ayrs 118 F4
Crossway Hereford 49 F8
Crossway Mon 35 C8
Crossway Powys 48 D2
Crossway Green Worcs 50 C3
Crossways Dorset 13 F5
Crosswell Pembs 45 F3
Crosswood Ceredig 47 B5
Crosthwaite Cumb 99 E6
Croston Lancs 86 C2
Crostwick Norf 69 C5
Crostwight Norf 69 B6
Crothair W Isles 154 D6
Crouch Kent 29 D7
Crouch Hill Dorset 12 C5
Crouch House Green Kent 28 E5
Croucheston Wilts 13 B8
Croughton Northants 52 F3
Crovie Aberds 153 B8
Crow Edge S Yorks 88 D2
Crow Hill Hereford 36 B3
Crowan Corn 2 C5
Crowborough E Sus 18 B2
Crowcombe Som 22 F3
Crowdecote Derbys 75 C8
Crowden Derbys 87 E8
Crowell Oxon 39 E7
Crowfield Northants 52 E4
Crowfield Suff 56 D5
Crowhurst E Sus 18 D4
Crowhurst Sur 28 E4
Crowhurst Lane End Sur 28 E4
Crowland Lincs 66 C2
Crowlas Corn 2 C4
Crowle N Lincs 89 C8
Crowle Worcs 50 D4
Crowmarsh Gifford Oxon 39 F6
Crown Corner Suff 57 B6
Crownhill Plym 6 D2
Crownland Suff 56 C4
Crownthorpe Norf 68 D3
Crowntown Corn 2 C5
Crows-an-wra Corn 2 D2
Crowshill Norf 68 D2
Crowsnest Shrops 60 D3
Crowthorne Brack 27 C6
Crowton Ches W 74 B2
Croxall Staffs 63 C5
Croxby Lincs 91 E5
Croxdale Durham 111 F5
Croxden Staffs 75 F7
Croxley Green Herts 40 E3
Croxton Cambs 54 C3
Croxton N Lincs 90 C4
Croxton Norf 67 F8
Croxton Staffs 74 F4
Croxton Kerrial Leics 64 B5
Croxtonbank Staffs 74 F4
Croy Highld 151 G10
Croy N Lanark 119 B7
Croyde Devon 20 F3
Croydon Cambs 54 E4
Croydon London 28 C4
Crubenmore Lodge Highld 138 E2
Cruckmeole Shrops 60 D4
Cruckton Shrops 60 C4
Cruden Bay Aberds 153 E10
Crudgington Telford 61 C6
Crudwell Wilts 37 E6
Crug Powys 48 B3
Crugmeer Corn 4 B4
Crugybar Carms 47 F5
Crulabhig W Isles 154 D6
Crumlin = Crymlyn Caerph 35 E6
Crumpsall Gtr Man 87 D6
Crundale Kent 30 E4
Crundale Pembs 44 D4
Cruwys Morchard Devon 10 C3
Crux Easton Hants 26 D2
Crwbin Carms 33 C5
Crya Orkney 159 H4
Cryers Hill Bucks 40 E1
Crymlyn = Crumlin Caerph 35 E6
Crymlyn Gwyn 83 D6
Crymych Pembs 45 F3
Crynant Neath 34 D1
Crynfryn Ceredig 46 C4
Cuaig Highld 149 C12
Cuan Argyll 124 D3
Cubbington Warks 51 C8
Cubeck N Yorks 100 F4
Cubert Corn 4 D2
Cubley S Yorks 88 D3
Cubley Common Derbys 75 F8
Cublington Bucks 39 B8
Cublington Hereford 49 F6
Cuckfield W Sus 17 B7
Cucklington Som 13 B5
Cuckney Notts 77 B5
Cuckoo Hill Notts 89 E8
Cuddesdon Oxon 39 D6
Cuddington Bucks 39 C7
Cuddington Ches W 74 B3
Cuddington Heath Ches W 73 E8
Cuddy Hill Lancs 92 F4
Cudham London 28 D5
Cudliptown Devon 6 B3
Cudworth S Yorks 88 D4
Cudworth Som 11 C8
Cuffley Herts 41 D6
Cuiashader W Isles 155 B10
Cuidhir W Isles 148 H1
Cuidhtinis W Isles 154 J5
Culbo Highld 151 E9
Culbokie Highld 151 F9
Culburnie Highld 150 G7
Culcabock Highld 151 G9
Culcairn Highld 151 E9
Culcharry Highld 151 F11
Culcheth Warr 86 E4
Culdrain Aberds 152 E5
Culduie Highld 149 D12
Culford Suff 56 B2
Culgaith Cumb 99 B8
Culham Oxon 39 E5
Culkein Highld 156 F3
Culkein Drumbeg Highld 156 F4
Culkerton Glos 37 E6
Cullachie Highld 139 B5
Cullen Moray 152 B5
Cullercoats T&W 111 B6
Cullicudden Highld 151 E9
Cullingworth W Yorks 94 F3
Cullipool Argyll 124 D3
Cullivoe Shetland 160 C7
Culloch Perth 127 C6
Culloden Highld 151 G10
Cullompton Devon 10 D5
Culmaily Highld 151 B11
Culmazie Dumfries 105 D7
Culmington Shrops 60 F4
Culmstock Devon 11 C6
Culnacraig Highld 156 J3
Culnaknock Highld 149 B10
Culpho Suff 57 E6
Culrain Highld 151 B8
Culross Fife 127 F8
Culroy S Ayrs 112 C3
Culsh Aberds 140 E2
Culsh Aberds 153 D8
Culshabbin Dumfries 105 D7
Culswick Shetland 160 J4
Cultercullen Aberds 141 B8
Cults Aberdeen 141 D7
Cults Aberds 152 E5
Cults Dumfries 105 E8
Culverstone Green Kent 29 C7
Culverthorpe Lincs 78 E3
Culworth Northants 52 E3
Culzie Lodge Highld 151 D8
Cumbernauld N Lanark 119 B7
Cumbernauld Village N Lanark 119 B7
Cumberworth Lincs 79 B8
Cuminestown Aberds 153 C8
Cumlewick Shetland 160 L6
Cummersdale Cumb 108 D3
Cummertrees Dumfries 107 C8
Cummingston Moray 152 B1
Cumnock E Ayrs 113 B5
Cumnor Oxon 38 D4
Cumrew Cumb 108 D5
Cumwhinton Cumb 108 D4
Cumwhitton Cumb 108 D5
Cundall N Yorks 95 B7
Cunninghamhead N Ayrs 118 E3
Cunnister Shetland 160 D7
Cupar Fife 129 C5
Cupar Muir Fife 129 C5
Cupernham Hants 14 B4
Curbar Derbys 76 B2
Curbridge Hants 15 C6
Curbridge Oxon 38 D3
Curdridge Hants 15 C6
Curdworth Warks 63 E5
Curland Som 11 C7
Curlew Green Suff 57 C7
Currarie S Ayrs 112 E1
Curridge W Berks 26 B2
Currie Edin 120 C4
Curry Mallet Som 11 B8
Curry Rivel Som 11 B8
Curtisden Green Kent 29 E8
Curtisknowle Devon 6 D5
Cury Corn 3 D5
Cushnie Aberds 153 B7
Cushuish Som 22 F3
Cusop Hereford 48 E4
Cutcloy Dumfries 105 F8
Cutcombe Som 21 F8
Cutgate Gtr Man 87 C6
Cutiau Gwyn 58 C3
Cutlers Green Essex 55 F6
Cutnall Green Worcs 50 C3
Cutsdean Glos 51 F5
Cutthorpe Derbys 76 B3
Cutts Shetland 160 K6
Cuxham Oxon 39 E6
Cuxton Medway 29 C8
Cuxwold Lincs 91 D5
Cwm Bl Gwent 35 D5
Cwm Denb 72 B4
Cwm Swansea 33 E7
Cwm-byr Carms 46 F5
Cwm-Cewydd Gwyn 59 C5
Cwm-cou Ceredig 45 E4
Cwm-Dulais Swansea 33 D7
Cwm-felin-fach Caerph 35 E5
Cwm Ffrwd-oer Torf 35 D6
Cwm-hesgen Gwyn 71 E8
Cwm-hwnt Rhondda 34 D3
Cwm Irfon Powys 47 E7
Cwm-Llinau Powys 58 D5
Cwm-mawr Carms 33 C6
Cwm-parc Rhondda 34 E3
Cwm Penmachno Conwy 71 C8
Cwm-y-glo Carms 33 C6
Cwm-y-glo Gwyn 82 E5
Cwmafan Neath 34 E1
Cwmaman Rhondda 34 E4
Cwmann Carms 46 E4
Cwmavon Torf 35 D6
Cwmbâch Rhondda 34 D4
Cwmbach Carms 32 B3
Cwmbach Carms 33 D5
Cwmbach Powys 48 D2
Cwmbach Powys 48 F3
Cwmbelan Powys 59 F6
Cwmbrân = Cwmbran Torf 35 E6
Cwmbran = Cwmbrân Torf 35 E6
Cwmbrwyno Ceredig 58 F4
Cwmcarn Caerph 35 E6
Cwmcarvan Mon 36 D1
Cwmcych Carms 45 F4
Cwmdare Rhondda 34 D3
Cwmderwen Powys 59 D6
Cwmdu Carms 46 F5
Cwmdu Powys 35 B5
Cwmdu Swansea 33 E7
Cwmduad Carms 46 F2
Cwmdwr Carms 47 F6
Cwmfelin Bridgend 34 F2
Cwmfelin M Tydf 34 D4
Cwmfelin Boeth Carms 32 C2
Cwmfelin Mynach Carms 32 B3
Cwmffrwd Carms 33 C5
Cwmgiedd Powys 34 C1
Cwmgors Neath 33 C8
Cwmgwili Carms 33 C6
Cwmgwrach Neath 34 D2
Cwmhiraeth Carms 46 F2
Cwmifor Carms 33 B7
Cwmisfael Carms 33 C5
Cwmllynfell Neath 33 C8
Cwmorgan Pembs 45 F4
Cwmpengraig Carms 46 F2
Cwmrhos Powys 35 B5
Cwmsychpant Ceredig 46 E3
Cwmtillery Bl Gwent 35 D6
Cwmwysg Powys 34 B2
Cwmyoy Mon 35 B6
Cwmystwyth Ceredig 47 B6
Cwrt Gwyn 58 D3
Cwrt-newydd Ceredig 46 E3
Cwrt-y-cadno Carms 47 E5
Cwrt-y-gollen Powys 35 C6
Cydweli = Kidwelly Carms 33 D5
Cyffordd Llandudno = Llandudno Junction Conwy 83 D7
Cyffylliog Denb 72 D4
Cyfronydd Powys 59 D8
Cymer Neath 34 E2
Cyncoed Cardiff 35 F5
Cynghordy Carms 47 E7
Cynheidre Carms 33 D5
Cynwyd Denb 72 E4
Cynwyl Elfed Carms 32 B4
Cywarch Gwyn 59 C5

D

Dacre Cumb 99 B6
Dacre N Yorks 94 C4
Dacre Banks N Yorks 94 C4
Daddry Shield Durham 109 F8
Dadford Bucks 52 F4
Dadlington Leics 63 E8
Dafarn Faig Gwyn 71 C5
Dafen Carms 33 D6
Daffy Green Norf 68 D2
Dagenham London 41 F7
Daglingworth Glos 37 D6
Dagnall Bucks 40 C2
Dail Beag W Isles 154 C7
Dail bho Dheas W Isles 155 A9
Dail bho Thuath W Isles 155 A9
Dail Mor W Isles 154 C7
Daill Argyll 142 B4
Dailly S Ayrs 112 D2
Dairsie or Osnaburgh Fife 129 C6
Daisy Hill Gtr Man 86 D4
Dalabrog W Isles 148 F2
Dalavich Argyll 125 D5
Dalbeattie Dumfries 106 C5
Dalblair E Ayrs 113 C6
Dalbog Angus 135 B5
Dalbury Derbys 76 F2
Dalby IoM 84 E2
Dalby N Yorks 96 B2
Dalchalloch Perth 132 C4
Dalchalm Highld 157 J12
Dalchenna Argyll 125 E6
Dalchirach Moray 152 E1
Dalchork Highld 157 H8
Dalchreichart Highld 137 C5
Dalchruin Perth 127 C6
Dalderby Lincs 78 C5
Dale Pembs 44 E3
Dale Abbey Derbys 76 F4
Dale Head Cumb 99 C6
Dale of Walls Shetland 160 H3
Dalelia Highld 147 E10
Daless Highld 151 H11
Dalfaber Highld 138 C5
Dalgarven N Ayrs 118 E2
Dalgety Bay Fife 128 F3
Dalginross Perth 127 B6
Dalguise Perth 133 E6
Dalhalvaig Highld 157 D11
Dalham Suff 55 C8
Dalinlongart Argyll 145 E10
Dalkeith Midloth 121 C6
Dallam Warr 86 E3
Dallas Moray 152 C1
Dalleagles E Ayrs 113 C5
Dallinghoo Suff 57 D6
Dallington E Sus 18 D3
Dallington Northants 52 C5
Dallow N Yorks 94 B4
Dalmadilly Aberds 141 C6
Dalmally Argyll 125 C7
Dalmarnock Glasgow 119 C6
Dalmary Stirling 126 E4
Dalmellington E Ayrs 112 D4
Dalmeny Edin 120 B4
Dalmigavie Highld 138 C3
Dalmigavie Lodge Highld 138 B3
Dalmore Highld 151 E9
Dalmuir W Dunb 118 B4
Dalnabreck Highld 147 E9
Dalnacardoch Lodge Perth 132 B4
Dalnacroich Highld 150 F6
Dalnaglar Castle Perth 133 C8
Dalnahaitnach Highld 138 B4
Dalnaspidal Lodge Perth 132 B3
Dalnavaid Perth 133 C7
Dalnavie Highld 151 D9
Dalnawillan Lodge Highld 157 E13
Dalness Highld 131 D5
Dalnessie Highld 157 H9
Dalqueich Perth 128 D2
Dalreavoch Highld 157 J10
Dalry N Ayrs 118 E2
Dalrymple E Ayrs 112 C3
Dalserf S Lanark 119 D8
Dalston Cumb 108 D3
Dalswinton Dumfries 114 F2
Dalton Dumfries 107 B8
Dalton Lancs 86 D2
Dalton N Yorks 95 B7
Dalton N Yorks 101 D6
Dalton Northumb 110 B4
Dalton Northumb 110 D2
Dalton S Yorks 89 E5
Dalton-in-Furness Cumb 92 B2
Dalton-le-Dale Durham 111 E7
Dalton-on-Tees N Yorks 101 D7
Dalton Piercy Hrtlpl 111 F7
Dalveich Stirling 126 B5
Dalvina Lodge Highld 157 E9
Dalwhinnie Highld 138 F2
Dalwood Devon 11 D7
Dalwyne S Ayrs 112 E3
Dam Green Norf 68 F3
Dam Side Lancs 92 E4
Damerham Hants 14 C2
Damgate Norf 69 D7
Damnaglaur Dumfries 104 F5
Damside Borders 120 E4
Danbury Essex 42 D3
Danby N Yorks 103 D5
Danby Wiske N Yorks 101 E8
Dandaleith Moray 152 D2
Danderhall Midloth 121 C6
Dane End Herts 41 B6
Danebridge Ches E 75 C6
Danehill E Sus 17 B8
Danemoor Green Norf 68 D3
Danesford Shrops 61 E7
Daneshill Hants 26 D4
Dangerous Corner Lancs 86 C3
Danskine E Loth 121 C8
Darcy Lever Gtr Man 86 D5
Darenth Kent 29 B6
Daresbury Halton 86 F3
Darfield S Yorks 88 D5
Darfoulds Notts 77 B5
Dargate Kent 30 C4
Darite Corn 5 C7
Darlaston W Mid 62 E3
Darley N Yorks 94 D5
Darley Bridge Derbys 76 C2
Darley Head N Yorks 94 D4
Darlingscott Warks 51 E7
Darlington Darl 101 C7
Darliston Shrops 74 F2
Darlton Notts 77 B7
Darnall S Yorks 88 F4
Darnick Borders 121 F8
Darowen Powys 58 D5
Darra Aberds 153 D7
Darracott Devon 20 F3
Darras Hall Northumb 110 B4
Darrington W Yorks 89 B5
Darsham Suff 57 C8
Dartford Kent 29 B6
Dartford Crossing Kent 29 B6
Dartington Devon 7 C5
Dartmeet Devon 6 B4
Dartmouth Devon 7 D6
Darton S Yorks 88 D4
Darvel E Ayrs 119 F5
Darwell Hole E Sus 18 D3
Darwen Blackburn 86 B4
Datchet Windsor 27 B7
Datchworth Herts 41 C5
Datchworth Green Herts 41 C5
Daubhill Gtr Man 86 D5
Daugh of Kinermony Moray 152 D2
Dauntsey Wilts 37 F6
Dava Moray 151 H13
Davenham Ches W 74 B3
Davenport Green Ches E 74 B5
Daventry Northants 52 C3
David's Well Powys 48 B2
Davidson's Mains Edin 120 B5
Davidstow Corn 8 F3
Davington Dumfries 115 D5
Daviot Aberds 141 B6
Daviot Highld 151 H10
Davoch of Grange Moray 152 C4
Davyhulme Gtr Man 87 E5
Dawley Telford 61 D6
Dawlish Devon 7 B7
Dawlish Warren Devon 7 B7
Dawn Conwy 83 D8
Daws Heath Essex 42 F4
Daw's House Corn 8 F5
Dawsmere Lincs 79 F7
Dayhills Staffs 75 F6
Daylesford Glos 38 B2
Ddôl-Cownwy Powys 59 C7
Ddrydwy Anglesey 82 D3
Deadwater Northumb 116 E2
Deaf Hill Durham 111 F6
Deal Kent 31 D7
Deal Hall Essex 43 E6
Dean Cumb 98 B2
Dean Devon 6 C5
Dean Devon 20 E4
Dean Dorset 13 C7
Dean Hants 15 C6
Dean Som 23 E8
Dean Prior Devon 6 C5
Dean Row Ches E 87 F6
Deanburnhaugh Borders 115 C6
Deane Gtr Man 86 D4
Deane Hants 26 D3
Deanich Lodge Highld 150 C6
Deanland Dorset 13 C7
Deans W Loth 120 C3
Deanscales Cumb 98 B2
Deanshanger Northants 53 F5
Deanston Stirling 127 D6
Dearham Cumb 107 F7
Debach Suff 57 D6
Debden Essex 41 E7
Debden Essex 55 F6
Debden Cross Essex 55 F6
Debenham Suff 57 C5
Dechmont W Loth 120 B3
Deddington Oxon 52 F2
Dedham Essex 56 F4
Dedham Heath Essex 56 F4
Deebank Aberds 141 E5
Deene Northants 65 E6
Deenethorpe Northants 65 E6
Deepcar S Yorks 88 E3
Deepcut Sur 27 D7
Deepdale Cumb 100 F2
Deeping Gate Lincs 65 D8
Deeping St James Lincs 65 D8
Deeping St Nicholas Lincs 66 C2
Deerhill Moray 152 C4
Deerhurst Glos 37 B5
Deerness Orkney 159 H6
Defford Worcs 50 E4
Defynnog Powys 34 B3
Deganwy Conwy 83 D7
Deighton N Yorks 102 D1
Deighton W Yorks 88 C2
Deighton York 96 E2
Deiniolen Gwyn 83 E5
Delabole Corn 8 F2
Delamere Ches W 74 C2
Delfrigs Aberds 141 B8
Dell Lodge Highld 139 C6
Delliefure Highld 151 H13
Delnabo Moray 139 C7
Delnadamph Aberds 139 D8
Delph Gtr Man 87 D7
Delves Durham 110 E4
Delvine Perth 133 E8
Dembleby Lincs 78 F3
Denaby Main S Yorks 89 E5
Denbigh = Dinbych Denb 72 C4
Denbury Devon 7 C6
Denby Derbys 76 E3
Denby Dale W Yorks 88 D3
Denchworth Oxon 38 E3
Dendron Cumb 92 B2
Denel End C Beds 53 F8
Denend Aberds 152 E6
Denford Northants 53 B7
Dengie Essex 43 D5
Denham Bucks 40 F3
Denham Suff 55 C8
Denham Suff 57 B5
Denham Street Suff 57 B5
Denhead Aberds 153 C9
Denhead Fife 129 C6
Denhead of Arbilot Angus 135 E5
Denhead of Gray Dundee 134 F3
Denholm Borders 115 C8
Denholme W Yorks 94 F3
Denholme Clough W Yorks 94 F3
Denio Gwyn 70 D4
Denmead Hants 15 C7
Denmore Aberdeen 141 C8
Denmoss Aberds 153 D6
Dennington Suff 57 C6
Denny Falk 127 F7
Denny Lodge Hants 14 D4
Dennyloanhead Falk 127 F7
Denshaw Gtr Man 87 C7
Denside Aberds 141 E7
Densole Kent 31 E6
Denston Suff 55 D8
Denstone Staffs 75 E8
Dent Cumb 100 F2
Denton Cambs 65 F8
Denton Darl 101 C7
Denton E Sus 17 D8
Denton Gtr Man 87 E7
Denton Kent 31 E6
Denton Lincs 77 F8
Denton N Yorks 94 E4
Denton Norf 69 F5
Denton Northants 53 D6
Denton Oxon 39 D5
Denton's Green Mers 86 E2
Denver Norf 67 D6
Denwick Northumb 117 C8
Deopham Norf 68 D3
Deopham Green Norf 68 E3
Depden Suff 55 D8
Depden Green Suff 55 D8
Deptford London 28 B4
Deptford Wilts 24 F5
Derby Derby 76 F3
Derbyhaven IoM 84 F2
Dereham Norf 68 C2
Deri Caerph 35 D5
Derril Devon 8 D5
Derringstone Kent 31 E6
Derrington Staffs 62 B2
Derriton Devon 8 D5
Derry Hill Wilts 24 B4
Derryguaig Argyll 146 H7
Derrythorpe N Lincs 90 D2
Dersingham Norf 80 D2
Dervaig Argyll 146 F7
Derwen Denb 72 D4
Derwenlas Powys 58 E4
Desborough Northants 64 F5
Desford Leics 63 D8
Detchant Northumb 123 F6
Detling Kent 29 D8
Deuddwr Powys 60 C2
Devauden Mon 36 E1
Devil's Bridge Ceredig 47 B6
Devizes Wilts 24 C5
Devol Invclyd 118 B3
Devonport Plym 6 D2
Devonside Clack 127 E8
Devoran Corn 3 C6
Dewar Borders 121 E6
Dewlish Dorset 13 E5
Dewsbury W Yorks 88 B3
Dewsbury Moor W Yorks 88 B3
Dewshall Court Hereford 49 F6
Dhoon IoM 84 D4
Dhoor IoM 84 C4
Dhowin IoM 84 B4
Dial Post W Sus 17 C5
Dibden Hants 14 D5
Dibden Purlieu Hants 14 D5
Dickleburgh Norf 68 F4
Didbrook Glos 51 F5
Didcot Oxon 39 F5
Diddington Cambs 54 C2
Diddlebury Shrops 60 F5
Didley Hereford 49 F6
Didling W Sus 16 C2
Didmarton Glos 37 F5
Didsbury Gtr Man 87 E6
Didworthy Devon 6 C4
Digby Lincs 78 D3
Digg Highld 149 B9
Diggle Gtr Man 87 D8
Digmoor Lancs 86 D2
Digswell Park Herts 41 C5
Dihewyd Ceredig 46 D3
Dilham Norf 69 B6
Dilhorne Staffs 75 E6
Dillarburn S Lanark 119 E8
Dillington Cambs 54 C2
Dilston Northumb 110 C2
Dilton Marsh Wilts 24 E3
Dilwyn Hereford 49 D6
Dinas Carms 45 F4
Dinas Gwyn 70 D3
Dinas Cross Pembs 45 F2
Dinas Dinlle Gwyn 82 F4
Dinas-Mawddwy Gwyn 59 C5
Dinas Powys V Glam 22 B3
Dinbych = Denbigh Denb 72 C4
Dinbych-Y-Pysgod = Tenby Pembs 32 D2
Dinder Som 23 E7
Dinedor Hereford 49 F7
Dingestow Mon 36 C1
Dingle Mers 85 F4
Dingleden Kent 18 B5
Dingley Northants 64 F4
Dingwall Highld 151 F8
Dinlabyre Borders 115 E8
Dinmael Conwy 72 E4
Dinnet Aberds 140 E3
Dinnington S Yorks 89 F6
Dinnington Som 12 C2
Dinnington T&W 110 B5
Dinorwic Gwyn 83 E5
Dinton Bucks 39 C7
Dinton Wilts 24 F5
Dinwoodie Mains Dumfries 114 E4
Dinworthy Devon 8 C5
Dippen N Ayrs 143 F11
Dippenhall Sur 27 E6
Dipple Moray 152 C3
Dipple S Ayrs 112 D2
Diptford Devon 6 D5
Dipton Durham 110 D4
Dirdhu Highld 139 B6
Dirleton E Loth 129 F7
Dirt Pot Northumb 109 E8
Discoed Powys 48 C4
Diseworth Leics 63 B8
Dishes Orkney 159 F7
Dishforth N Yorks 95 B6
Disley Ches E 87 F7
Diss Norf 56 B5
Disserth Powys 48 D2
Distington Cumb 98 B2
Ditchampton Wilts 25 F5
Ditcheat Som 23 F8
Ditchingham Norf 69 E6
Ditchling E Sus 17 C7
Ditherington Shrops 60 C5
Dittisham Devon 7 D6
Ditton Halton 86 F2
Ditton Kent 29 D8
Ditton Green Cambs 55 D7
Ditton Priors Shrops 61 F6
Divach Highld 137 B7
Divlyn Carms 47 F6
Dixton Glos 50 F4
Dixton Mon 36 C2
Dobcross Gtr Man 87 D7
Dobwalls Corn 5 C7
Doc Penfro = Pembroke Dock Pembs 44 E4
Doccombe Devon 10 F2
Dochfour Ho. Highld 151 H9
Dochgarroch Highld 151 G9
Docking Norf 80 D3
Docklow Hereford 49 D7
Dockray Cumb 99 B5
Dockroyd W Yorks 94 F3
Dodburn Borders 115 D7
Doddinghurst Essex 42 E1
Doddington Cambs 66 E3
Doddington Kent 30 D3
Doddington Lincs 78 B2
Doddington Northumb 123 F5
Doddington Shrops 49 B8
Doddiscombsleigh Devon 10 F3
Dodford Northants 52 C4
Dodford Worcs 50 B4
Dodington S Glos 24 A2
Dodleston Ches W 73 C7
Dods Leigh Staffs 75 F7
Dodworth S Yorks 88 D4
Doe Green Warr 86 F3
Doe Lea Derbys 76 C4
Dog Village Devon 10 E4
Dogdyke Lincs 78 D5
Dogmersfield Hants 27 D5
Dogridge Wilts 37 F7
Dogsthorpe Pboro 65 D8
Dol-fôr Powys 58 D5
Dôl-y-Bont Ceredig 58 F3
Dol-y-cannau Powys 48 E4
Dolanog Powys 59 C7
Dolau Powys 48 C3
Dolau Rhondda 34 F3
Dolbenmaen Gwyn 71 C6
Dolfach Powys 59 D6
Dolfor Powys 59 F8
Dolgarrog Conwy 83 E7
Dolgellau Gwyn 58 C4
Dolgran Carms 46 F3
Dolhelfa Powys 47 B8
Doll Highld 157 J11
Dollar Clack 127 E8
Dolley Green Powys 48 C4
Dollwen Ceredig 58 F3
Dolphin Flint 73 B5
Dolphinholme Lancs 92 D5
Dolphinton S Lanark 120 E4
Dolton Devon 9 C7
Dolwen Conwy 83 D8
Dolwen Powys 59 D6
Dolwyd Conwy 83 D8
Dolwyddelan Conwy 83 F7
Dolyhir Powys 48 D4
Doncaster S Yorks 89 D6
Dones Green Ches W 74 B3
Donhead St Andrew Wilts 13 B7
Donhead St Mary Wilts 13 B7
Donibristle Fife 128 F3
Donington Lincs 78 F5
Donington on Bain Lincs 91 F6
Donington South Ing Lincs 78 F5
Donisthorpe Leics 63 C7
Donkey Town Sur 27 C7
Donnington Glos 38 B1
Donnington Hereford 50 F2
Donnington Shrops 61 D5
Donnington Telford 61 C7
Donnington W Berks 26 C2
Donnington W Sus 16 D2
Donnington Wood Telford 61 C7
Donyatt Som 11 C8
Doonfoot S Ayrs 112 C3
Dorback Lodge Highld 139 C6
Dorchester Dorset 12 E4
Dorchester Oxon 39 E5
Dordon Warks 63 D6
Dore S Yorks 88 F4
Dores Highld 151 H8
Dorking Sur 28 E2
Dormansland Sur 28 E5
Dormanstown Redcar 102 B3
Dormington Hereford 49 E7
Dormston Worcs 50 D4
Dornal S Ayrs 105 B6
Dorney Bucks 27 B7
Dornie Highld 149 F13
Dornoch Highld 151 C10
Dornock Dumfries 108 C2
Dorrery Highld 158 E2
Dorridge W Mid 51 B6
Dorrington Lincs 78 D3
Dorrington Shrops 60 D4
Dorsington Warks 51 E6
Dorstone Hereford 48 E5
Dorton Bucks 39 C6
Dorusduain Highld 136 B2
Dosthill Staffs 63 E6
Dottery Dorset 12 E2
Doublebois Corn 5 C6
Dougarie N Ayrs 143 E9
Doughton Glos 37 E5
Douglas IoM 84 E3
Douglas S Lanark 119 F8
Douglas & Angus Dundee 134 F4
Douglas Water S Lanark 119 F8
Douglas West S Lanark 119 F8
Douglastown Angus 134 E4
Doulting Som 23 E8
Dounby Orkney 159 F3
Doune Highld 156 J7
Doune Stirling 127 D6
Doune Park Aberds 153 B7
Douneside Aberds 140 D3
Dounie Highld 151 B8
Dounreay Highld 157 C12
Dousland Devon 6 C3
Dovaston Shrops 60 B3
Dove Holes Derbys 75 B7
Dovenby Cumb 107 F7
Dover Kent 31 E7
Dovercourt Essex 57 F6
Doverdale Worcs 50 C3
Doveridge Derbys 75 F8
Doversgreen Sur 28 E3
Dowally Perth 133 E7
Dowbridge Lancs 92 F4
Dowdeswell Glos 37 C6
Dowlais M Tydf 34 D4
Dowland Devon 9 C7
Dowlish Wake Som 11 C8
Down Ampney Glos 37 E8
Down Hatherley Glos 37 B5
Down St Mary Devon 10 D2
Down Thomas Devon 6 D3
Downcraig Ferry N Ayrs 145 H10
Downderry Corn 5 D8
Downe London 28 C5
Downend IoW 15 F6
Downend S Glos 23 B8
Downend W Berks 26 B2
Downfield Dundee 134 F3
Downgate Corn 5 B8
Downham Essex 42 E3
Downham Lancs 93 E7
Downham Northumb 122 F4
Downham Market Norf 67 D6
Downhead Som 23 E8
Downhill Perth 133 F7
Downhill T&W 111 D6
Downholland Cross Lancs 85 D4
Downholme N Yorks 101 E6
Downies Aberds 141 E8
Downley Bucks 39 E8
Downside Som 23 E8
Downside Sur 28 D2
Downton Hants 14 E3
Downton Wilts 14 B2
Downton on the Rock Hereford 49 B6
Dowsby Lincs 65 B8
Dowsdale Lincs 66 C2
Dowthwaitehead Cumb 99 B5
Doxey Staffs 62 B3
Doxford Northumb 117 B7
Doxford Park T&W 111 D6
Doynton S Glos 24 B2
Draffan S Lanark 119 E7
Dragonby N Lincs 90 C3
Drakeland Corner Devon 6 D3
Drakemyre N Ayrs 118 D2
Drake's Broughton Worcs 50 E4
Drakes Cross Worcs 51 B5
Drakewalls Corn 6 B2
Draughton N Yorks 94 D3
Draughton Northants 53 B5
Drax N Yorks 89 B7
Draycote Warks 52 B2
Draycott Derbys 76 F4
Draycott Glos 51 F6
Draycott Som 23 D6
Draycott in the Clay Staffs 63 B5
Draycott in the Moors Staffs 75 E6
Drayford Devon 10 C2
Drayton Leics 64 E5
Drayton Lincs 78 F5
Drayton Norf 68 C4
Drayton Oxon 38 E4
Drayton Oxon 52 E2
Drayton Ptsmth 15 D7
Drayton Som 12 B2
Drayton Worcs 50 B4
Drayton Bassett Staffs 63 D5
Drayton Beauchamp Bucks 40 C2
Drayton Parslow Bucks 39 B8
Drayton St Leonard Oxon 39 E5
Dre-fach Carms 33 C7
Dre-fach Ceredig 46 E4
Drebley N Yorks 94 D3
Dreemskerry IoM 84 C4
Dreenhill Pembs 44 D4
Drefach Carms 33 C6
Drefach Carms 46 F2
Drefelin Carms 46 F2
Dreghorn N Ayrs 118 F3
Drellingore Kent 31 E6
Drem E Loth 121 B8
Dresden Stoke 75 E6
Dreumasdal W Isles 148 E2
Drewsteignton Devon 10 E2
Driby Lincs 79 B6
Driffield E Yorks 97 D6
Driffield Glos 37 E7
Drigg Cumb 98 E2
Drighlington W Yorks 88 B3
Drimnin Highld 147 F8
Drimpton Dorset 12 D2
Drimsynie Argyll 125 E7
Drinisiadar W Isles 154 H6
Drinkstone Suff 56 C3
Drinkstone Green Suff 56 C3
Drishaig Argyll 125 D7
Drissaig Argyll 124 D5
Drochil Borders 120 E4
Drointon Staffs 62 B4
Droitwich Spa Worcs 50 C3
Droman Highld 156 D4
Dron Perth 128 C3
Dronfield Derbys 76 B3
Dronfield Woodhouse Derbys 76 B3
Drongan E Ayrs 112 C4
Dronley Angus 134 F3
Droxford Hants 15 C7
Droylsden Gtr Man 87 E7
Druid Denb 72 E4
Druidston Pembs 44 D3
Druimarbin Highld 130 B4
Druimavuic Argyll 130 E4
Druimdrishaig Argyll 144 F6
Druimindarroch Highld 147 C9
Druimyeon More Argyll 143 C7
Drum Argyll 145 F8
Drum Perth 128 D2
Drumbeg Highld 156 F4
Drumblade Aberds 152 D5
Drumblair Aberds 153 D6
Drumbuie Dumfries 113 F5
Drumbuie Highld 149 E12
Drumburgh Cumb 108 D2
Drumburn Dumfries 107 C6
Drumchapel Glasgow 118 B5
Drumchardine Highld 151 G8
Drumchork Highld 155 J13
Drumclog S Lanark 119 F6
Drumderfit Highld 151 F9
Drumeldrie Fife 129 D6
Drumelzier Borders 120 F4
Drumfearn Highld 149 G11
Drumgask Highld 138 E2
Drumgley Angus 134 D4
Drumguish Highld 138 E3
Drumin Moray 152 E1
Drumlasie Aberds 140 D5
Drumlemble Argyll 143 G7
Drumligair Aberds 141 C8
Drumlithie Aberds 141 F6
Drummoddie Dumfries 105 E7
Drummond Highld 151 E9
Drummore Dumfries 104 F5
Drummuir Moray 152 D3
Drummuir Castle Moray 152 D3
Drumnadrochit Highld 137 B8
Drumnagorrach Moray 152 C5
Drumoak Aberds 141 E6
Drumpark Dumfries 107 A5
Drumphail Dumfries 105 C6
Drumrash Dumfries 106 B3
Drumrunie Highld 156 J4
Drums Aberds 141 B8
Drumsallie Highld 130 B3
Drumstinchall Dumfries 107 D5
Drumsturdy Angus 134 F4
Drumtochty Castle Aberds 135 B6
Drumtroddan Dumfries 105 E7
Drumuie Highld 149 D9
Drumuillie Highld 138 B5
Drumvaich Stirling 127 D5
Drumwhindle Aberds 153 E9
Drunkendub Angus 135 E6
Drury Flint 73 C6
Drury Square Norf 68 C2
Dry Doddington Lincs 77 E8
Dry Drayton Cambs 54 C4
Drybeck Cumb 100 C1
Drybridge Moray 152 B4
Drybridge N Ayrs 118 F3
Drybrook Glos 36 C3
Dryburgh Borders 121 F8
Dryhope Borders 115 B5
Drylaw Edin 120 B5
Drym Corn 2 C5
Drymen Stirling 126 F3
Drymuir Aberds 153 D9
Drynoch Highld 149 E9
Dryslwyn Carms 33 B6
Dryton Shrops 61 D5
Dubford Aberds 153 B8
Dubton Angus 135 D5
Duchally Highld 156 H6
Duchlage Argyll 126 F2
Duck Corner Suff 57 E7
Duckington Ches W 73 D8
Ducklington Oxon 38 D3
Duckmanton Derbys 76 B4
Duck's Cross Bedford 54 D2
Duddenhoe End Essex 55 F5
Duddingston Edin 121 B5
Duddington Northants 65 D6
Duddleswell E Sus 17 B8
Duddo Northumb 122 E5
Duddon Ches W 74 C2
Duddon Bridge Cumb 98 F4
Dudleston Shrops 73 F7
Dudleston Heath Shrops 73 F7
Dudley T&W 111 B5
Dudley W Mid 62 E3
Dudley Port W Mid 62 E3
Duffield Derbys 76 E3
Duffryn Neath 34 E2
Duffryn Newport 35 F6
Dufftown Moray 152 E3
Duffus Moray 152 B1
Dufton Cumb 100 B1
Duggleby N Yorks 96 C4
Duirinish Highld 149 E12
Duisdalemore Highld 149 G12
Duisky Highld 130 B4
Dukestown Bl Gwent 35 C5
Dukinfield Gtr Man 87 E7
Dulas Anglesey 82 C4
Dulcote Som 23 E7
Dulford Devon 11 D5
Dull Perth 133 E5
Dullatur N Lanark 119 B7
Dullingham Cambs 55 D7
Dulnain Bridge Highld 139 B5
Duloe Bedford 54 C2
Duloe Corn 5 D7
Dulsie Highld 151 G12
Dulverton Som 10 B4
Dulwich London 28 B4
Dumbarton W Dunb 118 B3
Dumbleton Glos 50 F5
Dumcrieff Dumfries 114 D4
Dumfries Dumfries 107 B6
Dumgoyne Stirling 126 F4
Dummer Hants 26 E3
Dumpford W Sus 16 B2
Dumpton Kent 31 C7
Dun Angus 135 D6
Dun Charlabhaigh W Isles 154 C6
Dunain Ho. Highld 151 G9
Dunalastair Perth 132 D4
Dunan Highld 149 F10
Dunans Argyll 145 D9
Dunball Som 22 E5
Dunbar E Loth 122 B2
Dunbeath Highld 158 H3
Dunbeg Argyll 124 B4
Dunblane Stirling 127 D6
Dunbog Fife 128 C4
Duncanston Highld 151 F8
Duncanstone Aberds 140 B4
Dunchurch Warks 52 B2
Duncote Northants 52 D4
Duncow Dumfries 114 F2
Duncraggan Stirling 126 D4
Duncrievie Perth 128 D3
Duncton W Sus 16 C3
Dundas Ho. Orkney 159 K5
Dundee Dundee 134 F4
Dundeugh Dumfries 113 F5
Dundon Som 23 F6
Dundonald S Ayrs 118 F3
Dundonnell Highld 150 C3
Dundonnell Hotel Highld 150 C3
Dundonnell House Highld 150 C4
Dundraw Cumb 108 E2
Dundreggan Highld 137 C6
Dundreggan Lodge Highld 137 C6
Dundrennan Dumfries 106 E4
Dundry N Som 23 C7
Dunecht Aberds 141 D6
Dunfermline Fife 128 F2
Dunfield Glos 37 E8
Dunford Bridge S Yorks 88 D2
Dungworth S Yorks 88 F3
Dunham Notts 77 B8
Dunham-on-the-Hill Ches W 73 B8

Felingwm uchaf Carms 33 B6
Felinwynt Ceredig 45 D4
Felixkirk N Yorks 102 F2
Felixstowe Suff 57 F6
Felixstowe Ferry Suff 57 F7
Felkington Northumb 122 E5
Felkirk W Yorks 88 C4
Fell Side Cumb 108 F3
Felling T&W 111 C5
Felmersham Bedford 53 D7
Felmingham Norf 81 E8
Felpham W Sus 16 E3
Felsham Suff 56 D3
Felsted Essex 42 B2
Feltham London 28 B2
Felthorpe Norf 68 C4
Felton Hereford 49 E7
Felton N Som 23 C7
Felton Northumb 117 D7
Felton Butler Shrops 60 C3
Feltwell Norf 67 E7
Fen Ditton Cambs 55 C5
Fen Drayton Cambs 54 C4
Fen End W Mid 51 B7
Fen Side Lincs 79 D6
Fenay Bridge W Yorks 88 C2
Fence Lancs 93 F8
Fence Houses T&W 111 D6
Fengate Norf 81 E7
Fengate Pboro 66 E2
Fenham Northumb 123 E6
Fenhouses Lincs 79 E5
Feniscliffe Blackburn 86 B4
Feniscowles Blackburn 86 B4
Feniton Devon 11 E6
Fenlake Bedford 53 E8
Fenny Bentley Derbys 75 D8
Fenny Bridges Devon 11 E6
Fenny Compton Warks 52 D2
Fenny Drayton Leics 63 E7
Fenny Stratford M Keynes 53 F6
Fenrother Northumb 117 E7
Fenstanton Cambs 54 C4
Fenton Cambs 54 B4
Fenton Lincs 77 B8
Fenton Lincs 77 D8
Fenton Stoke 75 E5
Fenton Barns E Loth 129 F7
Fenton Town Northumb 123 F5
Fenwick E Ayrs 118 E4
Fenwick Northumb 110 B3
Fenwick Northumb 123 E6
Fenwick S Yorks 89 C6
Feochaig Argyll 143 G8
Feock Corn 3 C7
Feolin Ferry Argyll 144 G3
Ferindonald Highld 149 H11
Feriniquarrie Highld 148 C6
Ferlochan Argyll 130 E3
Fern Angus 134 C4
Ferndale Rhondda 34 E4
Ferndown Dorset 13 D8
Ferness Highld 151 G12
Ferney Green Cumb 99 E6
Fernham Oxon 38 E2
Fernhill Heath Worcs 50 D3
Fernhurst W Sus 16 B2
Fernie Fife 128 C5
Ferniegair S Lanark 119 D7
Fernilea Highld 149 E8
Fernilee Derbys 75 B7
Ferrensby N Yorks 95 C6
Ferring W Sus 16 D4
Ferry Hill Cambs 66 F3
Ferry Point Highld 151 C10
Ferrybridge W Yorks 89 B5
Ferryden Angus 135 D7
Ferryhill Aberdeen 141 D8
Ferryhill Durham 111 F5
Ferryhill Station Durham 111 F6
Ferryside Carms 32 C4
Fersfield Norf 68 F3
Fersit Highld 131 B7
Ferwig Ceredig 45 E3
Feshiebridge Highld 138 D4
Fetcham Sur 28 D2
Fetterangus Aberds 153 C9
Fettercairn Aberds 135 B6
Fettes Highld 151 F8
Fewcott Oxon 39 B5
Fewston N Yorks 94 D4
Ffair-Rhos Ceredig 47 C6
Ffairfach Carms 33 B7
Ffaldybrenin Carms 46 E5
Ffarmers Carms 47 E5
Ffawyddog Powys 35 C6
Fforest Carms 33 D6
Fforest-fâch Swansea 33 E7
Ffos-y-ffin Ceredig 46 C3
Ffostrasol Ceredig 46 E2
Ffridd-Uchaf Gwyn 83 F5
Ffrith Wrex 73 D6
Ffrwd Gwyn 82 F4
Ffynnon ddrain Carms 33 B5
Ffynnon-oer Ceredig 46 D4
Ffynnongroyw Flint 85 F2
Fidden Argyll 146 J6
Fiddes Aberds 141 F7
Fiddington Glos 50 F4
Fiddington Som 22 E4
Fiddleford Dorset 13 C6
Fiddlers Hamlet Essex 41 D7
Field Staffs 75 F7
Field Broughton Cumb 99 F5
Field Dalling Norf 81 D6
Field Head Leics 63 D8
Fifehead Magdalen Dorset 13 B5
Fifehead Neville Dorset 13 C5
Fifield Oxon 38 C2
Fifield Wilts 25 D6
Fifield Windsor 27 B7
Fifield Bavant Wilts 13 B8
Figheldean Wilts 25 E6
Filands Wilts 37 F6
Filby Norf 69 C7
Filey N Yorks 97 A7
Filgrave M Keynes 53 E6
Filkins Oxon 38 D2
Filleigh Devon 9 B8
Filleigh Devon 10 C2
Fillingham Lincs 90 F3
Fillongley Warks 63 F6
Filton S Glos 23 B8
Fimber E Yorks 96 C4
Finavon Angus 134 D4
Finchairn Argyll 124 E5
Fincham Norf 67 D6
Finchampstead Wokingham 27 C5
Finchdean Hants 15 C8
Finchingfield Essex 55 F7
Finchley London 41 E5
Findern Derbys 76 F3
Findhorn Moray 151 E13
Findhorn Bridge Highld 138 B4
Findo Gask Perth 128 B2
Findochty Moray 152 B4
Findon Aberds 141 E8
Findon W Sus 16 D5
Findon Mains Highld 151 E9
Findrack Ho. Aberds 140 D5
Finedon Northants 53 B7
Fingal Street Suff 57 C6
Fingask Aberds 141 B6
Fingerpost Worcs 50 B2
Fingest Bucks 39 E7
Finghall N Yorks 101 F6
Fingland Cumb 108 D2
Fingland Dumfries 113 C7
Finglesham Kent 31 D7
Fingringhoe Essex 43 B6
Finlarig Stirling 132 F2
Finmere Oxon 52 F4
Finnart Perth 132 D2
Finningham Suff 56 C4
Finningley S Yorks 89 E7
Finnygaud Aberds 152 C5
Finsbury London 41 F6
Finstall Worcs 50 C4
Finsthwaite Cumb 99 F5
Finstock Oxon 38 C3
Finstown Orkney 159 G4
Fintry Aberds 153 C7
Fintry Dundee 134 F4
Fintry Stirling 126 F5
Finzean Aberds 140 E5
Fionnphort Argyll 146 J6
Fionnsbhagh W Isles 154 J5
Fir Tree Durham 110 F4
Firbeck S Yorks 89 F6
Firby N Yorks 96 C3
Firby N Yorks 101 F7
Firgrove Gtr Man 87 C7
Firsby Lincs 79 C7
Firsdown Wilts 25 F7
First Coast Highld 150 B2
Fishbourne IoW 15 E6
Fishbourne W Sus 16 D2
Fishburn Durham 111 F6
Fishcross Clack 127 E7
Fisher Place Cumb 99 C5
Fisherford Aberds 153 E6
Fisher's Pond Hants 15 B5
Fisherstreet W Sus 27 F7
Fisherton Highld 151 F10
Fisherton S Ayrs 112 C2
Fishguard = Abergwaun Pembs 44 B4
Fishlake S Yorks 89 C7
Fishleigh Barton Devon 9 B7
Fishponds Bristol 23 B8
Fishpool Glos 36 B3
Fishtoft Lincs 79 E6
Fishtoft Drove Lincs 79 E6
Fishtown of Usan Angus 135 D7
Fishwick Borders 122 D5
Fiskavaig Highld 149 E8
Fiskerton Lincs 78 B3
Fiskerton Notts 77 D7
Fitling E Yorks 97 F8
Fittleton Wilts 25 E6
Fittleworth W Sus 16 C4
Fitton End Cambs 66 C4
Fitz Shrops 60 C4
Fitzhead Som 11 B6
Fitzwilliam W Yorks 88 C5
Fiunary Highld 147 G9
Five Acres Glos 36 C2
Five Ashes E Sus 18 C2
Five Oak Green Kent 29 E7
Five Oaks Jersey 17
Five Oaks W Sus 16 B4
Five Roads Carms 33 D5
Fivecrosses Ches W 74 B2
Fivehead Som 11 B8
Flack's Green Essex 42 C3
Flackwell Heath Bucks 40 F1
Fladbury Worcs 50 E4
Fladdabister Shetland 160 K6
Flagg Derbys 75 C8
Flamborough E Yorks 97 B8
Flamstead Herts 40 C3
Flamstead End Herts 41 D6
Flansham W Sus 16 D3
Flanshaw W Yorks 88 B4
Flasby N Yorks 94 D2
Flash Staffs 75 C7
Flashader Highld 149 C8
Flask Inn N Yorks 103 D7
Flaunden Herts 40 D3
Flawborough Notts 77 E7
Flawith N Yorks 95 C7
Flax Bourton N Som 23 C7
Flaxby N Yorks 95 D6
Flaxholme Derbys 76 E3
Flaxley Glos 36 C3
Flaxpool Som 22 F3
Flaxton N Yorks 96 C2
Fleckney Leics 64 E3
Flecknoe Warks 52 C3
Fledborough Notts 77 B8
Fleet Hants 15 D8
Fleet Hants 27 D6
Fleet Lincs 66 B3
Fleet Hargate Lincs 66 B3
Fleetham Northumb 117 B7
Fleetlands Hants 15 D6
Fleetville Herts 40 D4
Fleetwood Lancs 92 E3
Flemingston V Glam 22 B2
Flemington S Lanark 119 D6
Flempton Suff 56 C2
Fleoideabhagh W Isles 154 J5
Fletchertown Cumb 108 E2
Fletching E Sus 17 B8
Flexbury Corn 8 D4
Flexford Sur 27 E7
Flimby Cumb 107 F7
Flimwell E Sus 18 B4
Flint = Y Fflint Flint 73 B6
Flint Mountain Flint 73 B6
Flintham Notts 77 E7
Flinton E Yorks 97 F8
Flintsham Hereford 48 D5
Flitcham Norf 80 E3
Flitton C Beds 53 F8
Flitwick C Beds 53 F8
Flixborough N Lincs 90 C2
Flixborough Stather N Lincs 90 C2
Flixton Gtr Man 86 E5
Flixton N Yorks 97 B6
Flixton Suff 69 F6
Flockton W Yorks 88 C3
Flodaigh W Isles 148 C3
Flodden Northumb 122 F5
Flodigarry Highld 149 A9
Flood's Ferry Cambs 66 E3
Flookburgh Cumb 92 B3
Florden Norf 68 E4
Flore Northants 52 C4
Flotterton Northumb 117 D5
Flowton Suff 56 E4
Flush House W Yorks 88 D2
Flushing Aberds 153 D10
Flushing Corn 3 C7
Flyford Flavell Worcs 50 D4
Foals Green Suff 57 B6
Fobbing Thurrock 42 F3
Fochabers Moray 152 C3
Fochriw Caerph 35 D5
Fockerby N Lincs 90 C2
Fodderletter Moray 139 B7
Fodderty Highld 151 F8
Foel Powys 59 C6
Foel-gastell Carms 33 C6
Foffarty Angus 134 E4
Foggathorpe E Yorks 96 F3
Fogo Borders 122 E3
Fogorig Borders 122 E3
Foindle Highld 156 E4
Folda Angus 134 C1
Fole Staffs 75 F7
Foleshill W Mid 63 F7
Folke Dorset 12 C4
Folkestone Kent 31 F6
Folkingham Lincs 78 F3
Folkington E Sus 18 E2
Folksworth Cambs 65 F8
Folkton N Yorks 97 B6
Folla Rule Aberds 153 E7
Follifoot N Yorks 95 D6
Folly Gate Devon 9 E7
Fonthill Bishop Wilts 24 F4
Fonthill Gifford Wilts 24 F4
Fontmell Magna Dorset 13 C6
Fontwell W Sus 16 D3
Foolow Derbys 75 B8
Foots Cray London 29 B5
Forbestown Aberds 140 C2
Force Mills Cumb 99 E5
Forcett N Yorks 101 C6
Ford Argyll 124 E4
Ford Bucks 39 D7
Ford Devon 9 B6
Ford Glos 37 B7
Ford Northumb 122 F5
Ford Shrops 60 C4
Ford Staffs 75 D7
Ford W Sus 16 D3
Ford Wilts 24 B3
Ford End Essex 42 C2
Ford Street Som 11 C6
Fordcombe Kent 29 E6
Fordell Fife 128 F3
Forden Powys 60 D2
Forder Green Devon 7 C5
Fordham Cambs 55 B7
Fordham Essex 43 B5
Fordham Norf 67 E6
Fordhouses W Mid 62 D3
Fordingbridge Hants 14 C2
Fordon E Yorks 97 B6
Fordoun Aberds 135 B7
Ford's Green Suff 56 C4
Fordstreet Essex 43 B5
Fordwells Oxon 38 C3
Fordwich Kent 31 D5
Fordyce Aberds 152 B5
Forebridge Staffs 62 B3
Forest Durham 109 F8
Forest Becks Lancs 93 D7
Forest Gate London 41 F7
Forest Green Sur 28 E2
Forest Hall Cumb 99 D7
Forest Head Cumb 109 D5
Forest Hill Oxon 39 D5
Forest Lane Head N Yorks 95 D6
Forest Lodge Argyll 131 E6
Forest Lodge Highld 139 C6
Forest Lodge Perth 133 B6
Forest Mill Clack 127 E8
Forest Row E Sus 28 F5
Forest Town Notts 77 C5
Forestburn Gate Northumb 117 E6
Foresterseat Moray 152 C1
Forestside W Sus 15 C8
Forfar Angus 134 D4
Forgandenny Perth 128 C2
Forge Powys 58 E4
Forge Side Torf 35 D6
Forgewood N Lanark 119 D7
Forgie Moray 152 C3
Forglen Ho. Aberds 153 C6
Formby Mers 85 D4
Forncett End Norf 68 E4
Forncett St Mary Norf 68 E4
Forncett St Peter Norf 68 E4
Forneth Perth 133 E7
Fornham All Saints Suff 56 C2
Fornham St Martin Suff 56 C2
Forres Moray 151 F13
Forrest Lodge Dumfries 113 F5
Forrestfield N Lanark 119 C8
Forsbrook Staffs 75 E6
Forse Highld 158 G4
Forse Ho. Highld 158 G4
Forsinain Highld 157 E12
Forsinard Highld 157 E11
Forsinard Station Highld 157 E11
Forston Dorset 12 E4
Fort Augustus Highld 137 D6
Fort George Guern 16
Fort George Highld 151 F10
Fort William Highld 131 B5
Forteviot Perth 128 C2
Forth S Lanark 120 D2
Forth Road Bridge Edin 120 B4
Forthampton Glos 50 F3
Fortingall Perth 132 E4
Forton Hants 26 E2
Forton Lancs 92 D4
Forton Shrops 60 C4
Forton Som 11 D8
Forton Staffs 61 B7
Forton Heath Shrops 60 C4
Fortrie Aberds 153 D6
Fortrose Highld 151 F10
Fortuneswell Dorset 12 G4
Forty Green Bucks 40 E2
Forty Hill London 41 E6
Forward Green Suff 56 D4
Fosbury Wilts 25 D8
Fosdyke Lincs 79 F6
Foss Perth 132 D4
Foss Cross Glos 37 D7
Fossebridge Glos 37 C7
Foster Street Essex 41 D7
Fosterhouses S Yorks 89 C7
Foston Derbys 75 F8
Foston Lincs 77 E8
Foston N Yorks 96 C2
Foston on the Wolds E Yorks 97 D7
Fotherby Lincs 91 E7
Fotheringhay Northants 65 E7
Foubister Orkney 159 H6
Foul Mile E Sus 18 D3
Foulby W Yorks 88 C4
Foulden Borders 122 D5
Foulden Norf 67 E7
Foulis Castle Highld 151 E8
Foulridge Lancs 93 E8
Foulsham Norf 81 E6
Fountainhall Borders 121 E7
Four Ashes Staffs 62 F2
Four Ashes Suff 56 B4
Four Crosses Powys 59 D7
Four Crosses Powys 60 C2
Four Crosses Wrex 73 D6
Four Elms Kent 29 E5
Four Forks Som 22 F4
Four Gotes Cambs 66 C4
Four Lane Ends Ches W 74 C2
Four Lanes Corn 3 C5
Four Marks Hants 26 F4
Four Mile Bridge Anglesey 82 D2
Four Oaks E Sus 19 C5
Four Oaks W Mid 62 E5
Four Oaks W Mid 63 F6
Four Roads Carms 33 D5
Four Roads IoM 84 F2
Four Throws Kent 18 C4
Fourlane Ends Derbys 76 D3
Fourlanes End Ches E 74 D5
Fourpenny Highld 151 B11
Fourstones Northumb 109 C8
Fovant Wilts 13 B8
Foveran Aberds 141 B8
Fowey Corn 5 D6
Fowley Common Warr 86 E4
Fowlis Angus 134 F3
Fowlis Wester Perth 127 B8
Fowlmere Cambs 54 E5
Fownhope Hereford 49 F7
Fox Corner Sur 27 D7
Fox Lane Hants 27 D6
Fox Street Essex 43 B6
Foxbar Renfs 118 C4
Foxcombe Hill Oxon 38 D4
Foxdale IoM 84 E2
Foxearth Essex 56 E2
Foxfield Cumb 98 F4
Foxham Wilts 24 B4
Foxhole Corn 4 D4
Foxhole Swansea 33 E7
Foxholes N Yorks 97 B6
Foxhunt Green E Sus 18 D2
Foxley Norf 81 E6
Foxley Wilts 37 F5
Foxt Staffs 75 E7
Foxton Cambs 54 E5
Foxton Durham 102 B1
Foxton Leics 64 E4
Foxup N Yorks 93 B8
Foxwist Green Ches W 74 C3
Foxwood Shrops 49 B8
Foy Hereford 36 B2
Foyers Highld 137 B7
Fraddam Corn 2 C4
Fraddon Corn 4 D4
Fradley Staffs 63 C5
Fradswell Staffs 75 F6
Fraisthorpe E Yorks 97 C7
Framfield E Sus 17 B8
Framingham Earl Norf 69 D5
Framingham Pigot Norf 69 D5
Framlingham Suff 57 C6
Frampton Dorset 12 E4
Frampton Lincs 79 F6
Frampton Cotterell S Glos 36 F3
Frampton Mansell Glos 37 D6
Frampton on Severn Glos 36 D4
Frampton West End Lincs 79 E5
Framsden Suff 57 D5
Framwellgate Moor Durham 111 E5
Franche Worcs 50 B3
Frankby Mers 85 F3
Frankley Worcs 62 F3
Frank's Bridge Powys 48 D3
Frankton Warks 52 B2
Frant E Sus 18 B2
Fraserburgh Aberds 153 B9
Frating Green Essex 43 B6
Fratton Ptsmth 15 E7
Freathy Corn 5 D8
Freckenham Suff 55 B7
Freckleton Lancs 86 B2
Freeby Leics 64 B5
Freehay Staffs 75 E7
Freeland Oxon 38 C4
Freester Shetland 160 H6
Freethorpe Norf 69 D7
Freiston Lincs 79 E6
Fremington Devon 20 F4
Fremington N Yorks 101 E5
Frenchay S Glos 23 B8
Frenchbeer Devon 9 F8
Frenich Stirling 126 D3
Frensham Sur 27 E6
Fresgoe Highld 157 C12
Freshfield Mers 85 D3
Freshford Bath 24 C2
Freshwater IoW 14 F4
Freshwater Bay IoW 14 F4
Freshwater East Pembs 32 E1
Fressingfield Suff 57 B6
Freston Suff 57 F5
Freswick Highld 158 D5
Fretherne Glos 36 D4
Frettenham Norf 68 C5
Freuchie Fife 128 D4
Freuchies Angus 134 C2
Freystrop Pembs 44 D4
Friar's Gate E Sus 29 F5
Friarton Perth 128 B3
Friday Bridge Cambs 66 D4
Friday Street E Sus 18 E3
Fridaythorpe E Yorks 96 D4
Friern Barnet London 41 E5
Friesland Argyll 146 F4
Friesthorpe Lincs 90 F4
Frieston Lincs 78 E2
Frieth Bucks 39 E7
Frilford Oxon 38 E4
Frilsham W Berks 26 B3
Frimley Sur 27 D6
Frimley Green Sur 27 D6
Frindsbury Medway 29 B8
Fring Norf 80 D3
Fringford Oxon 39 B6
Frinsted Kent 30 D2
Frinton-on-Sea Essex 43 B8
Friockheim Angus 135 E5
Friog Gwyn 58 C3
Frisby on the Wreake Leics 64 C3
Friskney Lincs 79 D7
Friskney Eaudike Lincs 79 D7
Friskney Tofts Lincs 79 D7
Friston E Sus 18 F2
Friston Suff 57 C8
Fritchley Derbys 76 D3
Frith Bank Lincs 79 E6
Frith Common Worcs 49 C8
Fritham Hants 14 C3
Frithelstock Devon 9 C6
Frithelstock Stone Devon 9 C6
Frithville Lincs 79 D6
Frittenden Kent 30 E2
Frittiscombe Devon 7 E6
Fritton Norf 68 E5
Fritton Norf 69 D7
Fritwell Oxon 39 B5
Frizinghall W Yorks 94 F4
Frizington Cumb 98 C2
Frocester Glos 36 D4
Frodesley Shrops 60 D5
Frodingham N Lincs 90 C2
Frodsham Ches W 74 B2
Frogden Borders 116 B3
Froggatt Derbys 76 B2
Froghall Staffs 75 E7
Frogmore Devon 7 E5
Frogmore Hants 27 D6
Frognall Lincs 65 C8
Frogshail Norf 81 D8
Frolesworth Leics 64 E2
Frome Som 24 E2
Frome St Quintin Dorset 12 D3
Fromes Hill Hereford 49 E8
Fron Denb 72 C4
Fron Gwyn 70 D4
Fron Gwyn 82 F5
Fron Powys 48 C2
Fron Powys 59 E8
Fron Powys 60 D2
Froncysyllte Wrex 73 E6
Frongoch Gwyn 72 F3
Frostenden Suff 69 F7
Frosterley Durham 110 F3
Frotoft Orkney 159 F5
Froxfield Wilts 25 C7
Froxfield Green Hants 15 B8
Froyle Hants 27 E5
Fryerning Essex 42 D2
Fryton N Yorks 96 B2
Fulbeck Lincs 78 D2
Fulbourn Cambs 55 D6
Fulbrook Oxon 38 C2
Fulford Som 11 B7
Fulford Staffs 75 F6
Fulford York 96 E2
Fulham London 28 B3
Fulking W Sus 17 C6
Full Sutton E Yorks 96 D3
Fullarton Glasgow 119 C6
Fullarton N Ayrs 118 F3
Fuller Street Essex 42 C3
Fuller's Moor Ches W 73 D8
Fullerton Hants 25 F8
Fulletby Lincs 79 B5
Fullwood E Ayrs 118 D4
Fulmer Bucks 40 F2
Fulmodestone Norf 81 D5
Fulnetby Lincs 78 B3
Fulstow Lincs 91 E7
Fulwell T&W 111 D6
Fulwood Lancs 92 F5
Fulwood S Yorks 88 F4
Fundenhall Norf 68 E4
Fundenhall Street Norf 68 E4
Funtington W Sus 15 D8
Funtley Hants 15 D6
Funtullich Perth 127 B6
Funzie Shetland 160 D8
Furley Devon 11 D7
Furnace Argyll 125 E6
Furnace Carms 33 D6
Furnace End Warks 63 E6
Furneaux Pelham Herts 41 B7
Furness Vale Derbys 87 F8
Furze Platt Windsor 40 F1
Furzehill Devon 21 E6
Fyfett Som 11 C7
Fyfield Essex 42 D1
Fyfield Glos 38 D2
Fyfield Hants 25 E7
Fyfield Oxon 38 E4
Fyfield Wilts 25 C6
Fylingthorpe N Yorks 103 D7
Fyvie Aberds 153 E7

G

Gabhsann bho Dheas W Isles 155 B9
Gabhsann bho Thuath W Isles 155 B9
Gablon Highld 151 B10
Gabroc Hill E Ayrs 118 D4
Gaddesby Leics 64 C3
Gadebridge Herts 40 D3
Gaer Powys 35 B5
Gaerllwyd Mon 35 E8
Gaerwen Anglesey 82 D4
Gagingwell Oxon 38 B4
Gaick Lodge Highld 138 F3
Gailey Staffs 62 C3
Gainford Durham 101 C6
Gainsborough Lincs 90 E2
Gainsborough Suff 57 E5
Gainsford End Essex 55 F8
Gairloch Highld 149 A13
Gairlochy Highld 136 F4
Gairney Bank Perth 128 E3
Gairnshiel Lodge Aberds 139 D8
Gaisgill Cumb 99 D8
Gaitsgill Cumb 108 E3
Galashiels Borders 121 F7
Galgate Lancs 92 D4
Galhampton Som 12 B4
Gallaberry Dumfries 114 F2
Gallachoille Argyll 144 E6
Gallanach Argyll 124 C4
Gallanach Argyll 146 E5
Gallantry Bank Ches E 74 D2
Gallatown Fife 128 E4
Galley Common Warks 63 E7
Galley Hill Cambs 54 C4
Galleyend Essex 42 D3
Galleywood Essex 42 D3
Gallin Perth 132 E2
Gallowfauld Angus 134 E4
Gallows Green Staffs 75 E7
Galltair Highld 149 F13
Galmisdale Highld 146 C7
Galmpton Devon 6 E4
Galmpton Torbay 7 D6
Galphay N Yorks 95 B5
Galston E Ayrs 118 F5
Galtrigill Highld 148 C6
Gamblesby Cumb 109 F6
Gamesley Derbys 87 E8
Gamlingay Cambs 54 D3
Gammersgill N Yorks 101 F5
Gamston Notts 77 B7
Ganarew Hereford 36 C2
Ganavan Argyll 124 B4
Garg Corn 5 C8
Ganllwyd Gwyn 71 E8
Gannochy Angus 135 B5
Gannochy Perth 128 B3
Gansclet Highld 158 F5
Ganstead E Yorks 97 F7
Ganthorpe N Yorks 96 B2
Ganton N Yorks 97 B5
Garbat Highld 150 E7
Garbhallt Argyll 125 F6
Garboldisham Norf 68 F3
Garden City Flint 73 C7
Garden Village W Yorks 95 F7
Garden Village Wrex 73 D7
Gardenstown Aberds 153 B7
Garderhouse Shetland 160 J5
Gardham E Yorks 97 E5
Gardin Shetland 160 G6
Gare Hill Som 24 E2
Garelochhead Argyll 145 D11
Garford Oxon 38 E4
Garforth W Yorks 95 F7
Gargrave N Yorks 94 D2
Gargunnock Stirling 127 E6
Garlic Street Norf 68 F5
Garlieston Dumfries 105 E8
Garlinge Green Kent 30 D5
Garlogie Aberds 141 D6
Garmond Aberds 153 C8
Garmony Argyll 147 G9
Garmouth Moray 152 B3
Garn-yr-erw Torf 35 C6
Garnant Carms 33 C7
Garndiffaith Torf 35 D6
Garndolbenmaen Gwyn 71 C5
Garnedd Conwy 83 F7
Garnett Bridge Cumb 99 E7
Garnfadryn Gwyn 70 D3
Garnkirk N Lanark 119 C6
Garnlydan Bl Gwent 35 C5
Garnswllt Swansea 33 D7
Garrabost W Isles 155 D10
Garraron Argyll 124 E4
Garras Corn 3 D6
Garreg Gwyn 71 C7
Garrick Perth 127 C7
Garrigill Cumb 109 E7
Garriston N Yorks 101 E6
Garroch Dumfries 113 F5
Garrogie Lodge Highld 137 C8
Garros Highld 149 B9
Garrow Perth 133 E5
Garryhorn Dumfries 113 E5
Garsdale Cumb 100 F2
Garsdale Head Cumb 100 E2
Garsdon Wilts 37 F6
Garshall Green Staffs 75 F6
Garsington Oxon 39 D5
Garstang Lancs 92 E4
Garston Mers 86 F2
Garswood Mers 86 E3
Gartcosh N Lanark 119 C6
Garth Bridgend 34 E2
Garth Gwyn 83 D5
Garth Powys 47 E8
Garth Shetland 160 H4
Garth Wrex 73 E6
Garth Row Cumb 99 E7
Garthamlock Glasgow 119 C6
Garthbrengy Powys 48 F2
Garthdee Aberdeen 141 D8
Gartheli Ceredig 46 D4
Garthmyl Powys 59 E8
Garthorpe Leics 64 B5
Garthorpe N Lincs 90 C2
Gartly Aberds 152 E5
Gartmore Stirling 126 E4
Gartnagrenach Argyll 144 H6
Gartness N Lanark 119 C7
Gartness Stirling 126 F4
Gartocharn W Dunb 126 F3
Garton E Yorks 97 F8
Garton-on-the-Wolds E Yorks 97 D5
Gartsherrie N Lanark 119 C7
Gartymore Highld 157 H13
Garvald E Loth 121 B8
Garvamore Highld 137 E8
Garvard Argyll 144 D2
Garvault Hotel Highld 157 F10
Garve Highld 150 E6
Garvestone Norf 68 D3
Garvock Aberds 135 B7
Garvock Invclyd 118 B2
Garway Hereford 36 B1
Garway Hill Hereford 35 B8
Gaskan Highld 130 B1
Gastard Wilts 24 C3
Gasthorpe Norf 68 F2
Gatcombe IoW 15 F5
Gate Burton Lincs 90 F2
Gate Helmsley N Yorks 96 D2
Gateacre Mers 86 F2
Gatebeck Cumb 99 F7
Gateford Notts 89 F6
Gateforth N Yorks 89 B6
Gatehead E Ayrs 118 F3
Gatehouse Northumb 116 F3
Gatehouse of Fleet Dumfries 106 D3
Gatelawbridge Dumfries 114 E2
Gateley Norf 81 E5
Gatenby N Yorks 101 F8
Gateshead T&W 111 C5
Gatesheath Ches W 73 C8
Gateside Aberds 140 C5
Gateside Angus 134 E4
Gateside E Renf 118 D4
Gateside Fife 128 D3
Gateside N Ayrs 118 D3
Gathurst Gtr Man 86 D3
Gatley Gtr Man 87 F6
Gattonside Borders 121 F8
Gatwick Airport W Sus 28 E3
Gaufron Powys 47 C8
Gaulby Leics 64 D3
Gauldry Fife 129 B5
Gaunt's Common Dorset 13 D8
Gautby Lincs 78 B4
Gavinton Borders 122 D3
Gawber S Yorks 88 D4
Gawcott Bucks 52 F4
Gawsworth Ches E 75 C5
Gawthorpe W Yorks 88 B3
Gawthrop Cumb 100 F1
Gawthwaite Cumb 98 F4
Gay Street W Sus 16 B4
Gaydon Warks 51 D8
Gayfield Orkney 159 C5
Gayhurst M Keynes 53 E6
Gayle N Yorks 100 F3
Gayles N Yorks 101 D6
Gayton Mers 85 F3
Gayton Norf 67 C7
Gayton Northants 52 D5
Gayton Staffs 62 B3
Gayton le Marsh Lincs 91 F8
Gayton le Wold Lincs 91 F6
Gayton Thorpe Norf 67 C7
Gaywood Norf 67 B6
Gazeley Suff 55 C8
Geanies House Highld 151 D11
Gearraidh Bhailteas W Isles 148 F2
Gearraidh Bhaird W Isles 155 E8
Gearraidh na h-Aibhne W Isles 154 D7
Gearraidh na Monadh W Isles 148 G2
Geary Highld 148 B7
Geddes House Highld 151 F11
Gedding Suff 56 D3
Geddington Northants 65 F5
Gedintailor Highld 149 E10
Gedling Notts 77 E6
Gedney Lincs 66 B4
Gedney Broadgate Lincs 66 B4
Gedney Drove End Lincs 66 B4
Gedney Dyke Lincs 66 B4
Gedney Hill Lincs 66 C3
Gee Cross Gtr Man 87 E7
Geilston Argyll 118 B3
Geirinis W Isles 148 D2
Geise Highld 158 D3
Geisiadar W Isles 154 D6
Geldeston Norf 69 E6
Gell Conwy 83 E8
Gelli Pembs 32 C1
Gelli Rhondda 34 E3
Gellideg M Tydf 34 D4
Gellifor Denb 72 C5
Gelligaer Caerph 35 E5
Gellilydan Gwyn 71 D7
Gellinudd Neath 33 D8
Gellyburn Perth 133 F7
Gellywen Carms 32 B3
Gelston Dumfries 106 D4
Gelston Lincs 78 E2
Gembling E Yorks 97 D7
Gentleshaw Staffs 62 C4
Geocrab W Isles 154 H6
George Green Bucks 40 F3
George Nympton Devon 10 B2
Georgefield Dumfries 115 E5
Georgeham Devon 20 F3
Georgetown Bl Gwent 35 D5
Gerlan Gwyn 83 E6
Germansweek Devon 9 E6
Germoe Corn 2 D4
Gerrans Corn 3 C7
Gerrards Cross Bucks 40 F3
Gestingthorpe Essex 56 F2
Geuffordd Powys 60 C2
Gib Hill Ches W 74 B3
Gibbet Hill Warks 64 F2
Gibbshill Dumfries 106 B4
Gidea Park London 41 F8
Gidleigh Devon 9 F8
Giffnock E Renf 119 D5
Gifford E Loth 121 C8
Giffordland N Ayrs 118 E2
Giffordtown Fife 128 C4
Giggleswick N Yorks 93 C8
Gilberdyke E Yorks 90 B2
Gilchriston E Loth 121 C7
Gilcrux Cumb 107 F8
Gildersome W Yorks 88 B3
Gildingwells S Yorks 89 F6
Gileston V Glam 22 C2
Gilfach Caerph 35 E5
Gilfach Goch Rhondda 34 F3
Gilfachrheda Ceredig 46 D3
Gillamoor N Yorks 102 F4
Gillar's Green Mers 86 E2
Gillen Highld 148 C7
Gilling East N Yorks 96 B2
Gilling West N Yorks 101 D6
Gillingham Dorset 13 B6
Gillingham Medway 29 C8
Gillingham Norf 69 E7
Gillock Highld 158 E4
Gillow Heath Staffs 75 D5
Gills Highld 158 C5
Gill's Green Kent 18 B4
Gilmanscleuch Borders 115 B6
Gilmerton Edin 121 C5
Gilmerton Perth 127 B7
Gilmonby Durham 100 C4
Gilmorton Leics 64 F2
Gilmourton S Lanark 119 E6
Gilsland Northumb 109 C6
Gilsland Spa Cumb 109 C6
Gilston Borders 121 D7
Gilston Herts 41 C7
Gilwern Mon 35 C6
Gimingham Norf 81 D8
Giosla W Isles 154 E6
Gipping Suff 56 C4
Gipsey Bridge Lincs 79 E5
Girdle Toll N Ayrs 118 E3
Girlsta Shetland 160 H6
Girsby N Yorks 102 D1
Girtford C Beds 54 D2
Girthon Dumfries 106 D3
Girton Cambs 54 C5
Girton Notts 77 C8
Girvan S Ayrs 112 E1
Gisburn Lancs 93 E8
Gisleham Suff 69 F8
Gislingham Suff 56 B4
Gissing Norf 68 F4
Gittisham Devon 11 E6
Gladestry Powys 48 D4
Gladsmuir E Loth 121 B7
Glais Swansea 33 D8
Glaisdale N Yorks 103 D5
Glame Highld 149 D10
Glamis Angus 134 E3
Glan Adda Gwyn 83 D5
Glan Conwy Conwy 83 D8
Glan-Conwy Conwy 83 F8
Glan-Duar Carms 46 E4
Glan-Dwyfach Gwyn 71 C5
Glan Gors Anglesey 82 D4
Glan-rhyd Gwyn 82 F4
Glan-traeth Anglesey 82 D2
Glan-y-don Flint 73 B5
Glan-y-nant Powys 59 F6
Glan-y-wern Gwyn 71 D7
Glan-yr-afon Anglesey 83 C6
Glan-yr-afon Gwyn 72 E3
Glan-yr-afon Gwyn 72 E4
Glanaman Carms 33 C7
Glandford Norf 81 C6
Glandwr Pembs 32 B2
Glandy Cross Carms 32 B2
Glandyfi Ceredig 58 E3
Glangrwyney Powys 35 C6
Glanmule Powys 59 E8
Glanrafon Ceredig 58 F3
Glanrhyd Gwyn 70 D3
Glanrhyd Pembs 45 E3
Glanton Northumb 117 C6
Glanton Pike Northumb 117 C6
Glanvilles Wootton Dorset 12 D4
Glapthorn Northants 65 E7
Glapwell Derbys 76 C4
Glas-allt Shiel Aberds 139 F8
Glasbury Powys 48 F3
Glaschoil Highld 151 H13
Glascoed Denb 72 B3
Glascoed Mon 35 D7
Glascoed Powys 59 C8
Glascorrie Aberds 140 E2
Glascote Staffs 63 D6
Glascwm Powys 48 D3
Glasdrum Argyll 130 E4
Glasfryn Conwy 72 D3
Glasgow Glasgow 119 C5
Glashvin Highld 149 B9
Glasinfryn Gwyn 83 E5
Glasnacardoch Highld 147 B9
Glasnakille Highld 149 G10
Glasphein Highld 148 D6
Glaspwll Powys 58 E4
Glassburn Highld 150 H6
Glasserton Dumfries 105 F8
Glassford S Lanark 119 E7
Glasshouse Hill Glos 36 B4
Glasshouses N Yorks 94 C4
Glasslie Fife 128 D4
Glasson Cumb 108 C2
Glasson Lancs 92 D4
Glassonby Cumb 109 F5
Glasterlaw Angus 135 D5
Glaston Rutland 65 D5
Glastonbury Som 23 F7
Glatton Cambs 65 F8
Glazebrook Warr 86 E4
Glazebury Warr 86 E4
Glazeley Shrops 61 F7
Gleadless S Yorks 88 F4
Gleadsmoss Ches E 74 C5
Gleann Tholàstaidh W Isles 155 C10
Gleaston Cumb 92 B2
Gleiniant Powys 59 E6
Glemsford Suff 56 E2
Glen Dumfries 106 B5
Glen Dumfries 106 D2
Glen Auldyn IoM 84 C4
Glen Bernisdale Highld 149 D9
Glen Ho Borders 121 F5
Glen Mona IoM 84 D4
Glen Nevis House Highld 131 B5
Glen Parva Leics 64 E2
Glen Sluain Argyll 125 F6
Glen Tanar House Aberds 140 E3
Glen Trool Lodge Dumfries 112 F4
Glen Village Falk 119 B8
Glen Vine IoM 84 E3
Glenamachrie Argyll 124 C5
Glenbarr Argyll 143 E7
Glenbeg Highld 139 B6
Glenbeg Highld 147 E8
Glenbervie Aberds 141 F6
Glenboig N Lanark 119 C7
Glenborrodale Highld 147 E9
Glenbranter Argyll 125 F7
Glenbreck Borders 114 B3
Glenbrein Lodge Highld 137 C7
Glenbrittle House Highld 149 F9
Glenbuchat Lodge Aberds 140 C2
Glenbuck E Ayrs 113 B7
Glenburn Renfs 118 C4
Glencalvie Lodge Highld 150 C7
Glencanisp Lodge Highld 156 G4
Glencaple Dumfries 107 C6
Glencarron Lodge Highld 150 F3
Glencarse Perth 128 B3
Glencassley Castle Highld 156 J7
Glenceitlein Highld 131 E5
Glencoe Highld 130 D4
Glencraig Fife 128 E3
Glencripesdale Highld 147 F9
Glencrosh Dumfries 113 F7
Glendavan Ho. Aberds 140 D3
Glendevon Perth 127 D8
Glendoe Lodge Highld 137 D7
Glendoebeg Highld 137 D7
Glendoick Perth 128 B4
Glendoll Lodge Angus 134 B2
Glendoune S Ayrs 112 E1
Glenduckie Fife 128 C4
Glendye Lodge Aberds 140 F5
Gleneagles Hotel Perth 127 C8
Gleneagles House Perth 127 D8
Glenegedale Argyll 142 C4
Glenelg Highld 149 G13
Glenernie Moray 151 G13
Glenfarg Perth 128 C3
Glenfarquhar Lodge Aberds 141 F6
Glenferness House Highld 151 G12
Glenfeshie Lodge Highld 138 E4
Glenfield Leics 64 D2
Glenfinnan Highld 147 C11
Glenfoot Perth 128 C3
Glenfyne Lodge Argyll 125 D8
Glengap Dumfries 106 D3
Glengarnock N Ayrs 118 D3
Glengorm Castle Argyll 146 F7
Glengrasco Highld 149 D9
Glenhead Farm Angus 134 C2
Glenhoul Dumfries 113 F6
Glenhurich Highld 130 C2
Glenkerry Borders 115 C5
Glenkiln Dumfries 106 B5
Glenkindie Aberds 140 C3
Glenlatterach Moray 152 C1
Glenlee Dumfries 113 F6
Glenlichorn Perth 127 C6
Glenlivet Moray 139 B7
Glenlochsie Perth 133 B7
Glenloig N Ayrs 143 E10
Glenluce Dumfries 105 D6
Glenmallan Argyll 125 F8
Glenmarksie Highld 150 F6
Glenmassan Argyll 145 E10
Glenmavis N Lanark 119 C7
Glenmaye IoM 84 E2
Glenmidge Dumfries 113 F8
Glenmore Argyll 124 D4
Glenmore Highld 149 D9
Glenmore Lodge Highld 139 D5
Glenmoy Angus 134 C4
Glenogil Angus 134 C4
Glenprosen Lodge Angus 134 C2
Glenprosen Village Angus 134 C3
Glenquiech Angus 134 C4
Glenreasdell Mains Argyll 145 H7
Glenree N Ayrs 143 F10
Glenridding Cumb 99 C5
Glenrossal Highld 156 J7
Glenrothes Fife 128 D4
Glensanda Highld 130 E2
Glensaugh Aberds 135 B6
Glenshero Lodge Highld 137 E8
Glenstockadale Dumfries 104 C4
Glenstriven Argyll 145 F9
Glentaggart S Lanark 113 B8
Glentham Lincs 90 E4
Glentirranmuir Stirling 127 E5
Glenton Aberds 140 B5
Glentress Borders 121 F5
Glentromie Lodge Highld 138 E3
Glentrool Village Dumfries 105 B7
Glentruan IoM 84 B4
Glentruim House Highld 138 E2
Glentworth Lincs 90 F3
Glenuig Highld 147 D9
Glenurquhart Highld 151 E10
Glespin S Lanark 113 B8
Gletness Shetland 160 H6
Glewstone Hereford 36 B2
Glinton Pboro 65 D8
Glooston Leics 64 E4
Glororum Northumb 123 F7
Glossop Derbys 87 E8
Gloster Hill Northumb 117 D8
Gloucester Glos 37 C5
Gloup Shetland 160 C7
Glusburn N Yorks 94 E3
Glutt Lodge Highld 157 F12
Glutton Bridge Staffs 75 C7
Glympton Oxon 38 B4
Glyn-Ceiriog Wrex 73 F6
Glyn-cywarch Gwyn 71 D7
Glyn Ebwy = Ebbw Vale Bl Gwent 35 D5
Glyn-neath = Glynedd Neath 34 D2
Glynarthen Ceredig 46 E2
Glynbrochan Powys 59 F6
Glyncoch Rhondda 34 E4
Glyncorrwg Neath 34 E2
Glynde E Sus 17 D8
Glyndebourne E Sus 17 C8
Glyndyfrdwy Denb 72 E5
Glynedd = Glyn-neath Neath 34 D2
Glynogwr Bridgend 34 F3
Glyntaff Rhondda 34 F4
Glyntawe Powys 34 C2
Gnosall Staffs 62 B2
Gnosall Heath Staffs 62 B2
Goadby Leics 64 E4
Goadby Marwood Leics 64 B4
Goat Lees Kent 30 E4
Goatacre Wilts 24 B5
Goathill Dorset 12 C4
Goathland N Yorks 103 D6
Goathurst Som 22 F4
Gobernuisgach Lodge Highld 156 E7
Gobhaig W Isles 154 G5
Gobowen Shrops 73 F7
Godalming Sur 27 E7
Godley Gtr Man 87 E7
Godmanchester Cambs 54 B3
Godmanstone Dorset 12 E4
Godmersham Kent 30 D4
Godney Som 23 E6
Godolphin Cross Corn 2 C5
Godre'r-graig Neath 34 D1
Godshill Hants 14 C2
Godshill IoW 15 F6
Godstone Sur 28 D4
Godwinscroft Hants 14 E2
Goetre Mon 35 D7
Goferydd Anglesey 82 C2
Goff's Oak Herts 41 D6
Gogar Edin 120 B4
Goginan Ceredig 58 F3
Golan Gwyn 71 C6
Golant Corn 5 D6
Golberdon Corn 5 B8
Golborne Gtr Man 86 E4
Golcar W Yorks 88 C2
Gold Hill Norf 66 E5
Goldcliff Newport 35 F7
Golden Cross E Sus 18 D2
Golden Green Kent 29 E7
Golden Grove Carms 33 C6

Hatherton Ches E 74 E3
Hatherton Staffs 62 C3
Hatley St George Cambs 54 D3
Hatt Corn 5 C8
Hattingley Hants 26 F4
Hatton Aberds 153 E10
Hatton Derbys 63 B6
Hatton Lincs 78 B4
Hatton Shrops 60 E4
Hatton Warks 51 C7
Hatton Warr 86 F3
Hatton Castle Aberds 153 D7
Hatton Heath Ches W 73 C8
Hatton of Fintray Aberds 141 C7
Hattoncrook Aberds 141 B7
Haugh E Ayrs 112 B4
Haugh Gtr Man 87 C7
Haugh Lincs 79 B7
Haugh Head Northumb 117 B6
Haugh of Glass Moray 152 E4
Haugh of Urr Dumfries 106 C5
Haugham Lincs 91 F7
Haughley Suff 56 C4
Haughley Green Suff 56 C4
Haughs of Clinterty Aberdeen 141 C7
Haughton Notts 77 B6
Haughton Shrops 60 B3
Haughton Shrops 61 C5
Haughton Shrops 61 D7
Haughton Shrops 61 E6
Haughton Staffs 62 B2
Haughton Castle Northumb 110 B2
Haughton Green Gtr Man 87 E7
Haughton Moss Ches E 74 D2
Haultwick Herts 41 B6
Haunn Argyll 146 G6
Haunn W Isles 148 G2
Haunton Staffs 63 C6
Hauxley Northumb 117 D8
Hauxton Cambs 54 D5
Havant Hants 15 D8
Haven Hereford 49 D6
Haven Bank Lincs 78 D5
Haven Side E Yorks 91 B5
Havenstreet IoW 15 E6
Havercroft W Yorks 88 C4
Haverfordwest = Hwlffordd Pembs 44 D4
Haverhill Suff 55 E7
Haverigg Cumb 92 B1
Havering-atte-Bower London 41 E8
Haveringland Norf 81 E7
Haversham M Keynes 53 E6
Haverthwaite Cumb 99 F5
Haverton Hill Stockton 102 B2
Hawarden = Penarlâg Flint 73 C7
Hawcoat Cumb 92 B2
Hawen Ceredig 46 E2
Hawes N Yorks 100 F3
Hawes' Green Norf 68 E5
Hawes Side Blackpool 92 F3
Hawford Worcs 50 C3
Hawick Borders 115 C8
Hawk Green Gtr Man 87 F7
Hawkchurch Devon 11 D8
Hawkedon Suff 55 D8
Hawkenbury Kent 18 B2
Hawkenbury Kent 30 E2
Hawkeridge Wilts 24 D3
Hawkerland Devon 11 F5
Hawkes End W Mid 63 F7
Hawkesbury S Glos 36 F4
Hawkesbury Warks 63 F7
Hawkesbury Upton S Glos 36 F4
Hawkhill Northumb 117 C8
Hawkhurst Kent 18 B4
Hawkinge Kent 31 F6
Hawkley Hants 15 B8
Hawkridge Som 21 F7
Hawkshead Cumb 99 E5
Hawkshead Hill Cumb 99 E5
Hawksland S Lanark 119 F8
Hawkswick N Yorks 94 B2
Hawksworth Notts 77 E7
Hawksworth W Yorks 94 E4
Hawksworth W Yorks 95 F5
Hawkwell Essex 42 E4
Hawley Hants 27 D6
Hawley Kent 29 B6
Hawling Glos 37 B7
Hawnby N Yorks 102 F3
Haworth W Yorks 94 F3
Hawstead Suff 56 D2
Hawthorn Durham 111 E7
Hawthorn Rhondda 35 F5
Hawthorn Wilts 24 C3
Hawthorn Hill Brack 27 B6
Hawthorn Hill Lincs 78 D5
Hawthorpe Lincs 65 B7
Hawton Notts 77 D7
Haxby York 96 D2
Haxey N Lincs 89 D8
Hay Green Norf 66 C5
Hay-on-Wye = Y Gelli Gandryll Powys 48 E4
Hay Street Herts 41 B6
Haydock Mers 86 E3
Haydon Dorset 12 C4
Haydon Bridge Northumb 109 C8
Haydon Wick Swindon 37 F8
Haye Corn 5 C8
Hayes London 28 C5
Hayes London 40 F4
Hayfield Derbys 87 F8
Hayfield Fife 128 E4
Hayhill E Ayrs 112 C4
Hayhillock Angus 135 E5
Hayle Corn 2 C4
Haynes C Beds 53 E8
Haynes Church End C Beds 53 E8
Hayscastle Pembs 44 C3
Hayscastle Cross Pembs 44 C4
Hayshead Angus 135 E6
Hayton Aberdeen 141 D8
Hayton Cumb 107 E8
Hayton Cumb 108 D5
Hayton E Yorks 96 E4
Hayton Notts 89 F8
Hayton's Bent Shrops 60 F5
Haytor Vale Devon 7 B5
Haywards Heath W Sus 17 B7
Haywood S Yorks 89 C6
Haywood Oaks Notts 77 D6
Hazel Grove Gtr Man 87 F7
Hazel Street Kent 18 B3
Hazelbank S Lanark 119 E8
Hazelbury Bryan Dorset 12 D5
Hazeley Hants 26 D5
Hazelhurst Gtr Man 87 D7
Hazelslade Staffs 62 C4
Hazelton Glos 37 C7
Hazelton Walls Fife 128 B5
Hazelwood Derbys 76 E3
Hazlemere Bucks 40 E1
Hazlerigg T&W 110 B5
Hazlewood N Yorks 94 D3
Hazon Northumb 117 D7
Heacham Norf 80 D2
Head of Muir Falk 127 F7
Headbourne Worthy Hants 26 F2
Headbrook Hereford 48 D5
Headcorn Kent 30 E2
Headingley W Yorks 95 F5
Headington Oxon 39 D5
Headlam Durham 101 C6
Headless Cross Worcs 50 C5
Headley Hants 26 C3
Headley Hants 27 F6
Headley Sur 28 D3
Headon Notts 77 B7
Heads S Lanark 119 E7
Heads Nook Cumb 108 D4
Heage Derbys 76 D3
Healaugh N Yorks 95 E7
Healaugh N Yorks 101 E5
Heald Green Gtr Man 87 F6
Heale Devon 20 E5
Heale Som 23 E8
Healey Gtr Man 87 C6
Healey N Yorks 101 F6
Healey Northumb 110 D3
Healing NE Lincs 91 C6
Heamoor Corn 2 C3
Heanish Argyll 146 G3
Heanor Derbys 76 E4
Heanton Punchardon Devon 20 F4
Heapham Lincs 90 F2
Hearthstane Borders 114 B4
Heasley Mill Devon 21 F6
Heast Highld 149 G11
Heath Cardiff 22 B3
Heath Derbys 76 C4
Heath and Reach C Beds 40 B2
Heath End Hants 26 C3
Heath End Sur 27 E6
Heath End Warks 51 C7
Heath Hayes Staffs 62 C4
Heath Hill Shrops 61 C7
Heath House Som 23 E6
Heath Town W Mid 62 E3
Heathcote Derbys 75 C8
Heather Leics 63 C7
Heatherfield Highld 149 D9
Heathfield Devon 7 B6
Heathfield E Sus 18 C2
Heathfield Som 11 B6
Heathhall Dumfries 107 B6
Heathrow Airport London 27 B8
Heathstock Devon 11 D7
Heathton Shrops 62 E2
Heatley Warr 86 F5
Heaton Lancs 92 C4
Heaton Staffs 75 C6
Heaton T&W 111 C5
Heaton W Yorks 94 F4
Heaton Moor Gtr Man 87 E6
Heaverham Kent 29 D6
Heaviley Gtr Man 87 F7
Heavitree Devon 10 E4
Hebburn T&W 111 C6
Hebden N Yorks 94 C3
Hebden Bridge W Yorks 87 B7
Hebron Anglesey 82 C4
Hebron Carms 32 B2
Hebron Northumb 117 F7
Heck Dumfries 114 F3
Heckfield Hants 26 C5
Heckfield Green Suff 57 B5
Heckfordbridge Essex 43 B5
Heckington Lincs 78 E4
Heckmondwike W Yorks 88 B3
Heddington Wilts 24 C4
Heddle Orkney 159 G4
Heddon-on-the-Wall Northumb 110 C4
Hedenham Norf 69 E6
Hedge End Hants 15 C5
Hedgerley Bucks 40 F2
Hedging Som 11 B8
Hedley on the Hill Northumb 110 D3
Hednesford Staffs 62 C4
Hedon E Yorks 91 B5
Hedsor Bucks 40 F2
Hedworth T&W 111 C6
Hegdon Hill Hereford 49 D7
Heggerscales Cumb 100 C3
Heglibister Shetland 160 H5
Heighington Darl 101 B7
Heighington Lincs 78 C3
Heights of Brae Highld 151 E8
Heights of Kinlochewe Highld 150 E3
Heilam Highld 156 C7
Heiton Borders 122 F3
Hele Devon 10 D4
Hele Devon 20 E4
Helensburgh Argyll 145 E11
Helford Corn 3 D6
Helford Passage Corn 3 D6
Helhoughton Norf 80 E4
Helions Bumpstead Essex 55 E7
Hellaby S Yorks 89 E6
Helland Corn 5 B5
Hellesdon Norf 68 C5
Hellidon Northants 52 D3
Hellifield N Yorks 93 D8
Hellingly E Sus 18 D2
Hellington Norf 69 D6
Hellister Shetland 160 J5
Helm Northumb 117 E7
Helmdon Northants 52 E3
Helmingham Suff 57 D5
Helmington Row Durham 110 F4
Helmsdale Highld 157 H13
Helmshore Lancs 87 B5
Helmsley N Yorks 102 F4
Helperby N Yorks 95 C7
Helperthorpe N Yorks 97 B5
Helpringham Lincs 78 E4
Helpston Pboro 65 D8
Helsby Ches W 73 B8
Helsey Lincs 79 B8
Helston Corn 3 D5
Helstone Corn 8 F2
Helton Cumb 99 B7
Helwith Bridge N Yorks 93 C8
Hemblington Norf 69 C6
Hemel Hempstead Herts 40 D3
Hemingbrough N Yorks 96 F2
Hemingby Lincs 78 B5
Hemingford Abbots Cambs 54 B3
Hemingford Grey Cambs 54 B3
Hemingstone Suff 57 D5
Hemington Leics 63 B8
Hemington Northants 65 F7
Hemington Som 24 D2
Hemley Suff 57 E6
Hemlington Mbro 102 C3
Hemp Green Suff 57 C7
Hempholme E Yorks 97 D6
Hempnall Norf 68 E5
Hempnall Green Norf 68 E5
Hempriggs House Highld 158 F5
Hempstead Essex 55 F7
Hempstead Medway 29 C8
Hempstead Norf 69 B7
Hempstead Norf 81 D7
Hempsted Glos 37 C5
Hempton Norf 80 E5
Hempton Oxon 52 F2
Hemsby Norf 69 C7
Hemswell Lincs 90 E3
Hemswell Cliff Lincs 90 F3
Hemsworth W Yorks 88 C5
Hemyock Devon 11 C6
Hen-feddau fawr Pembs 45 F4
Henbury Bristol 23 B7
Henbury Ches E 75 B5
Hendon London 41 F5
Hendon T&W 111 D7
Hendre Flint 73 C5
Hendre-ddu Conwy 83 E8
Hendreforgan Rhondda 34 F3
Hendy Carms 33 D6
Heneglwys Anglesey 82 D4
Henfield W Sus 17 C6
Henford Devon 9 E5
Henghurst Kent 19 B6
Hengoed Caerph 35 E5
Hengoed Powys 48 D4
Hengoed Shrops 73 F6
Hengrave Suff 56 C2
Henham Essex 41 B8
Heniarth Powys 59 D8
Henlade Som 11 B7
Henley Shrops 49 B7
Henley Som 23 F6
Henley Suff 57 D5
Henley W Sus 16 B2
Henley-in-Arden Warks 51 C6
Henley-on-Thames Oxon 39 F7
Henley's Down E Sus 18 D4
Henllan Ceredig 46 E2
Henllan Denb 72 C4
Henllan Amgoed Carms 32 B2
Henllys Torf 35 E6
Henlow C Beds 54 F2
Hennock Devon 10 F3
Henny Street Essex 56 F2
Henryd Conwy 83 D7
Henry's Moat Pembs 32 B1
Hensall N Yorks 89 B6
Henshaw Northumb 109 C7
Hensingham Cumb 98 C1
Henstead Suff 69 F7
Henstridge Som 12 C5
Henstridge Ash Som 12 B5
Henstridge Marsh Som 12 B5
Henton Oxon 39 D7
Henton Som 23 E6
Henwood Corn 5 B7
Heogan Shetland 160 J6
Heol-las Swansea 33 E7
Heol Senni Powys 34 B3
Heol-y-Cyw Bridgend 34 F3
Hepburn Northumb 117 B6
Hepple Northumb 117 D5
Hepscott Northumb 117 F8
Heptonstall W Yorks 87 B7
Hepworth Suff 56 B3
Hepworth W Yorks 88 D2
Herbrandston Pembs 44 E3
Hereford Hereford 49 E7
Heriot Borders 121 D6
Hermiston Edin 120 B4
Hermitage Borders 115 E8
Hermitage Dorset 12 D4
Hermitage W Berks 26 B3
Hermitage W Sus 15 D8
Hermon Anglesey 82 E3
Hermon Carms 33 B7
Hermon Carms 46 F2
Hermon Pembs 45 F4
Herne Kent 31 C5
Herne Bay Kent 31 C5
Herner Devon 9 B7
Hernhill Kent 30 C4
Herodsfoot Corn 5 C7
Herongate Essex 42 E2
Heronsford S Ayrs 104 A5
Herriard Hants 26 E4
Herringfleet Suff 69 E7
Herringswell Suff 55 B8
Hersden Kent 31 C6
Hersham Corn 8 D4
Hersham Sur 28 C2
Herstmonceux E Sus 18 D3
Herston Orkney 159 J5
Hertford Herts 41 C6
Hertford Heath Herts 41 C6
Hertingfordbury Herts 41 C6
Hesket Newmarket Cumb 108 F3
Hesketh Bank Lancs 86 B2
Hesketh Lane Lancs 93 E6
Heskin Green Lancs 86 C3
Hesleden Durham 111 F7
Hesleyside Northumb 116 F4
Heslington York 96 D2
Hessay York 95 D8
Hessenford Corn 5 D8
Hessett Suff 56 C3
Hessle E Yorks 90 B4
Hest Bank Lancs 92 C4
Heston London 28 B2
Hestwall Orkney 159 G3
Heswall Mers 85 F3
Hethe Oxon 39 B5
Hethersett Norf 68 D4
Hethersgill Cumb 108 C4
Hethpool Northumb 116 B4
Hett Durham 111 F5
Hetton N Yorks 94 D2
Hetton-le-Hole T&W 111 E6
Hetton Steads Northumb 123 F5
Heugh Northumb 110 B3
Heugh-head Aberds 140 C2
Heveningham Suff 57 B7
Hever Kent 29 E5
Heversham Cumb 99 F6
Hevingham Norf 81 E7
Hewas Water Corn 3 B8
Hewelsfield Glos 36 D2
Hewish N Som 23 C6
Hewish Som 12 D2
Heworth York 96 D2
Hexham Northumb 110 C2
Hextable Kent 29 B6
Hexton Herts 54 F2
Hexworthy Devon 6 B4
Hey Lancs 93 E8
Heybridge Essex 42 D4
Heybridge Essex 42 E2
Heybridge Basin Essex 42 D4
Heybrook Bay Devon 6 E3
Heydon Cambs 54 E5
Heydon Norf 81 E7
Heydour Lincs 78 F3
Heylipol Argyll 146 G2
Heylor Shetland 160 E4
Heysham Lancs 92 C4
Heyshott W Sus 16 C2
Heyside Gtr Man 87 D7
Heytesbury Wilts 24 E4
Heythrop Oxon 38 B3
Heywood Gtr Man 87 C6
Heywood Wilts 24 D3
Hibaldstow N Lincs 90 D3
Hickleton S Yorks 89 D5
Hickling Norf 69 B7
Hickling Notts 64 B3
Hickling Green Norf 69 B7
Hickling Heath Norf 69 B7
Hickstead W Sus 17 B6
Hidcote Boyce Glos 51 E6
High Ackworth W Yorks 88 C5
High Angerton Northumb 117 F6
High Bankhill Cumb 109 E5
High Barnes T&W 111 D6
High Beach Essex 41 E7
High Bentham N Yorks 93 C6
High Bickington Devon 9 B8
High Birkwith N Yorks 93 B7
High Blantyre S Lanark 119 D6
High Bonnybridge Falk 119 B8
High Bradfield S Yorks 88 E3
High Bray Devon 21 F5
High Brooms Kent 29 E6
High Bullen Devon 9 B7
High Buston Northumb 117 D8
High Callerton Northumb 110 B4
High Catton E Yorks 96 D3
High Cogges Oxon 38 D3
High Coniscliffe Darl 101 C7
High Cross Hants 15 B8
High Cross Herts 41 C6
High Easter Essex 42 C2
High Eggborough N Yorks 89 B6
High Ellington N Yorks 101 F6
High Ercall Telford 61 C5
High Etherley Durham 101 B6
High Garrett Essex 42 B3
High Grange Durham 110 F4
High Green Norf 68 D4
High Green S Yorks 88 E4
High Green Worcs 50 E3
High Halden Kent 19 B5
High Halstow Medway 29 B8
High Ham Som 23 F6
High Harrington Cumb 98 B2
High Hatton Shrops 61 B6
High Hawsker N Yorks 103 D7
High Hesket Cumb 108 E4
High Hesleden Durham 111 F7
High Hoyland S Yorks 88 C3
High Hunsley E Yorks 97 F5
High Hurstwood E Sus 17 B8
High Hutton N Yorks 96 C3
High Ireby Cumb 108 F2
High Kelling Norf 81 C7
High Kilburn N Yorks 95 B8
High Lands Durham 101 B6
High Lane Gtr Man 87 F7
High Lane Worcs 49 C8
High Laver Essex 41 D8
High Legh Ches E 86 F5
High Leven Stockton 102 C2
High Littleton Bath 23 D8
High Lorton Cumb 98 B3
High Marishes N Yorks 96 B4
High Marnham Notts 77 B8
High Melton S Yorks 89 D6
High Mickley Northumb 110 C3
High Mindork Dumfries 105 D7
High Newton Cumb 99 F6
High Newton-by-the-Sea Northumb 117 B8
High Nibthwaite Cumb 98 F4
High Offley Staffs 61 B7
High Ongar Essex 42 D1
High Onn Staffs 62 C2
High Roding Essex 42 C2
High Row Cumb 108 F3
High Salvington W Sus 16 D5
High Sellafield Cumb 98 D2
High Shaw N Yorks 100 E3
High Spen T&W 110 D4
High Stoop Durham 110 E4
High Street Corn 4 D4
High Street Kent 18 B4
High Street Suff 56 E2
High Street Suff 57 B8
High Street Suff 57 D8
High Street Green Suff 56 D4
High Throston Hrtlpl 111 F7
High Toynton Lincs 79 C5
High Trewhitt Northumb 117 D6
High Valleyfield Fife 128 F2
High Westwood Durham 110 D4
High Wray Cumb 99 E5
High Wych Herts 41 C7
High Wycombe Bucks 40 E1
Higham Derbys 76 D3
Higham Kent 29 B8
Higham Lancs 93 F8
Higham Suff 55 C8
Higham Suff 56 F4
Higham Dykes Northumb 110 B4
Higham Ferrers Northants 53 C7
Higham Gobion C Beds 54 F2
Higham on the Hill Leics 63 E7
Higham Wood Kent 29 E6
Highampton Devon 9 D6
Highbridge Highld 136 F4
Highbridge Som 22 E5
Highbrook W Sus 28 F4
Highburton W Yorks 88 C2
Highbury Som 23 E8
Highclere Hants 26 C2
Highcliffe Dorset 14 E3
Higher Ansty Dorset 13 D5
Higher Ashton Devon 10 F3
Higher Ballam Lancs 92 F3
Higher Bartle Lancs 92 F5
Higher Boscaswell Corn 2 C2
Higher Burwardsley Ches W 74 D2
Higher Clovelly Devon 8 B5
Higher End Gtr Man 86 D3
Higher Kinnerton Flint 73 C7
Higher Penwortham Lancs 86 B3
Higher Town Scilly 2 E4
Higher Walreddon Devon 6 B2
Higher Walton Lancs 86 B3
Higher Walton Warr 86 F3
Higher Wheelton Lancs 86 B4
Higher Whitley Ches W 86 F4
Higher Wincham Ches W 74 B3
Higher Wych Ches W 73 E8
Highfield E Yorks 96 F3
Highfield Gtr Man 86 D5
Highfield N Ayrs 118 D3
Highfield Oxon 39 B5
Highfield S Yorks 88 F4
Highfield T&W 110 D4
Highfields Cambs 54 D4
Highfields Northumb 123 D5
Highgate London 41 F5
Highlane Ches E 75 C5
Highlane Derbys 88 F5
Highlaws Cumb 107 E8
Highleadon Glos 36 B4
Highleigh W Sus 16 E2
Highley Shrops 61 F7
Highmoor Cross Oxon 39 F7
Highmoor Hill Mon 36 F1
Highnam Glos 36 C4
Highnam Green Glos 36 B4
Highsted Kent 30 C3
Highstreet Green Essex 55 F8
Hightae Dumfries 107 B7
Hightown Ches E 75 C5
Hightown Mers 85 D4
Hightown Green Suff 56 D3
Highway Wilts 24 B5
Highweek Devon 7 B6
Highworth Swindon 38 E2
Hilborough Norf 67 D8
Hilcote Derbys 76 D4
Hilcott Wilts 25 D6
Hilden Park Kent 29 E6
Hildenborough Kent 29 E6
Hildersham Cambs 55 E6
Hilderstone Staffs 75 F6
Hilderthorpe E Yorks 97 C7
Hilfield Dorset 12 D4
Hilgay Norf 67 E6
Hill Pembs 32 D2
Hill S Glos 36 E3
Hill W Mid 62 E5
Hill Brow W Sus 15 B8
Hill Dale Lancs 86 C2
Hill Dyke Lincs 79 E6
Hill End Durham 110 F3
Hill End Fife 128 E2
Hill End N Yorks 94 D3
Hill Head Hants 15 D6
Hill Head Northumb 110 C2
Hill Mountain Pembs 44 E4
Hill of Beath Fife 128 E3
Hill of Fearn Highld 151 D11
Hill of Mountblairy Aberds 153 C6
Hill Ridware Staffs 62 C4
Hill Top Durham 100 B4
Hill Top Hants 14 D5
Hill Top W Mid 62 E3
Hill Top W Yorks 88 C4
Hill View Dorset 13 E7
Hillam N Yorks 89 B6
Hillbeck Cumb 100 C2
Hillborough Kent 31 C6
Hillbrae Aberds 141 B6
Hillbrae Aberds 152 D6
Hillbutts Dorset 13 D7
Hillclifflane Derbys 76 E2
Hillcommon Som 11 B6
Hillend Fife 128 F3
Hillerton Devon 10 E2
Hillesden Bucks 39 B6
Hillesley Glos 36 F4
Hillfarance Som 11 B6
Hillhead Aberds 152 E5
Hillhead Devon 7 D7
Hillhead S Ayrs 112 C4
Hillhead of Auchentumb Aberds 153 C9
Hillhead of Cocklaw Aberds 153 D10
Hillhouse Borders 121 D8
Hilliclay Highld 158 D3
Hillingdon London 40 F3
Hillington Glasgow 118 C5
Hillington Norf 80 E3
Hillmorton Warks 52 B3
Hillockhead Aberds 140 C3
Hillockhead Aberds 140 D2
Hillside Aberds 141 E8
Hillside Angus 135 C7
Hillside Mers 85 C4
Hillside Orkney 159 J5
Hillside Shetland 160 G6
Hillswick Shetland 160 F4
Hillway IoW 15 F7
Hillwell Shetland 160 M5
Hilmarton Wilts 24 B5
Hilperton Wilts 24 D3
Hilsea Ptsmth 15 D7
Hilston E Yorks 97 F8
Hilton Aberds 153 E9
Hilton Cambs 54 C3
Hilton Cumb 100 B2
Hilton Derbys 76 F2
Hilton Dorset 13 D5
Hilton Durham 101 B6
Hilton Highld 151 C10
Hilton Shrops 61 E7
Hilton Stockton 102 C2
Hilton of Cadboll Highld 151 D11
Himbleton Worcs 50 D4
Himley Staffs 62 E2
Hincaster Cumb 99 F7
Hinckley Leics 63 E8
Hinderclay Suff 56 B4
Hinderton Ches W 73 B7
Hinderwell N Yorks 103 C5
Hindford Shrops 73 F7
Hindhead Sur 27 F6
Hindley Gtr Man 86 D4
Hindley Green Gtr Man 86 D4
Hindlip Worcs 50 D3
Hindolveston Norf 81 E6
Hindon Wilts 24 F4
Hindringham Norf 81 D5
Hingham Norf 68 D3
Hinstock Shrops 61 B6
Hintlesham Suff 56 E4
Hinton Hants 14 E3
Hinton Hereford 48 F5
Hinton Northants 52 D3
Hinton S Glos 24 B2
Hinton Shrops 60 D4
Hinton Ampner Hants 15 B6
Hinton Blewett Bath 23 D7
Hinton Charterhouse Bath 24 D2
Hinton-in-the-Hedges Northants 52 F3
Hinton Martell Dorset 13 D8
Hinton on the Green Worcs 50 E5
Hinton Parva Swindon 38 F2
Hinton St George Som 12 C2
Hinton St Mary Dorset 13 C5
Hinton Waldrist Oxon 38 E3
Hints Shrops 49 B8
Hints Staffs 63 D5
Hinwick Bedford 53 C7
Hinxhill Kent 30 E4
Hinxton Cambs 55 E5
Hinxworth Herts 54 E3
Hipperholme W Yorks 88 B2
Hipswell N Yorks 101 E6
Hirael Gwyn 83 D5
Hiraeth Carms 32 B2
Hirn Aberds 141 D6
Hirnant Powys 59 B7
Hirst N Lanark 119 C8
Hirst Northumb 117 F8
Hirst Courtney N Yorks 89 B7
Hirwaen Denb 72 C5
Hirwaun Rhondda 34 D3
Hiscott Devon 9 B7
Histon Cambs 54 C5
Hitcham Suff 56 D3
Hitchin Herts 40 B4
Hither Green London 28 B4
Hittisleigh Devon 10 E2
Hive E Yorks 96 F4
Hixon Staffs 62 B4
Hoaden Kent 31 D6
Hoaldalbert Mon 35 B7
Hoar Cross Staffs 62 B5
Hoarwithy Hereford 36 B2
Hoath Kent 31 C6
Hobarris Shrops 48 B5
Hobbister Orkney 159 H4
Hobkirk Borders 115 C8
Hobson Durham 110 D4
Hoby Leics 64 C3
Hockering Norf 68 C3
Hockerton Notts 77 D7
Hockley Essex 42 E4
Hockley Heath W Mid 51 B6
Hockliffe C Beds 40 B2
Hockwold cum Wilton Norf 67 F7
Hockworthy Devon 10 C5
Hoddesdon Herts 41 D6
Hoddlesden Blackburn 86 B5
Hoddom Mains Dumfries 107 B8
Hoddomcross Dumfries 107 B8
Hodgeston Pembs 32 E1
Hodley Powys 59 E8
Hodnet Shrops 61 B6
Hodthorpe Derbys 76 B5
Hoe Hants 15 C6
Hoe Norf 68 C2
Hoe Gate Hants 15 C7
Hoff Cumb 100 C1
Hog Patch Sur 27 E6
Hoggard's Green Suff 56 D2
Hoggeston Bucks 39 B8
Hogha Gearraidh W Isles 148 A2
Hoghton Lancs 86 B4
Hognaston Derbys 76 D2
Hogsthorpe Lincs 79 B8
Holbeach Lincs 66 B3
Holbeach Bank Lincs 66 B3
Holbeach Clough Lincs 66 B3
Holbeach Drove Lincs 66 C3
Holbeach Hurn Lincs 66 B3
Holbeach St Johns Lincs 66 C3
Holbeach St Marks Lincs 79 F6
Holbeach St Matthew Lincs 79 F7
Holbeck Notts 76 B5
Holbeck W Yorks 95 F5
Holbeck Woodhouse Notts 76 B5
Holberrow Green Worcs 50 D5
Holbeton Devon 6 D4
Holborn London 41 F6
Holbrook Derbys 76 E3
Holbrook S Yorks 88 F5
Holbrook Suff 57 F5
Holburn Northumb 123 F6
Holbury Hants 14 D5
Holcombe Devon 7 B7
Holcombe Som 23 E8
Holcombe Rogus Devon 11 C5
Holcot Northants 53 C5
Holden Lancs 93 E7
Holdenby Northants 52 C4
Holdenhurst Bmouth 14 E2
Holdgate Shrops 61 F5
Holdingham Lincs 78 E3
Holditch Dorset 11 D8
Hole-in-the-Wall Hereford 36 B3
Holefield Borders 122 F4
Holehouses Ches E 74 B4
Holemoor Devon 9 D6
Holestane Dumfries 113 E8
Holford Som 22 E3
Holgate York 95 D8
Holker Cumb 92 B3
Holkham Norf 80 C4
Hollacombe Devon 9 D5
Holland Orkney 159 C5
Holland Orkney 159 F7
Holland Fen Lincs 78 E5
Holland-on-Sea Essex 43 C8
Hollandstoun Orkney 159 C8
Hollee Dumfries 108 C2
Hollesley Suff 57 E7
Hollicombe Torbay 7 C6
Hollingbourne Kent 30 D2
Hollington Derbys 76 F2
Hollington E Sus 18 D4
Hollington Staffs 75 F7
Hollington Grove Derbys 76 F2
Hollingworth Gtr Man 87 E8
Hollins Gtr Man 87 D6
Hollins Green Warr 86 E4
Hollins Lane Lancs 92 D4
Hollinsclough Staffs 75 C7
Hollinwood Gtr Man 87 D7
Hollinwood Shrops 74 F2
Hollocombe Devon 9 C8
Hollow Meadows S Yorks 88 F3
Holloway Derbys 76 D3
Hollowell Northants 52 B4
Holly End Norf 66 D4
Holly Green Worcs 50 E3
Hollybush Caerph 35 D5
Hollybush E Ayrs 112 C3
Hollybush Worcs 50 F2
Hollym E Yorks 91 B7
Hollywood Worcs 51 B5
Holmbridge W Yorks 88 D2
Holmbury St Mary Sur 28 E2
Holmbush Corn 4 D5
Holmcroft Staffs 62 B3
Holme Cambs 65 F8
Holme Cumb 92 B5
Holme N Yorks 102 F1
Holme Notts 77 D8
Holme W Yorks 88 D2
Holme Chapel Lancs 87 B6
Holme Green N Yorks 95 E8
Holme Hale Norf 67 D8
Holme Lacy Hereford 49 F7
Holme Marsh Hereford 48 D5
Holme next the Sea Norf 80 C3
Holme-on-Spalding-Moor E Yorks 96 F4
Holme on the Wolds E Yorks 97 E5
Holme Pierrepont Notts 77 F6
Holme St Cuthbert Cumb 107 E8
Holme Wood W Yorks 94 F4
Holmer Hereford 49 E7
Holmer Green Bucks 40 E2
Holmes Chapel Ches E 74 C4
Holmesfield Derbys 76 B3
Holmeswood Lancs 86 C2
Holmewood Derbys 76 C4
Holmfirth W Yorks 88 D2
Holmhead Dumfries 113 F7
Holmhead E Ayrs 113 B5
Holmisdale Highld 148 D6
Holmpton E Yorks 91 B7
Holmrook Cumb 98 E2
Holmsgarth Shetland 160 J6
Holmwrangle Cumb 108 E5
Holne Devon 6 C5
Holnest Dorset 12 D4
Holsworthy Devon 8 D5
Holsworthy Beacon Devon 9 D5
Holt Dorset 13 D8
Holt Norf 81 D6
Holt Wilts 24 C3
Holt Worcs 50 C3
Holt Wrex 73 D8
Holt End Hants 26 F4
Holt End Worcs 51 C5
Holt Fleet Worcs 50 C3
Holt Heath Worcs 50 C3
Holt Park W Yorks 95 E5
Holtby York 96 D2
Holton Oxon 39 D6
Holton Som 12 B4
Holton Suff 57 B7
Holton cum Beckering Lincs 90 F5
Holton Heath Dorset 13 E7
Holton le Clay Lincs 91 D6
Holton le Moor Lincs 90 E4
Holton St Mary Suff 56 F4
Holwell Dorset 12 C5
Holwell Herts 54 F2
Holwell Leics 64 B4
Holwell Oxon 38 D2
Holwick Durham 100 B4
Holworth Dorset 13 F5
Holy Cross Worcs 50 B4
Holy Island Northumb 123 E7
Holybourne Hants 26 E5
Holyhead = Caergybi Anglesey 82 C2
Holymoorside Derbys 76 C3
Holyport Windsor 27 B6
Holystone Northumb 117 D5
Holytown N Lanark 119 C7
Holywell Cambs 54 B4
Holywell Corn 4 D2
Holywell Dorset 12 D3
Holywell E Sus 18 F2
Holywell = Treffynnon Flint 73 B5
Holywell Northumb 111 B6
Holywell Green W Yorks 87 C8
Holywell Lake Som 11 B6
Holywell Row Suff 55 B8
Holywood Dumfries 114 F2
Hom Green Hereford 36 B2
Homer Shrops 61 D6
Homersfield Suff 69 F5
Homington Wilts 14 B2
Honey Hill Kent 30 C5
Honey Street Wilts 25 C6
Honey Tye Suff 56 F3
Honeyborough Pembs 44 E4
Honeybourne Worcs 51 E6
Honeychurch Devon 9 D8
Honiley Warks 51 B7
Honing Norf 69 B6
Honingham Norf 68 C4
Honington Lincs 78 E2
Honington Suff 56 B3
Honington Warks 51 E7
Honiton Devon 11 D6
Honley W Yorks 88 C2
Hoo Green Ches E 86 F5
Hoo St Werburgh Medway 29 B8
Hood Green S Yorks 88 D4
Hooe E Sus 18 E3
Hooe Plym 6 D3
Hooe Common E Sus 18 D3
Hook E Yorks 89 B8
Hook Hants 26 D5
Hook London 28 C2
Hook Pembs 44 D4
Hook Wilts 37 F7
Hook Green Kent 18 B3
Hook Green Kent 29 C7
Hook Norton Oxon 51 F8
Hooke Dorset 12 E3
Hookgate Staffs 74 F4
Hookway Devon 10 E3
Hookwood Sur 28 E3
Hoole Ches W 73 C8
Hooley Sur 28 D3
Hoop Mon 36 D2
Hooton Ches W 73 B7
Hooton Levitt S Yorks 89 E6
Hooton Pagnell S Yorks 89 D5
Hooton Roberts S Yorks 89 E5
Hop Pole Lincs 65 C8
Hope Derbys 88 F2
Hope Devon 6 F4
Hope Highld 156 B7
Hope Powys 60 D2
Hope Shrops 60 D3
Hope Staffs 75 D8
Hope = Yr Hôb Flint 73 D7
Hope Bagot Shrops 49 B7
Hope Bowdler Shrops 60 E4
Hope End Green Essex 42 B1
Hope Green Ches E 87 F7
Hope Mansell Hereford 36 C3
Hope under Dinmore Hereford 49 D7
Hopeman Moray 152 B1
Hope's Green Essex 42 F3
Hopesay Shrops 60 F3
Hopley's Green Hereford 48 D5
Hopperton N Yorks 95 D7
Hopstone Shrops 61 E7
Hopton Shrops 60 B3
Hopton Shrops 61 B5
Hopton Staffs 62 B3
Hopton Suff 56 B3
Hopton Cangeford Shrops 60 F5
Hopton Castle Shrops 49 B5
Hopton on Sea Norf 69 D8
Hopton Wafers Shrops 49 B8
Hoptonheath Shrops 49 B5
Hopwas Staffs 63 D5
Hopwood Gtr Man 87 D6
Hopwood Worcs 50 B5
Horam E Sus 18 D2
Horbling Lincs 78 F4
Horbury W Yorks 88 C3
Horcott Glos 38 D1
Horden Durham 111 E7
Horderley Shrops 60 F4
Hordle Hants 14 E3
Hordley Shrops 73 F7
Horeb Carms 33 B6
Horeb Carms 33 D5
Horeb Ceredig 46 E2
Horfield Bristol 23 B8
Horham Suff 57 B6
Horkesley Heath Essex 43 B5
Horkstow N Lincs 90 C3
Horley Oxon 52 E2
Horley Sur 28 E3
Hornblotton Green Som 23 F7
Hornby Lancs 93 C5
Hornby N Yorks 101 E7
Hornby N Yorks 102 D1
Horncastle Lincs 79 C5
Hornchurch London 41 F8
Horncliffe Northumb 122 E5
Horndean Borders 122 E4
Horndean Hants 15 C8
Horndon Devon 6 B3
Horndon on the Hill Thurrock 42 F2
Horne Sur 28 E4
Horniehaugh Angus 134 C4
Horning Norf 69 C6
Horninghold Leics 64 E5
Horninglow Staffs 63 B6
Horningsea Cambs 55 C5
Horningsham Wilts 24 E3
Horningtoft Norf 80 E5
Horns Corner Kent 18 C4
Horns Cross Devon 9 B5
Horns Cross E Sus 18 C5
Hornsby Cumb 108 D5
Hornsea E Yorks 97 E8
Hornsea Bridge E Yorks 97 E8
Hornsey London 41 F6
Hornton Oxon 51 E8
Horrabridge Devon 6 C3
Horringer Suff 56 C2
Horringford IoW 15 F6
Horse Bridge Staffs 75 D6
Horsebridge Devon 6 B2
Horsebridge Hants 25 F8
Horsebrook Staffs 62 C2
Horsehay Telford 61 D6
Horseheath Cambs 55 E7
Horsehouse N Yorks 101 F5
Horsell Sur 27 D7
Horseman's Green Wrex 73 E8
Horseway Cambs 66 F4
Horsey Norf 69 B7
Horsford Norf 68 C4
Horsforth W Yorks 94 F5
Horsham W Sus 28 F2
Horsham Worcs 50 D2
Horsham St Faith Norf 68 C5
Horsington Lincs 78 C4
Horsington Som 12 B5
Horsley Derbys 76 E3
Horsley Glos 37 E5
Horsley Northumb 110 C3
Horsley Northumb 116 E4
Horsley Cross Essex 43 B7
Horsley Woodhouse Derbys 76 E3
Horsleycross Street Essex 43 B7
Horsleyhill Borders 115 C8
Horsleyhope Durham 110 E3
Horsmonden Kent 29 E7
Horspath Oxon 39 D5
Horstead Norf 69 C5
Horsted Keynes W Sus 17 B7
Horton Bucks 40 C2
Horton Dorset 13 D8
Horton Lancs 93 D8
Horton Northants 53 D6
Horton S Glos 36 F4
Horton Shrops 60 B4
Horton Som 11 C8
Horton Staffs 75 D6
Horton Swansea 33 F5
Horton Wilts 25 C5
Horton Windsor 27 B8
Horton-cum-Studley Oxon 39 C5
Horton Green Ches W 73 E8
Horton Heath Hants 15 C5
Horton in Ribblesdale N Yorks 93 B8
Horton Kirby Kent 29 C6
Hortonlane Shrops 60 C4
Horwich Gtr Man 86 C4
Horwich End Derbys 87 F8
Horwood Devon 9 B7
Hose Leics 64 B4
Hoselaw Borders 122 F4
Hoses Cumb 98 E4
Hosh Perth 127 B7
Hosta W Isles 148 A2
Hoswick Shetland 160 L6
Hotham E Yorks 96 F4
Hothfield Kent 30 E3
Hoton Leics 64 B2
Houbie Shetland 160 D8
Houdston S Ayrs 112 E1
Hough Ches E 74 D4
Hough Ches E 75 B5
Hough Green Halton 86 F2
Hough-on-the-Hill Lincs 78 E2
Hougham Lincs 77 E8
Houghton Cambs 54 B3
Houghton Cumb 108 D4
Houghton Hants 25 F8
Houghton Pembs 44 E4
Houghton W Sus 16 C4
Houghton Conquest C Beds 53 E8
Houghton Green E Sus 19 C6
Houghton Green Warr 86 E4
Houghton-le-Side Darl 101 B7
Houghton-Le-Spring T&W 111 E6
Houghton on the Hill Leics 64 D3
Houghton Regis C Beds 40 B3
Houghton St Giles Norf 80 D5
Houlland Shetland 160 F7
Houlland Shetland 160 H5
Houlsyke N Yorks 103 D5
Hound Hants 15 D5
Hound Green Hants 26 D5
Houndslow Borders 122 E2
Houndwood Borders 122 C4
Hounslow London 28 B2
Hounslow Green Essex 42 C2
Housay Shetland 160 F8
House of Daviot Highld 151 G10
House of Glenmuick Aberds 140 E2
Housetter Shetland 160 E5
Houss Shetland 160 K5
Houston Renfs 118 C4
Houstry Highld 158 G3
Houton Orkney 159 H4
Hove Brighton 17 D6
Hoveringham Notts 77 E6
Hoveton Norf 69 C6
Hovingham N Yorks 96 B2
How Cumb 108 D5
How Caple Hereford 49 F8
How End C Beds 53 E8
How Green Kent 29 E5
How Hill Norf 69 C6
Howbrook S Yorks 88 E4
Howden Borders 116 B2
Howden E Yorks 89 B8
Howden-le-Wear Durham 110 F4
Howe Highld 158 D5
Howe N Yorks 101 F8
Howe Norf 69 D5
Howe Bridge Gtr Man 86 D4
Howe Green Essex 42 D3
Howe of Teuchar Aberds 153 D7
Howe Street Essex 42 C2
Howe Street Essex 55 F7
Howell Lincs 78 E4
Howey Powys 48 D2
Howgate Midloth 120 D5
Howick Northumb 117 C8
Howle Durham 101 B5
Howle Telford 61 B6
Howlett End Essex 55 F6
Howley Som 11 D7
Hownam Borders 116 C3
Hownam Mains Borders 116 B3
Howpasley Borders 115 D6
Howsham N Lincs 90 D4
Howsham N Yorks 96 C3
Howslack Dumfries 114 D3
Howtel Northumb 122 F4
Howton Hereford 35 B8
Howtown Cumb 99 C6
Howwood Renfs 118 C3
Hoxne Suff 57 B5
Hoy Orkney 159 H3
Hoylake Mers 85 F3
Hoyland S Yorks 88 D4
Hoylandswaine S Yorks 88 D3
Hubberholme N Yorks 94 B2
Hubbert's Bridge Lincs 79 E5
Huby N Yorks 95 C8
Huby N Yorks 95 E5
Hucclecote Glos 37 C5
Hucking Kent 30 D2
Hucknall Notts 76 E5
Huddersfield W Yorks 88 C2
Huddington Worcs 50 D4
Hudswell N Yorks 101 D6
Huggate E Yorks 96 D4
Hugglescote Leics 63 C8
Hugh Town Scilly 2 E4
Hughenden Valley Bucks 40 E1
Hughley Shrops 61 E5
Huish Devon 9 C7
Huish Wilts 25 C6
Huish Champflower Som 11 B5
Huish Episcopi Som 12 B2
Huisinis W Isles 154 F4
Hulcott Bucks 40 C1
Hulland Derbys 76 E2
Hulland Ward Derbys 76 E2
Hullavington Wilts 37 F5
Hullbridge Essex 42 E4
Hulme Gtr Man 87 E6

Kirkton of Auchterhouse Angus 134 F3
Kirkton of Auchterless Aberds 153 D7
Kirkton of Barevan Highld 151 G11
Kirkton of Bourtie Aberds 141 B7
Kirkton of Collace Perth 134 F1
Kirkton of Craig Angus 135 D7
Kirkton of Culsalmond Aberds 153 E6
Kirkton of Durris Aberds 141 E6
Kirkton of Glenbuchat Aberds 140 C2
Kirkton of Glenisla Angus 134 C2
Kirkton of Kingoldrum Angus 134 D3
Kirkton of Largo Fife 129 D6
Kirkton of Lethendy Perth 133 E8
Kirkton of Logie Buchan Aberds 141 B8
Kirkton of Maryculter Aberds 141 E7
Kirkton of Menmuir Angus 135 C5
Kirkton of Monikie Angus 135 F5
Kirkton of Oyne Aberds 141 B5
Kirkton of Rayne Aberds 153 F6
Kirkton of Skene Aberds 141 D7
Kirkton of Tough Aberds 140 C5
Kirktonhill Borders 121 D7
Kirktown Aberds 153 C10
Kirktown of Alvah Aberds 153 B6
Kirktown of Deskford Moray 152 B5
Kirktown of Fetteresso Aberds 141 F7
Kirktown of Mortlach Moray 152 E3
Kirktown of Slains Aberds 141 B9
Kirkurd Borders 120 E4
Kirkwall Orkney 159 G5
Kirkwhelpington Northumb 117 F5
Kirmington N Lincs 90 C5
Kirmond le Mire Lincs 91 E5
Kirn Argyll 145 F10
Kirriemuir Angus 134 D3
Kirstead Green Norf 69 E5
Kirtlebridge Dumfries 108 B2
Kirtleton Dumfries 115 F5
Kirtling Cambs 55 D7
Kirtling Green Cambs 55 D7
Kirtlington Oxon 38 C4
Kirtomy Highld 157 C10
Kirton Lincs 79 F6
Kirton Notts 77 C6
Kirton Suff 57 F6
Kirton End Lincs 79 E5
Kirton Holme Lincs 79 E5
Kirton in Lindsey N Lincs 90 E3
Kislingbury Northants 52 D4
Kites Hardwick Warks 52 C2
Kittisford Som 11 B5
Kittle Swansea 33 F6
Kitt's Green W Mid 63 F5
Kitt's Moss Gtr Man 87 F6
Kittybrewster Aberdeen 141 D8
Kitwood Hants 26 F4
Kivernoll Hereford 49 F6
Kiveton Park S Yorks 89 F5
Knaith Lincs 90 F2
Knaith Park Lincs 90 F2
Knap Corner Dorset 13 B6
Knaphill Sur 27 D7
Knapp Perth 134 F2
Knapp Som 11 B8
Knapthorpe Notts 77 D7
Knapton Norf 81 D9
Knapton York 95 D8
Knapton Green Hereford 49 D6
Knapwell Cambs 54 C4
Knaresborough N Yorks 95 D6
Knarsdale Northumb 109 D6
Knauchland Moray 152 C5
Knaven Aberds 153 D8
Knayton N Yorks 102 F2
Knebworth Herts 41 B5
Knedlington E Yorks 89 B8
Kneesall Notts 77 C7
Kneesworth Cambs 54 E4
Kneeton Notts 77 E7
Knelston Swansea 33 F5
Knenhall Staffs 75 F6
Knettishall Suff 68 F2
Knightacott Devon 21 F5
Knightcote Warks 51 D8
Knightley Dale Staffs 62 B2
Knighton Devon 6 E3
Knighton Leicester 64 D2
Knighton = Tref-Y-Clawdd Powys 48 B4
Knighton Staffs 61 B7
Knighton Staffs 74 E4
Knightswood Glasgow 118 C5
Knightwick Worcs 50 D2
Knill Hereford 48 C4
Knipton Leics 77 F8
Knitsley Durham 110 E4
Kniveton Derbys 76 D2
Knock Argyll 147 H8
Knock Cumb 100 B1
Knock Moray 152 C5
Knockally Highld 158 H3
Knockan Highld 156 H5
Knockandhu Moray 139 B8
Knockando Moray 152 D1
Knockando Ho. Moray 152 D2
Knockbain Highld 151 F9
Knockbreck Highld 148 B7
Knockbrex Dumfries 106 E2
Knockdee Highld 158 D3
Knockdolian S Ayrs 104 A5
Knockenkelly N Ayrs 143 F11
Knockentiber E Ayrs 118 F3
Knockespock Ho. Aberds 140 B4
Knockfarrel Highld 151 F8
Knockglass Dumfries 104 D4
Knockholt Kent 29 D5
Knockholt Pound Kent 29 D5
Knockie Lodge Highld 137 C7
Knockin Shrops 60 B3
Knockinlaw E Ayrs 118 F4
Knocklearn Dumfries 106 B4
Knocknaha Argyll 143 G7
Knocknain Dumfries 104 C3
Knockrome Argyll 144 F4
Knocksharry IoM 84 D2
Knodishall Suff 57 C8
Knolls Green Ches E 74 B5
Knolton Wrex 73 F7
Knolton Bryn Wrex 73 F7
Knook Wilts 24 E4
Knossington Leics 64 D5
Knott End-on-Sea Lancs 92 E3
Knotting Bedford 53 C8
Knotting Green Bedford 53 C8
Knottingley W Yorks 89 B6
Knotts Cumb 99 B6
Knotts Lancs 93 D7
Knotty Ash Mers 86 E2
Knotty Green Bucks 40 E2
Knowbury Shrops 49 B7
Knowe Dumfries 105 B7
Knowehead Dumfries 113 E6
Knowes of Elrick Aberds 152 C6
Knowesgate Northumb 117 F5
Knoweton N Lanark 119 D7
Knowhead Aberds 153 C9
Knowl Hill Windsor 27 B6
Knowle Bristol 23 B8
Knowle Devon 10 D2
Knowle Devon 11 F5
Knowle Devon 20 F3
Knowle Shrops 49 B7
Knowle W Mid 51 B6
Knowle Green Lancs 93 F6
Knowle Park W Yorks 94 E3
Knowlton Dorset 13 C8
Knowlton Kent 31 D6
Knowsley Mers 86 E2
Knowstone Devon 10 B3
Knox Bridge Kent 29 E8
Knucklas Powys 48 B4
Knuston Northants 53 C7
Knutsford Ches E 74 B4
Knutton Staffs 74 E5
Knypersley Staffs 75 D5
Kuggar Corn 3 E6
Kyle of Lochalsh Highld 149 F12
Kyleakin Highld 149 F12
Kylerhea Highld 149 F12
Kylesknoydart Highld 147 B11
Kylesku Highld 156 F5
Kylesmorar Highld 147 B11
Kylestrome Highld 156 F5
Kyllachy House Highld 138 B3
Kynaston Shrops 60 B3
Kynnersley Telford 61 C6
Kyre Magna Worcs 49 C8

L

La Fontenelle Guern 16
La Planque Guern 16
Labost W Isles 155 C7
Lacasaidh W Isles 155 E8
Lacasdal W Isles 155 D9
Laceby NE Lincs 91 D6
Lacey Green Bucks 39 E8
Lach Dennis Ches W 74 B4
Lackford Suff 55 B8
Lacock Wilts 24 C4
Ladbroke Warks 52 D2
Laddingford Kent 29 E7
Lade Bank Lincs 79 D6
Ladock Corn 4 D3
Lady Orkney 159 D7
Ladybank Fife 128 C5
Ladykirk Borders 122 E4
Ladysford Aberds 153 B9
Laga Highld 147 E9
Lagalochan Argyll 124 D4
Lagavulin Argyll 142 D5
Lagg Argyll 144 F4
Lagg N Ayrs 143 F10
Laggan Argyll 142 C3
Laggan Highld 137 E5
Laggan Highld 138 E2
Laggan Highld 147 D10
Laggan S Ayrs 112 F2
Lagganulva Argyll 146 G7
Laide Highld 155 H13
Laigh Fenwick E Ayrs 118 E4
Laigh Glengall S Ayrs 112 C3
Laighmuir E Ayrs 118 E4
Laindon Essex 42 F2
Lair Highld 150 G3
Lairg Highld 157 J8
Lairg Lodge Highld 157 J8
Lairg Muir Highld 157 J8
Lairgmore Highld 151 H8
Laisterdyke W Yorks 94 F4
Laithes Cumb 108 F4
Lake IoW 15 F6
Lake Wilts 25 F6
Lakenham Norf 68 D5
Lakenheath Suff 67 F7
Lakesend Norf 66 E5
Lakeside Cumb 99 F5
Laleham Sur 27 C8
Laleston Bridgend 21 B7
Lamarsh Essex 56 F2
Lamas Norf 81 E8
Lambden Borders 122 E3
Lamberhurst Kent 18 B3
Lamberhurst Quarter Kent 18 B3
Lamberton Borders 123 D5
Lambeth London 28 B4
Lambhill Glasgow 119 C5
Lambley Northumb 109 D6
Lambley Notts 77 E6
Lamborough Hill Oxon 38 D4
Lambourn W Berks 25 B8
Lambourne End Essex 41 E7
Lambs Green W Sus 28 F3
Lambston Pembs 44 D4
Lambton T&W 111 D5
Lamerton Devon 6 B2
Lamesley T&W 111 D5
Laminess Orkney 159 E7
Lamington Highld 151 D10
Lamington S Lanark 120 F2
Lamlash N Ayrs 143 E11
Lamloch Dumfries 112 E5
Lamonby Cumb 108 F4
Lamorna Corn 2 D3
Lamorran Corn 3 B7
Lampardbrook Suff 57 C6
Lampeter = Llanbedr Pont Steffan Ceredig 46 E4
Lampeter Velfrey Pembs 32 C2
Lamphey Pembs 32 D1
Lamplugh Cumb 98 B2
Lamport Northants 53 B5
Lamyatt Som 23 F8
Lana Devon 8 E5
Lanark S Lanark 119 E8
Lancaster Lancs 92 C4
Lanchester Durham 110 E4
Lancing W Sus 17 D5
Landbeach Cambs 55 C5
Landcross Devon 9 B6
Landerberry Aberds 141 D6
Landford Wilts 14 C3
Landford Manor Wilts 14 B3
Landimore Swansea 33 E5
Landkey Devon 20 F4
Landore Swansea 33 E7
Landrake Corn 5 C8
Landscove Devon 7 C5
Landshipping Pembs 32 C1
Landshipping Quay Pembs 32 C1
Landulph Corn 6 C2
Landwade Suff 55 C7
Lane Corn 4 C3
Lane End Bucks 39 E8
Lane End Cumb 98 E3
Lane End Dorset 13 E6
Lane End Hants 15 B6
Lane End IoW 15 F7
Lane End Lancs 93 E8
Lane Ends Lancs 93 D7
Lane Ends Lancs 93 F7
Lane Ends N Yorks 94 E2
Lane Head Derbys 75 B8
Lane Head Durham 101 C6
Lane Head Gtr Man 86 E4
Lane Head W Yorks 88 D2
Lane Side Lancs 87 B5
Laneast Corn 8 F4
Laneham Notts 77 B8
Lanehead Durham 109 E8
Lanehead Northumb 116 F3
Lanercost Cumb 109 C5
Laneshaw Bridge Lancs 94 E2
Lanfach Caerph 35 E6
Langar Notts 77 F7
Langbank Renfs 118 B3
Langbar N Yorks 94 D3
Langburnshiels Borders 115 D8
Langcliffe N Yorks 93 C8
Langdale Highld 157 E9
Langdale End N Yorks 103 E7
Langdon Corn 8 F5
Langdon Beck Durham 109 F8
Langdon Hills Essex 42 F2
Langdyke Fife 128 D5
Langenhoe Essex 43 C6
Langford C Beds 54 E2
Langford Devon 10 D5
Langford Essex 42 D4
Langford Notts 77 D8
Langford Oxon 38 D2
Langford Budville Som 11 B6
Langham Essex 56 F4
Langham Norf 81 C6
Langham Rutland 64 C5
Langham Suff 56 C3
Langhaugh Borders 120 F5
Langho Lancs 93 F7
Langholm Dumfries 115 F6
Langleeford Northumb 117 B5
Langley Ches E 75 B6
Langley Hants 14 D5
Langley Herts 41 B5
Langley Kent 30 D2
Langley Northumb 109 C8
Langley Slough 27 B8
Langley W Sus 16 B2
Langley Warks 51 C6
Langley Burrell Wilts 24 B4
Langley Common Derbys 76 F2
Langley Heath Kent 30 D2
Langley Lower Green Essex 54 F5
Langley Marsh Som 11 B5
Langley Park Durham 110 E5
Langley Street Norf 69 D6
Langley Upper Green Essex 54 F5
Langney E Sus 18 E3
Langold Notts 89 F6
Langore Corn 8 F5
Langport Som 12 B2
Langrick Lincs 79 E5
Langridge Bath 24 C2
Langridge Ford Devon 9 B7
Langrigg Cumb 107 E8
Langrish Hants 15 B8
Langsett S Yorks 88 D3
Langshaw Borders 121 F8
Langside Perth 127 C6
Langskaill Orkney 159 D5
Langstone Hants 15 D8
Langstone Newport 35 E7
Langthorne N Yorks 101 E7
Langthorpe N Yorks 95 C6
Langthwaite N Yorks 101 D5
Langtoft E Yorks 97 C6
Langtoft Lincs 65 C8
Langton Durham 101 C6
Langton Lincs 78 C5
Langton Lincs 79 B6
Langton N Yorks 96 C3
Langton by Wragby Lincs 78 B4
Langton Green Kent 18 B2
Langton Green Suff 56 B5
Langton Herring Dorset 12 F4
Langton Matravers Dorset 13 G8
Langtree Devon 9 C6
Langwathby Cumb 109 F5
Langwell Ho. Highld 158 H3
Langwell Lodge Highld 156 J4
Langwith Derbys 76 C5
Langwith Junction Derbys 76 C5
Langworth Lincs 78 B3
Lanivet Corn 4 C5
Lanlivery Corn 5 D5
Lanner Corn 3 C6
Lanreath Corn 5 D6
Lansallos Corn 5 D6
Lansdown Glos 37 B6
Lanteglos Highway Corn 5 D6
Lanton Borders 116 B2
Lanton Northumb 122 F5
Lapford Devon 10 D2
Laphroaig Argyll 142 D4
Lapley Staffs 62 C2
Lapworth Warks 51 B6
Larachbeg Highld 147 G9
Larbert Falk 127 F7
Larden Green Ches E 74 D2
Largie Aberds 152 E6
Largiemore Argyll 145 E8
Largoward Fife 129 D6
Largs N Ayrs 118 D2
Largybeg N Ayrs 143 F11
Largymore N Ayrs 143 F11
Larkfield Involyd 118 B2
Larkhall S Lanark 119 D7
Larkhill Wilts 25 E6
Larling Norf 68 F2
Larriston Borders 115 E8
Lartington Durham 101 C5
Lary Aberds 140 D2
Lasham Hants 26 E4
Lashenden Kent 30 E2
Lassington Glos 36 B4
Lassodie Fife 128 E3
Lastingham N Yorks 103 E5
Latcham Som 23 E6
Latchford Herts 41 B6
Latchford Warr 86 F4
Latchingdon Essex 42 D4
Latchley Corn 6 B2
Lately Common Warr 86 E4
Lathbury M Keynes 53 E6
Latheron Highld 158 G3
Latheronwheel Highld 158 G3
Latheronwheel Ho. Highld 158 G3
Lathones Fife 129 D6
Latimer Bucks 40 E3
Latteridge S Glos 36 F3
Lattiford Som 12 B4
Latton Wilts 37 E7
Latton Bush Essex 41 D7
Lauchintilly Aberds 141 C6
Lauder Borders 121 E8
Laugharne Carms 32 C4
Laughterton Lincs 77 B8
Laughton E Sus 18 D2
Laughton Leics 64 F3
Laughton Lincs 78 F3
Laughton Lincs 90 E2
Laughton Common S Yorks 89 F6
Laughton en le Morthen S Yorks 89 F6
Launcells Corn 8 D4
Launceston Corn 8 F5
Launton Oxon 39 B6
Laurencekirk Aberds 135 B7
Laurieston Dumfries 106 C3
Laurieston Falk 120 B2
Lavendon M Keynes 53 D7
Lavenham Suff 56 E3
Laverhay Dumfries 114 E4
Laversdale Cumb 108 C4
Laverstock Wilts 25 F6
Laverstoke Hants 26 E2
Laverton Glos 51 F5
Laverton N Yorks 94 B5
Laverton Som 24 D2
Lavister Wrex 73 D7
Law S Lanark 119 D8
Lawers Perth 127 B6
Lawers Perth 132 F3
Lawford Essex 56 F4
Lawhitton Corn 9 F5
Lawkland N Yorks 93 C7
Lawley Telford 61 D6
Lawnhead Staffs 62 B2
Lawrenny Pembs 32 D1
Lawshall Suff 56 D2
Lawton Hereford 49 D6
Laxey IoM 84 D4
Laxfield Suff 57 B6
Laxfirth Shetland 160 H6
Laxfirth Shetland 160 J6
Laxford Bridge Highld 156 E5
Laxo Shetland 160 G6
Laxobigging Shetland 160 F6
Laxton E Yorks 89 B8
Laxton Northants 65 E6
Laxton Notts 77 C7
Laycock W Yorks 94 E3
Layer Breton Essex 43 C5
Layer de la Haye Essex 43 C5
Layer Marney Essex 43 C5
Layham Suff 56 E4
Laylands Green W Berks 25 C8
Laytham E Yorks 96 F3
Layton Blackpool 92 F3
Lazenby Redcar 102 B3
Lazonby Cumb 108 F5
Le Planel Guern 16
Le Skerne Haughton Darl 101 C8
Le Villocq Guern 16
Lea Derbys 76 D3
Lea Hereford 36 B3
Lea Lincs 90 F2
Lea Shrops 60 D4
Lea Shrops 60 F3
Lea Wilts 37 F6
Lea Marston Warks 63 E6
Lea Town Lancs 92 F4
Leabrooks Derbys 76 D4
Leac a Li W Isles 154 H6
Leachkin Highld 151 G9
Leadburn Midloth 120 D5
Leaden Roding Essex 42 C1
Leadenham Lincs 78 D2
Leadgate Cumb 109 E7
Leadgate Durham 110 D4
Leadgate T&W 110 D4
Leadhills S Lanark 113 C8
Leafield Oxon 38 C3
Leagrave Luton 40 B3
Leake N Yorks 102 E2
Leake Commonside Lincs 79 D6
Lealholm N Yorks 103 D5
Lealt Argyll 144 D5
Lealt Highld 149 B10
Leamington Hastings Warks 52 C2
Leamonsley Staffs 62 D5
Leamside Durham 111 E6
Leanaig Highld 151 F8
Leargybreck Argyll 144 F4
Leasgill Cumb 99 F6
Leasingham Lincs 78 E3
Leasingthorne Durham 101 B7
Leasowe Mers 85 E3
Leatherhead Sur 28 D2
Leatherhead Common Sur 28 D2
Leathley N Yorks 94 E5
Leaton Shrops 60 C4
Leaveland Kent 30 D4
Leavening N Yorks 96 C3
Leaves Green London 28 C5
Leazes Durham 110 D4
Lebberston N Yorks 103 F8
Lechlade-on-Thames Glos 38 E2
Leck Lancs 93 B6
Leckford Hants 25 F8
Leckfurin Highld 157 D10
Leckgruinart Argyll 142 B3
Leckhampstead Bucks 52 F5
Leckhampstead W Berks 26 B2
Leckhampstead Thicket W Berks 26 B2
Leckhampton Glos 37 C6
Leckie Highld 150 E3
Leckmelm Highld 150 B4
Leckwith V Glam 22 B3
Leconfield E Yorks 97 E6
Ledaig Argyll 124 B5
Ledburn Bucks 40 B2
Ledbury Hereford 50 F2
Ledcharrie Stirling 126 B4
Ledgemoor Hereford 49 D6
Ledicot Hereford 49 C6
Ledmore Highld 156 H5
Lednagullin Highld 157 C10
Ledsham Ches W 73 B7
Ledsham W Yorks 89 B5
Ledston W Yorks 88 B5
Ledston Luck W Yorks 95 F7
Ledwell Oxon 38 B4
Lee Argyll 146 J7
Lee Devon 20 E3
Lee Hants 14 C4
Lee Lancs 93 D5
Lee Shrops 73 F8
Lee Brockhurst Shrops 60 B5
Lee Clump Bucks 40 D2
Lee Mill Devon 6 D4
Lee Moor Devon 6 C3
Lee-on-the-Solent Hants 15 D6
Leeans Shetland 160 J5
Leebotten Shetland 160 L6
Leebotwood Shrops 60 E4
Leece Cumb 92 C2
Leechpool Pembs 44 D4
Leeds Kent 30 D2
Leeds W Yorks 95 F5
Leedstown Corn 2 C5
Leek Staffs 75 D6
Leek Wootton Warks 51 C7
Leekbrook Staffs 75 D6
Leeming N Yorks 101 F7
Leeming Bar N Yorks 101 E7
Lees Derbys 76 F2
Lees Gtr Man 87 D7
Lees W Yorks 94 F3
Leeswood Flint 73 C6
Legbourne Lincs 91 F7
Legerwood Borders 121 E8
Legsby Lincs 90 F5
Leicester Leicester 64 D2
Leicester Forest East Leics 64 D2
Leigh Dorset 12 D4
Leigh Glos 37 B5
Leigh Gtr Man 86 D4
Leigh Kent 29 E6
Leigh Shrops 60 D3
Leigh Sur 28 E3
Leigh Wilts 37 E7
Leigh Worcs 50 D2
Leigh Beck Essex 42 F4
Leigh Common Som 12 B5
Leigh Delamere Wilts 24 B3
Leigh Green Kent 19 B6
Leigh on Sea Southend 42 F4
Leigh Park Hants 15 D8
Leigh Sinton Worcs 50 D2
Leigh upon Mendip Som 23 E8
Leigh Woods N Som 23 B7
Leighswood W Mid 62 D4
Leighterton Glos 37 E5
Leighton N Yorks 94 B4
Leighton Powys 60 D2
Leighton Shrops 61 D6
Leighton Som 24 E2
Leighton Bromswold Cambs 54 B2
Leighton Buzzard C Beds 40 B2
Leinthall Earls Hereford 49 C6
Leinthall Starkes Hereford 49 C6
Leintwardine Hereford 49 B6
Leire Leics 64 E2
Leirinmore Highld 156 C7
Leiston Suff 57 C8
Leitfie Perth 134 E2
Leith Edin 121 B5
Leitholm Borders 122 E3
Lelant Corn 2 C4
Lelley E Yorks 97 F8
Lem Hill Worcs 50 B2
Lemmington Hall Northumb 117 C7
Lempitlaw Borders 122 F3
Lenchwick Worcs 50 E5
Lendalfoot S Ayrs 112 F1
Lendrick Lodge Stirling 126 D4
Lenham Kent 30 D2
Lenham Heath Kent 30 E3
Lennel Borders 122 E4
Lennoxtown E Dunb 119 B6
Lenton Lincs 78 F3
Lenton Nottingham 77 F5
Lentran Highld 151 G8
Lenwade Norf 68 C3
Leny Ho. Stirling 126 D5
Lenzie E Dunb 119 B6
Leoch Angus 134 F3
Leochel-Cushnie Aberds 140 C4
Leominster Hereford 49 D6
Leonard Stanley Glos 37 D5
Leorin Argyll 142 D4
Lepe Hants 15 E5
Lephin Highld 148 D6
Lephinchapel Argyll 145 D8
Lephinmore Argyll 145 D8
Leppington N Yorks 96 C3
Lepton W Yorks 88 C3
Lerryn Corn 5 D6
Lerwick Shetland 160 J6
Lesbury Northumb 117 C8
Leslie Aberds 140 B4
Leslie Fife 128 D4
Lesmahagow S Lanark 119 F8
Lesnewth Corn 8 E3
Lessendrum Aberds 152 D5
Lessingham Norf 69 B6
Lessonhall Cumb 108 D2
Leswalt Dumfries 104 C4
Letchmore Heath Herts 40 E4
Letchworth Herts 54 F3
Letcombe Bassett Oxon 38 F3
Letcombe Regis Oxon 38 F3
Letham Angus 135 E5
Letham Falk 127 F7
Letham Fife 128 C5
Letham Perth 128 B2
Letham Grange Angus 135 E6
Lethenty Aberds 153 D8
Letheringham Suff 57 D6
Letheringsett Norf 81 D6
Lettaford Devon 10 F2
Lettan Orkney 159 D8
Letterewe Highld 150 D2
Letterfearn Highld 149 F13
Letterfinlay Highld 137 E5
Lettermorar Highld 147 C10
Lettermore Argyll 146 G7
Letters Highld 150 C4
Letterston Pembs 44 C4
Lettoch Highld 139 C6
Lettoch Highld 151 H13
Letton Hereford 48 E5
Letton Hereford 49 B5
Letton Green Norf 68 D2
Letty Green Herts 41 C5
Letwell S Yorks 89 F6
Leuchars Fife 129 B6
Leuchars Ho. Moray 152 B2
Leumrabhagh W Isles 155 F8
Levan Involyd 118 B2
Levaneap Shetland 160 G6
Levedale Staffs 62 C2
Leven E Yorks 97 E7
Leven Fife 129 D5
Levencorroch N Ayrs 143 F11
Levens Cumb 99 F6
Levens Green Herts 41 B6
Levenshulme Gtr Man 87 E6
Levenwick Shetland 160 L6
Leverburgh = An t-Ob W Isles 154 J5
Leverington Cambs 66 C4
Leverton Lincs 79 E7
Leverton Highgate Lincs 79 E7
Leverton Lucasgate Lincs 79 E7
Leverton Outgate Lincs 79 E7
Levington Suff 57 F6
Levisham N Yorks 103 E6
Levishie Highld 137 C7
Lew Oxon 38 D3
Lewannick Corn 8 F4
Lewdown Devon 9 F6
Lewes E Sus 17 C8
Leweston Pembs 44 C4
Lewisham London 28 B4
Lewiston Highld 137 B8
Lewistown Bridgend 34 F3
Lewknor Oxon 39 E7
Leworthy Devon 8 D5
Leworthy Devon 21 F5
Lewtrenchard Devon 9 F6
Lexden Essex 43 B5
Ley Aberds 140 C4
Ley Corn 5 C6
Leybourne Kent 29 D7
Leyburn N Yorks 101 E6
Leyfields Staffs 63 D6
Leyhill Bucks 40 D2
Leyland Lancs 86 B3
Leylodge Aberds 141 C6
Leymoor W Yorks 88 C2
Leys Aberds 153 C10
Leys Perth 134 F2
Leys Castle Highld 151 G9
Leys of Cossans Angus 134 E3
Leysdown-on-Sea Kent 30 B4
Leysmill Angus 135 E6
Leysters Pole Hereford 49 C7
Leyton London 41 F6
Leytonstone London 41 F6
Lezant Corn 5 B8
Leziate Norf 67 C6
Lhanbryde Moray 152 B2
Liatrie Highld 150 H5
Libanus Powys 34 B3
Libberton S Lanark 120 E2
Liberton Edin 121 C5
Liceasto W Isles 154 H6
Lichfield Staffs 62 D5
Lickey Worcs 50 B4
Lickey End Worcs 50 B4
Lickfold W Sus 16 B3
Liddel Orkney 159 K5
Liddesdale Highld 130 D1
Liddington Swindon 38 F2
Lidgate Suff 55 D8
Lidget S Yorks 89 D7
Lidget Green W Yorks 94 F4
Lidgett Notts 77 C6
Lidlington C Beds 53 F7
Lidstone Oxon 38 B3
Lieurary Highld 158 D2
Liff Angus 134 F3
Lifton Devon 9 F5
Liftondown Devon 9 F5
Lighthorne Warks 51 D8
Lightwater Sur 27 C7
Lightwood Stoke 75 E6
Lightwood Green Ches E 74 E3
Lightwood Green Wrex 73 E7
Lilbourne Northants 52 B3
Lilburn Tower Northumb 117 B6
Lilleshall Telford 61 C7
Lilley Herts 40 B4
Lilley W Berks 26 B2
Lilliesleaf Borders 115 B8
Lillingstone Dayrell Bucks 52 F5
Lillingstone Lovell Bucks 52 E5
Lillington Dorset 12 C4
Lillington Warks 51 C8
Lilliput Poole 13 E8
Lilstock Som 22 E3
Lilyhurst Shrops 61 C7
Limbury Luton 40 B3
Limebrook Hereford 49 C5
Limefield Gtr Man 87 C6
Limekilnburn S Lanark 119 D7
Limekilns Fife 128 F2
Limerigg Falk 119 B8
Limerstone IoW 14 F5
Limington Som 12 B3
Limpenhoe Norf 69 D6
Limpley Stoke Wilts 24 C2
Limpsfield Sur 28 D5
Limpsfield Chart Sur 28 D5
Linby Notts 76 D5
Linchmere W Sus 27 F6
Lincluden Dumfries 107 B6
Lincoln Lincs 78 B2
Lincomb Worcs 50 C3
Lincombe Devon 6 D5
Lindal in Furness Cumb 92 B2
Lindale Cumb 99 F6
Lindean Borders 121 F7
Lindfield W Sus 17 B7
Lindford Hants 27 F6
Lindifferon Fife 128 C5
Lindley W Yorks 88 C2
Lindley Green N Yorks 94 E5
Lindores Fife 128 C4
Lindridge Worcs 49 C8
Lindsell Essex 42 B2
Lindsey Suff 56 E3
Linford Hants 14 D2
Linford Thurrock 29 B7
Lingague IoM 84 E2
Lingards Wood W Yorks 87 C8
Lingbob W Yorks 94 F3
Lingdale Redcar 102 C4
Lingen Hereford 49 C5
Lingfield Sur 28 E4
Lingreabhagh W Isles 154 J5
Lingwood Norf 69 D6
Linicro Highld 149 B8
Linkenholt Hants 25 D8
Linkhill Kent 18 C5
Linkinhorne Corn 5 B8
Linklater Orkney 159 K5
Linksness Orkney 159 H3
Linktown Fife 128 E4
Linley Shrops 60 E3
Linley Green Hereford 49 D8
Linlithgow W Loth 120 B3
Linlithgow Bridge W Loth 120 B2
Linshiels Northumb 116 D4
Linsiadar W Isles 154 D7
Linsidemore Highld 151 B8
Linslade C Beds 40 B2
Linstead Parva Suff 57 B7
Linstock Cumb 108 D4
Linthwaite W Yorks 88 C2
Lintlaw Borders 122 D4
Lintmill Moray 152 B5
Linton Borders 116 B3
Linton Cambs 55 E6
Linton Derbys 63 C6
Linton Hereford 36 B3
Linton Kent 29 E8
Linton N Yorks 94 C2
Linton Northumb 117 E8
Linton W Yorks 95 E6
Linton-on-Ouse N Yorks 95 C7
Linwood Hants 14 D2
Linwood Lincs 90 F5
Linwood Renfs 118 C4
Lionacleit W Isles 148 D2
Lional W Isles 155 A10
Liphook Hants 27 F6
Liscard Mers 85 E4
Liscombe Som 21 F7
Liskeard Corn 5 C7
L'Islet Guern 16
Liss Hants 15 B8
Liss Forest Hants 15 B8
Lissett E Yorks 97 D7
Lissington Lincs 90 F5
Lisvane Cardiff 35 F5
Liswerry Newport 35 F7
Litcham Norf 67 C8
Litchborough Northants 52 D4
Litchfield Hants 26 D2
Litherland Mers 85 E4
Litlington Cambs 54 E4
Litlington E Sus 18 E2
Little Abington Cambs 55 E6
Little Addington Northants 53 B7
Little Alne Warks 51 C6
Little Altcar Mers 85 D4
Little Asby Cumb 100 D1
Little Assynt Highld 156 G4
Little Aston Staffs 62 D4
Little Atherfield IoW 15 F5
Little Ayre Orkney 159 J4
Little-ayre Shetland 160 G5
Little Ayton N Yorks 102 C3
Little Baddow Essex 42 D3
Little Badminton S Glos 37 F5
Little Ballinluig Perth 133 D6
Little Bampton Cumb 108 D2
Little Bardfield Essex 55 F7
Little Barford Bedford 54 D2
Little Barningham Norf 81 D7
Little Barrington Glos 38 C2
Little Barrow Ches W 73 B8
Little Barugh N Yorks 96 B3
Little Bavington Northumb 110 B2
Little Bealings Suff 57 E6
Little Bedwyn Wilts 25 C7
Little Bentley Essex 43 B7
Little Berkhamsted Herts 41 D5
Little Billing Northants 53 C6
Little Birch Hereford 49 F7
Little Blakenham Suff 56 E5
Little Blencow Cumb 108 F4
Little Bollington Ches E 86 F5
Little Bookham Sur 28 D2
Little Bowden Leics 64 F4
Little Bradley Suff 55 D7
Little Brampton Shrops 60 F3
Little Brechin Angus 135 C5
Little Brickhill M Keynes 53 F7
Little Brington Northants 52 C4
Little Bromley Essex 43 B6
Little Broughton Cumb 107 F7
Little Budworth Ches W 74 C2
Little Burstead Essex 42 E2
Little Bytham Lincs 65 C7
Little Carlton Lincs 91 F7
Little Carlton Notts 77 D7
Little Casterton Rutland 65 D7
Little Cawthorpe Lincs 91 F7
Little Chalfont Bucks 40 E2
Little Chart Kent 30 E3
Little Chesterford Essex 55 E6
Little Cheverell Wilts 24 D4
Little Chishill Cambs 54 F5
Little Clacton Essex 43 C7
Little Clifton Cumb 98 B2
Little Colp Aberds 153 D7
Little Comberton Worcs 50 E4
Little Common E Sus 18 E4
Little Compton Warks 51 F7
Little Cornard Suff 56 F2
Little Cowarne Hereford 49 D8
Little Coxwell Oxon 38 E2
Little Crakehall N Yorks 101 E7
Little Cressingham Norf 67 D8
Little Crosby Mers 85 D4
Little Dalby Leics 64 C4
Little Dawley Telford 61 D6
Little Dens Aberds 153 D10
Little Dewchurch Hereford 49 F7
Little Downham Cambs 66 F5
Little Driffield E Yorks 97 D6
Little Dunham Norf 67 C8
Little Dunkeld Perth 133 E7
Little Dunmow Essex 42 B2
Little Easton Essex 42 B2
Little Eaton Derbys 76 E3
Little Eccleston Lancs 92 E4
Little Ellingham Norf 68 E3
Little End Essex 41 D8
Little Eversden Cambs 54 D4
Little Faringdon Oxon 38 D2
Little Fencote N Yorks 101 E7
Little Fenton N Yorks 95 F8
Little Finborough Suff 56 D4
Little Fransham Norf 68 C2
Little Gaddesden Herts 40 C2
Little Gidding Cambs 65 F8
Little Glemham Suff 57 D7
Little Glenshee Perth 133 F6
Little Gransden Cambs 54 D3
Little Green Som 24 E2
Little Grimsby Lincs 91 E7
Little Gruinard Highld 150 C2
Little Habton N Yorks 96 B3
Little Hadham Herts 41 B7
Little Hale Lincs 78 E4
Little Hallingbury Essex 41 C7
Little Hampden Bucks 40 D1
Little Harrowden Northants 53 B6
Little Haseley Oxon 39 D6
Little Hatfield E Yorks 97 E7
Little Hautbois Norf 81 E8
Little Haven Pembs 44 D3
Little Hay Staffs 62 D5
Little Hayfield Derbys 87 F8
Little Haywood Staffs 62 B4
Little Heath W Mid 63 F7
Little Hereford Hereford 49 C7
Little Horkesley Essex 56 F3
Little Horsted E Sus 17 C8
Little Horton W Yorks 94 F4
Little Horwood Bucks 53 F5
Little Houghton Northants 53 D6
Little Houghton S Yorks 88 D5
Little Hucklow Derbys 75 B8
Little Hulton Gtr Man 86 D5
Little Humber E Yorks 91 B5
Little Hungerford W Berks 26 B3
Little Irchester Northants 53 C7
Little Kimble Bucks 39 D8
Little Kineton Warks 51 D8
Little Kingshill Bucks 40 E1
Little Langdale Cumb 99 D5
Little Langford Wilts 25 F5
Little Laver Essex 41 D8
Little Leigh Ches W 74 B3
Little Leighs Essex 42 C3
Little Lever Gtr Man 87 D5
Little London Bucks 39 C6
Little London E Sus 18 D2
Little London Hants 25 E8
Little London Hants 26 D4
Little London Lincs 66 B2
Little London Lincs 66 B4
Little London Norf 81 E7
Little London Powys 59 F7
Little Longstone Derbys 75 B8
Little Lynturk Aberds 140 C4
Little Malvern Worcs 50 E2
Little Maplestead Essex 56 F2
Little Marcle Hereford 49 F8
Little Marlow Bucks 40 F1
Little Marsden Lancs 93 F8
Little Massingham Norf 80 E3
Little Melton Norf 68 D4
Little Mill Mon 35 D7
Little Milton Oxon 39 D6
Little Missenden Bucks 40 E2
Little Musgrave Cumb 100 C2
Little Ness Shrops 60 C4
Little Neston Ches W 73 B6
Little Newcastle Pembs 44 C4
Little Newsham Durham 101 C6
Little Oakley Essex 43 B8
Little Oakley Northants 65 F5
Little Orton Cumb 108 D3
Little Ouseburn N Yorks 95 C7
Little Paxton Cambs 54 C2
Little Petherick Corn 4 B4
Little Pitlurg Moray 152 D4
Little Plumpton Lancs 92 F3
Little Plumstead Norf 69 C6
Little Ponton Lincs 78 F2
Little Raveley Cambs 54 B3
Little Reedness E Yorks 90 B2
Little Ribston N Yorks 95 D6
Little Rissington Glos 38 C1
Little Ryburgh Norf 81 E5
Little Ryle Northumb 117 C6
Little Salkeld Cumb 109 F5
Little Sampford Essex 55 F7
Little Sandhurst Brack 27 C6
Little Saxham Suff 55 C8
Little Scatwell Highld 150 F6
Little Sessay N Yorks 95 B7
Little Shelford Cambs 54 D5
Little Singleton Lancs 92 F3
Little Skillymarno Aberds 153 C9
Little Smeaton N Yorks 89 C6
Little Snoring Norf 81 D5
Little Sodbury S Glos 36 F4
Little Somborne Hants 25 F8
Little Somerford Wilts 37 F6
Little Stainforth N Yorks 93 C8
Little Stainton Darl 101 B8
Little Stanney Ches W 73 B8
Little Staughton Bedford 54 C2
Little Steeping Lincs 79 C7
Little Stoke Staffs 75 F6
Little Stonham Suff 56 C5
Little Stretton Leics 64 D3
Little Stretton Shrops 60 E4
Little Strickland Cumb 99 C7
Little Stukeley Cambs 54 B3
Little Sutton Ches W 73 B7
Little Tew Oxon 38 B3
Little Thetford Cambs 55 B6
Little Thirkleby N Yorks 95 B7
Little Thurlow Suff 55 D7
Little Thurrock Thurrock 29 B7
Little Torboll Highld 151 B10
Little Torrington Devon 9 C6
Little Totham Essex 42 C4
Little Toux Aberds 152 C5
Little Town Cumb 98 C4
Little Town Lancs 93 F6
Little Urswick Cumb 92 B2
Little Wakering Essex 43 F5
Little Walden Essex 55 E6
Little Waldingfield Suff 56 E3
Little Walsingham Norf 80 D5
Little Waltham Essex 42 C3
Little Warley Essex 42 E2
Little Weighton E Yorks 97 F5
Little Weldon Northants 65 F6
Little Welnetham Suff 56 C2
Little Wenlock Telford 61 D6
Little Whittingham Green Suff 57 B6
Little Wilbraham Cambs 55 D6
Little Wishford Wilts 25 F5
Little Witley Worcs 50 C2
Little Wittenham Oxon 39 E5
Little Wolford Warks 51 F7
Little Wratting Suff 55 E7
Little Wymington Bedford 53 C7
Little Wymondley Herts 41 B5
Little Wyrley Staffs 62 D4
Little Yeldham Essex 55 F8
Littlebeck N Yorks 103 D6
Littleborough Gtr Man 87 C7
Littleborough Notts 90 F2
Littlebourne Kent 31 D6
Littlebredy Dorset 12 F3
Littlebury Essex 55 F6
Littlebury Green Essex 55 F5
Littledean Glos 36 C3
Littleferry Highld 151 B11
Littleham Devon 9 B6
Littleham Devon 10 F5
Littlehampton W Sus 16 D4
Littlehempston Devon 7 C6
Littlehoughton Northumb 117 C8
Littlemill Aberds 140 E2
Littlemill E Ayrs 112 C4
Littlemill Highld 151 F12
Littlemill Northumb 117 C8
Littlemoor Dorset 12 F4
Littlemore Oxon 39 D5
Littleover Derby 76 F3
Littleport Cambs 67 F5
Littlestone on Sea Kent 19 C7
Littlethorpe Leics 64 E2
Littlethorpe N Yorks 95 C6
Littleton Ches W 73 C8
Littleton Hants 26 F2
Littleton Perth 134 F2
Littleton Som 23 F6
Littleton Sur 27 C8
Littleton Sur 27 E7
Littleton Drew Wilts 37 F5
Littleton-on-Severn S Glos 36 F2
Littleton Pannell Wilts 24 D5
Littletown Durham 111 E6
Littlewick Green Windsor 27 B6
Littleworth Bedford 53 E8
Littleworth Glos 37 D5
Littleworth Oxon 38 E3
Littleworth Staffs 62 C4
Littleworth Worcs 50 D3
Litton Derbys 75 B8
Litton N Yorks 94 B2
Litton Som 23 D7
Litton Cheney Dorset 12 E3
Liurbost W Isles 155 E8
Liverpool Mers 85 E4
Liverpool Airport Mers 86 F2
Liversedge W Yorks 88 B3
Liverton Devon 7 B6
Liverton Redcar 103 C5
Livingston W Loth 120 C3
Livingston Village W Loth 120 C3
Lixwm Flint 73 B5
Lizard Corn 3 E6
Llaingoch Anglesey 82 C2
Llaithddu Powys 59 F7
Llan Powys 59 D5
Llan Ffestiniog Gwyn 71 C8
Llan-y-pwll Wrex 73 D7
Llanaber Gwyn 58 C3
Llanaelhaearn Gwyn 70 C4
Llanafan Ceredig 47 B5
Llanafan-fawr Powys 47 D8
Llanallgo Anglesey 82 C4
Llanandras = Presteigne Powys 48 C5
Llanarmon Gwyn 70 D5
Llanarmon Dyffryn Ceiriog Wrex 73 F5
Llanarmon-yn-Ial Denb 73 D5
Llanarth Ceredig 46 D3
Llanarth Mon 35 C7
Llanarthne Carms 33 B6
Llanasa Flint 85 F2
Llanbabo Anglesey 82 C3
Llanbadarn Fawr Ceredig 58 F3

Llanbadarn Fynydd Powys 48 B3
Llanbadarn-y-Garreg Powys 48 E3
Llanbadoc Mon 35 E7
Llanbadrig Anglesey 82 B3
Llanbeder Newport 35 E7
Llanbedr Gwyn 71 E6
Llanbedr Powys 35 B6
Llanbedr Powys 48 E3
Llanbedr-Dyffryn-Clwyd Denb 72 D5
Llanbedr Pont Steffan = Lampeter Ceredig 46 E4
Llanbedr-y-cennin Conwy 83 E7
Llanbedrgoch Anglesey 82 C5
Llanbedrog Gwyn 70 D4
Llanberis Gwyn 83 E5
Llanbethêry V Glam 22 C2
Llanbister Powys 48 B3
Llanblethian V Glam 21 B8
Llanboidy Carms 32 B3
Llanbradach Caerph 35 E5
Llanbrynmair Powys 59 D5
Llancarfan V Glam 22 B2
Llancayo Mon 35 D7
Llancloudy Hereford 36 B1
Llancynfelyn Ceredig 58 E3
Llandaff Cardiff 22 B3
Llandanwg Gwyn 71 E6
Llandarcy Neath 33 E8
Llandawke Carms 32 C3
Llanddaniel Fab Anglesey 82 D4
Llanddarog Carms 33 C6
Llanddeiniol Ceredig 46 B4
Llanddeiniolen Gwyn 82 E5
Llandderfel Gwyn 72 F3
Llanddeusant Anglesey 82 C3
Llanddeusant Carms 34 B1
Llanddew Powys 48 F2
Llanddewi Swansea 33 F5
Llanddewi-Brefi Ceredig 47 D5
Llanddewi Rhydderch Mon 35 C7
Llanddewi Velfrey Pembs 32 C2
Llanddewi'r Cwm Powys 48 E2
Llanddoged Conwy 83 E8
Llanddona Anglesey 83 D5
Llanddowror Carms 32 C3
Llanddulas Conwy 72 B3
Llanddwywe Gwyn 71 E6
Llanddyfynan Anglesey 82 D5
Llandefaelog Fach Powys 48 F2
Llandefaelog-tre'r-graig Powys 35 B5
Llandefalle Powys 48 F3
Llandegai Gwyn 83 D5
Llandegfan Anglesey 83 D5
Llandegla Denb 73 D5
Llandegley Powys 48 C3
Llandegveth Mon 35 E7
Llandegwning Gwyn 70 D3
Llandeilo Carms 33 B7
Llandeilo Graban Powys 48 E2
Llandeilo'r Fan Powys 47 F7
Llandeloy Pembs 44 C3
Llandenny Mon 35 D8
Llandevenny Mon 35 F8
Llandewednock Corn 3 E6
Llandewi Ystradenny Powys 48 C3
Llandinabo Hereford 36 B2
Llandinam Powys 59 F7
Llandissilio Pembs 32 B2
Llandogo Mon 36 D2
Llandough V Glam 21 B8
Llandough V Glam 22 B3
Llandovery = Llanymddyfri Carms 47 F6
Llandow V Glam 21 B8
Llandre Carms 47 E5
Llandre Ceredig 58 F3
Llandrillo Denb 72 F4
Llandrillo-yn-Rhos Conwy 83 C8
Llandrindod = Llandrindod Wells Powys 48 C2
Llandrindod Wells = Llandrindod Powys 48 C2
Llandrinio Powys 60 C2
Llandudno Conwy 83 C7
Llandudno Junction = Cyffordd Llandudno Conwy 83 D7
Llandwrog Gwyn 82 F4
Llandybie Carms 33 C7
Llandyfaelog Carms 33 C5
Llandyfan Carms 33 C7
Llandyfriog Ceredig 46 E2
Llandyfrydog Anglesey 82 C4
Llandygwydd Ceredig 45 E4
Llandynan Denb 73 E5
Llandyrnog Denb 72 C5
Llandysilio Powys 60 C2
Llandyssil Powys 59 E8
Llandysul Ceredig 46 E3
Llanedeyrn Cardiff 35 F6
Llanedi Carms 33 D6
Llaneglwys Powys 48 F2
Llanegryn Gwyn 58 D2
Llanegwad Carms 33 B6
Llaneilian Anglesey 82 B4
Llanelian-yn-Rhos Conwy 83 D8
Llanelidan Denb 72 D5
Llanelieu Powys 48 F3
Llanellen Mon 35 C7
Llanelli Carms 33 E6
Llanelltyd Gwyn 58 C4
Llanelly Mon 35 C6
Llanelly Hill Mon 35 C6
Llanelwedd Powys 48 D2
Llanelwy = St Asaph Denb 72 B4
Llanenddwyn Gwyn 71 E6
Llanengan Gwyn 70 E3
Llanerchymedd Anglesey 82 C4
Llanerfyl Powys 59 D7
Llanfachraeth Anglesey 82 C3
Llanfachreth Gwyn 71 E8
Llanfaelog Anglesey 82 D3
Llanfaelrhys Gwyn 70 E3
Llanfaenor Mon 35 C8
Llanfaes Anglesey 83 D6
Llanfaes Powys 34 B4
Llanfaethlu Anglesey 82 C3
Llanfaglan Gwyn 82 E4
Llanfair Gwyn 71 E6
Llanfair-ar-y-bryn Carms 47 F7
Llanfair Caereinion Powys 59 D8
Llanfair Clydogau Ceredig 46 D5
Llanfair-Dyffryn-Clwyd Denb 72 D5
Llanfair Kilgheddin Mon 35 D7
Llanfair-Nant-Gwyn Pembs 45 F3
Llanfair Talhaiarn Conwy 72 B3
Llanfair Waterdine Shrops 48 B4
Llanfair-Ym-Muallt = Builth Wells Powys 48 D2
Llanfairfechan Conwy 83 D6
Llanfairpwll-gwyngyll Anglesey 82 D5
Llanfairyneubwll Anglesey 82 D3
Llanfairynghornwy Anglesey 82 B3
Llanfallteg Carms 32 C2
Llanfaredd Powys 48 D2
Llanfarian Ceredig 46 B4
Llanfechain Powys 59 B8
Llanfechan Powys 47 D8
Llanfechell Anglesey 82 B3
Llanfendigaid Gwyn 58 D2
Llanferres Denb 73 C5
Llanfflewyn Anglesey 82 C3
Llanfihangel-ar-arth Carms 46 F3
Llanfihangel-Crucorney Mon 35 B7
Llanfihangel Glyn Myfyr Conwy 72 E3
Llanfihangel Nant Bran Powys 47 F8
Llanfihangel-nant-Melan Powys 48 D3
Llanfihangel Rhydithon Powys 48 C3
Llanfihangel Rogiet Mon 35 F8
Llanfihangel Tal-y-llyn Powys 35 B5
Llanfihangel-uwch-Gwili Carms 33 B5
Llanfihangel-y-Creuddyn Ceredig 47 B5
Llanfihangel-y-pennant Gwyn 58 D3
Llanfihangel-y-pennant Gwyn 71 C6
Llanfihangel-y-traethau Gwyn 71 D6
Llanfihangel-yn-Ngwynfa Powys 59 C7
Llanfihangel yn Nhowyn Anglesey 82 D3
Llanfilo Powys 48 F3
Llanfoist Mon 35 C6
Llanfor Gwyn 72 F3
Llanfrechfa Torf 35 E7
Llanfrothen Gwyn 71 C7
Llanfrynach Powys 34 B4
Llanfwrog Anglesey 82 C3
Llanfwrog Denb 72 D5
Llanfyllin Powys 59 C8
Llanfynydd Carms 33 B6
Llanfynydd Flint 73 D6
Llanfyrnach Pembs 45 F4
Llangadfan Powys 59 C7
Llangadog Carms 33 B8
Llangadwaladr Anglesey 82 E3
Llangadwaladr Powys 73 F5
Llangaffo Anglesey 82 E4
Llangain Carms 32 C4
Llangammarch Wells Powys 47 E8
Llangan V Glam 21 B8
Llangarron Hereford 36 B2
Llangasty Talyllyn Powys 35 B5
Llangathen Carms 33 B6
Llangattock Powys 35 C6
Llangattock Lingoed Mon 35 B7
Llangattock nigh Usk Mon 35 D7
Llangattock-Vibon-Avel Mon 36 C1
Llangedwyn Powys 59 B8
Llangefni Anglesey 82 D4
Llangeinor Bridgend 34 F3
Llangeitho Ceredig 46 D5
Llangeler Carms 46 F2
Llangelynin Gwyn 58 D2
Llangendeirne Carms 33 C5
Llangennech Carms 33 D6
Llangennith Swansea 33 E5
Llangenny Powys 35 C6
Llangernyw Conwy 83 E8
Llangian Gwyn 70 E3
Llanglydwen Carms 32 B2
Llangoed Anglesey 83 D6
Llangoedmor Ceredig 45 E3
Llangollen Denb 73 E6
Llangolman Pembs 32 B2
Llangors Powys 35 B5
Llangovan Mon 36 D1
Llangower Gwyn 72 F3
Llangrannog Ceredig 46 D2
Llangristiolus Anglesey 82 D4
Llangrove Hereford 36 C2
Llangua Mon 35 B7
Llangunllo Powys 48 B4
Llangunnor Carms 33 C5
Llangurig Powys 47 B8
Llangwm Conwy 72 E3
Llangwm Mon 35 D8
Llangwm Pembs 44 E4
Llangwnnadl Gwyn 70 D3
Llangwyfan Denb 72 C5
Llangwyfan-isaf Anglesey 82 E3
Llangwyllog Anglesey 82 D4
Llangwyryfon Ceredig 46 B4
Llangybi Ceredig 46 D5
Llangybi Gwyn 70 C5
Llangybi Mon 35 E7
Llangyfelach Swansea 33 E7
Llangynhafal Denb 72 C5
Llangynidr Powys 35 C5
Llangynin Carms 32 C3
Llangynog Carms 32 C4
Llangynog Powys 59 B7
Llangynwyd Bridgend 34 F2
Llanhamlach Powys 34 B4
Llanharan Rhondda 34 F4
Llanharry Rhondda 34 F4
Llanhennock Mon 35 E7
Llanhiledd = Llanhilleth Bl Gwent 35 D6
Llanhilleth = Llanhiledd Bl Gwent 35 D6
Llanidloes Powys 59 F6
Llaniestyn Gwyn 70 D3
Llanifyny Powys 59 F5
Llanigon Powys 48 F4
Llanilar Ceredig 46 B5
Llanilid Rhondda 34 F3
Llanilltud Fawr = Llantwit Major V Glam 21 C8
Llanishen Cardiff 35 F5
Llanishen Mon 36 D1
Llanllawddog Carms 33 B5
Llanllechid Gwyn 83 E6
Llanllowell Mon 35 E7
Llanllugan Powys 59 D7
Llanllwch Carms 32 C4
Llanllwchaiarn Powys 59 E8
Llanllwni Carms 46 F3
Llanllyfni Gwyn 82 F4
Llanmadoc Swansea 33 E5
Llanmaes V Glam 21 C8
Llanmartin Newport 35 F7
Llanmihangel V Glam 21 B8
Llanmorlais Swansea 33 E6
Llannefydd Conwy 72 B3
Llannon Carms 33 D6
Llannor Gwyn 70 D4
Llanon Ceredig 46 C4
Llanover Mon 35 D7
Llanpumsaint Carms 33 B5
Llanreithan Pembs 44 C3
Llanrhaeadr Denb 72 C4
Llanrhaeadr-ym-Mochnant Powys 59 B8
Llanrhian Pembs 44 B3
Llanrhidian Swansea 33 E5
Llanrhos Conwy 83 C7
Llanrhyddlad Anglesey 82 C3
Llanrhystud Ceredig 46 C4
Llanrosser Hereford 48 F4
Llanrothal Hereford 36 C1
Llanrug Gwyn 82 E5
Llanrumney Cardiff 35 F6
Llanrwst Conwy 83 E8
Llansadurnen Carms 32 C3
Llansadwrn Anglesey 83 D5
Llansadwrn Carms 47 F5
Llansaint Carms 32 D4
Llansamlet Swansea 33 E7
Llansannffraid-ym-Mechain Powys 60 B2
Llansannan Conwy 72 C3
Llansannor V Glam 21 B8
Llansantffraed Ceredig 46 C4
Llansantffraed Powys 35 B5
Llansantffraed Cwmdeuddwr Powys 47 C8
Llansantffraed-in-Elvel Powys 48 D2
Llansawel Carms 46 F5
Llansilin Powys 60 B2
Llansoy Mon 35 D8
Llanspyddid Powys 34 B4
Llanstadwell Pembs 44 E4
Llansteffan Carms 32 C4
Llanstephan Powys 48 E3
Llantarnam Torf 35 E7
Llanteg Pembs 32 C2
Llanthony Mon 35 B6
Llantilio Crossenny Mon 35 C7
Llantilio Pertholey Mon 35 C7
Llantood Pembs 45 E3
Llantrisant Anglesey 82 C3
Llantrisant Mon 35 E7
Llantrisant Rhondda 34 F4
Llantrithyd V Glam 22 B2
Llantwit Fardre Rhondda 34 F4
Llantwit Major = Llanilltud Fawr V Glam 21 C8
Llanuwchllyn Gwyn 72 F2
Llanvaches Newport 35 E8
Llanvair Discoed Mon 35 E8
Llanvapley Mon 35 C7
Llanvetherine Mon 35 C7
Llanveynoe Hereford 48 F5
Llanvihangel Gobion Mon 35 D7
Llanvihangel-Ystern-Llewern Mon 35 C8
Llanwarne Hereford 36 B2
Llanwddyn Powys 59 C7
Llanwenog Ceredig 46 E3
Llanwern Newport 35 F7
Llanwinio Carms 32 B3
Llanwnda Gwyn 82 F4
Llanwnda Pembs 44 B4
Llanwnnen Ceredig 46 E4
Llanwnog Powys 59 E7
Llanwrda Carms 47 F6
Llanwrin Powys 58 D4
Llanwrthwl Powys 47 C8
Llanwrtud = Llanwrtyd Wells Powys 47 E7
Llanwrtyd Powys 47 E7
Llanwrtyd Wells = Llanwrtud Powys 47 E7
Llanwyddelan Powys 59 D7
Llanyblodwel Shrops 60 B2
Llanybri Carms 32 C4
Llanybydder Carms 46 E4
Llanycefn Pembs 32 B1
Llanychaer Pembs 44 B4
Llanycil Gwyn 72 F3
Llanycrwys Carms 46 E5
Llanymawddwy Gwyn 59 C6
Llanymddyfri = Llandovery Carms 47 F6
Llanymynech Powys 60 B2
Llanynghenedl Anglesey 82 C3
Llanynys Denb 72 C5
Llanyre Powys 48 C2
Llanystumdwy Gwyn 71 D5
Llanywern Powys 35 B5
Llawhaden Pembs 32 C1
Llawnt Shrops 73 F6
Llawr Dref Gwyn 70 E3
Llawryglyn Powys 59 E6
Llay Wrex 73 D7
Llechcynfarwy Anglesey 82 C3
Llecheiddior Gwyn 71 C5
Llechfaen Powys 34 B4
Llechryd Caerph 35 D5
Llechryd Ceredig 45 E4
Llechrydau Powys 73 F6
Lledrod Ceredig 46 B5
Llenmerewig Powys 59 E8
Llethrid Swansea 33 E6
Llidiad Nenog Carms 46 F4
Llidiardau Gwyn 72 F2
Llidiart-y-parc Denb 72 E5
Llithfaen Gwyn 70 C4
Llong Flint 73 C6
Llowes Powys 48 E3
Llundain-fach Ceredig 46 D4
Llwydcoed Rhondda 34 D3
Llwyn Shrops 60 F2
Llwyn-du Mon 35 C6
Llwyn-hendy Carms 33 E6
Llwyn-têg Carms 33 D6
Llwyn-y-brain Carms 32 C2
Llwyn-y-groes Ceredig 46 D4
Llwyncelyn Ceredig 46 D3
Llwyndafydd Ceredig 46 D2
Llwynderw Powys 60 D2
Llwyndyrys Gwyn 70 C4
Llwyngwril Gwyn 58 D2
Llwynmawr Wrex 73 F6
Llwynypia Rhondda 34 E3
Llynclys Shrops 60 B2
Llynfaes Anglesey 82 D4
Llys-y-frân Pembs 32 B1
Llysfaen Conwy 83 D8
Llyswen Powys 48 F3
Llysworney V Glam 21 B8
Llywel Powys 47 F7
Loan Falk 120 B2
Loanend Northumb 122 D5
Loanhead Midloth 121 C5
Loans S Ayrs 118 F3
Loans of Tullich Highld 151 D11
Lobb Devon 20 F3
Loch a Charnain W Isles 148 D3
Loch a' Ghainmhich W Isles 155 E7
Loch Baghasdail = Lochboisdale W Isles 148 G2
Loch Choire Lodge Highld 157 F9
Loch Euphoirt W Isles 148 B3
Loch Head Dumfries 105 E7
Loch Loyal Lodge Highld 157 E9
Loch nam Madadh = Lochmaddy W Isles 148 B4
Loch Sgioport W Isles 148 E3
Lochailort Highld 147 C10
Lochaline Highld 147 G9
Lochanhully Highld 138 B5
Lochans Dumfries 104 D4
Locharbriggs Dumfries 114 F2
Lochassynt Lodge Highld 156 G4
Lochavich Ho Argyll 124 D5
Lochawe Argyll 125 C7
Lochboisdale = Loch Baghasdail W Isles 148 G2
Lochbuie Argyll 124 C2
Lochcarron Highld 149 E13
Lochdhu Highld 157 E13
Lochdochart House Stirling 126 B3
Lochdon Argyll 124 B3
Lochdrum Highld 150 D5
Lochead Argyll 144 F6
Lochearnhead Stirling 126 B4
Lochee Dundee 134 F3
Lochend Highld 151 H8
Lochend Highld 158 D4
Locherben Dumfries 114 E2
Lochfoot Dumfries 107 B5
Lochgair Argyll 145 D8
Lochgarthside Highld 137 C8
Lochgelly Fife 128 E3
Lochgilphead Argyll 145 E7
Lochgoilhead Argyll 125 E8
Lochhill Moray 152 B2
Lochindorb Lodge Highld 151 H12
Lochinver Highld 156 G3
Lochlane Perth 127 B7
Lochluichart Highld 150 E6
Lochmaben Dumfries 114 F3
Lochmaddy = Loch nam Madadh W Isles 148 B4
Lochmore Cottage Highld 158 F2
Lochmore Lodge Highld 156 F5
Lochore Fife 128 E3
Lochportain W Isles 148 A4
Lochranza N Ayrs 143 C10
Lochs Crofts Moray 152 B3
Lochside Aberds 135 C7
Lochside Highld 151 F11
Lochside Highld 156 D7
Lochside Highld 157 F11
Lochslin Highld 151 C11
Lochstack Lodge Highld 156 E5
Lochton Aberds 141 E6
Lochty Angus 135 C5
Lochty Fife 129 D7
Lochty Perth 128 B2
Lochuisge Highld 130 D1
Lochurr Dumfries 113 F7
Lochwinnoch Renfs 118 D3
Lochwood Dumfries 114 E3
Lochyside Highld 131 B5
Lockengate Corn 4 C5
Lockerbie Dumfries 114 F4
Lockeridge Wilts 25 C6
Lockerley Hants 14 B3
Locking N Som 23 D5
Lockinge Oxon 38 F4
Lockington E Yorks 97 E5
Lockington Leics 63 B8
Lockleywood Shrops 61 B6
Locks Heath Hants 15 D6
Lockton N Yorks 103 E6
Lockwood W Yorks 88 C2
Loddington Leics 64 D4
Loddington Northants 53 B6
Loddiswell Devon 6 E5
Loddon Norf 69 E6
Lode Cambs 55 C6
Loders Dorset 12 E2
Lodsworth W Sus 16 B3
Lofthouse N Yorks 94 B4
Lofthouse W Yorks 88 B4
Loftus Redcar 103 C5
Logan E Ayrs 113 B5
Logan Mains Dumfries 104 E4
Loganlea W Loth 120 C2
Loggerheads Staffs 74 F4
Logie Angus 135 C6
Logie Fife 129 B6
Logie Moray 151 F13
Logie Coldstone Aberds 140 D3
Logie Hill Highld 151 D10
Logie Newton Aberds 153 E6
Logie Pert Angus 135 C6
Logiealmond Lodge Perth 133 F6
Logierait Perth 133 D6
Login Carms 32 B2
Lolworth Cambs 54 C4
Lonbain Highld 149 C11
Londesborough E Yorks 96 E4
London Colney Herts 40 D4
Londonderry N Yorks 101 F8
Londonthorpe Lincs 78 F2
Londubh Highld 155 J13
Lonemore Highld 151 C10
Long Ashton N Som 23 B7
Long Bennington Lincs 77 E8
Long Bredy Dorset 12 E3
Long Buckby Northants 52 C4
Long Clawson Leics 64 B4
Long Common Hants 15 C6
Long Compton Staffs 62 B2
Long Compton Warks 51 F7
Long Crendon Bucks 39 D6
Long Crichel Dorset 13 C7
Long Ditton Sur 28 C2
Long Drax N Yorks 89 B7
Long Duckmanton Derbys 76 B4
Long Eaton Derbys 76 F4
Long Green Worcs 50 F3
Long Hanborough Oxon 38 C4
Long Itchington Warks 52 C2
Long Lawford Warks 52 B2
Long Load Som 12 B2
Long Marston Herts 40 C1
Long Marston N Yorks 95 D8
Long Marston Warks 51 E6
Long Marton Cumb 100 B1
Long Melford Suff 56 E2
Long Newnton Glos 37 E6
Long Newton E Loth 121 C8
Long Preston N Yorks 93 D8
Long Riston E Yorks 97 E7
Long Sight Gtr Man 87 D7
Long Stratton Norf 68 E4
Long Street M Keynes 53 E5
Long Sutton Hants 26 E5
Long Sutton Lincs 66 B4
Long Sutton Som 12 B2
Long Thurlow Suff 56 C4
Long Whatton Leics 63 B8
Long Wittenham Oxon 39 E5
Longbar N Ayrs 118 D3
Longbenton T&W 111 C5
Longborough Glos 38 B1
Longbridge W Mid 50 B5
Longbridge Warks 51 C7
Longbridge Deverill Wilts 24 E3
Longburton Dorset 12 C4
Longcliffe Derbys 76 D2
Longcot Oxon 38 E2
Longcroft Falk 119 B7
Longden Shrops 60 D4
Longdon Staffs 62 C4
Longdon Worcs 50 F3
Longdon Green Staffs 62 C4
Longdon on Tern Telford 61 C6
Longdown Devon 10 E3
Longdowns Corn 3 C6
Longfield Kent 29 C7
Longfield Shetland 160 M5
Longford Derbys 76 F2
Longford Glos 37 B5
Longford London 27 B8
Longford Shrops 74 F3
Longford Telford 61 C7
Longford W Mid 63 F7
Longfordlane Derbys 76 F2
Longforgan Perth 128 B5
Longformacus Borders 122 D2
Longframlington Northumb 117 D7
Longham Dorset 13 E8
Longham Norf 68 C2
Longhaven Aberds 153 E11
Longhill Aberds 153 C9
Longhirst Northumb 117 F8
Longhope Glos 36 C3
Longhope Orkney 159 J4
Longhorsley Northumb 117 E7
Longhoughton Northumb 117 C8
Longlane Derbys 76 F2
Longlane W Berks 26 B2
Longlevens Glos 37 B5
Longley W Yorks 88 D2
Longley Green Worcs 50 D2
Longmanhill Aberds 153 B7
Longmoor Camp Hants 27 F5
Longmorn Moray 152 C2
Longnewton Borders 115 B8
Longnewton Stockton 102 C1
Longney Glos 36 C4
Longniddry E Loth 121 B7
Longnor Shrops 60 D4
Longnor Staffs 75 C7
Longparish Hants 26 E2
Longport Stoke 75 E5
Longridge Lancs 93 F6
Longridge Staffs 62 C3
Longridge W Loth 120 C2
Longriggend N Lanark 119 B8
Longsdon Staffs 75 D6
Longshaw Gtr Man 86 D3
Longside Aberds 153 D10
Longstanton Cambs 54 C4
Longstock Hants 25 F8
Longstone Pembs 32 D2
Longstowe Cambs 54 D4
Longthorpe Pboro 65 E8
Longthwaite Cumb 99 B6
Longton Lancs 86 B2
Longton Stoke 75 E6
Longtown Cumb 108 C3
Longtown Hereford 35 B7
Longview Mers 86 E2
Longville in the Dale Shrops 60 E5
Longwick Bucks 39 D7
Longwitton Northumb 117 F6
Longwood Shrops 61 D6
Longworth Oxon 38 E3
Longyester E Loth 121 C8
Lonmay Aberds 153 C10
Lonmore Highld 148 D7
Looe Corn 5 D7
Loose Kent 29 D8
Loosley Row Bucks 39 D8
Lopcombe Corner Wilts 25 F7
Lopen Som 12 C2
Loppington Shrops 60 B4
Lopwell Devon 6 C2
Lorbottle Northumb 117 D6
Lorbottle Hall Northumb 117 D6
Lornty Perth 134 E1
Loscoe Derbys 76 E4
Losgaintir W Isles 154 H5
Lossiemouth Moray 152 A2
Lossit Argyll 142 C2
Lostford Shrops 74 F3
Lostock Gralam Ches W 74 B3
Lostock Green Ches W 74 B3
Lostock Hall Lancs 86 B3
Lostock Junction Gtr Man 86 D4
Lostwithiel Corn 5 D6
Loth Orkney 159 E7
Lothbeg Highld 157 H12
Lothersdale N Yorks 94 E2
Lothmore Highld 157 H12
Loudwater Bucks 40 E2
Loughborough Leics 64 C2
Loughor Swansea 33 E6
Loughton Essex 41 E7
Loughton M Keynes 53 F6
Loughton Shrops 61 F6
Lound Lincs 65 C7
Lound Notts 89 F7
Lound Suff 69 E8
Lount Leics 63 C7
Louth Lincs 91 F7
Love Clough Lancs 87 B6
Lovedean Hants 15 C7
Lover Wilts 14 B3
Loversall S Yorks 89 E6
Loves Green Essex 42 D2
Lovesome Hill N Yorks 102 E1
Loveston Pembs 32 D1
Lovington Som 23 F7
Low Ackworth W Yorks 89 C5
Low Barlings Lincs 78 B3
Low Bentham N Yorks 93 C6
Low Bradfield S Yorks 88 E3
Low Bradley N Yorks 94 E3
Low Braithwaite Cumb 108 E4
Low Brunton Northumb 110 B2
Low Burnham N Lincs 89 D8
Low Burton N Yorks 101 F7
Low Buston Northumb 117 D8
Low Catton E Yorks 96 D3
Low Clanyard Dumfries 104 F5
Low Coniscliffe Darl 101 C7
Low Crosby Cumb 108 D4
Low Dalby N Yorks 103 F6
Low Dinsdale Darl 101 C8
Low Ellington N Yorks 101 F7
Low Etherley Durham 101 B6
Low Fell T&W 111 D5
Low Fulney Lincs 66 B2
Low Garth N Yorks 103 D5
Low Gate Northumb 110 C2
Low Grantley N Yorks 94 B5
Low Habberley Worcs 50 B3
Low Ham Som 12 B2
Low Hesket Cumb 108 E4
Low Hesleyhurst Northumb 117 E6
Low Hutton N Yorks 96 C3
Low Laithe N Yorks 94 C4
Low Leighton Derbys 87 F8
Low Lorton Cumb 98 B3
Low Marishes N Yorks 96 B4
Low Marnham Notts 77 C8
Low Mill N Yorks 102 E4
Low Moor Lancs 93 E7
Low Moor W Yorks 88 B2
Low Moorsley T&W 111 E6
Low Newton Cumb 99 F6
Low Newton-by-the-Sea Northumb 117 B8
Low Row Cumb 108 F3
Low Row Cumb 109 C5
Low Row N Yorks 100 E4
Low Salchrie Dumfries 104 C4
Low Smerby Argyll 143 F8
Low Torry Fife 128 F2
Low Worsall N Yorks 102 D1
Low Wray Cumb 99 D5
Lowbridge House Cumb 99 D7
Lowca Cumb 98 B1
Lowdham Notts 77 E6
Lowe Shrops 74 F2
Lowe Hill Staffs 75 D6
Lower Aisholt Som 22 F4
Lower Arncott Oxon 39 C6
Lower Ashton Devon 10 F3
Lower Assendon Oxon 39 F7
Lower Badcall Highld 156 E4
Lower Bartle Lancs 92 F4
Lower Basildon W Berks 26 B4
Lower Beeding W Sus 17 B6
Lower Benefield Northants 65 F6
Lower Boddington Northants 52 D2
Lower Brailes Warks 51 F8
Lower Breakish Highld 149 F11
Lower Broadheath Worcs 50 D3
Lower Bullingham Hereford 49 F7
Lower Cam Glos 36 D4
Lower Chapel Powys 48 F2
Lower Chute Wilts 25 D8
Lower Cragabus Argyll 142 D4
Lower Crossings Derbys 87 F8
Lower Cumberworth W Yorks 88 D3
Lower Cwm-twrch Powys 34 C1
Lower Darwen Blackburn 86 B4
Lower Dean Bedford 53 C8
Lower Diabaig Highld 149 B12
Lower Dicker E Sus 18 D2
Lower Dinchope Shrops 60 F4
Lower Down Shrops 60 F3
Lower Drift Corn 2 D3
Lower Dunsforth N Yorks 95 C7
Lower Egleton Hereford 49 E8
Lower Elkstone Staffs 75 D7
Lower End C Beds 40 B2
Lower Everleigh Wilts 25 D6
Lower Farringdon Hants 26 F5
Lower Foxdale IoM 84 E2
Lower Frankton Shrops 73 F7
Lower Froyle Hants 27 E5
Lower Gledfield Highld 151 B8
Lower Green Norf 81 D5
Lower Hacheston Suff 57 D7
Lower Halistra Highld 148 C7
Lower Halstow Kent 30 C2
Lower Hardres Kent 31 D5
Lower Hawthwaite Cumb 98 F4
Lower Heath Ches E 75 C5
Lower Hempriggs Moray 151 E14
Lower Hergest Hereford 48 D4
Lower Heyford Oxon 38 B4
Lower Higham Kent 29 B8
Lower Holbrook Suff 57 F5
Lower Hordley Shrops 60 B3
Lower Horsebridge E Sus 18 D2
Lower Killeyan Argyll 142 D3
Lower Kingswood Sur 28 D3
Lower Kinnerton Ches W 73 C7
Lower Langford N Som 23 C6
Lower Largo Fife 129 D6
Lower Leigh Staffs 75 F7
Lower Lemington Glos 51 F7
Lower Lenie Highld 137 B8
Lower Lydbrook Glos 36 C2
Lower Lye Hereford 49 C6
Lower Machen Newport 35 F6
Lower Maes-coed Hereford 48 F5
Lower Mayland Essex 43 D5
Lower Midway Derbys 63 B7
Lower Milovaig Highld 148 C6
Lower Moor Worcs 50 E4
Lower Nazeing Essex 41 D6
Lower Netchwood Shrops 61 E6
Lower Ollach Highld 149 E10
Lower Penarth V Glam 22 B3
Lower Penn Staffs 62 E2
Lower Pennington Hants 14 E4
Lower Peover Ches W 74 B4
Lower Pexhill Ches E 75 B5
Lower Place Gtr Man 87 C7
Lower Quinton Warks 51 E6
Lower Rochford Worcs 49 C8
Lower Seagry Wilts 37 F6
Lower Shelton C Beds 53 E7
Lower Shiplake Oxon 27 B5
Lower Shuckburgh Warks 52 C2
Lower Slaughter Glos 38 B1
Lower Stanton St Quintin Wilts 37 F6
Lower Stoke Medway 30 B2
Lower Stondon C Beds 54 F2
Lower Stow Bedon Norf 68 E2
Lower Street Norf 69 C6
Lower Street Norf 81 D8
Lower Strensham Worcs 50 E4
Lower Stretton Warr 86 F4
Lower Sundon C Beds 40 B3
Lower Swanwick Hants 15 D5
Lower Swell Glos 38 B1
Lower Tean Staffs 75 F7
Lower Thurlton Norf 69 E7
Lower Tote Highld 149 B10
Lower Town Pembs 44 B4
Lower Tysoe Warks 51 E8
Lower Upham Hants 15 C6
Lower Vexford Som 22 F3
Lower Weare Som 23 D6
Lower Welson Hereford 48 D4
Lower Whitley Ches W 74 B3
Lower Wield Hants 26 E4
Lower Winchendon Bucks 39 C7
Lower Withington Ches E 74 C5
Lower Woodend Bucks 39 F8
Lower Woodford Wilts 25 F6
Lower Wyche Worcs 50 E2
Lowesby Leics 64 D4
Lowestoft Suff 69 E8
Loweswater Cumb 98 B3
Lowford Hants 15 C5
Lowgill Cumb 99 E8
Lowgill Lancs 93 C6
Lowick Northants 65 F6
Lowick Northumb 123 F6
Lowick Bridge Cumb 98 F4
Lowick Green Cumb 98 F4
Lowlands Torf 35 E6
Lowmoor Row Cumb 99 B8
Lownie Moor Angus 134 E4
Lowsonford Warks 51 C6
Lowther Cumb 99 B7
Lowthorpe E Yorks 97 C6
Lowton Gtr Man 86 E4
Lowton Common Gtr Man 86 E4
Loxbeare Devon 10 C4
Loxhill Sur 27 F8
Loxhore Devon 20 F5
Loxley Warks 51 D7
Loxton N Som 23 D5
Loxwood W Sus 27 F8
Lubcroy Highld 156 J6
Lubenham Leics 64 F4
Luccombe Som 21 E8
Luccombe Village IoW 15 G6
Lucker Northumb 123 F7
Luckett Corn 5 B8
Luckington Wilts 37 F5
Lucklawhill Fife 129 B6
Luckwell Bridge Som 21 F8
Lucton Hereford 49 C6
Ludag W Isles 148 G2
Ludborough Lincs 91 E6
Ludchurch Pembs 32 C2
Luddenden W Yorks 87 B8
Luddenden Foot W Yorks 87 B8
Luddesdown Kent 29 C7
Luddington N Lincs 90 C2
Luddington Warks 51 D6
Luddington in the Brook Northants 65 F8
Lude House Perth 133 C5
Ludford Lincs 91 F6
Ludford Shrops 49 B7
Ludgershall Bucks 39 C6
Ludgershall Wilts 25 D7
Ludgvan Corn 2 C4
Ludham Norf 69 C6
Ludlow Shrops 49 B7
Ludwell Wilts 13 B7
Ludworth Durham 111 E6
Luffincott Devon 8 E5
Lugar E Ayrs 113 B5
Lugg Green Hereford 49 C6
Luggate Burn E Loth 122 B2
Luggiebank N Lanark 119 B7
Lugton E Ayrs 118 D4
Lugwardine Hereford 49 E7
Luib Highld 149 F10
Lulham Hereford 49 E6
Lullenden Sur 28 E5
Lullington Derbys 63 C6
Lullington Som 24 D2
Lulsgate Bottom N Som 23 C7
Lulsley Worcs 50 D2
Lumb W Yorks 87 B8
Lumby N Yorks 95 F7
Lumloch E Dunb 119 C6
Lumphanan Aberds 140 D4
Lumphinnans Fife 128 E3
Lumsdaine Borders 122 C4
Lumsden Aberds 140 B3
Lunan Angus 135 D6
Lunanhead Angus 134 D4
Luncarty Perth 128 B2
Lund E Yorks 97 E5
Lund N Yorks 96 F2
Lund Shetland 160 C7
Lunderton Aberds 153 D11
Lundie Angus 134 F2
Lundie Highld 136 C4
Lundin Links Fife 129 D6
Lunga Argyll 124 E3
Lunna Shetland 160 G6
Lunning Shetland 160 G7
Lunnon Swansea 33 F6
Lunsford's Cross E Sus 18 D4
Lunt Mers 85 D4
Luntley Hereford 49 D5
Luppitt Devon 11 D6
Lupset W Yorks 88 C4
Lupton Cumb 99 F7
Lurgashall W Sus 16 B3
Lusby Lincs 79 C6
Luson Devon 6 E4
Luss Argyll 126 E2
Lussagiven Argyll 144 E5
Lusta Highld 149 C7
Lustleigh Devon 10 F2
Luston Hereford 49 C6
Luthermuir Aberds 135 C6
Luthrie Fife 128 C5
Luton Devon 7 B7
Luton Luton 40 B3
Luton Medway 29 C8
Lutterworth Leics 64 F2
Lutton Devon 6 D3
Lutton Lincs 66 B4
Lutton Northants 65 F8
Lutworthy Devon 10 C2
Luxborough Som 21 F8
Luxulyan Corn 5 D5
Lybster Highld 158 G4
Lydbury North Shrops 60 F3
Lydcott Devon 21 F5
Lydd Kent 19 C7
Lydd on Sea Kent 19 C7
Lydden Kent 31 E6
Lyddington Rutland 65 E5
Lyde Green Hants 26 D5
Lydeard St Lawrence Som 22 F3
Lydford Devon 9 F7
Lydford-on-Fosse Som 23 F7
Lydgate W Yorks 87 B7
Lydham Shrops 60 E3
Lydiard Green Wilts 37 F7
Lydiard Millicent Wilts 37 F7
Lydiate Mers 85 D4
Lydlinch Dorset 12 C5
Lydney Glos 36 D3
Lydstep Pembs 32 E1
Lye W Mid 62 F3
Lye Green Bucks 40 D2
Lye Green E Sus 18 B2
Lyford Oxon 38 E3
Lymbridge Green Kent 30 E5
Lyme Regis Dorset 11 E8
Lyminge Kent 31 E5
Lymington Hants 14 E4
Lyminster W Sus 16 D4
Lymm Warr 86 F4
Lymore Hants 14 E3
Lympne Kent 19 B8
Lympsham Som 22 D5
Lympstone Devon 10 F4
Lynchat Highld 138 D3
Lyndale Ho. Highld 149 C8
Lyndhurst Hants 14 D4
Lyndon Rutland 65 D6
Lyne Sur 27 C8
Lyne Down Hereford 49 F8
Lyne of Gorthleck Highld 137 B8
Lyne of Skene Aberds 141 C6
Lyneal Shrops 73 F8
Lyneham Oxon 38 B2
Lyneham Wilts 24 B5
Lynemore Highld 139 B6
Lynemouth Northumb 117 E8
Lyness Orkney 159 J4
Lyng Norf 68 C3
Lyng Som 11 B8
Lynmouth Devon 21 E6
Lynsted Kent 30 C3
Lynton Devon 21 E6
Lyon's Gate Dorset 12 D4
Lyonshall Hereford 48 D5
Lytchett Matravers Dorset 13 E7
Lytchett Minster Dorset 13 E7
Lyth Highld 158 D4
Lytham Lancs 85 B4
Lytham St Anne's Lancs 85 B4
Lythe N Yorks 103 C6
Lythes Orkney 159 K5

M

Mabe Burnthouse Corn 3 C6
Mabie Dumfries 107 B6
Mablethorpe Lincs 91 F9
Macclesfield Ches E 75 B6
Macclesfield Forest Ches E 75 B6
Macduff Aberds 153 B7
Mace Green Suff 56 E5
Macharioch Argyll 143 H8
Machen Caerph 35 F6
Machrihanish Argyll 143 F7
Machynlleth Powys 58 D4
Machynys Carms 33 E6
Mackerel's Common W Sus 16 B4
Mackworth Derbys 76 F3
Macmerry E Loth 121 B7
Madderty Perth 127 B8
Maddiston Falk 120 B2
Madehurst W Sus 16 C3
Madeley Staffs 74 E4
Madeley Telford 61 D6
Madeley Heath Staffs 74 E4
Madeley Park Staffs 74 E4
Madingley Cambs 54 C4
Madley Hereford 49 F6
Madresfield Worcs 50 E3
Madron Corn 2 C3
Maen-y-groes Ceredig 46 D2
Maenaddwyn Anglesey 82 C4
Maenclochog Pembs 32 B1
Maendy V Glam 22 B2
Maentwrog Gwyn 71 C7
Maer Staffs 74 F4
Maerdy Conwy 72 E4
Maerdy Rhondda 34 E3
Maes-Treylow Powys 48 C4
Maesbrook Shrops 60 B2
Maesbury Shrops 60 B3
Maesbury Marsh Shrops 60 B3
Maesgwyn-Isaf Powys 59 C8
Maesgwynne Carms 32 B3
Maeshafn Denb 73 C6
Maesllyn Ceredig 46 E2
Maesmynis Powys 48 E2
Maesteg Bridgend 34 E2
Maestir Ceredig 46 E4
Maesy cwmmer Caerph 35 E5
Maesybont Carms 33 C6
Maesycrugiau Carms 46 E3
Maesymeillion Ceredig 46 E3
Magdalen Laver Essex 41 D8
Maggieknockater Moray 152 D3
Magham Down E Sus 18 D3
Maghull Mers 85 D4
Magor Mon 35 F8
Magpie Green Suff 56 B4
Maiden Bradley Wilts 24 F3
Maiden Law Durham 110 E4
Maiden Newton Dorset 12 E3
Maiden Wells Pembs 44 F4
Maidencombe Torbay 7 C7
Maidenhall Suff 57 E5
Maidenhead Windsor 40 F1
Maidens S Ayrs 112 D2
Maiden's Green Brack 27 B6
Maidensgrave Suff 57 E6
Maidenwell Corn 5 B6
Maidenwell Lincs 79 B6
Maidford Northants 52 D4
Maids Moreton Bucks 52 F5
Maidstone Kent 29 D8
Maidwell Northants 52 B5
Mail Shetland 160 L6
Main Powys 59 C8
Maindee Newport 35 F7
Mains of Airies Dumfries 104 C3
Mains of Allardice Aberds 135 B8
Mains of Annochie Aberds 153 D9
Mains of Ardestie Angus 135 F5
Mains of Balhall Angus 135 C5
Mains of Ballindarg Angus 134 D4
Mains of Balnakettle Aberds 135 B6
Mains of Birness Aberds 153 E9
Mains of Burgie Moray 151 F13
Mains of Clunas Highld 151 G11
Mains of Crichie Aberds 153 D9
Mains of Dalvey Highld 151 H14
Mains of Dellavaird Aberds 141 F6
Mains of Drum Aberds 141 E7
Mains of Edingight Moray 152 C5
Mains of Fedderate Aberds 153 D8
Mains of Inkhorn Aberds 153 E9
Mains of Mayen Moray 152 D5
Mains of Melgund Angus 135 D5
Mains of Thornton Aberds 135 B6
Mains of Watten Highld 158 E4
Mainsforth Durham 111 F6
Mainsriddle Dumfries 107 D6
Mainstone Shrops 60 F2
Maisemore Glos 37 B5
Malacleit W Isles 148 A2
Malborough Devon 6 F5
Malcoff Derbys 87 F8
Maldon Essex 42 D4
Malham N Yorks 94 C2
Maligar Highld 149 B9
Mallaig Highld 147 B9
Malleny Mills Edin 120 C4
Malling Stirling 126 D4
Malltraeth Anglesey 82 E4
Mallwyd Gwyn 59 C5
Malmesbury Wilts 37 F6
Malmsmead Devon 21 E6
Malpas Ches W 73 E8
Malpas Corn 3 B7
Malpas Newport 35 E7
Malswick Glos 36 B4
Maltby S Yorks 89 E6
Maltby Stockton 102 C2
Maltby le Marsh Lincs 91 F8
Malting Green Essex 43 B5
Maltman's Hill Kent 30 E3
Malton N Yorks 96 B3
Malvern Link Worcs 50 E2
Malvern Wells Worcs 50 E2
Mamble Worcs 49 B8
Man-moel Caerph 35 D5
Manaccan Corn 3 D6
Manafon Powys 59 D8
Manais W Isles 154 J6

Manar Ho. Aberds 141 B6
Manaton Devon 10 F2
Manby Lincs 91 F7
Mancetter Warks 63 E7
Manchester Gtr Man 87 E6
Manchester Airport Gtr Man 87 F6
Mancot Flint 73 C7
Mandally Highld 137 D5
Manea Cambs 66 F4
Manfield N Yorks 101 C7
Mangaster Shetland 160 F5
Mangotsfield S Glos 23 B8
Mangurstadh W Isles 154 D5
Mankinholes W Yorks 87 B7
Manley Ches W 74 B2
Mannal Argyll 146 G2
Mannerston W Loth 120 B3
Manningford Bohune Wilts 25 D6
Manningford Bruce Wilts 25 D6
Manningham W Yorks 94 F4
Mannings Heath W Sus 17 B6
Mannington Dorset 13 D8
Manningtree Essex 56 F4
Mannofield Aberdeen 141 D8
Manor London 41 F7
Manor Estate S Yorks 88 F4
Manorbier Pembs 32 E1
Manordeilo Carms 33 B7
Manorhill Borders 122 F2
Manorowen Pembs 44 B4
Mansel Lacy Hereford 49 E6
Manselfield Swansea 33 F6
Mansell Gamage Hereford 49 E5
Mansergh Cumb 99 F8
Mansfield E Ayrs 113 C6
Mansfield Notts 76 C5
Mansfield Woodhouse Notts 76 C5
Mansriggs Cumb 98 F4
Manston Dorset 13 C6
Manston Kent 31 C7
Manston W Yorks 95 F6
Manswood Dorset 13 D7
Manthorpe Lincs 65 C7
Manthorpe Lincs 78 F2
Manton N Lincs 90 D3
Manton Notts 77 B5
Manton Rutland 65 D5
Manton Wilts 25 C6
Manuden Essex 41 B7
Maperton Som 12 B4
Maple Cross Herts 40 E3
Maplebeck Notts 77 C7
Mapledurham Oxon 26 B4
Mapledurwell Hants 26 D4
Maplehurst W Sus 17 B5
Maplescombe Kent 29 C6
Mapleton Derbys 75 E8
Mapperley Derbys 76 E4
Mapperley Park Nottingham 77 E5
Mapperton Dorset 12 E3
Mappleborough Green Warks 51 C5
Mappleton E Yorks 97 E8
Mappowder Dorset 12 D5
Mar Lodge Aberds 139 E6
Maraig W Isles 154 G6
Marazanvose Corn 4 D3
Marazion Corn 2 C4
Marbhig W Isles 155 F9
Marbury Ches E 74 E2
March Cambs 66 E4
March S Lanark 114 C2
Marcham Oxon 38 E4
Marchamley Shrops 61 B5
Marchington Staffs 75 F8
Marchington Woodlands Staffs 62 B5
Marchroes Gwyn 70 E4
Marchwiel Wrex 73 E7
Marchwood Hants 14 C4
Marcross V Glam 21 C8
Marden Hereford 49 E7
Marden Kent 29 E8
Marden T&W 111 B6
Marden Wilts 25 D5
Marden Beech Kent 29 E8
Marden Thorn Kent 29 E8
Mardy Mon 35 C7
Marefield Leics 64 D4
Mareham le Fen Lincs 79 C5
Mareham on the Hill Lincs 79 C5
Marehay Derbys 76 E3
Marehill W Sus 16 C4
Maresfield E Sus 17 B8
Marfleet Hull 90 B5
Marford Wrex 73 D7
Margam Neath 34 F1
Margaret Marsh Dorset 13 C6
Margaret Roding Essex 42 C1
Margaretting Essex 42 D2
Margate Kent 31 B7
Margnaheglish N Ayrs 143 E11
Margrove Park Redcar 102 C4
Marham Norf 67 C7
Marhamchurch Corn 8 D4
Marholm Pboro 65 D8
Mariandyrys Anglesey 83 C6
Marianglas Anglesey 82 C5
Mariansleigh Devon 10 B2
Marionburgh Aberds 141 D6
Marishader Highld 149 B9
Marjoriebanks Dumfries 114 F3
Mark Dumfries 104 D5
Mark S Ayrs 104 B4
Mark Som 23 E5
Mark Causeway Som 23 E5
Mark Cross E Sus 17 C8
Mark Cross E Sus 18 B2
Markbeech Kent 29 E5
Markby Lincs 79 B7
Market Bosworth Leics 63 D8
Market Deeping Lincs 65 D8
Market Drayton Shrops 74 F3
Market Harborough Leics 64 F4
Market Lavington Wilts 24 D5
Market Overton Rutland 65 C5
Market Rasen Lincs 90 F5
Market Stainton Lincs 78 B5
Market Warsop Notts 77 C5
Market Weighton E Yorks 96 E4
Market Weston Suff 56 B3
Markethill Perth 134 F2
Markfield Leics 63 C8
Markham Caerph 35 D5
Markham Moor Notts 77 B7
Markinch Fife 128 D4
Markington N Yorks 95 C5
Marks Tey Essex 43 B5
Marksbury Bath 23 C8
Markyate Herts 40 C3
Marland Gtr Man 87 C6
Marlborough Wilts 25 C6
Marlbrook Hereford 49 D7
Marlbrook Worcs 50 B4
Marlcliff Warks 51 D5
Marldon Devon 7 C6
Marlesford Suff 57 D7
Marley Green Ches E 74 E2
Marley Hill T&W 110 D5
Marley Mount Hants 14 E3
Marlingford Norf 68 D4
Marloes Pembs 44 E2
Marlow Bucks 39 F8
Marlow Hereford 49 B6
Marlow Bottom Bucks 40 F1
Marlpit Hill Kent 28 E5
Marlpool Derbys 76 E4
Marnhull Dorset 13 C5
Marnoch Aberds 152 C5
Marnock N Lanark 119 C7
Marple Gtr Man 87 F7
Marple Bridge Gtr Man 87 F7
Marr S Yorks 89 D6
Marrel Highld 157 H13
Marrick N Yorks 101 E5
Marrister Shetland 160 G7
Marros Carms 32 D3
Marsden T&W 111 C6
Marsden W Yorks 87 C8
Marsett N Yorks 100 F4
Marsh Devon 11 C7
Marsh W Yorks 94 F3
Marsh Baldon Oxon 39 E5
Marsh Gibbon Bucks 39 B6
Marsh Green Devon 10 E5
Marsh Green Kent 28 E5
Marsh Green Staffs 75 D5
Marsh Lane Derbys 76 B4
Marsh Street Som 21 E8
Marshall's Heath Herts 40 C4
Marshalsea Dorset 11 D8
Marshalswick Herts 40 D4
Marsham Norf 81 E7
Marshaw Lancs 93 D5
Marshborough Kent 31 D7
Marshbrook Shrops 60 F4
Marshchapel Lincs 91 E7
Marshfield Newport 35 F6
Marshfield S Glos 24 B2
Marshgate Corn 8 E3
Marshland St James Norf 66 D5
Marshside Mers 85 C4
Marshwood Dorset 11 E8
Marske N Yorks 101 D6
Marske-by-the-Sea Redcar 102 B4
Marston Ches W 74 B3
Marston Hereford 49 D5
Marston Lincs 77 E8
Marston Oxon 39 D5
Marston Staffs 62 B3
Marston Staffs 62 C2
Marston Warks 63 E6
Marston Wilts 24 D4
Marston Doles Warks 52 D2
Marston Green W Mid 63 F5
Marston Magna Som 12 B3
Marston Meysey Wilts 37 E8
Marston Montgomery Derbys 75 F8
Marston Moretaine C Beds 53 E7
Marston on Dove Derbys 63 B6
Marston St Lawrence Northants 52 E3
Marston Stannett Hereford 49 D7
Marston Trussell Northants 64 F3
Marstow Hereford 36 C2
Marsworth Bucks 40 C2
Marten Wilts 25 D7
Marthall Ches E 74 B5
Martham Norf 69 C7
Martin Hants 13 C8
Martin Kent 31 E7
Martin Lincs 78 C5
Martin Lincs 78 D4
Martin Dales Lincs 78 C4
Martin Drove End Hants 13 B8
Martin Hussingtree Worcs 50 C3
Martin Mill Kent 31 E7
Martinhoe Devon 21 E5
Martinhoe Cross Devon 21 E5
Martinscroft Warr 86 F4
Martinstown Dorset 12 F4
Martlesham Suff 57 E6
Martlesham Heath Suff 57 E6
Martletwy Pembs 32 C1
Martley Worcs 50 D2
Martock Som 12 C2
Marton Ches E 75 C5
Marton E Yorks 97 F7
Marton Lincs 90 F2
Marton Mbro 102 C3
Marton N Yorks 95 C7
Marton N Yorks 103 F5
Marton Shrops 60 B4
Marton Shrops 60 D2
Marton Warks 52 C2
Marton-le-Moor N Yorks 95 B6
Martyr Worthy Hants 26 F3
Martyr's Green Sur 27 D8
Marwick Orkney 159 F3
Marwood Devon 20 F4
Mary Tavy Devon 6 B3
Marybank Highld 150 F7
Maryburgh Highld 151 F8
Maryhill Glasgow 119 C5
Marykirk Aberds 135 C6
Marylebone Gtr Man 86 D3
Marypark Moray 152 E1
Maryport Cumb 107 F7
Maryport Dumfries 104 F5
Maryton Angus 135 D6
Marywell Aberds 140 E4
Marywell Aberds 141 E8
Marywell Angus 135 E6
Masham N Yorks 101 F7
Mashbury Essex 42 C2
Masongill N Yorks 93 B6
Masonhill S Ayrs 112 B3
Mastin Moor Derbys 76 B4
Mastrick Aberdeen 141 D7
Matching Essex 41 C8
Matching Green Essex 41 C8
Matching Tye Essex 41 C8
Matfen Northumb 110 B3
Matfield Kent 29 E7
Mathern Mon 36 E2
Mathon Hereford 50 E2
Mathry Pembs 44 B3
Matlaske Norf 81 D7
Matlock Derbys 76 C2
Matlock Bath Derbys 76 D2
Matson Glos 37 C5
Matterdale End Cumb 99 B5
Mattersey Notts 89 F7
Mattersey Thorpe Notts 89 F7
Mattingley Hants 26 D5
Mattishall Norf 68 C3
Mattishall Burgh Norf 68 C3
Mauchline E Ayrs 112 B4
Maud Aberds 153 D9
Maugersbury Glos 38 B2
Maughold IoM 84 C4
Mauld Highld 150 H7
Maulden C Beds 53 F8
Maulds Meaburn Cumb 99 C8
Maunby N Yorks 102 F1
Maund Bryan Hereford 49 D7
Maundown Som 11 B5
Mautby Norf 69 C7
Mavis Enderby Lincs 79 C6
Maw Green Ches E 74 D4
Mawbray Cumb 107 E7
Mawdesley Lancs 86 C2
Mawdlam Bridgend 34 F2
Mawgan Corn 3 D6
Mawla Corn 3 B6
Mawnan Corn 3 D6
Mawnan Smith Corn 3 D6
Mawsley Northants 53 B6
Maxey Pboro 65 D8
Maxstoke Warks 63 F6
Maxton Borders 122 F2
Maxton Kent 31 E7
Maxwellheugh Borders 122 F3
Maxwelltown Dumfries 107 B6
Maxworthy Corn 8 E4
May Bank Staffs 75 E5
Mayals Swansea 33 E7
Maybole S Ayrs 112 D3
Mayfield E Sus 18 C2
Mayfield Midloth 121 C6
Mayfield Staffs 75 E8
Mayfield W Loth 120 C2
Mayford Sur 27 D7
Mayland Essex 43 D5
Maynard's Green E Sus 18 D2
Maypole Mon 36 C1
Maypole Scilly 2 E4
Maypole Green Essex 43 B5
Maypole Green Norf 69 E7
Maypole Green Suff 57 C6
Maywick Shetland 160 L5
Meadle Bucks 39 D8
Meadowtown Shrops 60 D3
Meaford Staffs 75 F5
Meal Bank Cumb 99 E7
Mealabost W Isles 155 D9
Mealabost Bhuirgh W Isles 155 B9
Mealsgate Cumb 108 E2
Meanwood W Yorks 95 F5
Mearbeck N Yorks 93 C8
Meare Som 23 E6
Meare Green Som 11 B8
Mears Ashby Northants 53 C6
Measham Leics 63 C7
Meath Green Sur 28 E3
Meathop Cumb 99 F6
Meaux E Yorks 97 F6
Meavy Devon 6 C3
Medbourne Leics 64 E4
Medburn Northumb 110 B4
Meddon Devon 8 C4
Meden Vale Notts 77 C5
Medlam Lincs 79 D6
Medmenham Bucks 39 F8
Medomsley Durham 110 D4
Medstead Hants 26 F4
Meer End W Mid 51 B7
Meerbrook Staffs 75 C6
Meers Bridge Lincs 91 F8
Meesden Herts 54 F5
Meeth Devon 9 D7
Meggethead Borders 114 B4
Meidrim Carms 32 B3
Meifod Denb 72 D4
Meifod Powys 59 C8
Meigle N Ayrs 118 C1
Meigle Perth 134 E2
Meikle Earnock S Lanark 119 D7
Meikle Ferry Highld 151 C10
Meikle Forter Angus 134 C1
Meikle Gluich Highld 151 C9
Meikle Pinkerton E Loth 122 B3
Meikle Strath Aberds 135 B6
Meikle Tarty Aberds 141 B8
Meikle Wartle Aberds 153 E7
Meikleour Perth 134 F1
Meinciau Carms 33 C5
Meir Stoke 75 E6
Meir Heath Staffs 75 E6
Melbourn Cambs 54 E4
Melbourne Derbys 63 B7
Melbourne E Yorks 96 E3
Melbourne S Lanark 120 E3
Melbury Abbas Dorset 13 B6
Melbury Bubb Dorset 12 D3
Melbury Osmond Dorset 12 D3
Melbury Sampford Dorset 12 D3
Melby Shetland 160 H3
Melchbourne Bedford 53 C8
Melcombe Bingham Dorset 13 D5
Melcombe Regis Dorset 12 F4
Meldon Devon 9 E7
Meldon Northumb 117 F7
Meldreth Cambs 54 E4
Meldrum Ho. Aberds 141 B7
Melfort Argyll 124 D4
Melgarve Highld 137 E7
Meliden Denb 72 A4
Melin-y-coed Conwy 83 E8
Melin-y-ddôl Powys 59 D7
Melin-y-grug Powys 59 D7
Melin-y-Wig Denb 72 E4
Melinbyrhedyn Powys 58 E5
Melincourt Neath 34 D2
Melkinthorpe Cumb 99 B7
Melkridge Northumb 109 C7
Melksham Wilts 24 C4
Melldalloch Argyll 145 F8
Melling Lancs 93 B5
Melling Mers 85 D4
Melling Mount Mers 86 D2
Mellis Suff 56 B5
Mellon Charles Highld 155 H13
Mellon Udrigle Highld 155 H13
Mellor Gtr Man 87 F7
Mellor Lancs 93 F6
Mellor Brook Lancs 93 F6
Mells Som 24 E2
Melmerby Cumb 109 F6
Melmerby N Yorks 95 B6
Melmerby N Yorks 101 F5
Melplash Dorset 12 E2
Melrose Borders 121 F8
Melsetter Orkney 159 K3
Melsonby N Yorks 101 D6
Meltham W Yorks 88 C2
Melton Suff 57 D6
Melton Constable Norf 81 D6
Melton Mowbray Leics 64 C4
Melton Ross N Lincs 90 C4
Meltonby E Yorks 96 D3
Melvaig Highld 155 J12
Melverley Shrops 60 C3
Melverley Green Shrops 60 C3
Melvich Highld 157 C11
Membury Devon 11 D7
Memsie Aberds 153 B9
Memus Angus 134 D4
Menabilly Corn 5 D5
Menai Bridge = Porthaethwy Anglesey 83 D5
Mendham Suff 69 F5
Mendlesham Suff 56 C5
Mendlesham Green Suff 56 C4
Menheniot Corn 5 C7
Mennock Dumfries 113 D8
Menston W Yorks 94 E4
Menstrie Clack 127 E7
Menthorpe N Yorks 96 F2
Mentmore Bucks 40 C2
Meoble Highld 147 C10
Meole Brace Shrops 60 C4
Meols Mers 85 E3
Meonstoke Hants 15 C7
Meopham Kent 29 C7
Meopham Station Kent 29 C7
Mepal Cambs 66 F4
Meppershall C Beds 54 F2
Merbach Hereford 48 E5
Mere Ches E 86 F5
Mere Wilts 24 F3
Mere Brow Lancs 86 C2
Mere Green W Mid 62 E5
Mereclough Lancs 93 F8
Mereside Blackpool 92 F3
Mereworth Kent 29 D7
Mergie Aberds 141 F6
Meriden W Mid 63 F6
Merkadale Highld 149 E8
Merkland Dumfries 106 B4
Merkland S Ayrs 112 E2
Merkland Lodge Highld 156 G7
Merley Poole 13 E8
Merlin's Bridge Pembs 44 D4
Merrington Shrops 60 B4
Merrion Pembs 44 F4
Merriott Som 12 C2
Merrivale Devon 6 B3
Merrow Sur 27 D8
Merrymeet Corn 5 C7
Mersham Kent 19 B7
Merstham Sur 28 D3
Merston W Sus 16 D2
Merstone IoW 15 F6
Merther Corn 3 B7
Merthyr Carms 32 B4
Merthyr Cynog Powys 47 F8
Merthyr-Dyfan V Glam 22 C3
Merthyr Mawr Bridgend 21 B7
Merthyr Tudful = Merthyr Tydfil M Tydf 34 D4
Merthyr Tydfil = Merthyr Tudful M Tydf 34 D4
Merthyr Vale M Tydf 34 E4
Merton Devon 9 C7
Merton London 28 B3
Merton Norf 68 E2
Merton Oxon 39 C5
Mervinslaw Borders 116 C2
Meshaw Devon 10 C2
Messing Essex 42 C4
Messingham N Lincs 90 D2
Metfield Suff 69 F5
Metheringham Lincs 78 C3
Methil Fife 129 E5
Methlem Gwyn 70 D2
Methley W Yorks 88 B4
Methlick Aberds 153 E8
Methven Perth 128 B2
Methwold Norf 67 E7
Methwold Hythe Norf 67 E7
Mettingham Suff 69 F6
Mevagissey Corn 3 B9
Mewith Head N Yorks 93 C7
Mexborough S Yorks 89 D5
Mey Highld 158 C4
Meysey Hampton Glos 37 E8
Miabhag W Isles 154 G5
Miabhag W Isles 154 H6
Miabhig W Isles 154 D5
Michaelchurch Hereford 36 B2
Michaelchurch Escley Hereford 48 F5
Michaelchurch on Arrow Powys 48 D4
Michaelston-le-Pit V Glam 22 B3
Michaelston-y-Fedw Newport 35 F6
Michaelstow Corn 5 B5
Michealston-super-Ely Cardiff 22 B3
Micheldever Hants 26 F3
Michelmersh Hants 14 B4
Mickfield Suff 56 C5
Mickle Trafford Ches W 73 C8
Micklebring S Yorks 89 E6
Mickleby N Yorks 103 C6
Mickleham Sur 28 D2
Mickleover Derby 76 F3
Micklethwaite W Yorks 94 E4
Mickleton Durham 100 B4
Mickleton Glos 51 E6
Mickletown W Yorks 88 B4
Mickley N Yorks 95 B5
Mickley Square Northumb 110 C3
Mid Ardlaw Aberds 153 B9
Mid Auchinlech Invclyd 118 B3
Mid Beltie Aberds 140 D5
Mid Calder W Loth 120 C3
Mid Cloch Forbie Aberds 153 C7
Mid Clyth Highld 158 G4
Mid Lavant W Sus 16 D2
Mid Main Highld 150 H7
Mid Urchany Highld 151 G11
Mid Walls Shetland 160 H4
Mid Yell Shetland 160 D7
Midbea Orkney 159 D5
Middle Assendon Oxon 39 F7
Middle Aston Oxon 38 B4
Middle Barton Oxon 38 B4
Middle Cairncake Aberds 153 D8
Middle Claydon Bucks 39 B7
Middle Drums Angus 135 D5
Middle Handley Derbys 76 B4
Middle Littleton Worcs 51 E5
Middle Maes-coed Hereford 48 F5
Middle Mill Pembs 44 C3
Middle Rasen Lincs 90 F4
Middle Rigg Perth 128 D2
Middle Tysoe Warks 51 E8
Middle Wallop Hants 25 F7
Middle Winterslow Wilts 25 F7
Middle Woodford Wilts 25 F6
Middlebie Dumfries 108 B2
Middleforth Green Lancs 86 B3
Middleham N Yorks 101 F6
Middlehope Shrops 60 F4
Middlemarsh Dorset 12 D4
Middlemuir Aberds 141 B8
Middlesbrough Mbro 102 B2
Middleshaw Cumb 99 F7
Middleshaw Dumfries 107 B8
Middlesmoor N Yorks 94 B3
Middlestone Durham 111 F5
Middlestone Moor Durham 110 F5
Middlestown W Yorks 88 C3
Middlethird Borders 122 E2
Middleton Aberds 141 C7
Middleton Argyll 146 G2
Middleton Cumb 99 F8
Middleton Derbys 75 C8
Middleton Derbys 76 D2
Middleton Essex 56 F2
Middleton Gtr Man 87 D6
Middleton Hants 26 E2
Middleton Hereford 49 C7
Middleton Lancs 92 D4
Middleton Midloth 121 D6
Middleton N Yorks 94 E4
Middleton N Yorks 103 F5
Middleton Norf 67 C6
Middleton Northants 64 F5
Middleton Northumb 117 F6
Middleton Northumb 123 F7
Middleton Perth 128 D3
Middleton Perth 133 E8
Middleton Shrops 49 B7
Middleton Shrops 60 B3
Middleton Shrops 60 E2
Middleton Suff 57 C8
Middleton Swansea 33 F5
Middleton W Yorks 88 B3
Middleton Warks 63 E5
Middleton Cheney Northants 52 E2
Middleton Green Staffs 75 F6
Middleton Hall Northumb 117 B5
Middleton-in-Teesdale Durham 100 B4
Middleton Moor Suff 57 C8
Middleton-on-Leven N Yorks 102 D2
Middleton-on-Sea W Sus 16 D3
Middleton on the Hill Hereford 49 C7
Middleton-on-the-Wolds E Yorks 96 E5
Middleton One Row Darl 102 C1
Middleton Priors Shrops 61 E6
Middleton Quernham N Yorks 95 B6
Middleton Scriven Shrops 61 F6
Middleton St George Darl 101 C8
Middleton Stoney Oxon 39 B5
Middleton Tyas N Yorks 101 D7
Middletown Cumb 98 D1
Middletown Powys 60 C3
Middlewich Ches E 74 C3
Middlewood Green Suff 56 C4
Middlezoy Som 23 F5
Middridge Durham 101 B7
Midfield Highld 157 C8
Midge Hall Lancs 86 B3
Midgeholme Cumb 109 D6
Midgham W Berks 26 C3
Midgley W Yorks 87 B8
Midgley W Yorks 88 C3
Midhopestones S Yorks 88 E3
Midhurst W Sus 16 B2
Midlem Borders 115 B8
Midmar Aberds 141 D5
Midsomer Norton Bath 23 D8
Midton Invclyd 118 B2
Midtown Highld 155 J13
Midtown Highld 157 C8
Midtown of Buchromb Moray 152 D3
Midville Lincs 79 D6
Midway Ches E 87 F7
Migdale Highld 151 B9
Migvie Aberds 140 D3
Milarrochy Stirling 126 E3
Milborne Port Som 12 C4
Milborne St Andrew Dorset 13 E6
Milborne Wick Som 12 B4
Milbourne Northumb 110 B4
Milburn Cumb 100 B1
Milbury Heath S Glos 36 E3
Milcombe Oxon 52 F2
Milden Suff 56 E3
Mildenhall Suff 55 B8
Mildenhall Wilts 25 C7
Mile Cross Norf 68 C5
Mile Elm Wilts 24 C4
Mile End Essex 43 B5
Mile End Glos 36 C2
Mile Oak Brighton 17 D6
Milebrook Powys 48 B5
Milebush Kent 29 E8
Mileham Norf 68 C2
Milesmark Fife 128 F2
Milfield Northumb 122 F5
Milford Derbys 76 E3
Milford Devon 8 B4
Milford Powys 59 E7
Milford Staffs 62 B3
Milford Sur 27 E7
Milford Wilts 14 B2
Milford Haven = Aberdaugleddau Pembs 44 E4
Milford on Sea Hants 14 E3
Milkwall Glos 36 D2
Milkwell Wilts 13 B7
Mill Bank W Yorks 87 B8
Mill Common Suff 69 F7
Mill End Bucks 39 F7
Mill End Herts 54 F4
Mill Green Essex 42 D2
Mill Green Norf 68 F4
Mill Green Suff 56 E3
Mill Hill London 41 E5
Mill Lane Hants 27 D5
Mill of Kingoodie Aberds 141 B7
Mill of Muiresk Aberds 153 D6
Mill of Sterin Aberds 140 E2
Mill of Uras Aberds 141 F7
Mill Place N Lincs 90 D3
Mill Side Cumb 99 F6
Mill Street Norf 68 C3
Milland W Sus 16 B2
Millarston Renfs 118 C4
Millbank Aberds 153 D11
Millbank Highld 158 D3
Millbeck Cumb 98 B4
Millbounds Orkney 159 E6
Millbreck Aberds 153 D10
Millbridge Sur 27 E6
Millbrook C Beds 53 F8
Millbrook Corn 6 D2
Millbrook Soton 14 C4
Millburn S Ayrs 112 B4
Millcombe Devon 7 E6
Millcorner E Sus 18 C5
Milldale Staffs 75 D8
Millden Lodge Angus 135 B5
Milldens Angus 135 D5
Millerhill Midloth 121 C6
Miller's Dale Derbys 75 B8
Miller's Green Derbys 76 D2
Millgreen Shrops 61 B6
Millhalf Hereford 48 E4
Millhayes Devon 11 D7
Millhead Lancs 92 B4
Millheugh S Lanark 119 D7
Millholme Cumb 99 E7
Millhouse Argyll 145 F8
Millhouse Cumb 108 F3
Millhouse Green S Yorks 88 D3
Millhousebridge Dumfries 114 F4
Millhouses S Yorks 88 F4
Millikenpark Renfs 118 C4
Millin Cross Pembs 44 D4
Millington E Yorks 96 D4
Millmeece Staffs 74 F5
Millom Cumb 98 F3
Millook Corn 8 E3
Millpool Corn 5 B6
Millport N Ayrs 145 H10
Millquarter Dumfries 113 F6
Millthorpe Lincs 78 F4
Millthrop Cumb 100 E1
Milltimber Aberdeen 141 D7
Milltown Corn 5 D6
Milltown Derbys 76 C3
Milltown Devon 20 F4
Milltown Dumfries 108 B3
Milltown of Aberdalgie Perth 128 B2
Milltown of Auchindoun Moray 152 D3
Milltown of Craigston Aberds 153 C7
Milltown of Edinvillie Moray 152 D2
Milltown of Kildrummy Aberds 140 C3
Milltown of Rothiemay Moray 152 D5
Milltown of Towie Aberds 140 C3
Milnathort Perth 128 D3
Milner's Heath Ches W 73 C8
Milngavie E Dunb 119 B5
Milnrow Gtr Man 87 C7
Milnshaw Lancs 87 B5
Milnthorpe Cumb 99 F6
Milo Carms 33 C6
Milson Shrops 49 B8
Milstead Kent 30 D3
Milston Wilts 25 E6
Milton Angus 134 E3
Milton Cambs 55 C5
Milton Cumb 109 C5
Milton Derbys 63 B7
Milton Dumfries 105 D6
Milton Dumfries 106 B5
Milton Dumfries 113 F8
Milton Highld 150 F6
Milton Highld 150 H7
Milton Highld 151 D10
Milton Highld 151 G8
Milton Highld 158 E5
Milton Moray 152 B5
Milton N Som 22 C5
Milton Notts 77 B7
Milton Oxon 38 E4
Milton Oxon 52 F2
Milton Pembs 32 D1
Milton Perth 127 C8
Milton Ptsmth 15 E7
Milton Stirling 126 D4
Milton Stoke 75 D6
Milton W Dunb 118 B4
Milton Abbas Dorset 13 D6
Milton Abbot Devon 6 B2
Milton Bridge Midloth 120 C5
Milton Bryan C Beds 53 F7
Milton Clevedon Som 23 F8
Milton Coldwells Aberds 153 E9
Milton Combe Devon 6 C2
Milton Damerel Devon 9 C5
Milton End Glos 37 D8
Milton Ernest Bedford 53 D8
Milton Green Ches W 73 D8
Milton Hill Oxon 38 E4
Milton Keynes M Keynes 53 F6
Milton Keynes Village M Keynes 53 F6
Milton Lilbourne Wilts 25 C6
Milton Malsor Northants 52 D5
Milton Morenish Perth 132 F3
Milton of Auchinhove Aberds 140 D4
Milton of Balgonie Fife 128 D5
Milton of Buchanan Stirling 126 E3
Milton of Campfield Aberds 140 D5
Milton of Campsie E Dunb 119 B6
Milton of Corsindae Aberds 141 D5
Milton of Cushnie Aberds 140 C4
Milton of Dalcapon Perth 133 D6
Milton of Edradour Perth 133 D6
Milton of Gollanfield Highld 151 F10
Milton of Lesmore Aberds 140 B3
Milton of Logie Aberds 140 D3
Milton of Murtle Aberdeen 141 D7
Milton of Noth Aberds 140 B4
Milton of Tullich Aberds 140 E2
Milton on Stour Dorset 13 B5
Milton Regis Kent 30 C3
Milton under Wychwood Oxon 38 C2
Miltonduff Moray 152 B1
Miltonhill Moray 151 E13
Miltonise Dumfries 105 B5
Milverton Som 11 B6
Milverton Warks 51 C8
Milwich Staffs 75 F6
Minard Argyll 125 F5
Minchinhampton Glos 37 D5
Mindrum Northumb 122 F4
Minehead Som 21 E8
Minera Wrex 73 D6
Minety Wilts 37 E7
Minffordd Gwyn 58 C4
Minffordd Gwyn 71 D6
Minffordd Gwyn 83 D5
Miningsby Lincs 79 C6
Minions Corn 5 B7
Minishant S Ayrs 112 C3
Minllyn Gwyn 59 C5
Minnes Aberds 141 B8
Minngearraidh W Isles 148 F2
Minnigaff Dumfries 105 C8
Minnonie Aberds 153 B7
Minskip N Yorks 95 C6
Minstead Hants 14 C3
Minsted W Sus 16 B2
Minster Kent 30 B3
Minster Kent 31 C7
Minster Lovell Oxon 38 C3
Minsterley Shrops 60 D3
Minsterworth Glos 36 C4
Minterne Magna Dorset 12 D4
Minting Lincs 78 B4
Mintlaw Aberds 153 D9
Minto Borders 115 B8
Minton Shrops 60 E4
Minwear Pembs 32 C1
Minworth W Mid 63 E5
Mirbister Orkney 159 F4
Mirehouse Cumb 98 C1
Mireland Highld 158 D5
Mirfield W Yorks 88 C3
Miserden Glos 37 D6
Miskin Rhondda 34 F4
Misson Notts 89 E7
Misterton Leics 64 F2
Misterton Notts 89 E8
Misterton Som 12 D2
Mistley Essex 56 F5
Mitcham London 28 C3
Mitchel Troy Mon 36 C1
Mitcheldean Glos 36 C3
Mitchell Corn 4 D3
Mitcheltroy Common Mon 36 D1
Mitford Northumb 117 F7
Mithian Corn 4 D2
Mitton Staffs 62 C2
Mixbury Oxon 52 F4
Moat Cumb 108 B4
Moats Tye Suff 56 D4
Mobberley Ches E 74 B4
Mobberley Staffs 75 E7
Moccas Hereford 49 E5
Mochdre Conwy 83 D8
Mochdre Powys 59 F7
Mochrum Dumfries 105 E7
Mockbeggar Hants 14 D2
Mockerkin Cumb 98 B2
Modbury Devon 6 D4
Moddershall Staffs 75 F6
Moelfre Anglesey 82 C5
Moelfre Powys 59 B8
Moffat Dumfries 114 D3
Moggerhanger C Beds 54 E2
Moira Leics 63 C7
Mol-chlach Highld 149 G9
Molash Kent 30 D4
Mold = Yr Wyddgrug Flint 73 C6
Moldgreen W Yorks 88 C2
Molehill Green Essex 42 B1
Molescroft E Yorks 97 E6
Molesden Northumb 117 F7
Molesworth Cambs 53 B8
Moll Highld 149 E10
Molland Devon 10 B3
Mollington Ches W 73 B7
Mollington Oxon 52 E2
Mollinsburn N Lanark 119 B7
Monachty Ceredig 46 C4
Monachylemore Stirling 126 C3
Monar Lodge Highld 150 G5
Monaughty Powys 48 C4
Monboddo House Aberds 135 B7
Mondynes Aberds 135 B7
Monevechadan Argyll 125 E7
Monewden Suff 57 D6
Moneydie Perth 128 B2
Moniaive Dumfries 113 E7
Monifieth Angus 134 F4
Monikie Angus 135 F4
Monimail Fife 128 C4
Monington Pembs 45 E3
Monk Bretton S Yorks 88 D4
Monk Fryston N Yorks 89 B6
Monk Sherborne Hants 26 D4
Monk Soham Suff 57 C6
Monk Street Essex 42 B2
Monken Hadley London 41 E5
Monkhopton Shrops 61 E6
Monkland Hereford 49 D6
Monkleigh Devon 9 B6
Monknash V Glam 21 B8
Monkokehampton Devon 9 D7
Monks Eleigh Suff 56 E3
Monk's Gate W Sus 17 B6
Monks Heath Ches E 74 B5
Monks Kirby Warks 63 F8
Monks Risborough Bucks 39 D8
Monkseaton T&W 111 B6
Monkshill Aberds 153 D7
Monksilver Som 22 F2
Monkspath W Mid 51 B6
Monkswood Mon 35 D7
Monkton Devon 11 D6
Monkton Kent 31 C6
Monkton Pembs 44 E4
Monkton S Ayrs 112 B3
Monkton Combe Bath 24 C2
Monkton Deverill Wilts 24 F3
Monkton Farleigh Wilts 24 C3
Monkton Heathfield Som 11 B7
Monkton Up Wimborne Dorset 13 C8
Monkwearmouth T&W 111 D6
Monkwood Hants 26 F4
Monmouth = Trefynwy Mon 36 C2
Monmouth Cap Mon 35 B7
Monnington on Wye Hereford 49 E5
Monreith Dumfries 105 E7
Monreith Mains Dumfries 105 E7
Mont Saint Guern 16
Montacute Som 12 C2
Montcoffer Ho. Aberds 153 B6
Montford Argyll 145 G10
Montford Shrops 60 C4
Montford Bridge Shrops 60 C4
Montgarrie Aberds 140 C4
Montgomery = Trefaldwyn Powys 60 E2
Montrave Fife 129 D5
Montrose Angus 135 D7
Montsale Essex 43 E6
Monxton Hants 25 E8
Monyash Derbys 75 C8
Monymusk Aberds 141 C5
Monzie Perth 127 B7
Monzie Castle Perth 127 B7
Moodiesburn N Lanark 119 B6
Moonzie Fife 128 C5
Moor Allerton W Yorks 95 F5
Moor Crichel Dorset 13 D7
Moor End E Yorks 96 F4
Moor End York 96 D2
Moor Monkton N Yorks 95 D8
Moor of Granary Moray 151 F13
Moor of Ravenstone Dumfries 105 E7
Moor Row Cumb 98 C2
Moor Street Kent 30 C2
Moorby Lincs 79 C5
Moordown Bmouth 13 E8
Moore Halton 86 F3
Moorend Glos 36 D4
Moorends S Yorks 89 C7
Moorgate S Yorks 88 E5
Moorgreen Notts 76 E4
Moorhall Derbys 76 B3
Moorhampton Hereford 49 E5
Moorhead W Yorks 94 F4
Moorhouse Cumb 108 D3
Moorhouse Notts 77 C7
Moorlinch Som 23 F5
Moorsholm Redcar 102 C4
Moorside Gtr Man 87 D7
Moorthorpe W Yorks 89 C5
Moortown Hants 14 D2
Moortown IoW 14 F5
Moortown Lincs 90 E4
Morangie Highld 151 C10
Morar Highld 147 B9
Morborne Cambs 65 E8
Morchard Bishop Devon 10 D2
Morcombelake Dorset 12 E2
Morcott Rutland 65 D6
Morda Shrops 60 B2
Morden Dorset 13 E7
Morden London 28 C3
Mordiford Hereford 49 F7
Mordon Durham 101 B8
More Shrops 60 E3
Morebath Devon 10 B4
Morebattle Borders 116 B3
Morecambe Lancs 92 C4
Morefield Highld 150 B4
Moreleigh Devon 7 D5
Morenish Perth 132 F2
Moresby Cumb 98 B1
Moresby Parks Cumb 98 C1
Morestead Hants 15 B6
Moreton Dorset 13 F6
Moreton Essex 41 D8
Moreton Mers 85 E3
Moreton Oxon 39 D6
Moreton Staffs 61 C7
Moreton Corbet Shrops 61 B5
Moreton-in-Marsh Glos 51 F7
Moreton Jeffries Hereford 49 E8
Moreton Morrell Warks 51 D8
Moreton on Lugg Hereford 49 E7
Moreton Pinkney Northants 52 E3
Moreton Say Shrops 74 F3
Moreton Valence Glos 36 D4
Moretonhampstead Devon 10 F2
Morfa Carms 33 C6
Morfa Carms 33 E6
Morfa Bach Carms 32 C4
Morfa Bychan Gwyn 71 D6
Morfa Dinlle Gwyn 82 F4
Morfa Glas Neath 34 D2
Morfa Nefyn Gwyn 70 C3
Morfydd Denb 72 E5
Morgan's Vale Wilts 14 B2
Moriah Ceredig 46 B5
Morland Cumb 99 B7
Morley Derbys 76 E3
Morley Durham 101 B6
Morley W Yorks 88 B3
Morley Green Ches E 87 F6
Morley St Botolph Norf 68 E3
Morningside Edin 120 B5
Morningside N Lanark 119 D8
Morningthorpe Norf 68 E5
Morpeth Northumb 117 F8
Morphie Aberds 135 C7
Morrey Staffs 62 C5
Morris Green Essex 55 F8
Morriston Swansea 33 E7
Morston Norf 81 C6
Mortehoe Devon 20 E3
Mortimer W Berks 26 C4
Mortimer West End Hants 26 C4
Mortimer's Cross Hereford 49 C6
Mortlake London 28 B3
Morton Cumb 108 D3
Morton Derbys 76 C4
Morton Lincs 65 B7
Morton Lincs 77 C8
Morton Lincs 90 E2
Morton Norf 68 C4
Morton Notts 77 D7
Morton S Glos 36 E3
Morton Shrops 60 B2
Morton Bagot Warks 51 C6
Morton-on-Swale N Yorks 101 E8
Morvah Corn 2 C3
Morval Corn 5 D7
Morvich Highld 136 B2
Morvich Highld 157 J10
Morville Shrops 61 E6
Morville Heath Shrops 61 E6
Morwenstow Corn 8 C4
Mosborough S Yorks 88 F5
Moscow E Ayrs 118 E4
Mosedale Cumb 108 F3
Moseley W Mid 62 E3
Moseley W Mid 62 F4
Moseley Worcs 50 D3
Moss Argyll 146 G2
Moss Highld 147 E9
Moss S Yorks 89 C6
Moss Wrex 73 D7
Moss Bank Mers 86 E3
Moss Edge Lancs 92 E4
Moss End Brack 27 B6
Moss of Barmuckity Moray 152 B2
Moss Pit Staffs 62 B3
Moss-side Highld 151 F11
Moss Side Lancs 92 F3
Mossat Aberds 140 C3
Mossbank Shetland 160 F6
Mossbay Cumb 98 B1
Mossblown S Ayrs 112 B4
Mossbrow Gtr Man 86 F5
Mossburnford Borders 116 C2
Mossdale Dumfries 106 B3
Mossend N Lanark 119 C7
Mosser Cumb 98 B3
Mossfield Highld 151 D9
Mossgiel E Ayrs 112 B4
Mosside Angus 134 D4
Mossley Ches E 75 C5
Mossley Gtr Man 87 D7
Mossley Hill Mers 85 F4
Mosstodloch Moray 152 B3
Mosston Angus 135 E5
Mossy Lea Lancs 86 C3
Mosterton Dorset 12 D2
Moston Gtr Man 87 D6
Moston Shrops 61 B5
Moston Green Ches E 74 C4
Mostyn Flint 85 F2
Mostyn Quay Flint 85 F2
Motcombe Dorset 13 B6
Mothecombe Devon 6 E4
Motherby Cumb 99 B6
Motherwell N Lanark 119 D7
Mottingham London 28 B5
Mottisfont Hants 14 B4
Mottistone IoW 14 F5
Mottram in Longdendale Gtr Man 87 E7
Mottram St Andrew Ches E 75 B5
Mouilpied Guern 16
Mouldsworth Ches W 74 B2
Moulin Perth 133 D6
Moulsecoomb Brighton 17 D7
Moulsford Oxon 39 F5
Moulsoe M Keynes 53 E7
Moulton Ches W 74 C3
Moulton Lincs 66 B3
Moulton N Yorks 101 D7
Moulton Northants 53 C5
Moulton Suff 55 C7
Moulton V Glam 22 B2
Moulton Chapel Lincs 66 C2
Moulton Eaugate Lincs 66 C3
Moulton Seas End Lincs 66 B3
Moulton St Mary Norf 69 D6
Mounie Castle Aberds 141 B6
Mount Corn 4 D2
Mount Corn 5 C6
Mount Highld 151 G12
Mount Bures Essex 56 F3
Mount Canisp Highld 151 D10
Mount Hawke Corn 3 B6
Mount Pleasant Ches E 74 D5
Mount Pleasant Derbys 63 C6
Mount Pleasant Derbys 76 E3
Mount Pleasant Flint 73 B6
Mount Pleasant Hants 14 E3
Mount Pleasant W Yorks 88 B3
Mount Sorrel Wilts 13 B8
Mount Tabor W Yorks 87 B8
Mountain W Yorks 94 F3
Mountain Ash = Aberpennar Rhondda 34 E4
Mountain Cross Borders 120 E4

196 Mou–Nor

Mountain Water Pembs 44 C4
Mountbenger Borders 115 B6
Mountfield E Sus 18 C4
Mountgerald Highld 151 E8
Mountjoy Corn 4 C3
Mountnessing Essex 42 E2
Mounton Mon 36 E2
Mountsorrel Leics 64 C2
Mousehole Corn 2 D3
Mousen Northumb 123 F7
Mouswald Dumfries 107 B7
Mow Cop Ches E 75 D5
Mowhaugh Borders 116 B4
Mowsley Leics 64 F3
Moxley W Mid 62 E3
Moy Highld 137 F7
Moy Highld 151 H10
Moy Hall Highld 151 H10
Moy Ho. Moray 151 E13
Moy Lodge Highld 137 F7
Moyles Court Hants 14 D2
Moylgrove Pembs 45 E3
Muasdale Argyll 143 D7
Much Birch Hereford 49 F7
Much Cowarne Hereford 49 E8
Much Dewchurch Hereford 49 F6
Much Hadham Herts 41 C7
Much Hoole Lancs 86 B2
Much Marcle Hereford 49 F8
Much Wenlock Shrops 61 D6
Muchalls Aberds 141 E8
Muchelney Som 12 B2
Muchlarnick Corn 5 D7
Muchrachd Highld 150 H5
Muckernich Highld 151 F8
Mucking Thurrock 42 F2
Muckleford Dorset 12 E4
Mucklestone Staffs 74 F4
Muckleton Shrops 61 B5
Muckletown Aberds 140 B4
Muckley Corner Staffs 62 D4
Muckton Lincs 91 F7
Mudale Highld 157 F8
Muddiford Devon 20 F4
Mudeford Dorset 14 E2
Mudford Som 12 C3
Mudgley Som 23 E6
Mugdock Stirling 119 B5
Mugeary Highld 149 E9
Mugginton Derbys 76 E2
Muggleswick Durham 110 E3
Muie Highld 157 J9
Muir Aberds 139 F6
Muir of Fairburn Highld 150 F7
Muir of Fowlis Aberds 140 C4
Muir of Ord Highld 151 F8
Muir of Pert Angus 134 F4
Muirden Aberds 153 C7
Muirdrum Angus 135 F5
Muirhead Angus 134 F3
Muirhead Fife 128 D4
Muirhead N Lanark 119 C6
Muirhead S Ayrs 118 F3
Muirhouselaw Borders 116 B2
Muirhouses Falk 128 F2
Muirkirk E Ayrs 113 B6
Muirmill Stirling 127 F6
Muirshearlich Highld 136 F4
Muirskie Aberds 141 E7
Muirtack Aberds 153 E9
Muirton Highld 151 E10
Muirton Perth 127 C8
Muirton Perth 128 B3
Muirton Mains Highld 150 F7
Muirton of Ardblair Perth 134 E1
Muirton of Ballochy Angus 135 C6
Muiryfold Aberds 153 C7
Muker N Yorks 100 E4
Mulbarton Norf 68 D4
Mulben Moray 152 C3
Mulindry Argyll 142 C4
Mullardoch House Highld 150 H5
Mullion Corn 3 E5
Mullion Cove Corn 3 E5
Mumby Lincs 79 B8
Munderfield Row Hereford 49 D8
Munderfield Stocks Hereford 49 D8
Mundesley Norf 81 D9
Mundford Norf 67 E8
Mundham Norf 69 E6
Mundon Essex 42 D4
Mundurno Aberdeen 141 C8
Munerigie Highld 137 D5
Muness Shetland 160 C8
Mungasdale Highld 150 B2
Mungrisdale Cumb 108 F3
Munlochy Highld 151 F9
Munsley Hereford 49 E8
Munslow Shrops 60 F5
Murchington Devon 9 F8
Murcott Oxon 39 C5
Murkle Highld 158 D3
Murlaggan Highld 136 E3
Murlaggan Highld 137 F6
Murra Orkney 159 H3
Murrayfield Edin 120 B5
Murrow Cambs 66 D3
Mursley Bucks 39 B8
Murthill Angus 134 D4
Murthly Perth 133 F7
Murton Cumb 100 B2
Murton Durham 111 E6
Murton Northumb 123 E5
Murton York 96 D2
Musbury Devon 11 E7
Muscoates N Yorks 102 F4
Musdale Argyll 124 C5
Musselburgh E Loth 121 B6
Muston Leics 77 F8
Muston N Yorks 97 B6
Mustow Green Worcs 50 B3
Mutehill Dumfries 106 E3
Mutford Suff 69 F7
Muthill Perth 127 C7
Mutterton Devon 10 D5
Muxton Telford 61 C7
Mybster Highld 158 E3
Myddfai Carms 34 B1
Myddle Shrops 60 B4
Mydroilyn Ceredig 46 D3
Myerscough Lancs 92 F4
Mylor Bridge Corn 3 C7
Mynachlog-ddu Pembs 45 F3
Myndtown Shrops 60 F3
Mynydd Bach Ceredig 47 B6
Mynydd-bach Mon 36 E1
Mynydd Bodafon Anglesey 82 C4
Mynydd-isa Flint 73 C6
Mynyddygarreg Carms 33 D5
Mynytho Gwyn 70 D4
Myrebird Aberds 141 E6
Myrelandhorn Highld 158 E4
Myreside Perth 128 B4
Myrtle Hill Carms 47 F6
Mytchett Sur 27 D6
Mytholm W Yorks 87 B7
Mytholmroyd W Yorks 87 B8
Myton-on-Swale N Yorks 95 C7
Mytton Shrops 60 C4

N

Na Gearrannan W Isles 154 C6
Naast Highld 155 J13
Naburn York 95 E8
Nackington Kent 31 D5
Nacton Suff 57 E6
Nafferton E Yorks 97 D6
Nailbridge Glos 36 C3
Nailsbourne Som 11 B7
Nailsea N Som 23 B6
Nailstone Leics 63 D8
Nailsworth Glos 37 E5
Nairn Highld 151 F11
Nalderswood Sur 28 E3
Nancegollan Corn 2 C5
Nancledra Corn 2 C3
Nanhoron Gwyn 70 D3
Nannau Gwyn 71 E8
Nannerch Flint 73 C5
Nanpantan Leics 64 C2
Nanpean Corn 4 D4
Nanstallon Corn 4 C5
Nant-ddu Powys 34 C4
Nant-glas Powys 47 C8
Nant Peris Gwyn 83 F6
Nant Uchaf Denb 72 D4
Nant-y-Bai Carms 47 E6
Nant-y-cafn Neath 34 D2
Nant-y-derry Mon 35 D7
Nant-y-ffin Carms 46 F4
Nant-y-moel Bridgend 34 E3
Nant-y-pandy Conwy 83 D6
Nanternis Ceredig 46 D2
Nantgaredig Carms 33 B5
Nantgarw Rhondda 35 F5
Nantglyn Denb 72 C4
Nantgwyn Powys 47 B8
Nantlle Gwyn 82 F5
Nantmawr Shrops 60 B2
Nantmel Powys 48 C2
Nantmor Gwyn 71 C7
Nantwich Ches E 74 D3
Nantycaws Carms 33 C5
Nantyffyllon Bridgend 34 E2
Nantyglo Bl Gwent 35 C5
Naphill Bucks 39 E8
Nappa N Yorks 93 D8
Napton on the Hill Warks 52 C2
Narberth = Arberth Pembs 32 C2
Narborough Leics 64 E2
Narborough Norf 67 C7
Nasareth Gwyn 82 F4
Naseby Northants 52 B4
Nash Bucks 53 F5
Nash Hereford 48 C5
Nash Newport 35 F7
Nash Shrops 49 B8
Nash Lee Bucks 39 D8
Nassington Northants 65 E7
Nasty Herts 41 B6
Nateby Cumb 100 D2
Nateby Lancs 92 E4
Natland Cumb 99 F7
Naughton Suff 56 E4
Naunton Glos 37 B8
Naunton Worcs 50 F3
Naunton Beauchamp Worcs 50 D4
Navenby Lincs 78 D2
Navestock Heath Essex 41 E8
Navestock Side Essex 42 E1
Navidale Highld 157 H13
Nawton N Yorks 102 F4
Nayland Suff 56 F3
Nazeing Essex 41 D7
Neacroft Hants 14 E2
Neal's Green Warks 63 F7
Neap Shetland 160 H7
Near Sawrey Cumb 99 E5
Neasham Darl 101 C8
Neath = Castell-Nedd Neath 33 E8
Neath Abbey Neath 33 E8
Neatishead Norf 69 B6
Nebo Anglesey 82 B4
Nebo Ceredig 46 C4
Nebo Conwy 83 F8
Nebo Gwyn 82 F4
Necton Norf 67 D8
Nedd Highld 156 F4
Nedderton Northumb 117 F8
Nedging Tye Suff 56 E4
Needham Norf 68 F5
Needham Market Suff 56 D4
Needingworth Cambs 54 B4
Needwood Staffs 63 B5
Neen Savage Shrops 49 B8
Neen Sollars Shrops 49 B8
Neenton Shrops 61 F6
Nefyn Gwyn 70 C4
Neilston E Renf 118 D4
Neinthirion Powys 59 D6
Neithrop Oxon 52 E2
Nelly Andrews Green Powys 60 D2
Nelson Caerph 35 E5
Nelson Lancs 93 F8
Nelson Village Northumb 111 B5
Nemphlar S Lanark 119 E8
Nempnett Thrubwell N Som 23 C7
Nene Terrace Lincs 66 D2
Nenthall Cumb 109 E7
Nenthead Cumb 109 E7
Nenthorn Borders 122 F2
Nerabus Argyll 142 C3
Nercwys Flint 73 C6
Nerston S Lanark 119 D6
Nesbit Northumb 123 F5
Ness Ches W 73 B7
Nesscliffe Shrops 60 C3
Neston Ches W 73 B6
Neston Wilts 24 C3
Nether Alderley Ches E 74 B5
Nether Blainslie Borders 121 E8
Nether Booth Derbys 88 F2
Nether Broughton Leics 64 B3
Nether Burrow Lancs 93 B6
Nether Cerne Dorset 12 E4
Nether Compton Dorset 12 C3
Nether Crimond Aberds 141 B7
Nether Dalgliesh Borders 115 D5
Nether Dallachy Moray 152 B3
Nether Exe Devon 10 D4
Nether Glasslaw Aberds 153 C8
Nether Handwick Angus 134 E3
Nether Haugh S Yorks 88 E5
Nether Heage Derbys 76 D3
Nether Heyford Northants 52 D4
Nether Hindhope Borders 116 C3
Nether Howecleuch S Lanark 114 C3
Nether Kellet Lancs 92 C5
Nether Kinmundy Aberds 153 D10
Nether Langwith Notts 76 B5
Nether Leask Aberds 153 E10
Nether Lenshie Aberds 153 D6
Nether Monynut Borders 122 C3
Nether Padley Derbys 76 B2
Nether Park Aberds 153 C10
Nether Poppleton York 95 D8
Nether Silton N Yorks 102 E2
Nether Stowey Som 22 F3
Nether Urquhart Fife 128 D3
Nether Wallop Hants 25 F8
Nether Wasdale Cumb 98 D3
Nether Whitacre Warks 63 E6
Nether Worton Oxon 52 F2
Netheravon Wilts 25 E6
Netherbrae Aberds 153 C7
Netherbrough Orkney 159 G4
Netherburn S Lanark 119 E8
Netherbury Dorset 12 E2
Netherby Cumb 108 B3
Netherby N Yorks 95 E6
Nethercote Warks 52 C3
Nethercott Devon 20 F3
Netherend Glos 36 D2
Netherfield E Sus 18 D4
Netherhampton Wilts 14 B2
Netherlaw Dumfries 106 E4
Netherley Aberds 141 E7
Netherley Mers 86 F2
Nethermill Dumfries 114 F3
Nethermuir Aberds 153 D9
Netherplace E Renf 118 D5
Netherseal Derbys 63 C6
Netherthird E Ayrs 113 C5
Netherthong W Yorks 88 D2
Netherthorpe S Yorks 89 F6
Netherton Angus 135 D5
Netherton Devon 7 B6
Netherton Hants 25 D8
Netherton Mers 85 D4
Netherton Northumb 117 D5
Netherton Oxon 38 E4
Netherton Perth 133 D8
Netherton Stirling 119 B5
Netherton W Mid 62 F3
Netherton W Yorks 88 C2
Netherton W Yorks 88 C3
Netherton Worcs 50 E4
Nethertown Cumb 98 D1
Nethertown Highld 158 C5
Netherwitton Northumb 117 E7
Netherwood E Ayrs 113 B6
Nethy Bridge Highld 139 B6
Netley Hants 15 D5
Netley Marsh Hants 14 C4
Netteswell Essex 41 C7
Nettlebed Oxon 39 F7
Nettlebridge Som 23 E8
Nettlecombe Dorset 12 E3
Nettleden Herts 40 C3
Nettleham Lincs 78 B3
Nettlestead Kent 29 D7
Nettlestead Green Kent 29 D7
Nettlestone IoW 15 E7
Nettlesworth Durham 111 E5
Nettleton Lincs 90 D5
Nettleton Wilts 24 B3
Neuadd Carms 33 B7
Nevendon Essex 42 E3
Nevern Pembs 45 E2
New Abbey Dumfries 107 C6
New Aberdour Aberds 153 B8
New Addington London 28 C4
New Alresford Hants 26 F3
New Alyth Perth 134 E2
New Arley Warks 63 F6
New Ash Green Kent 29 C7
New Barn Kent 29 C7
New Barnetby N Lincs 90 C4
New Barton Northants 53 C6
New Bewick Northumb 117 B6
New-bigging Angus 134 E2
New Bilton Warks 52 B2
New Bolingbroke Lincs 79 D6
New Boultham Lincs 78 B2
New Bradwell M Keynes 53 E6
New Brancepeth Durham 110 E5
New Bridge Wrex 73 E6
New Brighton Flint 73 C6
New Brighton Mers 85 E4
New Brinsley Notts 76 D4
New Broughton Wrex 73 D7
New Buckenham Norf 68 E3
New Byth Aberds 153 C8
New Catton Norf 68 C5
New Cheriton Hants 15 B6
New Costessey Norf 68 C4
New Cowper Cumb 107 E8
New Cross Ceredig 46 B5
New Cross London 28 B4
New Cumnock E Ayrs 113 C6
New Deer Aberds 153 D8
New Delaval Northumb 111 B5
New Duston Northants 52 C5
New Earswick York 96 D2
New Edlington S Yorks 89 E6
New Elgin Moray 152 B2
New Ellerby E Yorks 97 F7
New Eltham London 28 B5
New End Worcs 51 D5
New Farnley W Yorks 94 F5
New Ferry Mers 85 F4
New Fryston W Yorks 89 B5
New Galloway Dumfries 106 B3
New Gilston Fife 129 D6
New Grimsby Scilly 2 E3
New Hainford Norf 68 C5
New Hartley Northumb 111 B6
New Haw Sur 27 C8
New Hedges Pembs 32 D2
New Herrington T&W 111 D6
New Hinksey Oxon 39 D5
New Holkham Norf 80 D4
New Holland N Lincs 90 B4
New Houghton Derbys 76 C4
New Houghton Norf 80 E3
New Houses N Yorks 93 B8
New Humberstone Leicester 64 D3
New Hutton Cumb 99 E7
New Hythe Kent 29 D8
New Inn Carms 46 F3
New Inn Mon 36 D1
New Inn Pembs 45 F2
New Inn Torf 35 E7
New Invention Shrops 48 B4
New Invention W Mid 62 D3
New Kelso Highld 150 G2
New Kingston Notts 64 B2
New Lanark S Lanark 119 E8
New Lane Lancs 86 C2
New Lane End Warr 86 E4
New Leake Lincs 79 D7
New Leeds Aberds 153 C9
New Longton Lancs 86 B3
New Luce Dumfries 105 C5
New Malden London 28 C3
New Marske Redcar 102 B4
New Marton Shrops 73 F7
New Micklefield W Yorks 95 F7
New Mill Aberds 141 F6
New Mill Herts 40 C2
New Mill W Yorks 88 D2
New Mill Wilts 25 C6
New Mills Ches E 87 F5
New Mills Corn 4 D3
New Mills Derbys 87 F7
New Mills Powys 59 D7
New Milton Hants 14 E3
New Moat Pembs 32 B1
New Ollerton Notts 77 C6
New Oscott W Mid 62 E4
New Park N Yorks 95 D5
New Pitsligo Aberds 153 C8
New Polzeath Corn 4 B4
New Quay = Ceinewydd Ceredig 46 D2
New Rackheath Norf 69 C5
New Radnor Powys 48 C4
New Rent Cumb 108 F4
New Ridley Northumb 110 D3
New Road Side N Yorks 94 E2
New Romney Kent 19 C7
New Rossington S Yorks 89 E7
New Row Ceredig 47 B6
New Row Lancs 93 F6
New Row N Yorks 102 C4
New Sarum Wilts 25 F6
New Silksworth T&W 111 D6
New Stevenston N Lanark 119 D7
New Street Staffs 75 D7
New Street Lane Shrops 74 F3
New Swanage Dorset 13 F8
New Totley S Yorks 76 B3
New Town E Loth 121 B7
New Tredegar = Tredegar Newydd Caerph 35 D5
New Trows S Lanark 119 F8
New Ulva Argyll 144 E6
New Walsoken Cambs 66 D4
New Waltham NE Lincs 91 D6
New Whittington Derbys 76 B3
New Wimpole Cambs 54 E4
New Winton E Loth 121 B7
New Yatt Oxon 38 C3
New York Lincs 78 D5
New York N Yorks 94 C4
Newall W Yorks 94 E4
Newark Orkney 159 D8
Newark Pboro 66 D2
Newark-on-Trent Notts 77 D7
Newarthill N Lanark 119 D7
Newbarns Cumb 92 B2
Newbattle Midloth 121 C6
Newbiggin Cumb 92 C2
Newbiggin Cumb 98 E2
Newbiggin Cumb 99 B6
Newbiggin Cumb 99 B8
Newbiggin Cumb 109 E5
Newbiggin Durham 100 B4
Newbiggin N Yorks 100 E4
Newbiggin N Yorks 100 F4
Newbiggin-by-the-Sea Northumb 117 F9
Newbiggin-on-Lune Cumb 100 D2
Newbigging Angus 134 F4
Newbigging Angus 134 F4
Newbigging S Lanark 120 E3
Newbold Derbys 76 B3
Newbold Leics 63 C8
Newbold on Avon Warks 52 B2
Newbold on Stour Warks 51 E7
Newbold Pacey Warks 51 D7
Newbold Verdon Leics 63 D8
Newborough Anglesey 82 E4
Newborough Pboro 66 D2
Newborough Staffs 62 B5
Newbottle Northants 52 F3
Newbottle T&W 111 D6
Newbourne Suff 57 E6
Newbridge Caerph 35 E6
Newbridge Ceredig 46 D4
Newbridge Corn 2 C3
Newbridge Corn 5 C8
Newbridge Dumfries 107 B6
Newbridge Edin 120 B4
Newbridge Hants 14 C3
Newbridge IoW 14 F5
Newbridge Pembs 44 B4
Newbridge Green Worcs 50 F3
Newbridge-on-Usk Mon 35 E7
Newbridge on Wye Powys 48 D2
Newbrough Northumb 109 C8
Newbuildings Devon 10 D2
Newburgh Aberds 141 B8
Newburgh Aberds 153 C9
Newburgh Borders 115 C6
Newburgh Fife 128 C4
Newburgh Lancs 86 C2
Newburn T&W 110 C4
Newbury W Berks 26 C2
Newbury Park London 41 F7
Newby Cumb 99 B7
Newby Lancs 93 E8
Newby N Yorks 93 B7
Newby N Yorks 102 C3
Newby N Yorks 103 E8
Newby Bridge Cumb 99 F5
Newby East Cumb 108 D4
Newby West Cumb 108 D3
Newby Wiske N Yorks 102 F1
Newcastle Mon 35 C8
Newcastle Shrops 60 F2
Newcastle Emlyn = Castell Newydd Emlyn Carms 46 E2
Newcastle-under-Lyme Staffs 74 E5
Newcastle Upon Tyne T&W 110 C5
Newcastleton or Copshaw Holm Borders 115 F7
Newchapel Pembs 45 F4
Newchapel Powys 59 F6
Newchapel Staffs 75 D5
Newchapel Sur 28 E4
Newchurch Carms 32 B4
Newchurch IoW 15 F6
Newchurch Kent 19 B7
Newchurch Lancs 93 F8
Newchurch Mon 36 E1
Newchurch Powys 48 D4
Newchurch Staffs 62 B5
Newcott Devon 11 D7
Newcraighall Edin 121 B6
Newdigate Sur 28 E2
Newell Green Brack 27 B6
Newenden Kent 18 C5
Newent Glos 36 B4
Newerne Glos 36 D3
Newfield Durham 110 F5
Newfield Highld 151 D10
Newford Scilly 2 E4
Newfound Hants 26 D3
Newgale Pembs 44 C3
Newgate Norf 81 C6
Newgate Street Herts 41 D6
Newhall Ches E 74 E3
Newhall Derbys 63 B6
Newhall House Highld 151 E9
Newhall Point Highld 151 E10
Newham Northumb 117 B7
Newham Hall Northumb 117 B7
Newhaven Derbys 75 D8
Newhaven E Sus 17 D8
Newhaven Edin 121 B5
Newhey Gtr Man 87 C7
Newholm N Yorks 103 C6
Newhouse N Lanark 119 C7
Newick E Sus 17 B8
Newingreen Kent 19 B8
Newington Kent 19 B8
Newington Kent 30 C2
Newington Kent 31 C7
Newington Notts 89 E7
Newington Oxon 39 E6
Newington Shrops 60 F4
Newland Glos 36 D2
Newland Hull 97 F6
Newland N Yorks 89 B7
Newland Worcs 50 E2
Newlandrig Midloth 121 C6
Newlands Borders 115 E8
Newlands Highld 151 G10
Newlands Moray 152 C3
Newlands Northumb 110 D3
Newland's Corner Sur 27 E8
Newlands of Geise Highld 158 D2
Newlands of Tynet Moray 152 B3
Newlands Park Anglesey 82 C2
Newlandsmuir S Lanark 119 D6
Newlot Orkney 159 G6
Newlyn Corn 2 D3
Newmachar Aberds 141 C7
Newmains N Lanark 119 D8
Newmarket Suff 55 C7
Newmarket W Isles 155 D9
Newmill Borders 115 C7
Newmill Corn 2 C3
Newmill Moray 152 C4
Newmill of Inshewan Angus 134 C4
Newmills of Boyne Aberds 152 C5
Newmiln Perth 133 F8
Newmilns E Ayrs 118 F5
Newnham Cambs 54 D5
Newnham Glos 36 C3
Newnham Hants 26 D5
Newnham Herts 54 F3
Newnham Kent 30 D3
Newnham Northants 52 D3
Newnham Bridge Worcs 49 C8
Newpark Fife 129 C6
Newport Devon 20 F4
Newport E Yorks 96 F4
Newport Essex 55 F6
Newport Highld 158 H3
Newport IoW 15 F6
Newport = Casnewydd Newport 35 F7
Newport Norf 69 C8
Newport = Trefdraeth Pembs 45 F2
Newport Telford 61 C7
Newport-on-Tay Fife 129 B6
Newport Pagnell M Keynes 53 E6
Newpound Common W Sus 16 B4
Newquay Corn 4 C3
Newsbank Ches E 74 C5
Newseat Aberds 153 D10
Newseat Aberds 153 E7
Newsham N Yorks 101 C6
Newsham N Yorks 102 F1
Newsham Northumb 111 B6
Newsholme E Yorks 89 B8
Newsholme Lancs 93 D8
Newsome W Yorks 88 C2
Newstead Borders 121 F8
Newstead Northumb 117 B7
Newstead Notts 76 D5
Newthorpe N Yorks 95 F7
Newton Argyll 125 F6
Newton Borders 116 B2
Newton Bridgend 21 B7
Newton Cambs 54 E5
Newton Cambs 66 C4
Newton Cardiff 22 B4
Newton Ches W 73 C8
Newton Ches W 74 B2
Newton Ches W 74 D2
Newton Cumb 92 B2
Newton Derbys 76 D4
Newton Dorset 13 C5
Newton Dumfries 108 B2
Newton Dumfries 114 E4
Newton Gtr Man 87 E7
Newton Hereford 48 F5
Newton Hereford 49 D7
Newton Highld 151 E10
Newton Highld 151 G10
Newton Highld 156 F5
Newton Highld 158 F5
Newton Lancs 92 F4
Newton Lancs 93 B5
Newton Lancs 93 D6
Newton Lincs 78 F3
Newton Moray 152 B1
Newton Norf 67 C8
Newton Northants 65 F5
Newton Northumb 110 C3
Newton Notts 77 E6
Newton Perth 133 F5
Newton S Lanark 119 C6
Newton S Lanark 120 F2
Newton S Yorks 89 D6
Newton Staffs 62 B4
Newton Suff 56 E3
Newton Swansea 33 F7
Newton W Loth 120 B3
Newton Warks 52 B3
Newton Wilts 14 B3
Newton Abbot Devon 7 B6
Newton Arlosh Cumb 107 D8
Newton Aycliffe Durham 101 B7
Newton Bewley Hrtlpl 102 B2
Newton Blossomville M Keynes 53 D7
Newton Bromswold Northants 53 C7
Newton Burgoland Leics 63 D7
Newton by Toft Lincs 90 F4
Newton Ferrers Devon 6 E3
Newton Flotman Norf 68 E5
Newton Hall Northumb 110 C3
Newton Harcourt Leics 64 E3
Newton Heath Gtr Man 87 D6
Newton Ho. Aberds 141 B5
Newton Kyme N Yorks 95 E7
Newton-le-Willows Mers 86 E3
Newton-le-Willows N Yorks 101 F7
Newton Longville Bucks 53 F6
Newton Mearns E Renf 118 D5
Newton Morrell N Yorks 101 D7
Newton Mulgrave N Yorks 103 C5
Newton of Ardtoe Highld 147 D9
Newton of Balcanquhal Perth 128 C3
Newton of Falkland Fife 128 D4
Newton on Ayr S Ayrs 112 B3
Newton on Ouse N Yorks 95 D8
Newton-on-Rawcliffe N Yorks 103 E6
Newton-on-the-Moor Northumb 117 D7
Newton on Trent Lincs 77 B8
Newton Park Argyll 145 G10
Newton Poppleford Devon 11 F5
Newton Purcell Oxon 52 F4
Newton Regis Warks 63 D6
Newton Reigny Cumb 108 F4
Newton Solney Derbys 63 B6
Newton St Cyres Devon 10 E3
Newton St Faith Norf 68 C5
Newton St Loe Bath 24 C2
Newton St Petrock Devon 9 C6
Newton Stacey Hants 26 E2
Newton Stewart Dumfries 105 C8
Newton Tony Wilts 25 E7
Newton Tracey Devon 9 B7
Newton under Roseberry Redcar 102 C3
Newton upon Derwent E Yorks 96 E3
Newton Valence Hants 26 F5
Newtonairds Dumfries 113 F8
Newtongrange Midloth 121 C6
Newtonhill Aberds 141 E8
Newtonhill Highld 151 G8
Newtonmill Angus 135 C6
Newtonmore Highld 138 E3
Newtown Argyll 125 E6
Newtown Ches W 74 B2
Newtown Corn 3 D6
Newtown Cumb 107 E7
Newtown Cumb 108 C5
Newtown Derbys 87 F7
Newtown Devon 10 B2
Newtown Glos 36 D3
Newtown Glos 50 F4
Newtown Hants 14 B4
Newtown Hants 14 C3
Newtown Hants 15 C6
Newtown Hants 15 C7
Newtown Hants 15 D5
Newtown Hants 26 C2
Newtown Hereford 49 E8
Newtown Highld 137 D6
Newtown IoM 84 E3
Newtown IoW 14 E5
Newtown Northumb 117 B6
Newtown Northumb 117 D6
Newtown Northumb 123 F5
Newtown Poole 13 E8
Newtown = Y Drenewydd Powys 59 E8
Newtown Shrops 73 F8
Newtown Staffs 75 C6
Newtown Staffs 75 C7
Newtown Wilts 13 B7
Newtown Linford Leics 64 D2
Newtown St Boswells Borders 121 F8
Newtown Unthank Leics 63 D8
Newtyle Angus 134 E2
Neyland Pembs 44 E4
Niarbyl IoM 84 E2
Nibley S Glos 36 F3
Nibley Green Glos 36 E4
Nibon Shetland 160 F5
Nicholashayne Devon 11 C6
Nicholaston Swansea 33 F6
Nidd N Yorks 95 C6
Nigg Aberdeen 141 D8
Nigg Highld 151 D11
Nigg Ferry Highld 151 E10
Nightcott Som 10 B3
Nilig Denb 72 D4
Nine Ashes Essex 42 D1
Nine Mile Burn Midloth 120 D4
Nine Wells Pembs 44 C2
Ninebanks Northumb 109 D7
Ninfield E Sus 18 D4
Ningwood IoW 14 F4
Nisbet Borders 116 B2
Nisthouse Orkney 159 G4
Nisthouse Shetland 160 G7
Niton IoW 15 G6
Nitshill Glasgow 118 C5
No Man's Heath Ches W 74 E2
No Man's Heath Warks 63 D6
Noak Hill London 41 E8
Noblethorpe S Yorks 88 D3
Nobottle Northants 52 C4
Nocton Lincs 78 C3
Noke Oxon 39 C5
Nolton Pembs 44 D3
Nolton Haven Pembs 44 D3
Nomansland Devon 10 C3
Nomansland Wilts 14 C3
Noneley Shrops 60 B4
Nonikiln Highld 151 D9
Nonington Kent 31 D6
Noonsbrough Shetland 160 H4
Norbreck Blackpool 92 E3
Norbridge Hereford 50 E2
Norbury Ches E 74 E2
Norbury Derbys 75 E8
Norbury Shrops 60 E3
Norbury Staffs 61 B7
Nordelph Norf 67 D5
Norden Gtr Man 87 C6
Norden Heath Dorset 13 F7
Nordley Shrops 61 E6
Norham Northumb 122 E5
Norley Ches W 74 B2
Norleywood Hants 14 E4
Norman Cross Cambs 65 E8
Normanby N Lincs 90 C2
Normanby N Yorks 103 F5
Normanby Redcar 102 C3
Normanby-by-Spital Lincs 90 F4
Normanby by Stow Lincs 90 F2
Normanby le Wold Lincs 90 E5
Normandy Sur 27 D7
Norman's Bay E Sus 18 E3
Norman's Green Devon 11 D5
Normanstone Suff 69 E8
Normanton Derby 76 F3
Normanton Leics 77 E8
Normanton Lincs 78 E2
Normanton Notts 77 D7
Normanton Rutland 65 D6
Normanton W Yorks 88 B4
Normanton le Heath Leics 63 C7
Normanton on Soar Notts 64 B2
Normanton-on-the-Wolds Notts 77 F6
Normanton on Trent Notts 77 C7
Normoss Lancs 92 F3
Norney Sur 27 E7
Norrington Common Wilts 24 C3
Norris Green Mers 85 E4
Norris Hill Leics 63 C7
North Anston S Yorks 89 F6
North Aston Oxon 38 B4
North Baddesley Hants 14 C4
North Ballachulish Highld 130 C4
North Barrow Som 12 B4
North Barsham Norf 80 D5
North Benfleet Essex 42 F3
North Bersted W Sus 16 D3
North Berwick E Loth 129 F7
North Boarhunt Hants 15 C7
North Bovey Devon 10 F2
North Bradley Wilts 24 D3
North Brentor Devon 9 F6
North Brewham Som 24 F2
North Buckland Devon 20 E3
North Burlingham Norf 69 C6
North Cadbury Som 12 B4
North Cairn Dumfries 104 B3
North Carlton Lincs 78 B2
North Carrine Argyll 143 H7
North Cave E Yorks 96 F4
North Cerney Glos 37 D7
North Charford Wilts 14 C2
North Charlton Northumb 117 B7
North Cheriton Som 12 B4
North Cliff E Yorks 97 E8
North Cliffe E Yorks 96 F4
North Clifton Notts 77 B8
North Cockerington Lincs 91 E7
North Coker Som 12 C3
North Collafirth Shetland 160 E5
North Common E Sus 17 B7
North Connel Argyll 124 B5
North Cornelly Bridgend 34 F2
North Cotes Lincs 91 D7
North Cove Suff 69 F7
North Cowton N Yorks 101 D7
North Crawley M Keynes 53 E7
North Cray London 29 B5
North Creake Norf 80 D4
North Curry Som 11 B8
North Dalton E Yorks 96 D5
North Dawn Orkney 159 H5
North Deighton N Yorks 95 D6
North Duffield N Yorks 96 F2
North Elkington Lincs 91 E6
North Elmham Norf 81 E5
North Elmshall W Yorks 89 C5
North End Bucks 39 B8
North End E Yorks 97 F8
North End Essex 42 C2
North End Hants 26 C2
North End Lincs 78 E5
North End N Som 23 C6
North End Ptsmth 15 D7
North End Som 11 B7
North End W Sus 16 D5
North Erradale Highld 155 J12
North Fambridge Essex 42 E4
North Fearns Highld 149 E10
North Featherstone W Yorks 88 B5
North Ferriby E Yorks 90 B3
North Frodingham E Yorks 97 D7
North Gluss Shetland 160 F5
North Gorley Hants 14 C2
North Green Norf 68 F5
North Green Suff 57 C7
North Greetwell Lincs 78 B3
North Grimston N Yorks 96 C4
North Halley Orkney 159 H6
North Halling Medway 29 C8
North Hayling Hants 15 D8
North Hazelrigg Northumb 123 F6
North Heasley Devon 21 F6
North Heath W Sus 16 B4
North Hill Cambs 55 B5
North Hill Corn 5 B7
North Hinksey Oxon 38 D4
North Holmwood Sur 28 E2
North Howden E Yorks 96 F3
North Huish Devon 6 D5
North Hykeham Lincs 78 C2
North Johnston Pembs 44 D4
North Kelsey Lincs 90 D4
North Kelsey Moor Lincs 90 D4
North Kessock Highld 151 G9
North Killingholme N Lincs 90 C5
North Kilvington N Yorks 102 F2
North Kilworth Leics 64 F3
North Kirkton Aberds 153 C11
North Kiscadale N Ayrs 143 F11
North Kyme Lincs 78 D4
North Lancing W Sus 17 D5
North Lee Bucks 39 D8
North Leigh Oxon 38 C3
North Leverton with Habblesthorpe Notts 89 F8
North Littleton Worcs 51 E5
North Lopham Norf 68 F3
North Luffenham Rutland 65 D6
North Marden W Sus 16 C2
North Marston Bucks 39 B7
North Middleton Midloth 121 D6
North Middleton Northumb 117 B6
North Molton Devon 10 B2
North Moreton Oxon 39 F5
North Mundham W Sus 16 D2
North Muskham Notts 77 D7
North Newbald E Yorks 96 F5
North Newington Oxon 52 F2
North Newnton Wilts 25 D6
North Newton Som 22 F4
North Nibley Glos 36 E4
North Oakley Hants 26 D3
North Ockendon London 42 F1
North Ormesby Mbro 102 B3
North Ormsby Lincs 91 E6
North Otterington N Yorks 102 F1
North Owersby Lincs 90 E4
North Perrott Som 12 D2
North Petherton Som 22 F4
North Petherwin Corn 8 F4
North Pickenham Norf 67 D8
North Piddle Worcs 50 D4
North Poorton Dorset 12 E3
North Port Argyll 125 C6
North Queensferry Fife 128 F3
North Radworthy Devon 21 F6
North Rauceby Lincs 78 E3
North Reston Lincs 91 F7
North Rigton N Yorks 95 E5
North Rode Ches E 75 C5
North Roe Shetland 160 E5
North Runcton Norf 67 C6
North Sandwick Shetland 160 D7
North Scale Cumb 92 C1
North Scarle Lincs 77 C8
North Seaton Northumb 117 F8
North Shian Argyll 130 E3
North Shields T&W 111 C6
North Shoebury Southend 43 F5
North Shore Blackpool 92 F3
North Side Cumb 98 B2
North Side Pboro 66 E2
North Skelton Redcar 102 C4
North Somercotes Lincs 91 E8
North Stainley N Yorks 95 B5
North Stainmore Cumb 100 C3
North Stifford Thurrock 42 F2
North Stoke Bath 24 C2
North Stoke Oxon 39 F6
North Stoke W Sus 16 C4
North Street Hants 26 F4
North Street Kent 30 D4
North Street Medway 30 B2
North Street W Berks 26 B4
North Sunderland Northumb 123 F8
North Tamerton Corn 8 E5
North Tawton Devon 9 D8
North Thoresby Lincs 91 E6
North Tidworth Wilts 25 E7
North Togston Northumb 117 D8
North Tuddenham Norf 68 C3
North Walbottle T&W 110 C4
North Walsham Norf 81 D8
North Waltham Hants 26 E3
North Warnborough Hants 26 D5
North Water Bridge Angus 135 C6
North Watten Highld 158 E4
North Weald Bassett Essex 41 D7
North Wheatley Notts 89 F8
North Whilborough Devon 7 C6
North Wick Bath 23 C7
North Willingham Lincs 91 F5
North Wingfield Derbys 76 C4
North Witham Lincs 65 B6
North Woolwich London 28 B5
North Wootton Dorset 12 C4
North Wootton Norf 67 B6
North Wootton Som 23 E7
North Wraxall Wilts 24 B3
North Wroughton Swindon 38 F1
Northacre Norf 68 E2
Northallerton N Yorks 102 E1
Northam Devon 9 B6
Northam Soton 14 C5
Northampton Northants 53 C5
Northaw Herts 41 D5
Northbeck Lincs 78 E3
Northborough Pboro 65 D8
Northbourne Kent 31 D7
Northbridge Street E Sus 18 C4
Northchapel W Sus 16 B3
Northchurch Herts 40 D2
Northcott Devon 8 E5
Northdown Kent 31 B7
Northdyke Orkney 159 F3
Northend Bath 24 C2
Northend Bucks 39 E7
Northend Warks 51 D8
Northenden Gtr Man 87 E6
Northfield Aberdeen 141 D8
Northfield Borders 122 C5
Northfield E Yorks 90 B4
Northfield W Mid 50 B5
Northfields Lincs 65 D7
Northfleet Kent 29 B7
Northgate Lincs 65 B8
Northhouse Borders 115 D7
Northiam E Sus 18 C5
Northill C Beds 54 E2
Northington Hants 26 F3
Northlands Lincs 79 D6
Northlea Durham 111 D7
Northleach Glos 37 C8
Northleigh Devon 11 E6
Northlew Devon 9 E7
Northmoor Oxon 38 D4
Northmoor Green or Moorland Som 22 F5
Northmuir Angus 134 D3
Northney Hants 15 D8
Northolt London 40 F4
Northop Flint 73 C6
Northop Hall Flint 73 C6
Northorpe Lincs 65 C7
Northorpe Lincs 78 F5
Northorpe Lincs 90 E2
Northover Som 12 B3
Northover Som 23 F6
Northowram W Yorks 88 B2
Northport Dorset 13 F7
Northpunds Shetland 160 L6
Northrepps Norf 81 D8
Northtown Orkney 159 J5
Northway Glos 50 F4
Northwich Ches W 74 B3
Northwick S Glos 36 F2
Northwold Norf 67 E7
Northwood Derbys 76 C2
Northwood IoW 15 E5
Northwood Kent 31 C7
Northwood London 40 E3
Northwood Shrops 73 F8
Northwood Green Glos 36 C4
Norton E Sus 17 D8
Norton Glos 37 B5
Norton Halton 86 F3
Norton Herts 54 F3
Norton IoW 14 F4
Norton Mon 35 C8
Norton Northants 52 C4
Norton Notts 77 B5
Norton Powys 48 C5
Norton S Yorks 89 C6
Norton Shrops 60 F4
Norton Shrops 61 D5
Norton Shrops 61 E7
Norton Stockton 102 B2
Norton Suff 56 C3
Norton W Sus 16 D3
Norton W Sus 16 E2
Norton Wilts 37 F5
Norton Worcs 50 D3
Norton Worcs 50 E5
Norton Bavant Wilts 24 E4
Norton Bridge Staffs 75 F5
Norton Canes Staffs 62 D4
Norton Canon Hereford 49 E5
Norton Corner Norf 81 E6
Norton Disney Lincs 77 D8
Norton East Staffs 62 D4
Norton Ferris Wilts 24 F2
Norton Fitzwarren Som 11 B6
Norton Green IoW 14 F4
Norton Hawkfield Bath 23 C7
Norton Heath Essex 42 D2
Norton in Hales Shrops 74 F4
Norton-in-the-Moors Stoke 75 D5
Norton-Juxta-Twycross Leics 63 D7
Norton-le-Clay N Yorks 95 B7
Norton Lindsey Warks 51 C7
Norton Malreward Bath 23 C8
Norton Mandeville Essex 42 D1
Norton-on-Derwent N Yorks 96 B3
Norton St Philip Som 24 D2
Norton sub Hamdon Som 12 C2
Norton Woodseats S Yorks 88 F4

Ros–Shi 199

Rosehall Highld 156 J7
Rosehaugh Mains Highld 151 F9
Rosehearty Aberds 153 B9
Rosehill Shrops 74 F3
Roseisle Moray 152 B1
Roselands E Sus 18 E3
Rosemarket Pembs 44 E4
Rosemarkie Highld 151 F10
Rosemary Lane Devon 11 C6
Rosemount Perth 134 E1
Rosenannon Corn 4 C4
Rosewell Midloth 121 C5
Roseworth Stockton 102 B2
Roseworthy Corn 2 C5
Rosgill Cumb 99 C7
Roshven Highld 147 D10
Roskhill Highld 149 D7
Roskill House Highld 151 F9
Rosley Cumb 108 E3
Roslin Midloth 121 C5
Rosliston Derbys 63 C6
Rosneath Argyll 145 E11
Ross Dumfries 106 E3
Ross Northumb 123 F7
Ross Perth 127 B6
Ross-on-Wye Hereford 36 B3
Rossett Wrex 73 D7
Rossett Green N Yorks 95 D6
Rossie Ochill Perth 128 C2
Rossie Priory Perth 134 F2
Rossington S Yorks 89 E7
Rosskeen Highld 151 E9
Rossland Renfs 118 B4
Roster Highld 158 G4
Rostherne Ches E 86 F5
Rosthwaite Cumb 98 C4
Roston Derbys 75 E8
Rosyth Fife 128 F3
Rothbury Northumb 117 D6
Rotherby Leics 64 C3
Rotherfield E Sus 18 C2
Rotherfield Greys Oxon 39 F7
Rotherfield Peppard Oxon 39 F7
Rotherham S Yorks 88 E5
Rothersthorpe Northants 52 D5
Rotherwick Hants 26 D5
Rothes Moray 152 D2
Rothesay Argyll 145 G9
Rothiebrisbane Aberds 153 E7
Rothienorman Aberds 153 E7
Rothiesholm Orkney 159 F7
Rothley Leics 64 C2
Rothley Northumb 117 F6
Rothley Shield East Northumb 117 E6
Rothmaise Aberds 153 E6
Rothwell Lincs 91 E5
Rothwell Northants 64 F5
Rothwell W Yorks 88 B4
Rothwell Haigh W Yorks 88 B4
Rotsea E Yorks 97 D6
Rottal Angus 134 C3
Rotten End Suff 57 C7
Rottingdean Brighton 17 D7
Rottington Cumb 98 C1
Roud IoW 15 F6
Rough Close Staffs 75 F6
Rough Common Kent 30 D5
Rougham Norf 80 E4
Rougham Suff 56 C3
Rougham Green Suff 56 C3
Roughburn Highld 137 F6
Roughlee Lancs 93 E8
Roughley W Mid 62 E5
Roughsike Cumb 108 B5
Roughton Lincs 78 C5
Roughton Norf 81 D8
Roughton Shrops 61 E7
Roughton Moor Lincs 78 C5
Roundhay W Yorks 95 F6
Roundstonefoot Dumfries 114 D4
Roundstreet Common W Sus 16 B4
Roundway Wilts 24 C5
Rous Lench Worcs 50 D5
Rousdon Devon 11 E7
Routenburn N Ayrs 118 C1
Routh E Yorks 97 E6
Row Corn 5 B5
Row Cumb 99 F6
Row Heath Essex 43 C7
Rowanburn Dumfries 108 B4
Rowardennan Stirling 126 E2
Rowde Wilts 24 C4
Rowen Conwy 83 D7
Rowfoot Northumb 109 C6
Rowhedge Essex 43 B6
Rowhook W Sus 28 F2
Rowington Warks 51 C7
Rowland Derbys 76 B2
Rowlands Castle Hants 15 C8
Rowlands Gill T&W 110 D4
Rowledge Sur 27 E6
Rowlestone Hereford 35 B7
Rowley E Yorks 97 F5
Rowley Shrops 60 D3
Rowley Hill W Yorks 88 C2
Rowley Regis W Mid 62 F3
Rowly Sur 27 E8
Rowney Green Worcs 50 B5
Rownhams Hants 14 C4
Rowrah Cumb 98 C2
Rowsham Bucks 39 C8
Rowsley Derbys 76 C2
Rowstock Oxon 38 F4
Rowston Lincs 78 D3
Rowton Ches W 73 C8
Rowton Shrops 60 C3
Rowton Telford 61 C6
Roxburgh Borders 122 F3
Roxby N Lincs 90 C3
Roxby N Yorks 103 C5
Roxton Bedford 54 D2
Roxwell Essex 42 D2
Royal Leamington Spa Warks 51 C8
Royal Oak Darl 101 B7
Royal Oak Lancs 86 D2
Royal Tunbridge Wells Kent 18 B2
Royal Wootton Bassett Wilts 37 F7
Roybridge Highld 137 F5
Roydhouse W Yorks 88 C3
Roydon Essex 41 D7
Roydon Norf 68 F3
Roydon Norf 80 E3
Roydon Hamlet Essex 41 D7
Royston Herts 54 E4
Royston S Yorks 88 C4
Royton Gtr Man 87 D7
Rozel Jersey 17
Ruabon = Rhiwabon Wrex 73 E7
Ruaig Argyll 146 G3
Ruan Lanihorne Corn 3 B7
Ruan Minor Corn 3 E6
Ruarach Highld 136 B2
Ruardean Glos 36 C3
Ruardean Woodside Glos 36 C3
Rubery Worcs 50 B4
Ruckcroft Cumb 108 E5
Ruckhall Hereford 49 F6
Ruckinge Kent 19 B7
Ruckland Lincs 79 B6
Ruckley Shrops 60 D5
Rudbaxton Pembs 44 C4
Rudby N Yorks 102 D2
Ruddington Notts 77 F5
Rudford Glos 36 B4
Rudge Shrops 62 E2
Rudge Som 24 D3
Rudgeway S Glos 36 F3
Rudgwick W Sus 27 F8
Rudhall Hereford 36 B3
Rudheath Ches W 74 B3
Rudley Green Essex 42 D4
Rudry Caerph 35 F5
Rudston E Yorks 97 C6
Rudyard Staffs 75 D6
Rufford Lancs 86 C2
Rufforth York 95 D8
Rugby Warks 52 B3
Rugeley Staffs 62 C4
Ruglen S Ayrs 112 D2
Ruilick Highld 151 G8
Ruishton Som 11 B7
Ruisigearraidh W Isles 154 J4
Ruislip London 40 F3
Ruislip Common London 40 F3
Rumbling Bridge Perth 128 E2
Rumburgh Suff 69 F6
Rumford Corn 4 B3
Rumney Cardiff 22 B4
Runcorn Halton 86 F3
Runcton W Sus 16 D2
Runcton Holme Norf 67 D6
Rundlestone Devon 6 B3
Runfold Sur 27 E6
Runhall Norf 68 D3
Runham Norf 69 C7
Runham Norf 69 D8
Runnington Som 11 B6
Runsell Green Essex 42 D3
Runswick Bay N Yorks 103 C6
Runwell Essex 42 E3
Ruscombe Wokingham 27 B5
Rush Green London 41 F8
Rush-head Aberds 153 D8
Rushall Hereford 49 F8
Rushall Norf 68 F4
Rushall W Mid 62 D4
Rushall Wilts 25 D6
Rushbrooke Suff 56 C2
Rushbury Shrops 60 E5
Rushden Herts 54 F4
Rushden Northants 53 C7
Rushenden Kent 30 B3
Rushford Norf 68 F2
Rushlake Green E Sus 18 D3
Rushmere Suff 69 F7
Rushmere St Andrew Suff 57 E6
Rushmoor Sur 27 E6
Rushock Worcs 50 B3
Rusholme Gtr Man 87 E6
Rushton Ches W 74 C2
Rushton Northants 64 F5
Rushton Shrops 61 D6
Rushton Spencer Staffs 75 C6
Rushwick Worcs 50 D3
Rushyford Durham 101 B7
Ruskie Stirling 126 D5
Ruskington Lincs 78 D3
Rusland Cumb 99 F5
Rusper W Sus 28 F3
Ruspidge Glos 36 C3
Russell's Water Oxon 39 F7
Russel's Green Suff 57 B6
Rusthall Kent 18 B2
Rustington W Sus 16 D4
Ruston N Yorks 103 F7
Ruston Parva E Yorks 97 C6
Ruswarp N Yorks 103 D6
Rutherford Borders 122 F2
Rutherglen S Lanark 119 C6
Ruthernbridge Corn 4 C5
Ruthin = Rhuthun Denb 72 D5
Ruthrieston Aberdeen 141 D8
Ruthven Aberds 152 D5
Ruthven Angus 134 E2
Ruthven Highld 138 E3
Ruthven Highld 151 H11
Ruthven House Angus 134 E3
Ruthvoes Corn 4 C4
Ruthwell Dumfries 107 C7
Ruyton-XI-Towns Shrops 60 B3
Ryal Northumb 110 B3
Ryal Fold Blackburn 86 B4
Ryall Dorset 12 E2
Ryarsh Kent 29 D7
Rydal Cumb 99 D5
Ryde IoW 15 E6
Rye E Sus 19 C6
Rye Foreign E Sus 19 C5
Rye Harbour E Sus 19 D6
Rye Park Herts 41 C6
Rye Street Worcs 50 F2
Ryecroft Gate Staffs 75 C6
Ryehill E Yorks 91 B6
Ryhall Rutland 65 C7
Ryhill W Yorks 88 C4
Ryhope T&W 111 D7
Rylstone N Yorks 94 D2
Ryme Intrinseca Dorset 12 C3
Ryther N Yorks 95 F8
Ryton Glos 50 F2
Ryton N Yorks 96 B3
Ryton Shrops 61 D7
Ryton T&W 110 C4
Ryton-on-Dunsmore Warks 51 B8

S

Sabden Lancs 93 F7
Sacombe Herts 41 C6
Sacriston Durham 110 E5
Sadberge Darl 101 C8
Saddell Argyll 143 E8
Saddington Leics 64 E3
Saddle Bow Norf 67 C6
Saddlescombe W Sus 17 C6
Sadgill Cumb 99 D6
Saffron Walden Essex 55 F6
Sageston Pembs 32 D1
Saham Hills Norf 68 D2
Saham Toney Norf 68 D2
Saighdinis W Isles 148 B3
Saighton Ches W 73 C8
St Abbs Borders 122 C5
St Abb's Haven Borders 122 C5
St Agnes Corn 4 D2
St Agnes Scilly 2 F3
St Albans Herts 40 D4
St Allen Corn 4 D3
St Andrews Fife 129 C7
St Andrew's Major V Glam 22 B3
St Anne Ald 16
St Annes Lancs 85 B4
St Ann's Dumfries 114 E3
St Ann's Chapel Corn 6 B2
St Ann's Chapel Devon 6 E4
St Anthony-in-Meneage Corn 3 D6
St Anthony's Hill E Sus 18 E3
St Arvans Mon 36 E2
St Asaph = Llanelwy Denb 72 B4
St Athan V Glam 22 C2
St Aubin Jersey 17
St Austell Corn 4 D5
St Bees Cumb 98 C1
St Blazey Corn 5 D5
St Boswells Borders 121 F8
St Brelade Jersey 17
St Breock Corn 4 B4
St Breward Corn 5 B5
St Briavels Glos 36 D2
St Bride's Pembs 44 D3
St Brides Major V Glam 21 B7
St Bride's Netherwent Mon 35 F8
St Brides super Ely V Glam 22 B2
St Brides Wentlooge Newport 35 F6
St Budeaux Plym 6 D2
St Buryan Corn 2 D3
St Catherine Bath 24 B2
St Catherine's Argyll 125 E7
St Clears = Sanclêr Carms 32 C3
St Cleer Corn 5 C7
St Clement Corn 3 B7
St Clements Jersey 17
St Clether Corn 8 F4
St Colmac Argyll 145 G9
St Columb Major Corn 4 C4
St Columb Minor Corn 4 C3
St Columb Road Corn 4 D4
St Combs Aberds 153 B10
St Cross South Elmham Suff 69 F5
St Cyrus Aberds 135 C7
St David's Perth 127 B8
St David's = Tyddewi Pembs 44 C2
St Day Corn 3 B6
St Dennis Corn 4 D4
St Devereux Hereford 49 F6
St Dogmaels Pembs 45 E3
St Dogwells Pembs 44 C4
St Dominick Corn 6 C2
St Donat's V Glam 21 C8
St Edith's Wilts 24 C4
St Endellion Corn 4 B4
St Enoder Corn 4 D3
St Erme Corn 4 D3
St Erney Corn 5 D8
St Erth Corn 2 C4
St Ervan Corn 4 B3
St Eval Corn 4 C3
St Ewe Corn 3 B8
St Fagans Cardiff 22 B3
St Fergus Aberds 153 C10
St Fillans Perth 127 B5
St Florence Pembs 32 D1
St Genny's Corn 8 E3
St George Conwy 72 B3
St George's V Glam 22 B2
St Germans Corn 5 D8
St Giles Lincs 78 B2
St Giles in the Wood Devon 9 C7
St Giles on the Heath Devon 9 E5
St Harmon Powys 47 B8
St Helen Auckland Durham 101 B6
St Helena Warks 63 D6
St Helen's E Sus 18 D5
St Helens IoW 15 F7
St Helens Mers 86 E3
St Helier Jersey 17
St Helier London 28 C3
St Hilary Corn 2 C4
St Hilary V Glam 22 B2
Saint Hill W Sus 28 F4
St Illtyd Bl Gwent 35 D6
St Ippollytts Herts 40 B4
St Ishmael's Pembs 44 E3
St Issey Corn 4 B4
St Ive Corn 5 C8
St Ives Cambs 54 B4
St Ives Corn 2 B4
St Ives Dorset 14 D2
St James South Elmham Suff 69 F6
St Jidgey Corn 4 C4
St John Corn 6 D2
St John's IoM 84 D2
St John's Jersey 17
St John's Sur 27 D7
St John's Worcs 50 D3
St John's Chapel Durham 109 F8
St John's Fen End Norf 66 C5
St John's Highway Norf 66 C5
St John's Town of Dalry Dumfries 113 F6
St Judes IoM 84 C3
St Just Corn 2 C2
St Just in Roseland Corn 3 C7
St Katherine's Aberds 153 E7
St Keverne Corn 3 D6
St Kew Corn 4 B5
St Kew Highway Corn 4 B5
St Keyne Corn 5 C7
St Lawrence Corn 4 C5
St Lawrence Essex 43 D5
St Lawrence IoW 15 G6
St Leonard's Bucks 40 D2
St Leonards Dorset 14 D2
St Leonards E Sus 18 E4
Saint Leonards S Lanark 119 D6
St Levan Corn 2 D2
St Lythans V Glam 22 B3
St Mabyn Corn 4 B5
St Madoes Perth 128 B3
St Margaret's Hereford 49 F5
St Margarets Herts 41 C6
St Margaret's at Cliffe Kent 31 E7
St Margaret's Hope Orkney 159 J5
St Margaret South Elmham Suff 69 F6
St Mark's IoM 84 E2
St Martin Corn 5 D7
St Martins Corn 3 D6
St Martin's Jersey 17
St Martins Perth 134 F1
St Martin's Shrops 73 F7
St Mary Bourne Hants 26 D2
St Mary Church V Glam 22 B2
St Mary Cray London 29 C5
St Mary Hill V Glam 21 B8
St Mary Hoo Medway 30 B2
St Mary in the Marsh Kent 19 C7
St Mary's Jersey 17
St Mary's Orkney 159 H5
St Mary's Bay Kent 19 C7
St Maughans Mon 36 C1
St Mawes Corn 3 C7
St Mawgan Corn 4 C3
St Mellion Corn 5 C8
St Mellons Cardiff 35 F6
St Merryn Corn 4 B3
St Mewan Corn 4 D4
St Michael Caerhays Corn 3 B8
St Michael Penkevil Corn 3 B7
St Michael South Elmham Suff 69 F6
St Michael's Kent 19 B5
St Michaels Worcs 49 C7
St Michael's on Wyre Lancs 92 E4
St Minver Corn 4 B4
St Monans Fife 129 D7
St Neot Corn 5 C6
St Neots Cambs 54 C2
St Newlyn East Corn 4 D3
St Nicholas Pembs 44 B3
St Nicholas V Glam 22 B2
St Nicholas at Wade Kent 31 C6
St Ninians Stirling 127 E6
St Osyth Essex 43 C7
St Osyth Heath Essex 43 C7
St Ouens Jersey 17
St Owens Cross Hereford 36 B2
St Paul's Cray London 29 C5
St Paul's Walden Herts 40 B4
St Peter Port Guern 16
St Peter's Jersey 17
St Peter's Kent 31 C7
St Petrox Pembs 44 F4
St Pinnock Corn 5 C7
St Quivox S Ayrs 112 B3
St Ruan Corn 3 E6
St Sampson Guern 16
St Stephen Corn 4 D4
St Stephen's Corn 8 F5
St Stephens Corn 6 D2
St Stephens Herts 40 D4
St Teath Corn 8 F2
St Thomas Devon 10 E4
St Tudy Corn 5 B5
St Twynnells Pembs 44 F4
St Veep Corn 5 D6
St Vigeans Angus 135 E6
St Wenn Corn 4 C4
St Weonards Hereford 36 B1
Saintbury Glos 51 F6
Salcombe Devon 6 F5
Salcombe Regis Devon 11 F6
Salcott Essex 43 C5
Sale Gtr Man 87 E5
Sale Green Worcs 50 D4
Saleby Lincs 79 B7
Salehurst E Sus 18 C4
Salem Carms 33 B7
Salem Ceredig 58 F3
Salen Argyll 147 G8
Salen Highld 147 E9
Salesbury Lancs 93 F6
Salford C Beds 53 F7
Salford Gtr Man 87 E6
Salford Oxon 38 B2
Salford Priors Warks 51 D5
Salfords Sur 28 E3
Salhouse Norf 69 C6
Saline Fife 128 E2
Salisbury Wilts 14 B2
Sallachan Highld 130 C3
Sallachy Highld 150 H2
Sallachy Highld 157 J8
Salle Norf 81 E7
Salmonby Lincs 79 B6
Salmond's Muir Angus 135 F5
Salperton Glos 37 B7
Salph End Bedford 53 D8
Salsburgh N Lanark 119 C8
Salt Staffs 62 B3
Salt End E Yorks 91 B5
Saltaire W Yorks 94 F4
Saltash Corn 6 D2
Saltburn Highld 151 E10
Saltburn-by-the-Sea Redcar 102 B4
Saltby Leics 65 B5
Saltcoats Cumb 98 E2
Saltcoats N Ayrs 118 E2
Saltdean Brighton 17 D7
Salter Lancs 93 C6
Salterforth Lancs 93 E8
Salterswall Ches W 74 C3
Saltfleet Lincs 91 E8
Saltfleetby All Saints Lincs 91 E8
Saltfleetby St Clements Lincs 91 E8
Saltfleetby St Peter Lincs 91 F8
Saltford Bath 23 C8
Salthouse Norf 81 C6
Saltmarshe E Yorks 89 B8
Saltney Flint 73 C7
Salton N Yorks 96 B3
Saltwick Northumb 110 B4
Saltwood Kent 19 B8
Salum Argyll 146 G3
Salvington W Sus 16 D5
Salwarpe Worcs 50 C3
Salwayash Dorset 12 E2
Sambourne Warks 51 C5
Sambrook Telford 61 B7
Samhla W Isles 148 B2
Samlesbury Lancs 93 F5
Samlesbury Bottoms Lancs 86 B4
Sampford Arundel Som 11 C6
Sampford Brett Som 22 E2
Sampford Courtenay Devon 9 D8
Sampford Peverell Devon 10 C5
Sampford Spiney Devon 6 B3
Sampool Bridge Cumb 99 F6
Samuelston E Loth 121 B7
Sanachan Highld 149 D13
Sanaigmore Argyll 142 A3
Sanclêr = St Clears Carms 32 C3
Sancreed Corn 2 D3
Sancton E Yorks 96 F5
Sand Highld 150 B2
Sand Shetland 160 J5
Sand Hole E Yorks 96 F4
Sand Hutton N Yorks 96 D2
Sandaig Highld 149 H12
Sandal Magna W Yorks 88 C4
Sandale Cumb 108 E2
Sandbach Ches E 74 C4
Sandbank Argyll 145 E10
Sandbanks Poole 13 F8
Sandend Aberds 152 B5
Sanderstead London 28 C4
Sandfields Glos 37 B6
Sandford Cumb 100 C2
Sandford Devon 10 D3
Sandford Dorset 13 F7
Sandford IoW 15 F6
Sandford N Som 23 D6
Sandford S Lanark 119 E7
Sandford Shrops 74 F2
Sandford on Thames Oxon 39 D5
Sandford Orcas Dorset 12 B4
Sandford St Martin Oxon 38 B4
Sandfordhill Aberds 153 D11
Sandgate Kent 19 B8
Sandgreen Dumfries 106 D2
Sandhaven Aberds 153 B9
Sandhead Dumfries 104 E4
Sandhills Sur 27 F7
Sandhoe Northumb 110 C2
Sandholme E Yorks 96 F4
Sandholme Lincs 79 F6
Sandhurst Brack 27 C6
Sandhurst Glos 37 B5
Sandhurst Kent 18 C4
Sandhurst Cross Kent 18 C4
Sandhutton N Yorks 102 F1
Sandiacre Derbys 76 F4
Sandilands Lincs 91 F9
Sandilands S Lanark 119 F8
Sandiway Ches W 74 B3
Sandleheath Hants 14 C2
Sandling Kent 29 D8
Sandlow Green Ches E 74 C4
Sandness Shetland 160 H3
Sandon Essex 42 D3
Sandon Herts 54 F4
Sandon Staffs 75 F6
Sandown IoW 15 F6
Sandplace Corn 5 D7
Sandridge Herts 40 C4
Sandridge Wilts 24 C4
Sandringham Norf 67 B6
Sandsend N Yorks 103 C6
Sandside Ho. Highld 157 C12
Sandsound Shetland 160 J5
Sandtoft N Lincs 89 D8
Sandway Kent 30 D2
Sandwell W Mid 62 F4
Sandwich Kent 31 D7
Sandwick Cumb 99 C6
Sandwick Orkney 159 K5
Sandwick Shetland 160 L6
Sandwith Cumb 98 C1
Sandy C Beds 54 E2
Sandy Carms 33 D5
Sandy Bank Lincs 79 D5
Sandy Haven Pembs 44 E3
Sandy Lane Wilts 24 C4
Sandy Lane Wrex 73 E7
Sandycroft Flint 73 C7
Sandyford Dumfries 114 E5
Sandyford Stoke 75 D5
Sandygate IoM 84 C3
Sandyhills Dumfries 107 D5
Sandylands Lancs 92 C4
Sandypark Devon 10 F2
Sandysike Cumb 108 C3
Sangobeg Highld 156 C7
Sangomore Highld 156 C7
Sanna Highld 146 E7
Sanndabhaig W Isles 148 D3
Sanndabhaig W Isles 155 D9
Sannox N Ayrs 143 D11
Sanquhar Dumfries 113 D7
Santon N Lincs 90 C3
Santon Bridge Cumb 98 D3
Santon Downham Suff 67 F8
Sapcote Leics 63 E8
Sapey Common Hereford 50 C2
Sapiston Suff 56 B3
Sapley Cambs 54 B3
Sapperton Glos 37 D6
Sapperton Lincs 78 F3
Saracen's Head Lincs 66 B3
Sarclet Highld 158 F5
Sardis Carms 33 D6
Sarn Bridgend 34 F3
Sarn Powys 60 E2
Sarn Bach Gwyn 70 E4
Sarn Meyllteyrn Gwyn 70 D3
Sarnau Carms 32 C4
Sarnau Ceredig 46 D2
Sarnau Gwyn 72 F3
Sarnau Powys 48 F2
Sarnau Powys 60 C2
Sarnesfield Hereford 49 D5
Saron Carms 33 C7
Saron Carms 46 F2
Saron Denb 72 C4
Saron Gwyn 82 E5
Saron Gwyn 82 F4
Sarratt Herts 40 E3
Sarre Kent 31 C6
Sarsden Oxon 38 B2
Sarsgrum Highld 156 C6
Satley Durham 110 E4
Satron N Yorks 100 E4
Satterleigh Devon 9 B8
Satterthwaite Cumb 99 E5
Satwell Oxon 39 F7
Sauchen Aberds 141 C5
Saucher Perth 134 F1
Sauchie Clack 127 E7
Sauchieburn Aberds 135 C6
Saughall Ches W 73 B7
Saughtree Borders 115 E8
Saul Glos 36 D4
Saundby Notts 89 F8
Saundersfoot Pembs 32 D2
Saunderton Bucks 39 D7
Saunton Devon 20 F3
Sausthorpe Lincs 79 C6
Saval Highld 157 J8
Savary Highld 147 G9
Savile Park W Yorks 87 B8
Sawbridge Warks 52 C3
Sawbridgeworth Herts 41 C7
Sawdon N Yorks 103 F7
Sawley Derbys 76 F4
Sawley Lancs 93 E7
Sawley N Yorks 94 C5
Sawston Cambs 55 E5
Sawtry Cambs 65 F8
Saxby Leics 64 C5
Saxby Lincs 90 F4
Saxby All Saints N Lincs 90 C3
Saxelbye Leics 64 B4
Saxham Street Suff 56 C4
Saxilby Lincs 77 B8
Saxlingham Norf 81 D6
Saxlingham Green Norf 68 E5
Saxlingham Nethergate Norf 68 E5
Saxlingham Thorpe Norf 68 E5
Saxmundham Suff 57 C7
Saxon Street Cambs 55 D7
Saxondale Notts 77 F6
Saxtead Suff 57 C6
Saxtead Green Suff 57 C6
Saxthorpe Norf 81 D7
Saxton N Yorks 95 F7
Sayers Common W Sus 17 C6
Scackleton N Yorks 96 B2
Scadabhagh W Isles 154 H6
Scaftworth Notts 89 E7
Scagglethorpe N Yorks 96 B4
Scaitcliffe Lancs 87 B5
Scalasaig Argyll 144 D2
Scalby E Yorks 90 B2
Scalby N Yorks 103 E8
Scaldwell Northants 53 B5
Scale Houses Cumb 109 E5
Scaleby Cumb 108 C4
Scaleby Hill Cumb 108 C4
Scales Cumb 92 B2
Scales Cumb 99 B5
Scales Lancs 92 F4
Scalford Leics 64 B4
Scaling Redcar 103 C5
Scallastle Argyll 124 B2
Scalloway Shetland 160 K6
Scalpay W Isles 154 H7
Scalpay Ho. Highld 149 F11
Scalpsie Argyll 145 H9
Scamadale Highld 147 B10
Scamblesby Lincs 79 B5
Scamodale Highld 130 B2
Scampston N Yorks 96 B4
Scampton Lincs 78 B2
Scapa Orkney 159 H5
Scapegoat Hill W Yorks 87 C8
Scar Orkney 159 D7
Scarborough N Yorks 103 F8
Scarcliffe Derbys 76 C4
Scarcroft W Yorks 95 E6
Scarcroft Hill W Yorks 95 E6
Scardroy Highld 150 F5
Scarff Shetland 160 E4
Scarfskerry Highld 158 C4
Scargill Durham 101 C5
Scarinish Argyll 146 G3
Scarisbrick Lancs 85 C4
Scarning Norf 68 C2
Scarrington Notts 77 E7
Scartho NE Lincs 91 D6
Scarwell Orkney 159 F3
Scatness Shetland 160 M5
Scatraig Highld 151 H10
Scawby N Lincs 90 D3
Scawsby S Yorks 89 D6
Scawton N Yorks 102 F3
Scayne's Hill W Sus 17 B7
Scethrog Powys 35 B5
Scholar Green Ches E 74 D5
Scholes W Yorks 88 B2
Scholes W Yorks 88 D2
Scholes W Yorks 95 F6
School Green Ches W 74 C3
Scleddau Pembs 44 B4
Sco Ruston Norf 81 E8
Scofton Notts 89 F7
Scole Norf 56 B5
Scolpaig W Isles 148 A2
Scone Perth 128 B3
Sconser Highld 149 E10
Scoonie Fife 129 D5
Scoor Argyll 146 K7
Scopwick Lincs 78 D3
Scoraig Highld 150 B3
Scorborough E Yorks 97 E6
Scorrier Corn 3 B6
Scorton Lancs 92 E5
Scorton N Yorks 101 D7
Scotbheinn W Isles 148 C3
Scotby Cumb 108 D4
Scotch Corner N Yorks 101 D7
Scotforth Lancs 92 D4
Scothern Lincs 78 B3
Scotland Gate Northumb 117 F8
Scotlandwell Perth 128 D3
Scotsburn Highld 151 D10
Scotscalder Station Highld 158 E2
Scotscraig Fife 129 B6
Scots' Gap Northumb 117 F6
Scotston Aberds 135 B7
Scotston Perth 133 E6
Scotstoun Glasgow 118 C5
Scotstown Highld 130 C2
Scotswood T&W 110 C4
Scottas Highld 149 H12
Scotter Lincs 90 D2
Scotterthorpe Lincs 90 D2
Scottlethorpe Lincs 65 B7
Scotton Lincs 90 E2
Scotton N Yorks 95 D6
Scotton N Yorks 101 E6
Scottow Norf 81 E8
Scoughall E Loth 129 F8
Scoulag Argyll 145 H10
Scoulton Norf 68 D2
Scourie Highld 156 E4
Scourie More Highld 156 E4
Scousburgh Shetland 160 M5
Scrabster Highld 158 C2
Scrafield Lincs 79 C6
Scrainwood Northumb 117 D5
Scrane End Lincs 79 E6
Scraptoft Leics 64 D3
Scratby Norf 69 C8
Scrayingham N Yorks 96 C3
Scredington Lincs 78 E3
Scremby Lincs 79 C7
Scremerston Northumb 123 E6
Screveton Notts 77 E7
Scrivelsby Lincs 79 C5
Scriven N Yorks 95 D6
Scrooby Notts 89 E7
Scropton Derbys 75 F8
Scrub Hill Lincs 78 D5
Scruton N Yorks 101 E7
Sculcoates Hull 97 F6
Sculthorpe Norf 80 D4
Scunthorpe N Lincs 90 C2
Scurlage Swansea 33 F5
Sea Palling Norf 69 B7
Seaborough Dorset 12 D2
Seacombe Mers 85 E4
Seacroft Lincs 79 C8
Seacroft W Yorks 95 F6
Seadyke Lincs 79 F6
Seafield S Ayrs 112 B3
Seafield W Loth 120 C3
Seaford E Sus 17 E8
Seaforth Mers 85 E4
Seagrave Leics 64 C3
Seaham Durham 111 E7
Seahouses Northumb 123 F8
Seal Kent 29 D6
Sealand Flint 73 C7
Seale Sur 27 E6
Seamer N Yorks 102 C2
Seamer N Yorks 103 F8
Seamill N Ayrs 118 E2
Searby Lincs 90 D4
Seasalter Kent 30 C4
Seascale Cumb 98 D2
Seathorne Lincs 79 C8
Seathwaite Cumb 98 C4
Seathwaite Cumb 98 E4
Seatoller Cumb 98 C4
Seaton Corn 5 D8
Seaton Cumb 107 F7
Seaton Devon 11 F7
Seaton Durham 111 D6
Seaton E Yorks 97 E7
Seaton Northumb 111 B6
Seaton Rutland 65 E6
Seaton Burn T&W 110 B5
Seaton Carew Hrtlpl 102 B3
Seaton Delaval Northumb 111 B6
Seaton Ross E Yorks 96 E3
Seaton Sluice Northumb 111 B6
Seatown Aberds 152 B5
Seatown Dorset 12 E2
Seave Green N Yorks 102 D3
Seaview IoW 15 E7
Seaville Cumb 107 D8
Seavington St Mary Som 12 C2
Seavington St Michael Som 12 C2
Sebergham Cumb 108 E3
Seckington Warks 63 D6
Second Coast Highld 150 B2
Sedbergh Cumb 100 E1
Sedbury Glos 36 E2
Sedbusk N Yorks 100 E3
Sedgeberrow Worcs 50 F5
Sedgebrook Lincs 77 F8
Sedgefield Durham 102 B1
Sedgeford Norf 80 D3
Sedgehill Wilts 13 B6
Sedgley W Mid 62 E3
Sedgwick Cumb 99 F7
Sedlescombe E Sus 18 D4
Sedlescombe Street E Sus 18 D4
Seend Wilts 24 C4
Seend Cleeve Wilts 24 C4
Seer Green Bucks 40 E2
Seething Norf 69 E6
Sefton Mers 85 D4
Seghill Northumb 111 B5
Seifton Shrops 60 F4
Seighford Staffs 62 B2
Seilebost W Isles 154 H5
Seion Gwyn 82 E5
Seisdon Staffs 62 E2
Seisiadar W Isles 155 D10
Selattyn Shrops 73 F6
Selborne Hants 26 F5
Selby N Yorks 96 F2
Selham W Sus 16 B3
Selhurst London 28 C4
Selkirk Borders 115 B7
Sellack Hereford 36 B2
Sellafirth Shetland 160 D7
Sellibister Orkney 159 D8
Sellindge Kent 19 B7
Sellindge Lees Kent 19 B8
Selling Kent 30 D4
Sells Green Wilts 24 C4
Selly Oak W Mid 62 F4
Selmeston E Sus 18 E2
Selsdon London 28 C4
Selsey W Sus 16 E2
Selsfield Common W Sus 28 F4
Selsted Kent 31 E6
Selston Notts 76 D4
Selworthy Som 21 E8
Semblister Shetland 160 H5
Semer Suff 56 E3
Semington Wilts 24 C3
Semley Wilts 13 B6
Send Sur 27 D8
Send Marsh Sur 27 D8
Senghenydd Caerph 35 E5
Sennen Corn 2 D2
Sennen Cove Corn 2 D2
Sennybridge = Pont Senni Powys 34 B3
Serlby Notts 89 F7
Sessay N Yorks 95 B7
Setchey Norf 67 C6
Setley Hants 14 D4
Setter Shetland 160 E6
Setter Shetland 160 H5
Setter Shetland 160 J7
Settiscarth Orkney 159 G4
Settle N Yorks 93 C8
Settrington N Yorks 96 B4
Seven Kings London 41 F7
Seven Sisters Neath 34 D2
Sevenhampton Glos 37 B7
Sevenoaks Kent 29 D6
Sevenoaks Weald Kent 29 D6
Severn Beach S Glos 36 F2
Severn Stoke Worcs 50 E3
Severnhampton Swindon 38 E2
Sevington Kent 30 E4
Sewards End Essex 55 F6
Sewardstone Essex 41 E6
Sewardstonebury Essex 41 E6
Sewerby E Yorks 97 C7
Seworgan Corn 3 C6
Sewstern Leics 65 B5
Sezincote Glos 51 F6
Sgarasta Mhor W Isles 154 H5
Sgiogarstaigh W Isles 155 A10
Shabbington Bucks 39 D6
Shackerstone Leics 63 D7
Shackleford Sur 27 E7
Shade W Yorks 87 B7
Shadforth Durham 111 E6
Shadingfield Suff 69 F7
Shadoxhurst Kent 19 B6
Shadsworth Blackburn 86 B5
Shadwell Norf 68 F2
Shadwell W Yorks 95 F6
Shaftesbury Dorset 13 B6
Shafton S Yorks 88 C4
Shalbourne Wilts 25 C8
Shalcombe IoW 14 F4
Shalden Hants 26 E4
Shaldon Devon 7 B7
Shalfleet IoW 14 F5
Shalford Essex 42 B3
Shalford Sur 27 E8
Shalford Green Essex 42 B3
Shallowford Devon 21 E6
Shalmsford Street Kent 30 D4
Shalstone Bucks 52 F4
Shamley Green Sur 27 E8
Shandon Argyll 145 E11
Shandwick Highld 151 D11
Shangton Leics 64 E4
Shankhouse Northumb 111 B5
Shanklin IoW 15 F6
Shanquhar Aberds 152 E5
Shanzie Perth 134 D2
Shap Cumb 99 C7
Shapwick Dorset 13 D7
Shapwick Som 23 F6
Shardlow Derbys 76 F4
Shareshill Staffs 62 D3
Sharlston W Yorks 88 C4
Sharlston Common W Yorks 88 C4
Sharnbrook Bedford 53 D7
Sharnford Leics 63 E8
Sharoe Green Lancs 92 F5
Sharow N Yorks 95 B6
Sharp Street Norf 69 B6
Sharpenhoe C Beds 53 F8
Sharperton Northumb 117 D5
Sharpness Glos 36 D3
Sharpthorne W Sus 28 F4
Sharrington Norf 81 D6
Shatterford Worcs 61 F7
Shaugh Prior Devon 6 C3
Shavington Ches E 74 D4
Shaw Gtr Man 87 D7
Shaw W Berks 26 C2
Shaw Wilts 24 C3
Shaw Green Lancs 86 C3
Shaw Mills N Yorks 95 C5
Shawbury Shrops 61 B5
Shawdon Hall Northumb 117 C6
Shawell Leics 64 F2
Shawford Hants 15 B5
Shawforth Lancs 87 B6
Shawhead Dumfries 107 B5
Shawhill Dumfries 108 C2
Shawton S Lanark 119 E6
Shawtonhill S Lanark 119 E6
Shear Cross Wilts 24 E3
Shearington Dumfries 107 C7
Shearsby Leics 64 E3
Shebbear Devon 9 D6
Shebdon Staffs 61 B7
Shebster Highld 157 C13
Sheddens E Renf 119 D5
Shedfield Hants 15 C6
Sheen Staffs 75 C8
Sheepscar W Yorks 95 F6
Sheepscombe Glos 37 C5
Sheepstor Devon 6 C3
Sheepwash Devon 9 D6
Sheepway N Som 23 B6
Sheepy Magna Leics 63 D7
Sheepy Parva Leics 63 D7
Sheering Essex 41 C8
Sheerness Kent 30 B3
Sheet Hants 15 B8
Sheffield S Yorks 88 F4
Sheffield Bottom W Berks 26 C4
Sheffield Green E Sus 17 B8
Shefford C Beds 54 F2
Shefford Woodlands W Berks 25 B8
Sheigra Highld 156 C4
Sheinton Shrops 61 D6
Shelderton Shrops 49 B6
Sheldon Derbys 75 C8
Sheldon Devon 11 D6
Sheldon W Mid 63 F5
Sheldwich Kent 30 D4
Shelf W Yorks 88 B2
Shelfanger Norf 68 F4
Shelfield W Mid 62 D4
Shelfield Warks 51 C6
Shelford Notts 77 E6
Shellacres Northumb 122 E4
Shelley Essex 42 D1
Shelley Suff 56 F4
Shelley W Yorks 88 C3
Shellingford Oxon 38 E3
Shellow Bowells Essex 42 D2
Shelsley Beauchamp Worcs 50 C2
Shelsley Walsh Worcs 50 C2
Shelthorpe Leics 64 C2
Shelton Bedford 53 C8
Shelton Norf 68 E5
Shelton Notts 77 E7
Shelton Shrops 60 C4
Shelton Green Norf 68 E5
Shelve Shrops 60 E3
Shelwick Hereford 49 E7
Shenfield Essex 42 E2
Shenington Oxon 51 E8
Shenley Herts 40 D4
Shenley Brook End M Keynes 53 F6
Shenley Church End M Keynes 53 F6
Shenleybury Herts 40 D4
Shenmore Hereford 49 F5
Shennanton Dumfries 105 C7
Shenstone Staffs 62 D5
Shenstone Worcs 50 B3
Shenton Leics 63 D7
Shenval Highld 137 B7
Shenval Moray 139 B8
Shepeau Stow Lincs 66 C3
Shephall Herts 41 B5
Shepherd's Green Oxon 39 F7
Shepherd's Port Norf 80 D2
Shepherdswell Kent 31 E6
Shepley W Yorks 88 D2
Shepperdine S Glos 36 E3
Shepperton Sur 27 C8
Shepreth Cambs 54 E4
Shepshed Leics 63 C8
Shepton Beauchamp Som 12 C2
Shepton Mallet Som 23 E8
Shepton Montague Som 23 F8
Shepway Kent 29 D8
Sheraton Durham 111 F7
Sherborne Dorset 12 C4
Sherborne Glos 38 C1
Sherborne St John Hants 26 D4
Sherbourne Warks 51 C7
Sherburn Durham 111 E6
Sherburn N Yorks 97 B5
Sherburn Hill Durham 111 E6
Sherburn in Elmet N Yorks 95 F7
Shere Sur 27 E8
Shereford Norf 80 E4
Sherfield English Hants 14 B3
Sherfield on Loddon Hants 26 D4
Sherford Devon 7 E5
Sheriff Hutton N Yorks 96 C2
Sheriffhales Shrops 61 C7
Sheringham Norf 81 C7
Sherington M Keynes 53 E6
Shernal Green Worcs 50 C4
Shernborne Norf 80 D3
Sherrington Wilts 24 F4
Sherston Wilts 37 F5
Sherwood Green Devon 9 B7
Shettleston Glasgow 119 C6
Shevington Gtr Man 86 D3
Shevington Moor Gtr Man 86 C3
Shevington Vale Gtr Man 86 D3
Sheviock Corn 5 D8
Shide IoW 15 F5
Shiel Bridge Highld 136 C2
Shieldaig Highld 149 A13
Shieldaig Highld 149 C13
Shieldhill Dumfries 114 F3
Shieldhill Falk 119 B8
Shieldhill S Lanark 120 E3
Shielfoot Highld 147 E9
Shielhill Angus 134 D4
Shielhill Involyd 118 B2
Shifford Oxon 38 D3
Shifnal Shrops 61 D7
Shilbottle Northumb 117 D7
Shildon Durham 101 B7
Shillingford Devon 10 B4
Shillingford Oxon 39 E5
Shillingford St George Devon 10 F4
Shillingstone Dorset 13 C6
Shillington C Beds 54 F2
Shillmoor Northumb 116 D4
Shilton Oxon 38 D2
Shilton Warks 63 F8
Shilvington Northumb 117 F7
Shimpling Norf 68 F4
Shimpling Suff 56 D2
Shimpling Street Suff 56 D2
Shincliffe Durham 111 E5
Shiney Row T&W 111 D6
Shinfield Wokingham 26 C5
Shingham Norf 67 D7
Shingle Street Suff 57 E7
Shinner's Bridge Devon 7 C5
Shinness Highld 157 H8
Shipbourne Kent 29 D6
Shipdham Norf 68 D2
Shipham Som 23 D6
Shiphay Torbay 7 C6
Shiplake Oxon 27 B5
Shipley Derbys 76 E4
Shipley Northumb 117 C7
Shipley Shrops 62 E2
Shipley W Sus 16 B5
Shipley W Yorks 94 F4
Shipley Shiels Northumb 116 E3
Shipmeadow Suff 69 F6
Shippea Hill Station Cambs 67 F6
Shippon Oxon 38 E4
Shipston-on-Stour Warks 51 E7
Shipton Glos 37 C7
Shipton N Yorks 95 D8
Shipton Shrops 61 E5
Shipton Bellinger Hants 25 E7
Shipton Gorge Dorset 12 E2
Shipton Green W Sus 16 D2
Shipton Moyne Glos 37 F5
Shipton on Cherwell Oxon 38 C4
Shipton Solers Glos 37 C7
Shipton-under-Wychwood Oxon 38 C2
Shiptonthorpe E Yorks 96 E4
Shirburn Oxon 39 E6
Shirdley Hill Lancs 85 C4
Shirebrook Derbys 76 C5

Stoke sub Hamdon Som 12 C2
Stoke Talmage Oxon 39 E6
Stoke Trister Som 12 B5
Stoke Wake Dorset 13 D5
Stokeford Dorset 13 F6
Stokeham Notts 77 B7
Stokeinteignhead Devon 7 B7
Stokenchurch Bucks 39 E7
Stokenham Devon 7 E6
Stokesay Shrops 60 F4
Stokesby Norf 69 C7
Stokesley N Yorks 102 D3
Stolford Som 22 E4
Ston Easton Som 23 D8
Stondon Massey Essex 42 D1
Stone Bucks 39 C7
Stone Glos 36 E3
Stone Kent 19 C6
Stone Kent 29 B6
Stone S Yorks 89 F6
Stone Staffs 75 F6
Stone Worcs 50 B3
Stone Allerton Som 23 D6
Stone Bridge Corner Pboro 66 D2
Stone Chair W Yorks 88 B2
Stone Cross E Sus 18 E3
Stone Cross Kent 31 D7
Stone-edge Batch N Som 23 B6
Stone House Cumb 100 F2
Stone Street Kent 29 D6
Stone Street Suff 56 F3
Stone Street Suff 69 F6
Stonebroom Derbys 76 D4
Stoneferry Hull 97 F7
Stonefield S Lanark 119 D6
Stonegate E Sus 18 C3
Stonegate N Yorks 103 D5
Stonegrave N Yorks 96 B2
Stonehaugh Northumb 109 B7
Stonehaven Aberds 141 F7
Stonehouse Glos 37 D5
Stonehouse Northumb 109 D6
Stonehouse S Lanark 119 E7
Stoneleigh Warks 51 B8
Stonely Cambs 54 C2
Stoner Hill Hants 15 B8
Stone's Green Essex 43 B7
Stonesby Leics 64 B5
Stonesfield Oxon 38 C3
Stonethwaite Cumb 98 C4
Stoney Cross Hants 14 C3
Stoney Middleton Derbys 76 B2
Stoney Stanton Leics 63 E8
Stoney Stoke Som 24 F2
Stoney Stratton Som 23 F8
Stoney Stretton Shrops 60 D3
Stoneybreck Shetland 160 N8
Stoneyburn W Loth 120 C2
Stoneygate Aberds 153 E10
Stoneygate Leicester 64 D3
Stoneyhills Essex 43 E5
Stoneykirk Dumfries 104 D4
Stoneywood Aberdeen 141 C7
Stoneywood Falk 127 F6
Stonganess Shetland 160 C7
Stonham Aspal Suff 56 D5
Stonnall Staffs 62 D4
Stonor Oxon 39 F7
Stonton Wyville Leics 64 E4
Stony Cross Hereford 50 E2
Stony Stratford M Keynes 53 E5
Stonyfield Highld 151 D9
Stoodleigh Devon 10 C4
Stopes S Yorks 88 F3
Stopham W Sus 16 C4
Stopsley Luton 40 B4
Stores Corner Suff 57 E7
Storeton Mers 85 F4
Stornoway W Isles 155 D9
Storridge Hereford 50 E2
Storrington W Sus 16 C4
Storrs Cumb 99 E5
Storth Cumb 99 F6
Storwood E Yorks 96 E3
Stotfield Moray 152 A2
Stotfold C Beds 54 F3
Stottesdon Shrops 61 F6
Stoughton Leics 64 D3
Stoughton Sur 27 D7
Stoughton W Sus 16 C2
Stoul Highld 147 B10
Stoulton Worcs 50 E4
Stour Provost Dorset 13 B5
Stour Row Dorset 13 B6
Stourbridge W Mid 62 F3
Stourpaine Dorset 13 D6
Stourport on Severn Worcs 50 B3
Stourton Staffs 62 F2
Stourton Warks 51 F7
Stourton Wilts 24 F2
Stourton Caundle Dorset 12 C5
Stove Orkney 159 E7
Stove Shetland 160 L6
Stoven Suff 69 F7
Stow Borders 121 E7
Stow Lincs 78 F3
Stow Lincs 90 F2
Stow Bardolph Norf 67 D6
Stow Bedon Norf 68 E2
Stow cum Quy Cambs 55 C6
Stow Longa Cambs 54 B2
Stow Maries Essex 42 E4
Stow-on-the-Wold Glos 38 B1
Stowbridge Norf 67 D6
Stowe Shrops 48 B5
Stowe-by-Chartley Staffs 62 B4
Stowe Green Glos 36 D2
Stowell Som 12 B4
Stowford Devon 9 F6
Stowlangtoft Suff 56 C3
Stowmarket Suff 56 D4
Stowting Kent 30 E4
Stowupland Suff 56 D4
Straad Argyll 145 G9
Strachan Aberds 141 E5
Stradbroke Suff 57 B6
Stradishall Suff 55 D8
Stradsett Norf 67 D6
Stragglethorpe Lincs 78 D2
Straid S Ayrs 112 E1
Straith Dumfries 113 F8
Straiton Edin 121 C5
Straiton S Ayrs 112 D3
Straloch Aberds 141 B7
Straloch Perth 133 C7
Stramshall Staffs 75 F7
Strang IoM 84 E3
Stranraer Dumfries 104 C4
Stratfield Mortimer W Berks 26 C4
Stratfield Saye Hants 26 C4
Stratfield Turgis Hants 26 D4
Stratford London 41 F6
Stratford St Andrew Suff 57 C7
Stratford St Mary Suff 56 F4
Stratford Sub Castle Wilts 25 F6
Stratford Tony Wilts 13 B8
Stratford-upon-Avon Warks 51 D6
Strath Highld 149 A12
Strath Highld 158 E4
Strathan Highld 136 E2
Strathan Highld 156 G3
Strathan Highld 157 C8
Strathaven S Lanark 119 E7
Strathblane Stirling 119 B5
Strathcanaird Highld 156 J4
Strathcarron Highld 150 G2
Strathcoil Argyll 124 B2
Strathdon Aberds 140 C2
Strathellie Aberds 153 B10
Strathkinness Fife 129 C6
Strathmashie House Highld 137 E8
Strathmiglo Fife 128 C4
Strathmore Lodge Highld 158 F3
Strathpeffer Highld 150 F7
Strathrannoch Highld 150 D6
Strathtay Perth 133 D6
Strathvaich Lodge Highld 150 D6
Strathwhillan N Ayrs 143 E11
Strathy Highld 157 C11
Strathyre Stirling 126 C4
Stratton Corn 8 D4
Stratton Dorset 12 E4
Stratton Glos 37 D7
Stratton Audley Oxon 39 B6
Stratton on the Fosse Som 23 D8
Stratton St Margaret Swindon 38 F1
Stratton St Michael Norf 68 E5
Stratton Strawless Norf 81 E8
Stravithie Fife 129 C7
Streat E Sus 17 C7
Streatham London 28 B4
Streatley C Beds 40 B3
Streatley W Berks 39 F5
Street Lancs 92 D5
Street N Yorks 103 D5
Street Som 23 F6
Street Dinas Shrops 73 F7
Street End Kent 30 D5
Street End W Sus 16 E2
Street Gate T&W 110 D5
Street Lydan Wrex 73 F8
Streethay Staffs 62 C5
Streetlam N Yorks 101 E8
Streetly W Mid 62 E4
Streetly End Cambs 55 E7
Strefford Shrops 60 F4
Strelley Notts 76 E5
Strensall York 96 C2
Stretcholt Som 22 E4
Strete Devon 7 E6
Stretford Gtr Man 87 E6
Strethall Essex 55 F5
Stretham Cambs 55 B6
Strettington W Sus 16 D2
Stretton Ches W 73 D8
Stretton Derbys 76 C3
Stretton Rutland 65 C6
Stretton Staffs 62 C2
Stretton Staffs 63 B6
Stretton Warr 86 F4
Stretton Grandison Hereford 49 E8
Stretton-on-Dunsmore Warks 52 B2
Stretton-on-Fosse Warks 51 F7
Stretton Sugwas Hereford 49 E6
Stretton under Fosse Warks 63 F8
Stretton Westwood Shrops 61 E5
Strichen Aberds 153 C9
Strines Gtr Man 87 F7
Stringston Som 22 E3
Strixton Northants 53 C7
Stroat Glos 36 E2
Stromeferry Highld 149 E13
Stromemore Highld 149 E13
Stromness Orkney 159 H3
Stronaba Highld 136 F5
Stronachlachar Stirling 126 C3
Stronchreggan Highld 130 B4
Stronchrubie Highld 156 H5
Strone Argyll 145 E10
Strone Highld 136 F4
Strone Highld 137 B8
Strone Involyd 118 B2
Stronmilchan Argyll 125 C7
Strontian Highld 130 C2
Strood Medway 29 C8
Strood Green Sur 28 E3
Strood Green W Sus 16 B4
Strood Green W Sus 28 F2
Stroud Glos 37 D5
Stroud Hants 15 B8
Stroud Green Essex 42 E4
Stroxton Lincs 78 F2
Struan Highld 149 E8
Struan Perth 133 C5
Strubby Lincs 91 F8
Strumpshaw Norf 69 D6
Strutherhill S Lanark 119 E7
Struy Highld 150 H6
Stryt-issa Wrex 73 E6
Stuartfield Aberds 153 D9
Stub Place Cumb 98 E2
Stubbington Hants 15 D6
Stubbins Lancs 87 C5
Stubbs Cross Kent 19 B6
Stubb's Green Norf 69 E5
Stubbs Green Norf 69 E6
Stubhampton Dorset 13 C7
Stubton Lincs 77 E8
Stuckgowan Argyll 126 D2
Stuckton Hants 14 C2
Stud Green Windsor 27 B6
Studham C Beds 40 C3
Studland Dorset 13 F8
Studley Warks 51 C5
Studley Wilts 24 B4
Studley Roger N Yorks 95 B5
Stump Cross Essex 55 E6
Stuntney Cambs 55 B6
Sturbridge Staffs 74 F5
Sturmer Essex 55 E7
Sturminster Marshall Dorset 13 D7
Sturminster Newton Dorset 13 C5
Sturry Kent 31 C5
Sturton N Lincs 90 D3
Sturton by Stow Lincs 90 F2
Sturton le Steeple Notts 89 F8
Stuston Suff 56 B5
Stutton N Yorks 95 E7
Stutton Suff 57 F5
Styal Ches E 87 F6
Styrrup Notts 89 E7
Suainebost W Isles 155 A10
Suardail W Isles 155 D9
Succoth Aberds 152 E4
Succoth Argyll 125 E8
Suckley Worcs 50 D2
Suckquoy Orkney 159 K5
Sudborough Northants 65 F6
Sudbourne Suff 57 D8
Sudbrook Lincs 78 E2
Sudbrook Mon 36 F2
Sudbrooke Lincs 78 B3
Sudbury Derbys 75 F8
Sudbury London 40 F4
Sudbury Suff 56 E2
Suddie Highld 151 F9
Sudgrove Glos 37 D6
Suffield N Yorks 103 E7
Suffield Norf 81 D8
Sugnall Staffs 74 F4
Suladale Highld 149 C8
Sulaisiadar W Isles 155 D10
Sulby IoM 84 C3
Sulgrave Northants 52 E3
Sulham W Berks 26 B4
Sulhamstead W Berks 26 C4
Sulland Orkney 159 D6
Sullington W Sus 16 C4
Sullom Shetland 160 F5
Sullom Voe Oil Terminal Shetland 160 F5
Sully V Glam 22 C3
Sumburgh Shetland 160 N6
Summer Bridge N Yorks 94 C5
Summer-house Darl 101 C7
Summercourt Corn 4 D3
Summerfield Norf 80 D3
Summergangs Hull 97 F7
Summerleaze Mon 35 F8
Summersdale W Sus 16 D2
Summerseat Gtr Man 87 C5
Summertown Oxon 39 D5
Summit Gtr Man 87 D7
Sunbury-on-Thames Sur 28 C2
Sundaywell Dumfries 113 F8
Sunderland Argyll 142 B3
Sunderland Cumb 107 F8
Sunderland T&W 111 D6
Sunderland Bridge Durham 111 F5
Sundhope Borders 115 B6
Sundon Park Luton 40 B3
Sundridge Kent 29 D5
Sunipol Argyll 146 F6
Sunk Island E Yorks 91 C6
Sunningdale Windsor 27 C7
Sunninghill Windsor 27 C7
Sunningwell Oxon 38 D4
Sunniside Durham 110 F4
Sunniside T&W 110 D5
Sunnyhurst Blackburn 86 B4
Sunnylaw Stirling 127 E6
Sunnyside W Sus 28 F4
Sunton Wilts 25 D7
Surbiton London 28 C2
Surby IoM 84 E2
Surfleet Lincs 66 B2
Surfleet Seas End Lincs 66 B2
Surlingham Norf 69 D6
Sustead Norf 81 D7
Susworth Lincs 90 D2
Sutcombe Devon 8 C5
Suton Norf 68 E3
Sutors of Cromarty Highld 151 E11
Sutterby Lincs 79 B6
Sutterton Lincs 79 F5
Sutton C Beds 54 E3
Sutton Cambs 54 B5
Sutton Kent 31 E7
Sutton London 28 C3
Sutton Mers 86 E3
Sutton N Yorks 89 B5
Sutton Norf 69 B6
Sutton Notts 77 F7
Sutton Notts 89 F7
Sutton Oxon 38 D4
Sutton Pboro 65 E7
Sutton S Yorks 89 C6
Sutton Shrops 61 F7
Sutton Shrops 74 F3
Sutton Som 23 F8
Sutton Staffs 61 B7
Sutton Suff 57 E7
Sutton Sur 27 E8
Sutton W Sus 16 C3
Sutton at Hone Kent 29 B6
Sutton Bassett Northants 64 E4
Sutton Benger Wilts 24 B4
Sutton Bonington Notts 64 B2
Sutton Bridge Lincs 66 B4
Sutton Cheney Leics 63 D8
Sutton Coldfield W Mid 62 E5
Sutton Courtenay Oxon 39 E5
Sutton Crosses Lincs 66 B4
Sutton Grange N Yorks 95 B5
Sutton Green Sur 27 D8
Sutton Howgrave N Yorks 95 B6
Sutton In Ashfield Notts 76 D4
Sutton-in-Craven N Yorks 94 E3
Sutton in the Elms Leics 64 E2
Sutton Ings Hull 97 F7
Sutton Lane Ends Ches E 75 B6
Sutton Leach Mers 86 E3
Sutton Maddock Shrops 61 D7
Sutton Mallet Som 23 F5
Sutton Mandeville Wilts 13 B7
Sutton Manor Mers 86 E3
Sutton Montis Som 12 B4
Sutton on Hull Hull 97 F7
Sutton on Sea Lincs 91 F9
Sutton-on-the-Forest N Yorks 95 C8
Sutton on the Hill Derbys 76 F2
Sutton on Trent Notts 77 C7
Sutton Scarsdale Derbys 76 C4
Sutton Scotney Hants 26 F2
Sutton St Edmund Lincs 66 C3
Sutton St James Lincs 66 C3
Sutton St Nicholas Hereford 49 E7
Sutton under Brailes Warks 51 F8
Sutton-under-Whitestonecliffe N Yorks 102 F2
Sutton upon Derwent E Yorks 96 E3
Sutton Valence Kent 30 E2
Sutton Veny Wilts 24 E3
Sutton Waldron Dorset 13 C6
Sutton Weaver Ches W 74 B2
Sutton Wick Bath 23 D7
Swaby Lincs 79 B6
Swadlincote Derbys 63 C7
Swaffham Norf 67 D8
Swaffham Bulbeck Cambs 55 C6
Swaffham Prior Cambs 55 C6
Swafield Norf 81 D8
Swainby N Yorks 102 D2
Swainshill Hereford 49 E6
Swainsthorpe Norf 68 D5
Swainswick Bath 24 C2
Swalcliffe Oxon 51 F8
Swalecliffe Kent 30 C5
Swallow Lincs 91 D5
Swallowcliffe Wilts 13 B7
Swallowfield Wokingham 26 C5
Swallownest S Yorks 89 F5
Swallows Cross Essex 42 E2
Swan Green Ches W 74 B4
Swan Green Suff 57 B6
Swanage Dorset 13 G8
Swanbister Orkney 159 H4
Swanbourne Bucks 39 B8
Swanland E Yorks 90 B3
Swanley Kent 29 C6
Swanley Village Kent 29 C6
Swanmore Hants 15 C6
Swannington Leics 63 C8
Swannington Norf 68 C4
Swanscombe Kent 29 B7
Swansea = Abertawe Swansea 33 E7
Swanton Abbott Norf 81 E8
Swanton Morley Norf 68 C3
Swanton Novers Norf 81 D6
Swanton Street Kent 30 D2
Swanwick Derbys 76 D4
Swanwick Hants 15 D6
Swarby Lincs 78 E3
Swardeston Norf 68 D5
Swarister Shetland 160 E7
Swarkestone Derbys 63 B7
Swarland Northumb 117 D7
Swarland Estate Northumb 117 D7
Swarthmoor Cumb 92 B2
Swathwick Derbys 76 C3
Swaton Lincs 78 F4
Swavesey Cambs 54 C4
Sway Hants 14 E3
Swayfield Lincs 65 B6
Swaythling Soton 14 C5
Sweet Green Worcs 49 C8
Sweetham Devon 10 E3
Sweethouse Corn 5 C5
Sweffling Suff 57 C7
Swepstone Leics 63 C7
Swerford Oxon 51 F8
Swettenham Ches E 74 C5
Swetton N Yorks 94 B4
Swffryd Caerph 35 E6
Swiftsden E Sus 18 C4
Swilland Suff 57 D5
Swillington W Yorks 95 F6
Swimbridge Devon 9 B8
Swimbridge Newland Devon 20 F5
Swinbrook Oxon 38 C2
Swinderby Lincs 77 C8
Swindon Glos 37 B6
Swindon Staffs 62 E2
Swindon Swindon 38 F1
Swine E Yorks 97 F7
Swinefleet E Yorks 89 B8
Swineshead Bedford 53 C8
Swineshead Lincs 78 E5
Swineshead Bridge Lincs 78 E5
Swiney Highld 158 G4
Swinford Leics 52 B3
Swinford Oxon 38 D4
Swingate Notts 76 E5
Swingfield Minnis Kent 31 E6
Swingfield Street Kent 31 E6
Swinhoe Northumb 117 B8
Swinhope Lincs 91 E6
Swining Shetland 160 G6
Swinithwaite N Yorks 101 F5
Swinnow Moor W Yorks 94 F5
Swinscoe Staffs 75 E8
Swinside Hall Borders 116 C3
Swinstead Lincs 65 B7
Swinton Borders 122 E4
Swinton Gtr Man 87 D5
Swinton N Yorks 94 B5
Swinton N Yorks 96 B3
Swinton S Yorks 88 E5
Swintonmill Borders 122 E4
Swithland Leics 64 C2
Swordale Highld 151 E8
Swordland Highld 147 B10
Swordly Highld 157 C10
Sworton Heath Ches E 86 F4
Swydd-ffynnon Ceredig 47 C5
Swynnerton Staffs 75 F5
Swyre Dorset 12 F3
Sychtyn Powys 59 D6
Syde Glos 37 C6
Sydenham London 28 B4
Sydenham Oxon 39 D7
Sydenham Damerel Devon 6 B2
Syderstone Norf 80 D4
Sydling St Nicholas Dorset 12 E4
Sydmonton Hants 26 D2
Syerston Notts 77 E7
Syke Gtr Man 87 C6
Sykehouse S Yorks 89 C7
Sykes Lancs 93 D6
Syleham Suff 57 B6
Sylen Carms 33 D6
Symbister Shetland 160 G7
Symington S Ayrs 118 F3
Symington S Lanark 120 F2
Symonds Yat Hereford 36 C2
Symondsbury Dorset 12 E2
Synod Inn Ceredig 46 D3
Syre Highld 157 E9
Syreford Glos 37 B7
Syresham Northants 52 E4
Syston Leics 64 C3
Syston Lincs 78 E2
Sytchampton Worcs 50 C3
Sywell Northants 53 C6

T

Taagan Highld 150 E3
Tàbost W Isles 155 A10
Tabost W Isles 155 F8
Tackley Oxon 38 B4
Tacleit W Isles 154 D6
Tacolneston Norf 68 E4
Tadcaster N Yorks 95 E7
Taddington Derbys 75 B8
Taddiport Devon 9 C6
Tadley Hants 26 C4
Tadlow C Beds 54 E3
Tadmarton Oxon 51 F8
Tadworth Sur 28 D3
Tafarn-y-gelyn Denb 73 C5
Tafarnau-bach Bl Gwent 35 C5
Taff's Well Rhondda 35 F5
Tafolwern Powys 59 D5
Tai Conwy 83 E7
Tai-bach Powys 59 B8
Tai-mawr Conwy 72 E3
Tai-Ucha Denb 72 D4
Taibach Neath 33 E8
Taigh a Ghearraidh W Isles 148 A2
Tain Highld 151 C10
Tain Highld 158 D4
Tainant Wrex 73 E6
Tainlon Gwyn 82 F4
Tairbeart = Tarbert W Isles 154 G6
Tai'r-Bull Powys 34 B3
Tairgwaith Neath 33 C8
Takeley Essex 42 B1
Takeley Street Essex 41 B8
Tal-sarn Ceredig 46 D4
Tal-y-bont Ceredig 58 F3
Tal-y-Bont Conwy 83 E7
Tal-y-bont Gwyn 71 E6
Tal-y-bont Gwyn 83 D6
Tal-y-cafn Conwy 83 D7
Tal-y-llyn Gwyn 58 D4
Tal-y-wern Powys 58 D5
Talachddu Powys 48 F2
Talacre Flint 85 F2
Talardd Gwyn 59 B5
Talaton Devon 11 E5
Talbenny Pembs 44 D3
Talbot Green Rhondda 34 F4
Talbot Village Poole 13 E8
Tale Devon 11 D5
Talerddig Powys 59 D6
Talgarreg Ceredig 46 D3
Talgarth Powys 48 F3
Talisker Highld 149 E8
Talke Staffs 74 D5
Talkin Cumb 109 D5
Talla Linnfoots Borders 114 B4
Talladale Highld 150 D2
Tallarn Green Wrex 73 E8
Tallentire Cumb 107 F8
Talley Carms 46 F5
Tallington Lincs 65 D7
Talmine Highld 157 C8
Talog Carms 32 B4
Talsarn Carms 34 B1
Talsarnau Gwyn 71 D7
Talskiddy Corn 4 C4
Talwrn Anglesey 82 D4
Talwrn Wrex 73 E6
Talybont-on-Usk Powys 35 B5
Talygarn Rhondda 34 F4
Talyllyn Powys 35 B5
Talysarn Gwyn 82 F4
Talywain Torf 35 D6
Tame Bridge N Yorks 102 D3
Tamerton Foliot Plym 6 C2
Tamworth Staffs 63 D6
Tan Hinon Powys 59 F5
Tan-lan Conwy 83 E7
Tan-lan Gwyn 71 C7
Tan-y-bwlch Gwyn 71 C7
Tan-y-fron Conwy 72 C3
Tan-y-graig Anglesey 82 D5
Tan-y-graig Gwyn 70 D4
Tan-y-groes Ceredig 45 E4
Tan-y-pistyll Powys 59 B7
Tan-yr-allt Gwyn 82 F4
Tandem W Yorks 88 C2
Tanden Kent 19 B6
Tandridge Sur 28 D4
Tanerdy Carms 33 B5
Tanfield Durham 110 D4
Tanfield Lea Durham 110 D4
Tangasdal W Isles 148 J1
Tangiers Pembs 44 D4
Tangley Hants 25 D8
Tanglwst Carms 46 F2
Tangmere W Sus 16 D3
Tangwick Shetland 160 F4
Tankersley S Yorks 88 D4
Tankerton Kent 30 C5
Tannach Highld 158 F5
Tannachie Aberds 141 F6
Tannadice Angus 134 D4
Tannington Suff 57 C6
Tansley Derbys 76 D3
Tansley Knoll Derbys 76 C3
Tansor Northants 65 E7
Tantobie Durham 110 D4
Tanton N Yorks 102 C3
Tanworth-in-Arden Warks 51 B6
Tanygrisiau Gwyn 71 C7
Tanyrhydiau Ceredig 47 C6
Taobh a Chaolais W Isles 148 G2
Taobh a Thuath Loch Aineort W Isles 148 F2
Taobh a Tuath Loch Baghasdail W Isles 148 F2
Taobh a'Ghlinne W Isles 155 F8
Taobh Tuath W Isles 154 J4
Taplow Bucks 40 F2
Tapton Derbys 76 B3
Tarbat Ho. Highld 151 D10
Tarbert Argyll 143 C7
Tarbert Argyll 144 E5
Tarbert Argyll 145 G7
Tarbert = Tairbeart W Isles 154 G6
Tarbet Argyll 126 D2
Tarbet Highld 147 B10
Tarbet Highld 156 E4
Tarbock Green Mers 86 F2
Tarbolton S Ayrs 112 B4
Tarbrax S Lanark 120 D3
Tardebigge Worcs 50 C5
Tarfside Angus 134 B4
Tarland Aberds 140 D3
Tarleton Lancs 86 B2
Tarlogie Highld 151 C10
Tarlscough Lancs 86 C2
Tarlton Glos 37 E6
Tarnbrook Lancs 93 D5
Tarporley Ches W 74 C2
Tarr Som 22 F3
Tarrant Crawford Dorset 13 D7
Tarrant Gunville Dorset 13 C7
Tarrant Hinton Dorset 13 C7
Tarrant Keyneston Dorset 13 D7
Tarrant Launceston Dorset 13 D7
Tarrant Monkton Dorset 13 D7
Tarrant Rawston Dorset 13 D7
Tarrant Rushton Dorset 13 D7
Tarrel Highld 151 C11
Tarring Neville E Sus 17 D8
Tarrington Hereford 49 E8
Tarsappie Perth 128 B3
Tarskavaig Highld 149 H10
Tarves Aberds 153 E8
Tarvie Highld 150 F7
Tarvie Perth 133 C7
Tarvin Ches W 73 C8
Tasburgh Norf 68 E5
Tasley Shrops 61 E6
Taston Oxon 38 B3
Tatenhill Staffs 63 B6
Tathall End M Keynes 53 E6
Tatham Lancs 93 C6
Tathwell Lincs 91 F7
Tatling End Bucks 40 F3
Tatsfield Sur 28 D5
Tattenhall Ches W 73 D8
Tattenhoe M Keynes 53 F6
Tatterford Norf 80 E4
Tattersett Norf 80 D4
Tattershall Lincs 78 D5
Tattershall Bridge Lincs 78 D4
Tattershall Thorpe Lincs 78 D5
Tattingstone Suff 56 F5
Tatworth Som 11 D8
Taunton Som 11 B7
Taverham Norf 68 C4
Tavernspite Pembs 32 C2
Tavistock Devon 6 B2
Taw Green Devon 9 E8
Tawstock Devon 9 B7
Taxal Derbys 75 B7
Tay Bridge Dundee 129 B6
Tayinloan Argyll 143 D7
Taymouth Castle Perth 132 E4
Taynish Argyll 144 E6
Taynton Glos 36 B4
Taynton Oxon 38 C2
Taynuilt Argyll 125 B6
Tayport Fife 129 B6
Tayvallich Argyll 144 E6
Tealby Lincs 91 E5
Tealing Angus 134 F4
Teangue Highld 149 H11
Teanna Mhachair W Isles 148 B2
Tebay Cumb 99 D8
Tebworth C Beds 40 B2
Tedburn St Mary Devon 10 E3
Teddington Glos 50 F4
Teddington London 28 B2
Tedstone Delamere Hereford 49 D8
Tedstone Wafre Hereford 49 D8
Teeton Northants 52 B4
Teffont Evias Wilts 24 F4
Teffont Magna Wilts 24 F4
Tegryn Pembs 45 F4
Teigh Rutland 65 C5
Teigncombe Devon 9 F8
Teigngrace Devon 7 B6
Teignmouth Devon 7 B7
Telford Telford 61 D6
Telham E Sus 18 D4
Tellisford Som 24 D3
Telscombe E Sus 17 D8
Telscombe Cliffs E Sus 17 D7
Templand Dumfries 114 F3
Temple Corn 5 B6
Temple Glasgow 118 C5
Temple Midloth 121 D6
Temple Balsall W Mid 51 B7
Temple Bar Carms 33 C6
Temple Bar Ceredig 46 D4
Temple Cloud Bath 23 D8
Temple Combe Som 12 B5
Temple Ewell Kent 31 E6
Temple Grafton Warks 51 D6
Temple Guiting Glos 37 B7
Temple Herdewyke Warks 51 D8
Temple Hirst N Yorks 89 B7
Temple Normanton Derbys 76 C4
Temple Sowerby Cumb 99 B8
Templehall Fife 128 E4
Templeton Devon 10 C3
Templeton Pembs 32 C2
Templeton Bridge Devon 10 C3
Templetown Durham 110 D4
Tempsford C Beds 54 D2
Ten Mile Bank Norf 67 E6
Tenbury Wells Worcs 49 C7
Tenby = Dinbych-Y-Pysgod Pembs 32 D2
Tendring Essex 43 B7
Tendring Green Essex 43 B7
Tenston Orkney 159 G3
Tenterden Kent 19 B5
Terling Essex 42 C3
Ternhill Shrops 74 F3
Terregles Banks Dumfries 107 B6
Terrick Bucks 39 D8
Terrington N Yorks 96 B2
Terrington St Clement Norf 66 C5
Terrington St John Norf 66 C5
Teston Kent 29 D8
Testwood Hants 14 C4
Tetbury Glos 37 E5
Tetbury Upton Glos 37 E5
Tetchill Shrops 73 F7
Tetcott Devon 8 E5
Tetford Lincs 79 B6
Tetney Lincs 91 D7
Tetney Lock Lincs 91 D7
Tetsworth Oxon 39 D6
Tettenhall W Mid 62 E2
Teuchan Aberds 153 E10
Teversal Notts 76 C4
Teversham Cambs 55 D5
Teviothead Borders 115 D7
Tewel Aberds 141 F7
Tewin Herts 41 C5
Tewkesbury Glos 50 F3
Teynham Kent 30 C3
Thackthwaite Cumb 98 B3
Thainston Aberds 135 B6
Thakeham W Sus 16 C5
Thame Oxon 39 D7
Thames Ditton Sur 28 C2
Thames Haven Thurrock 42 F3
Thamesmead London 41 F7
Thanington Kent 30 D5
Thankerton S Lanark 120 F2
Tharston Norf 68 E4
Thatcham W Berks 26 C3
Thatto Heath Mers 86 E3
Thaxted Essex 55 F7
The Aird Highld 149 C9
The Arms Norf 67 E8
The Bage Hereford 48 E4
The Balloch Perth 127 C7
The Barony Orkney 159 F3
The Bog Shrops 60 E3
The Bourne Sur 27 E6
The Braes Highld 149 E10
The Broad Hereford 49 C6
The Butts Som 24 E2
The Camp Glos 37 D6
The Camp Herts 40 D4
The Chequer Wrex 73 E8
The City Bucks 39 E7
The Common Wilts 25 F7
The Craigs Highld 150 B7
The Cronk IoM 84 C3
The Dell Suff 69 E7
The Den N Ayrs 118 D3
The Eals Northumb 116 F3
The Eaves Glos 36 D3
The Flatt Cumb 109 B5
The Four Alls Shrops 74 F3
The Garths Shetland 160 B8
The Green Cumb 98 F3
The Green Wilts 24 F3
The Grove Dumfries 107 B6
The Hall Shetland 160 D8
The Haven W Sus 27 F8
The Heath Norf 81 E7
The Heath Suff 56 F5
The Hill Cumb 98 F3
The Howe Cumb 99 F6
The Howe IoM 84 F1
The Hundred Hereford 49 C7
The Lee Bucks 40 D2
The Lhen IoM 84 B3
The Marsh Powys 60 E3
The Marsh Wilts 37 F7
The Middles Durham 110 D5
The Moor Kent 18 C4
The Mumbles = Y Mwmbwls Swansea 33 F7
The Murray S Lanark 119 D6
The Neuk Aberds 141 E6
The Oval Bath 24 C2
The Pole of Itlaw Aberds 153 C6
The Quarry Glos 36 E4
The Rhos Pembs 32 C1
The Rock Telford 61 D6
The Ryde Herts 41 D5
The Sands Sur 27 E6
The Stocks Kent 19 C6
The Throat Wokingham 27 C6
The Vauld Hereford 49 E7
The Wyke Shrops 61 D7
Theakston N Yorks 101 F8
Thealby N Lincs 90 C2
Theale Som 23 E6
Theale W Berks 26 B4
Thearne E Yorks 97 F6
Theberton Suff 57 C8
Theddingworth Leics 64 F3
Theddlethorpe All Saints Lincs 91 F8
Theddlethorpe St Helen Lincs 91 F8
Thelbridge Barton Devon 10 C2
Thelnetham Suff 56 B4
Thelveton Norf 68 F4
Thelwall Warr 86 F4
Themelthorpe Norf 81 E6
Thenford Northants 52 E3
Therfield Herts 54 F4
Thetford Lincs 65 C8
Thetford Norf 67 F8
Theydon Bois Essex 41 E7
Thickwood Wilts 24 B3
Thimbleby Lincs 78 C5
Thimbleby N Yorks 102 E2
Thingwall Mers 85 F3
Thirdpart N Ayrs 118 E1
Thirlby N Yorks 102 F2
Thirlestane Borders 121 E8
Thirn N Yorks 101 F7
Thirsk N Yorks 102 F2
Thirtleby E Yorks 97 F7
Thistleton Lancs 92 F4
Thistleton Rutland 65 C6
Thistley Green Suff 55 B7
Thixendale N Yorks 96 C4
Thockrington Northumb 110 B2
Tholomas Drove Cambs 66 D3
Tholthorpe N Yorks 95 C7
Thomas Chapel Pembs 32 D2
Thomas Close Cumb 108 E4
Thomastown Aberds 152 E5
Thompson Norf 68 E2
Thomshill Moray 152 C2
Thong Kent 29 B7
Thongsbridge W Yorks 88 D2
Thoralby N Yorks 101 F5
Thoresway Lincs 91 E5
Thorganby Lincs 91 E6
Thorganby N Yorks 96 E2
Thorgill N Yorks 103 E5
Thorington Suff 57 B8
Thorington Street Suff 56 F4
Thorlby N Yorks 94 D2
Thorley Herts 41 C7
Thorley Street Herts 41 C7
Thorley Street IoW 14 F4
Thormanby N Yorks 95 B7
Thornaby-on-Tees Stockton 102 C2
Thornage Norf 81 D6
Thornborough Bucks 52 F5
Thornborough N Yorks 95 B5
Thornbury Devon 9 D6
Thornbury Hereford 49 D8
Thornbury S Glos 36 E3
Thornbury W Yorks 94 F4
Thornby Northants 52 B4
Thorncliffe Staffs 75 D7
Thorncombe Dorset 11 D8
Thorncombe Dorset 13 D6
Thorncombe Street Sur 27 E8
Thorncote Green C Beds 54 E2
Thorncross IoW 14 F5
Thorndon Suff 56 C5
Thorndon Cross Devon 9 E7
Thorne S Yorks 89 C7
Thorne St Margaret Som 11 B5
Thorner W Yorks 95 E6
Thorney Notts 77 B8
Thorney Pboro 66 D2
Thorney Crofts E Yorks 91 B6
Thorney Green Suff 56 C4
Thorney Hill Hants 14 E2
Thorney Toll Pboro 66 D3
Thornfalcon Som 11 B7
Thornford Dorset 12 C4
Thorngumbald E Yorks 91 B6
Thornham Norf 80 C3
Thornham Magna Suff 56 B5
Thornham Parva Suff 56 B5
Thornhaugh Pboro 65 D7
Thornhill Cardiff 35 F5
Thornhill Cumb 98 D2
Thornhill Derbys 88 F2
Thornhill Dumfries 113 E8
Thornhill Soton 15 C5
Thornhill Stirling 127 E5
Thornhill W Yorks 88 C3
Thornhill Edge W Yorks 88 C3
Thornhill Lees W Yorks 88 C3
Thornholme E Yorks 97 C7
Thornley Durham 110 F4
Thornley Durham 111 F6
Thornliebank E Renf 118 D5
Thorns Suff 55 D8
Thorns Green Ches E 87 F5
Thornsett Derbys 87 F8
Thornthwaite Cumb 98 B4
Thornthwaite N Yorks 94 D4
Thornton Angus 134 E3
Thornton Bucks 53 F5
Thornton E Yorks 96 E3
Thornton Fife 128 E4
Thornton Lancs 92 E3
Thornton Leics 63 D8
Thornton Lincs 78 C5
Thornton Mbro 102 C2
Thornton Mers 85 D4
Thornton Northumb 123 E5
Thornton Pembs 44 E4
Thornton W Yorks 94 F4
Thornton Curtis N Lincs 90 C4
Thornton Heath London 28 C4
Thornton Hough Mers 85 F4
Thornton in Craven N Yorks 94 E2
Thornton-le-Beans N Yorks 102 E1
Thornton-le-Clay N Yorks 96 C2
Thornton-le-Dale N Yorks 103 F6
Thornton le Moor Lincs 90 E4
Thornton-le-Moor N Yorks 102 F1
Thornton-le-Moors Ches W 73 B8
Thornton-le-Street N Yorks 102 F2
Thornton Rust N Yorks 100 F4
Thornton Steward N Yorks 101 F6
Thornton Watlass N Yorks 101 F7
Thorntonhall S Lanark 119 D5
Thorntonloch E Loth 122 B3
Thorntonpark Northumb 122 E5
Thornwood Common Essex 41 D7
Thornydykes Borders 122 E2
Thoroton Notts 77 E7
Thorp Arch W Yorks 95 E7
Thorpe Derbys 75 D8
Thorpe E Yorks 97 E5
Thorpe Lincs 91 F8
Thorpe N Yorks 94 C3
Thorpe Norf 69 E7
Thorpe Notts 77 E7
Thorpe Sur 27 C8
Thorpe Abbotts Norf 57 B5
Thorpe Acre Leics 64 B2
Thorpe Arnold Leics 64 B4
Thorpe Audlin W Yorks 89 C5
Thorpe Bassett N Yorks 96 B4
Thorpe Bay Southend 43 F5
Thorpe by Water Rutland 65 E5
Thorpe Common Suff 57 F6
Thorpe Constantine Staffs 63 D6
Thorpe Culvert Lincs 79 C7
Thorpe End Norf 69 C5
Thorpe Fendykes Lincs 79 C7
Thorpe Green Essex 43 B7
Thorpe Green Suff 56 D3
Thorpe Hesley S Yorks 88 E4
Thorpe in Balne S Yorks 89 C6
Thorpe in the Fallows Lincs 90 F3
Thorpe Langton Leics 64 E4
Thorpe Larches Durham 102 B1
Thorpe-le-Soken Essex 43 B7
Thorpe le Street E Yorks 96 E4
Thorpe Malsor Northants 53 B6
Thorpe Mandeville Northants 52 E3
Thorpe Market Norf 81 D8
Thorpe Marriot Norf 68 C4
Thorpe Morieux Suff 56 D3
Thorpe on the Hill Lincs 78 C2
Thorpe Salvin S Yorks 89 F6
Thorpe Satchville Leics 64 C4
Thorpe St Andrew Norf 69 D5
Thorpe St Peter Lincs 79 C7
Thorpe Thewles Stockton 102 B2
Thorpe Tilney Lincs 78 D4
Thorpe Underwood N Yorks 95 D7
Thorpe Waterville Northants 65 F7
Thorpe Willoughby N Yorks 95 F8
Thorpeness Suff 57 D8
Thorrington Essex 43 C6
Thorverton Devon 10 D4
Thrandeston Suff 56 B5
Thrapston Northants 53 B7
Thrashbush N Lanark 119 C7
Threapland Cumb 107 F8
Threapland N Yorks 94 C2
Threapwood Ches W 73 E8
Threapwood Staffs 75 E7
Three Ashes Hereford 36 B2
Three Bridges W Sus 28 F3
Three Burrows Corn 3 B6
Three Chimneys Kent 18 B5
Three Cocks Powys 48 F3
Three Crosses Swansea 33 E6
Three Cups Corner E Sus 18 C3
Three Holes Norf 66 D5
Three Leg Cross E Sus 18 B3
Three Legged Cross Dorset 13 D8
Three Oaks E Sus 18 D5
Threehammer Common Norf 69 C6
Threekingham Lincs 78 F3
Threemile Cross Wokingham 26 C5
Threemilestone Corn 3 B6
Threemiletown W Loth 120 B3
Threlkeld Cumb 99 B5
Threshfield N Yorks 94 C2
Thrigby Norf 69 C7
Thringarth Durham 100 B4
Thringstone Leics 63 C8
Thrintoft N Yorks 101 E8
Thriplow Cambs 54 E5
Throckenholt Lincs 66 D3
Throcking Herts 54 F4
Throckley T&W 110 C4
Throckmorton Worcs 50 E4
Throphill Northumb 117 F7
Thropton Northumb 117 D6
Throsk Stirling 127 E7
Throwleigh Devon 9 E8
Throwley Kent 30 D3
Thrumpton Notts 76 F5
Thrumster Highld 158 F5
Thrunton Northumb 117 C6
Thrupp Glos 37 D5
Thrupp Oxon 38 C4
Thrushelton Devon 9 F6
Thrussington Leics 64 C3
Thruxton Hants 25 E7
Thruxton Hereford 49 F6
Thrybergh S Yorks 89 E5
Thulston Derbys 76 F4
Thundergay N Ayrs 143 D9
Thundersley Essex 42 F3
Thundridge Herts 41 C6
Thurcaston Leics 64 C2
Thurcroft S Yorks 89 F5
Thurgarton Norf 81 D7
Thurgarton Notts 77 E6
Thurgoland S Yorks 88 D3
Thurlaston Leics 64 E2
Thurlaston Warks 52 B2
Thurlbear Som 11 B7
Thurlby Lincs 65 C8
Thurlby Lincs 78 C2
Thurleigh Bedford 53 D8
Thurlestone Devon 6 E4
Thurloxton Som 22 F4
Thurlstone S Yorks 88 D3
Thurlton Norf 69 E7
Thurlwood Ches E 74 D5
Thurmaston Leics 64 D3
Thurnby Leics 64 D3
Thurne Norf 69 C7
Thurnham Kent 30 D2
Thurnham Lancs 92 D4
Thurning Norf 81 E6
Thurning Northants 65 F7
Thurnscoe S Yorks 89 D5
Thurnscoe East S Yorks 89 D5
Thursby Cumb 108 D3
Thursford Norf 81 D5
Thursley Sur 27 F7
Thurso Highld 158 D3
Thurso East Highld 158 D3
Thurstaston Mers 85 F3
Thurston Suff 56 C3
Thurstonfield Cumb 108 D3
Thurstonland W Yorks 88 C2
Thurton Norf 69 D6
Thurvaston Derbys 76 F2
Thuxton Norf 68 D3
Thwaite N Yorks 100 E3

U

V

W